Amending the Past

Critical Human Rights

Series Editors

Steve J. Stern ❧ Scott Straus

Books in the series **Critical Human Rights** emphasize research that opens new ways to think about and understand human rights. The series values in particular empirically grounded and intellectually open research that eschews simplified accounts of human rights events and processes.

While tribunals, truth commissions, and community-based justice currently dominate human rights debate and scholarship, this book trains an analytical lens on a different form of transitional justice: the historical commission. Convened around the world to deal with contested, high-stakes episodes of the past, historical commissions are an important and understudied development in human rights discourse and praxis. In *Amending the Past*, the first book comparing and assessing the Holocaust historical commissions, Alexander Karn considers their various methods, challenges, and contributions. While acknowledging the limitations of historical commissions, Karn emphasizes their potential for transcending partisan narratives by bringing rival perspectives into dialogue and upholding high standards of evidence. The book thus contributes to multiple intersecting fields and disciplines, including peace and conflict studies, human rights, conflict resolution, and Holocaust studies.

Amending the Past

*Europe's Holocaust Commissions
and the Right to History*

Alexander Karn

The University of Wisconsin Press

The University of Wisconsin Press
1930 Monroe Street, 3rd Floor
Madison, Wisconsin 53711-2059
uwpress.wisc.edu

3 Henrietta Street, Covent Garden
London WC2E 8LU, United Kingdom
eurospanbookstore.com

Printed in the United States of America

This book may be available in a digital edition.

Library of Congress Cataloging-in-Publication Data

Karn, Alexander.
Amending the past: Europe's Holocaust commissions and the right to history / Alexander Karn.
    pages   cm — (Critical human rights)
    Includes bibliographical references and index.
    ISBN 978-0-299-30550-5 (cloth: alk. paper)
1. Holocaust, Jewish (1939–1945)—Historiography.   2. Truth commissions—Europe.
    I. Title.   II. Series: Critical human rights.
D804.348.K383   2015
940.53´1807204—dc23
2015008382

ISBN 978-0-299-31324-1 (pbk.: alk. paper)

forwarded with a grant from

Figure Foundation

time does fact the schematic

For JEM, BHK, and SEK

Contents

Acknowledgments

I cannot properly or adequately thank the full list of people who helped bring this project to fruition. There are some individuals, however, who deserve special mention.

Elazar Barkan took me under his wing when my academic trajectory looked decidedly shaky. His guidance and encouragement led me across numerous intellectual crevasses into which I almost certainly would have stumbled if left to my own devices. Besides reading and commenting on several sections of this book, he has improved my work enormously over the years by sharing his own.

Jonathan Petropoulos and Bill Jones read and commented on the dissertation that helped spawn this project and, together, promised me there was a feasible book project somewhere inside when I doubted that was the case.

Colgate University, in Central New York, has been my home base since 2007, and I am extremely fortunate to have landed among such capable students and supportive colleagues. In the Department of History, special thanks go to Kira Stevens, who hired me; David Robinson, who retained me; and Andy Rotter, who pointed out career opportunities to which I was hitherto oblivious. Rob Nemes and Ray Douglas, my fellow Europeanists, deserve special mention, too. Their work and interests have stimulated my own, and both have given me tremendous support over the years. I am also grateful to my colleagues in Colgate's Peace and Conflict Studies Program, particularly Nancy Ries, who reviewed and commented on the prospectus that led to this book being published, and Dan Monk, who opened a door for me when I hesitated to do this for myself.

Being an outsider to the commissions that are the subject of this study, I have benefitted enormously from conversations and e-mail exchanges with various commission personnel. All of these individuals saved me from propagating misinformation and helped me to better understand the subtleties of the commissions they worked for: Bjarte Bruland, Claire Andrieu, Diane Afoumado, Anne Grynberg, Regula Ludi, Natalia Indrimi, Ilaria Pavan, Michael Marrus, and Ariella Lang. Their input and perspectives have greatly improved the work. Of course, any mistakes that remain are mine alone.

A number of scholars working on topics related to mine answered my queries and pointed me toward helpful source material. In addition to Alexis Herr, Robert Paxton, Robert Gordon, and John Foot, I want to thank Jan Gross, who discussed his research with me at considerable length, even after it became clear that my interpretations contrasted sharply with his. Though I am critical of certain aspects of his work, I would be greatly remiss were I not to acknowledge what his scholarship has contributed in terms of "amending the past."

In order for new fields of academic study to emerge, it is crucial that like-minded individuals be given the opportunity to meet and exchange perspectives. Participation in the 2013 Summer Research Workshop "The Politics of Repair: Restitution and Reparations in the Wake of the Holocaust" at the United States Holocaust Memorial Museum's Center for Advanced Holocaust Studies contributed greatly to the development of this project. I want to thank, in particular, Krista Hegburg and Nicole Frechette for the work that went into planning and organizing that program.

I am also indebted to the Colgate University Research Council for funding provided in the final stages of preparing the manuscript.

Unlike the books that pour out of their authors in one powerful torrent, this one was composed in drips and drops. The overall project was improved by the comments and suggestions made by peer reviewers at the *Journal of International Affairs* and *Rethinking History*, where I submitted earlier work on topics related to what is covered here. Klaus Neumann also commented on an unpublished essay, which is partially incorporated here. The external reviewers for the University of Wisconsin Press have also left an indelible mark on this project. Their encouragement to expand and develop several of the book's principal themes has given it more substance and depth than it would have had otherwise.

I would be greatly remiss if I failed to mention the tremendous support I have received from the University of Wisconsin Press. I want to thank, first of all, Steve Stern and Scott Straus for including my work in what is widely regarded as one of the most challenging and compelling book series on the subject of human rights. Gwen Walker, the press's acquisitions editor, has been a patient advocate and keen reader for this project throughout its long gestation. Her assistant, Matthew Cosby, has helped to manage the sorts of details that authors normally try to avoid. Adam Mehring and Sheila McMahon have provided expert guidance throughout the production process. Others, including Sheila Leary, Carla Marolt, Mary Sutherland, and Jonah Horvitz, have made important contributions as well.

Finally, this book would not have seen the light of day except for the support of my family and the many sacrifices they have made. I cannot count the number of times that my writerly ambitions intruded on what was supposed to have been an occasion for frivolity or simple relaxation. Others who work on grim subject matter know what it means to be rejuvenated by those who give freely of their love and receive ours so easily. With humble thanks and all my love, I dedicate this book to the women in my life: Jen, Beatrix, and Sylvie.

Abbreviations

ADSS	*Actes et documents du Saint-Siège relatifs à la période de la Seconde Guerre Mondiale*
ANC	African National Conference
ATS	Austrian schilling
CDU	Christian Democratic Union
CHL	Commission of the Historians of Latvia
CIVS	Commission for the Compensation of Victims of Spoliation Resulting from Anti-Semitic Legislation (Drai Commission)
CPL	Centro Primo Levi
CRIF	Conseil Représentatif des Institutions juives de France (Representative Council of French Jewish Institutions)
DBPJ	Declaration of Basic Principles of Justice for Victims of Crime and Abuse of Power
DM	deutsche mark (Germany)
DNSAP	Deutsche Nationalsozialistische Arbeiterpartei (German National Socialist Workers Party) (Austria)
ECHR	European Court of Human Rights
FLD	Provincial Financial Directorate
FMS	Foundation for the Memory of the Shoah
FPÖ	Freiheitliche Partei Österreichs (Freedom Party of Austria)
GDR	German Democratic Republic
GEI	Georg Eckert Institute for International Textbook Research
GSF	General Settlement Fund
IACHR	Inter-American Court of Human Rights
ICE	Independent Commission of Experts
ICEP	Independent Commission of Eminent Persons (Volcker Commission)

ICHEIC	International Commission on Holocaust-Era Insurance Claims
ICJHC	International Catholic-Jewish Historical Commission
ICL	International Commission for the Evaluation of the Crimes of the Nazi and Soviet Occupation Regimes in Lithuania
ICTY	International Criminal Tribunal for the Former Yugoslavia
IHJR	Institute for Historical Justice and Reconciliation
IOM	International Organization for Migration
IPN	Instytut Pamięci Narodowej (Institute of National Remembrance)
KVSG	Kriegs- und Verfolgungssachschädengesetz (War and Persecution Material Damages Act)
LLRC	Lessons Learned and Reconciliation Commission
MOU	Memorandum of Understanding
MP	member of parliament
NAIC	National Association of Insurance Commissioners
NKVD	Narodnyĭ Kommissariat Vnutrennikh Del (People's Commissariat of Internal Affairs)
NSDAP	Nationalsozialistische Deutsche Arbeiterpartei (National Socialist German Workers' Party) (Nazis)
PS	Parti Socialiste (Socialist Party) (France)
PSK	Österreichische Postsparkasse (Austrian Postal Savings Bank)
PZPR	Polska Zjednoczona Partia Robotnicza (Polish United Workers' Party)
RM	reichsmark (Germany)
RSI	Repubblica Sociale Italiana (Italian Social Republic)
SD	Sicherheitsdienst (Security Service, intelligence agency of the SS)
SPÖ	Sozialdemokratische Partei Österreichs (Social Democratic Party of Austria)
SS	Schutzstaffel (Protection Squadrons)
TRC	truth and reconciliation commissions
UDHR	Universal Declaration of Human Rights
UNESCO	United Nations Educational, Scientific, and Cultural Organization
USHMM	United States Holocaust Memorial Museum
VOEST	steel company (now voestalpine AG)
WJC	World Jewish Congress

Amending the Past

Introduction

Confronting the Holocaust as Historical Injustice

For Swiss banks, 1995–96 was a disastrous year. Faced with a crescendo of questions and accusations concerning the fate of plundered assets transferred to Switzerland before, during, and immediately after World War II, Swiss bank officials at first invoked an inviolable principle of secrecy. There followed a chorus of increasingly strenuous denials, including some that came from the upper echelons of the Swiss government. When the World Jewish Congress (WJC) claimed to have uncovered more than 100,000 documents and artifacts suggestive of wrongdoing, Switzerland's president, Jean-Pascal Delamuraz, sounded off in the *Tribune de Genève*, calling the WJC's demands for speedy compensation "nothing less than extortion and blackmail."[1] Rather than accede to the demands for payback, which he likened to "an admission of guilt," Delamuraz suggested that foreign critics ought to withhold judgment pending the results of a "sweeping study," which was to be conducted by a nine-member panel of Swiss and international historians.

Established in December 1996 through a legislative decree of the Swiss Federal Council, this panel came to be known as the Independent Commission of Experts (ICE). According to its official mandate, the ICE was convened "to obtain the historical truth and to shed light on the extent and fate of assets which reached Switzerland as a result of the National-Socialist regime."[2] The commission was given a hefty budget for this purpose and was instructed to prepare a detailed report on the results of its inquiry within five years' time. In the course of its work, the ICE would come up against a thoroughly debunked, but still powerfully seductive and therefore persistent, nationalist myth regarding Switzerland's strict neutrality during World War II and the impeccable conduct of its leaders and functionaries. The ICE turned out to be the first in a wave of national Holocaust commissions, which were launched in Europe during the second half of the 1990s and the early 2000s. In 1998, as part of a larger project on Holocaust restitution, the United States Holocaust Memorial Museum (USHMM) compiled an international list of "Current Activities Regarding Holocaust-Era Assets," which included several dozen historical commissions charged with clarifying the circumstances under which Jewish spoliation took place and the extent to which lost and stolen assets had been dutifully returned—or not, as was often the case.[3] In June 1998 at the organizing seminar for the Washington Conference on Holocaust-Era Assets, Stuart Eizenstat, President Clinton's undersecretary of state and the "point man" for international initiatives related to Holocaust-era injustices, summarized what became the guiding ethos for most of these commissions:

> It is dispiriting that, for nearly half a century, the fate of Holocaust-era assets remained largely obscured. At the same time, it is inspiring that over the last several years, after the Cold War, and with the end of this century approaching, these issues have come to command the world's attention and touch the conscience of humanity. There is no doubt that this is a painful undertaking: it is not easy for any country to confront periods or issues in its recent history that reopen old wounds. But I believe that this can be a healing process, which can strengthen each of our countries and bring this century to a close on a high note of justice.[4]

Of course, this is the kind of buoyant perspective that one expects to encounter in the context of a fresh diplomatic initiative. The reality of the Holocaust commissions, however, proved to be more complicated than what Eizenstat, or anyone else, envisioned.

Although there is growing interest in understanding their work, historical commissions have been less thoroughly studied compared to other mechanisms that aim to secure justice for the victims of past atrocities (e.g., tribunals and truth commissions), and they have been largely ignored in terms of assessing their potential for supporting the still-evolving program of human rights. Broadly defined, historical commissions are investigative bodies charged with providing new understanding(s) of past events on the basis of fresh archival research. These commissions appear, in most cases, where difficult and shameful historical episodes have been suppressed in the public discourse, or where these events have become the fodder for destabilizing political debates. To an important extent, the work of these commissions has aligned with a burgeoning "right to history," which is discussed later in this chapter. While most historical commissions have arisen through official channels, as was the case with Switzerland, some have been created by unofficial organizations working within civil society. The majority of historical commissions have been national or local initiatives, although there are bilateral and international commissions to consider as well. With respect to the Holocaust commissions, which are the specific focus of this study, the most compelling aspect of their work is the promise they have shown for bringing the perspectives of rival groups more closely together in cases where divergent and conflicting memories of the same events have taken root. On the other hand, the ability of these commissions to cultivate intergroup dialogue and reconciliation is normally constrained, at least to some degree, both by the course of normal politics and also by what we might call the politics of knowledge. In December 1996, when the ICE was launched in Switzerland, nobody yet realized how this commission would become, in the words of its chairman, Jean-François Bergier, "a plaything for the political parties and different domestic and foreign groups *du pression.*"[5]

This book contributes to the interdisciplinary scholarship on the complex theme of reckoning with historical injustices and past atrocities. The following chapters treat more than a dozen commissions created to confront the legacies of World War II and, in particular, the Holocaust, which Saul Friedlander has called "the most extreme case of mass criminality" and "the most radical form of genocide encountered in history."[6] These commissions have a great deal to teach about the ways in which responsible historical scholarship can be blended with political advocacy and peace-building, and they tell us something new and important about the ways in which human rights are currently discussed and exercised (or not). Throughout the book, I explore the various ways that social memory has impeded deep historical understanding of the Holocaust, and I analyze recent Holocaust commissions in a broad, comparative framework in order to bring scholars, as well as nonspecialists, to a set of questions that now, more than ever, demand our attention. What role can historians play in societies where the past has been intensely and dangerously politicized? What contribution can historical clarification make to the achievement of justice? How might history be leveraged, responsibly, to ameliorate intergroup conflicts, where competing claims about the past represent a crucial dimension of the conflict? Just below the surface of these questions, I am engaged with another set of issues, which are to some degree "philosophical" but are also concrete in terms of what they mean for our ability to get along in the world in the aftermath of mass violence and large-scale human rights violations. What does it mean to be responsible for past injustices, and which forms of responsibility can be fairly applied to the present? How can we differentiate between explanation and exculpation, where historical narratives depicting past atrocities are concerned? In attempting to understand the experiences of the victims, while still engaging the perspectives of perpetrators and others who contributed to the violence, which historical comparisons are morally acceptable and which are untenable? Finally, how can we narrow the scope of disagreement on painful aspects of the past, while also leaving room for and encouraging further discussion, debate, and exchange of perspectives? To the extent that readers, at the end of this book, are able to come at these questions from new directions and with the benefit of fresh empirical data, this will be a good way to gauge the overall success of the work.

Prospects for a Mediating History

Historians have learned to tread lightly around the question of objectivity. Since the 1960s, philosophers like Hans-Georg Gadamer, Michel Foucault, and Jacques Derrida have pushed back against the claim that historical knowledge can reliably inform us about the past.[7] According to these skeptics, there is no given past to which historians have access, so it is impossible to know whether a particular interpretation of the past is valid. Foucault, in particular, succeeded in attenuating the empirical claims of historians by highlighting the roles of discourse and power in the construction of historical knowledge.[8] In the wake of these critiques, history has been engulfed by politics to the point that historians no longer blanch when called upon to admit as much. Previously seen as something shocking, Foucault's edict now passes for common knowledge: there is no history outside politics.

Despite the postmodernist critiques against it, however, history remains moored in the social sciences. Professional (i.e., academic) historians conduct their research and publish their findings in the belief that their representations of the past are both accurate and useful. The past also exerts a strong hold over the popular culture, and epic histories (for example, *Braveheart* or *Gladiator*) rate especially well. Even in the United States, where secondary school students consistently struggle on tests of basic historical knowledge, there is still a powerful appetite for stories that represent the past, especially on a grandiose scale.[9] For tens of millions of moviegoers, television viewers, readers, and video-gamers, the past supplies endless fascination. For historians, it is pleasant to believe that such popularity arises from a strong conviction that the past is a useful tool for making sense of the present, but there are also less satisfying ways to interpret this trend.

The past can also be a source of bitter conflict. The politics of history have proven to be just as divisive as the "Beltway" debates over fiscal policy, the future of federal entitlement programs, or the role of the state in the lives of its citizens. Battles over the past and its significance are commonplace in both the United States and the rest of the world, and popular media outlets rarely miss a chance to cover these debates and dustups. Whether it is the content of history textbooks in Texas,[10] a visit to a war shrine by Japan's prime minister,[11] the limits of free speech in countries that supported Nazism,[12] or discussions of caliphate revivalism in the Muslim world,[13] the past has a pronounced ability to pit large groups against each other and fan the flames of conflict. The so-called history wars are fought tooth and nail because the stakes for group identity are exceedingly high.[14] History is the moral glue that in-groups rely on to bind together their members, and at the same time it is the wedge they use to distance and distinguish themselves from outsiders. Without a unique history that differentiates them, groups lose not only the essence of their shared identity but also the compass that enables them to orient themselves and make decisions for the future. This helps to explain why groups sometimes play fast and loose with the past, by conjuring narratives that do not accord well with the facts, or that distort the facts to make historical conflicts appear more one-sided than they actually were.

Looking around the globe, one sees that history appears at the center of many of the most serious conflicts. Traditional theories of war and peace emphasize the importance of governance and resource competition or the anarchic character of international relations to explain why groups engage in violent conflict, but there are intellectual and emotional dimensions to these phenomena as well. History and memory pervade many of the seemingly intractable conflicts in the world today. This is true of manifest conflicts or "hot" wars like the one being fought between Israel and various Palestinian factions. It is also true with respect to latent conflicts, that is, simmering feuds with a potential to reignite, like the Sino-Japanese rivalry. Partisans in these contests weaponize the past in order to legitimate their interests and support their claims to moral superiority.[15] They place their political goals ahead of the disciplinary standards of professional history in order to construct narratives that validate and valorize their experience. Of course, one expects to encounter some degree of subjectivity in every historical narrative, given the ways in which the values and desires of the narrator intersect with her investigations of the past. But where and how does one draw a line between ordinary subjectivity, the sort that arises when responsible historians assemble carefully selected facts into a narrative built on hypothetical lines of causality, and irresponsible subjectivity, which partisans peddle to further their own interests?

While they may claim to have a monopoly on truth, the partisans, when they see their perspective contrasted against that of their rivals, oftentimes will embrace a relativist framework, since this maneuver removes the debate from the realm of science and pushes it onto the political terrain where they feel comfortable. Simo Drljača, a Bosnian Serb police chief and accused war criminal, made this kind of pivot after his indictment in 1997 by the International Criminal Tribunal for the former Yugoslavia (ICTY): "You have your facts. We have our facts. You have the complete right to choose between the two versions."[16] While Drljača grants that outsiders may freely conduct their own analysis of the facts, the hallmark of partisan history here is his unwillingness to be included in a conversation with his rivals: "You have your facts. We have ours." Negotiation and dialogue are antithetical to partisan discourse.

Changing the dynamic that confines partisans in their isolated silos of understanding is difficult work, to say the least. Partisans are disinclined to accept negotiations with their rivals, and their claims to objectivity "often veil a desire to silence competitors."[17] In open societies, where political jousting is the norm, the history wars are often viewed as an extension of grand debates over national values. Partisans of different political stripes have developed characteristic tactics, but the possibility for abuse always remains the same. In conservative nationalist circles, one observes a preference for laudatory and celebratory (i.e., triumphalist) narratives that emphasize the authenticity and wisdom of one particular cultural group or model over the others. On the Left, liberals have their own narrative, which embraces a new (or seemingly new) multicultural reality, but they can also be disingenuous about the way this narrative threatens the core identity of their rivals. Really, neither side has been shy about marshaling history for political gain, although attachment to tradition in conservative circles may foster greater inflexibility there.

Setting aside political differences, it seems clear that the partisans have overstepped academic historians in their bid to influence and sway public opinion. There are several reasons for this, including the tendency of partisans to package their judgments of the past in decontextualized, highly seductive "sound bites" and the readiness of mass media to propagate these. The most salient explanation for the inability of historians to compete effectively against partisan narratives, however, is the deep aversion they have shown toward any direct political engagement. This is largely a self-imposed restriction. Since the discipline was professionalized in the nineteenth century, history's academic gatekeepers have maintained a stringent boundary between scholarship and activism. With very few exceptions, scholars who have attempted to cross this line have seen their work roundly criticized and disparaged by their peers. While a few scholars have worked effectively against this current, a professional code that discourages instrumental history (i.e., history in the service of ideology) has remained in place for reasons both good and bad. As a consequence, historians inclined toward activism have been mostly marginalized within the profession. Except for an allegation of plagiarism, the surest way to discredit historical scholarship in the academy today is to claim that the author has allowed her ideological commitments to overdetermine the data.

For historians charged with political bias, the reflexive defense is to rearticulate the disciplinary oath, under which "knowledge workers" pledge to be guided by the evidence and to check their ideological predilections at the door. The recitation of this oath is understandable, considering the importance of protecting one's credibility and professional standing, but it is also problematic, since the historian's interpretive framework arises, unavoidably, from her subjectivity. Determined to abide by impossible rules, scholars find themselves pulled between the ideals and realities of historical praxis. Historians know that their identities and politics are deeply enmeshed in their interpretations of the past, yet they strive to produce an objective narrative that captures the essential qualities of the past. The partisan set, of course, never confronts this challenge, as these individuals routinely put what is politically expedient above consensus-based standards of objectivity. The Rankean imperative to represent the past "as it actually happened" (*wie es eigentlich gewesen*) exerts pressure on responsible historians that partisans do not so much ignore as fail to register in the first place.

To wrest power away from the partisan narratives that stymie responsible inquiry, historians will need to extricate themselves from the web of metaphysical and epistemological concerns that they have woven around the question of objectivity. This does not mean that historians can abandon the professional standards of their discipline. Historiography, to a remarkable extent, manages to apply consistent rules regarding how factual claims may be established, what degree of latitude historians enjoy when situating such facts into a broader context, how to assess different theories of causation, how to demarcate the limits of interpretation, and how to weigh competing interpretations of the same events. Strict methodological accountability is paramount if historians want to compete with the partisan narratives that feed conflict. At the same time, though, historians must be willing to engage the political debates they have previously tried to sidestep, and they must reckon more fully with the bugaboos of ideology and subjectivity if they want to contribute to a dialogue that can reconcile the divergent memories of historical rivals. If they insist on staying above the fray, or if they stick to the mantra that history and politics cannot be responsibly mingled, academic historians will only forfeit to the partisans whatever influence they might have over the public.

Charles Maier has engaged these problems more deeply than most historians, and his work over the past three decades points the way to a potential route forward. In his study of the *Historikerstreit* (historians' dispute), the highly publicized scuffle of the 1980s in which prominent German intellectuals raked through the Nazi past from opposing political perspectives, Maier brings the discipline to a critical juncture. After tracing the outlines of the debate, which, among other issues, raised the question of the Holocaust's uniqueness and the willingness of ordinary Germans to accept responsibility for this chapter in their nation's history, Maier unpacks the ideological agendas of the main participants and then sketches one possible roadway by which to escape the controversy: "The question becomes how history can mediate ideology methodologically. By mediate I do not mean just cover over or state indirectly. I mean incorporate, but transcend. For the historian, this requires a rigorous analysis of presuppositions from all contending points of view, indeed to see the stakes even for parties who may have been muffled or absent."[18] Maier envisions a process through which the past might be depolarized and partisan viewpoints brought to the heel of an adjudicating perspective. By excavating the assumptions and values that give them their skeletal support, Maier contends that historians can undercut the ideological agendas that partisans smuggle into their narratives of the past. This would entail a working through of the moral consequences that arise whenever we harness our identity to a particular version of history. Fully implemented, Maier's technique would bring all subjectivity to the surface so that representations of the past could be assessed on two axes simultaneously: one measuring empirical depth and rigor, and another that gauges the practical implications (i.e., the political and moral consequences) of a given narrative. The pairing of empirical and practical factors would create a new basis for judgment and critique by encouraging a broader line of questioning. Instead of limiting themselves to the customary questions (e.g., "Does the argument accord with the evidence?"), historians could look down other alleyways, where, previously, they had hesitated to venture, for example, "What state of affairs would arise if this (or that) argument were to prevail?" By adding a pragmatic dimension to the inquiry, mediating history carves out a new role for the historian. In addition to being an arbiter of plain facts, the historian would become an arbiter of the world into which the facts are fitted and according to which that world is shaped.

Maier's program recalls the techniques that Jacques Derrida, Jean-François Lyotard, and others in the poststructuralist camp have used to pick apart the major philosophical claims of the Western tradition. But while Maier may share a certain degree of skepticism with these French theorists, it is important to see that his mediating project strives at more than delegitimation of what the partisans hold dear. Besides "deconstruction," Maier's history also includes a positive program for us to consider. Through critical arbitration, a new reading of the past can emerge, which reframes the conversation, highlights points of potential agreement, and suggests new contours for subsequent inquiry. Maier's approach to the past seeks out the presuppositions that enable competing groups to wrap themselves in nonnegotiable cloaks of (mis)understanding. His mediating history strives for clarification and truth validation, but at the same time it seeks to expose the ideological scaffolding that supports each contending array of facts. The point is not that Maier's project can fully overcome the problem of subjectivity, but rather that his proposal for mediating history recognizes and addresses its own subjectivity, whereas the partisans pretend to live in a world where epistemological problems do not exist. You have your facts. We have ours.

The mediating history that Maier has outlined in broad strokes can come to fruition only where there is serious commitment to dialogue. This requires historians to engage with partisan perspectives rather than reject them out of hand because of their ideological overtones. The potential of mediating history rests in our ability to identify and overcome the cognitive (or sometimes emotional) blocks that lead partisans to reject the data and narratives that threaten their identity and worldview. Partisans will eschew the representations of history that do not accord with their facts, unless some aspect of their perspective is included (within limits) in the process of representation. Given the role historians have played in accommodating a relativist framework for interpretation, they must now live with the consequences of their own insights. This means exchanging the metaphysics that served as the standard currency of the profession (i.e., the search for objectivity) for a practical epistemology, which is more flexible and more in keeping with the style of inquiry that Maier believes can "incorporate, but transcend" ideology. In other words, mediating history aims to broaden, deepen, and add texture to our understanding of the past by engaging different and sometimes mutually opposing perspectives in a dialogue that allows for some degree of negotiation. By "negotiation," I do not mean the bargaining or compromise implied by a diplomatic definition of the word. Instead, I want to describe a dialogue that applies social scientific criteria for judgment while also looking for the narrative elements that could contribute to a shared understanding of the past. What we are aiming for is a history characterized by multivocality, although, as we shall see, there are limits to what this sort of approach can achieve. When dealing with individuals and groups whose view of the past depends on denial and rationalization, accommodating the needs and values of such parties moves us down a dangerous path that would undermine the potential of history to foster reconciliation.

Mediating history cannot give every interpretive claim equal consideration or create a roundtable at which every party, regardless of disposition, is entitled to a seat. Argument from the facts trumps the desire for myths of convenience, and mediation calls upon historians to invalidate certain perspectives. At the end of the day, history makes itself useful and distinguishes itself from partisan speech only insofar as it upholds the rhetorical and methodological rules of scientific inquiry.[19] Any possibility that historians will contribute to a new model of conflict management depends entirely on this point. Once in danger of being pitched onto its own proverbial dust heap, historical narrative returns here to claim a place within the tradition of philosophical pragmatism. Received as true, history has the potential to transform the world and domesticate the conflicts into which it has been drawn. The historical mode of knowledge cannot completely overcome the problem of subjectivity, but it can generate intersubjective agreement. The fact of such agreement testifies to the power of scholars, including historians, to make the world more as they wish to see it.[20] By injecting an idealist component into realist political discourse, a mediating history based on principled dialogue can effect justice, which is to say, broad agreement about what kinds of debt have accrued from the past and how to go about paying these down.

The Contribution of Historical Commissions

Successful engagement with the politics of the past requires careful analysis of existing conflict mediation tools, including some that are unconventional. While no single volume can address all of the mechanisms for confronting the past, there are trends worth examining, both for what they suggest in terms of best practices and because they highlight what is at stake when partisans wield the past irresponsibly. The rise of historical commissions since the end of the Cold War is one of these. Similar in some respects to the truth and reconciliation commissions that have been deployed in transitional settings, historical commissions, as previously stated, aim at clarifying the facts related to contentious and/or poorly understood episodes from the past.[21] Unlike the truth commissions, however, which address more recent events and collect oral testimonies from living victims and witnesses, the historical commissions normally investigate more distant episodes for which there are fewer direct witnesses. Consequently, the historical commissions have relied more heavily on written records. In certain cases, historical commissions have been able to access previously unexamined archives. More often, though, their work has entailed recontextualization of previously available materials. In general, historical commissions do not make shocking revelations that turn the past on its head. Where they have made an impact, they have typically done so by ascribing new meaning(s) to facts that have been the subject of interpretative debate or have been glossed over in societies where historical myths have helped to protect the collective self-image. As one member of Switzerland's ICE explained, "The main value added was in putting earlier findings on a firmer basis, adding perspectives, and providing a broader context."[22] Broadly speaking, then, the work of these commissions represents the possibility of amending the past. While this description paints their work in somewhat mundane terms, even a modest reconfiguration of context can have a powerful conciliatory effect where groups are divided over the past. In the case of Switzerland, the ICE's work produced a point of contact between Holocaust victims, who sought to impose maximum penalties against the banks that had unjustly acquired their assets, and the officers of these firms, who sought to satisfy these claims while also ensuring the long-term viability of their companies. In the end, Switzerland righted the wrongs it committed and, to a large extent, repaired its image abroad by negotiating its debt with the victims of Nazi-era spoliation and setting up a compensation fund that was pegged to the findings of expert historians.

The full genealogy of the historical commissions has not been recovered, although various commissions of inquiry established in the first several decades of the twentieth century offer a good starting point.[23] Over the last twenty-five years, historical commissions have been convened around the world to deal with contested events and memories. Some of these commissions have engaged history of mainly local significance; others have attempted to sort through major historical events with global implications. All of the commissions have tackled emotionally charged issues in settings where animosity and divergent memories have seriously unsettled intergroup relations. In the United States, commissions were convened to address the history of twentieth-century race riots, including large-scale violence and destruction in Tulsa, Oklahoma (1921), and Rosewood, Florida (1923).[24] In Uganda, members of civil society have tried to bring together government officials and representatives for the Acholi to assess the role that historical memory has played in stoking that country's civil wars.[25] At the heart of the Ugandan project, several groups of scholars, representing different ethnic populations, have used the historical record as a "bonding space" to write joint narratives that examined the origins of recent violence and documented past instances of interethnic cooperation.[26] In the Caucasus region of Eurasia, the Institute for Historical Justice and Reconciliation (IHJR) has tried to encourage Turkish-Armenian mutual understanding. Since 2009, the IHJR has sponsored a series of meetings, the Journey Toward Understanding Project, which it touts as a confidence-building exercise aimed at introducing Turkish and Armenian scholars who want to contemplate the history of their respective nations through a shared lens.[27] A similar project in the Balkans, the Scholars' Initiative for the Former Yugoslavia, has endeavored to narrow the "perceptual gap" that has reinforced cultural cleavages and generated distinctive histories for the ethnonational communities living there.[28] As one participant put it: "The Scholars' Initiative stemmed from the conviction that native historians and social scientists are best positioned to challenge the tendentious nationalistic narratives that have succeeded so well in dividing the peoples of [Southeastern] Europe."[29] These are just a few examples of recent commissions that have attempted to mediate the past in order to foster reconciliation. New initiatives spring up regularly, and although the efficacy of these commissions for promoting peace and understanding is by no means proven, their appeal for groups seeking a creative mechanism for historical clarification and redress seems undeniable. At the same time, the historical commission model can be unscrupulously exploited by regimes eager to hide their own records of abuse and to castigate their rivals.[30]

As the title of this book suggests, this study treats a large subset of historical commissions, which were convened in Europe during the 1990s and early 2000s to reexamine the history of the Holocaust, and confront the myths and misunderstandings that had stymied the efforts of its victims to achieve justice and have their history acknowledged. Although each of the commissions presented here was unique and operated in accordance with a distinctive mandate, for the purposes of this study I have chosen to divide these initiatives into two broad categories.[31] The first category, which represents the predominant model, consists of the national Holocaust commissions. In general, these commissions were launched in countries where complicity with the Nazi regime during the Holocaust era was either poorly documented or poorly integrated into the official historical narratives that reached the public. Like Switzerland, these countries embraced a mythology for the wartime era that emphasized the suffering of their own nationals and the acts of resistance undertaken by their citizens above and against the harmful policies, compromises, and capitulations that facilitated and amplified the Nazi genocide. To different degrees, the national commissions strove to confront these myths and counter them with new narratives that took a fuller account of the harmful and unjust policies implemented in their countries during and immediately after the Nazi era. The principal challenge that these commissions faced was how to explore and delineate the gradations of culpability that characterized each case without suggesting false equivalencies. This required a careful approach, capable of developing the theme of responsibility in a nuanced manner that could cover the many different forms of collaboration. It also entailed, at times, using the history of World War II and the Holocaust to a construct a pan-European narrative, which gave the countries implicated in these events a chance to manage their historical debts and build toward a common future.[32] As many of the national Holocaust commissions emerged against the backdrop of European Union enlargement, their work raised important questions about the flexibility and limitations of group identity (e.g., the desire for a strong nationalist identity at a moment of increasing integration).

In part I, I present seven national commissions: Switzerland, France, Poland, Austria, Italy, Lithuania, and Latvia. While this list is far from comprehensive, these cases have been selected for the way they combine unique attributes with emblematic qualities that highlight critical issues. The national commissions were primarily (but not exclusively) government-appointed bodies that received state funding. In some cases, this made it more difficult for the commissions to assert their independence. It also required careful attention to public perception, something the commissions did not always handle well. Can a commission that receives its funding and mandate from the state produce a credible and valid history that the public does not reflexively reject as the government's truth? As we shall see, each commission had to develop its own strategy for handling outside interference, and the outcomes were highly variable.

In addition to the national commissions, there are also bilateral and international commissions to consider. In part II, I take up six of these: Germany-France, Germany-Poland, Germany-Czech (which sponsored two separate, but also overlapping, commissions to deal with long-standing tensions between the two countries, as well as one very specific diplomatic crisis), the International Commission on Holocaust-Era Insurance Claims (ICHEIC), and the International Catholic-Jewish Historical Commission (ICJHC). Compared to the national commissions, these multiparty commissions are often more explicit in their commitment to conflict mediation, although there are clearly some failures to account for as well. These commissions have also tended to arise through different channels, for example through the initiatives of nongovernmental organizations (NGOs) and civil society. Because they engage debates in which large ethnonational groups are divided over seemingly small differences of interpretation, the success of these commissions can hinge on the way(s) their members understand the concept of closure. To the extent that commissions are able to establish their own evaluative criteria—some are prescribed such criteria in their mandate, while others generate their own—they need to be careful about how they define and measure success. Of course, not every commission has achieved success, even at a minimal standard. The ICJHC (see chap. 7) struggled badly from the outset, and the literature describing its work can best be characterized as a postmortem. The principal question for this study is whether anything useful can be gleaned from such failures.

I want to suggest that there are important lessons to be learned from all of the commissions presented here, including those that performed poorly. Close analysis suggests that historical commissions are an underutilized tool for mediating conflict and promoting reconciliation. Deployed intelligently, these commissions can foster an approach to history that deepens democratic commitment, encourages intergroup cooperation, and enriches the current conception of human rights. The most adept commissions have (1) clarified the historical record, that is, convincingly documented the truth about what happened; (2) confronted and delegitimated partisan narratives, which groups have used to support their claims to moral superiority and advance their political interests; (3) facilitated justice and apportioned guilt responsibly where past harms have been insufficiently investigated; (4) raised the question of appropriate redress where victims of past injustice and/or their close relatives have been left uncompensated; and (5) opened new possibilities for cooperation and reconciliation between groups divided by their shared history.

While the historical commissions have not garnered the same degree of attention from scholars as the truth and reconciliation commissions they partly resemble, there is rising interest in understanding their work and assessing their capabilities. Already, there have been a number of major academic conferences devoted to the subject. In November 2002, the National D-Day Museum (New Orleans) hosted the conference "Commissioning History in the United States, Germany, and Austria: Historical Commissions, Victims, and World War II Restitution."[33] The following month, Yad Vashem (Jerusalem) convened "The International Conference on Confronting History: The Historical Commissions of Inquiry."[34] In March 2010, Columbia University organized "Historical Commissions: Comparative Perspectives."[35] This two-day conference, organized by the Center for the Study of Human Rights, treated European commissions (including Poland, Ukraine, the Baltic States, and Romania), as well as examples from East Asia (China, Japan, and Korea) and the Armenian-Turkish case cited earlier. As the conference's title suggests, participants engaged in a comparative analysis of commissions whose work was already complete, but the organizers also sought to identify lessons for future commissions. This study continues that project, and it shares a set of working premises:

(1) Historical discourse is not monopolized by dispassionate scholars but is an inherently political enterprise in which a variety of groups and constituencies each have a stake;
(2) Historical narratives are embedded in the political discourse, where different groups aim to utilize the past for their own purposes; and
(3) In spite of these complications, there is a methodology rooted in the norms of social scientific inquiry, which provides a tool for the management of these debates and conflicts.

It is important to understand that the best commissions have strived to provide more than just good historical description. "Getting the facts straight" is only part of what these bodies can achieve. What makes the commissions compelling is the methodology they utilize, which represents an effort to bridge the scholarly and political discourses.[36] If the work of these commissions resonated only with scholars, there would be little point in probing their significance for the larger public, or for the purposes of conflict resolution. This does not mean, of course, that the historical commissions should strive for sensationalism or public titillation. Rather, it means that the commissions must be ready to highlight and explain the kinds of methodological choices that tend to be purposely obfuscated in partisan discourse. This includes how historians establish their factual claims (e.g., based on what kinds of evidence); the latitude (and restraints) that historians have when situating these claims in a broader, explanatory context; the narrative choices historians make in the course of interpreting their data; and the criteria according to which historians weigh competing interpretations of the same events. Only by presenting these considerations openly and self-consciously can the historical commissions hope to persuade scholars or the general public to accept—or even just care about—their findings. This is not to say that the commissions must win universal public acceptance in order to be successful. Indeed, there may be a great deal to gain where these investigations produce further disagreement. This may be exactly what is required to break social taboos that encourage silence, allow rivals to air their mutual grievances and vent their frustrations, and develop a common language for further inquiry. Even if the commissions do not always succeed in producing reconciliation "in one fell swoop," they can still nurture a culture that values tolerance for divergent perspectives. If the commissions contribute to a historical dialogue that accepts legitimate disagreements without allowing these to boil over into overt hostility and aggression, they will already have shifted the discourse onto a more conciliatory terrain. While the promise of these commissions is sometimes overexaggerated, they can supplement the process of reconciliation where rapprochement at the official level struggles to trickle down to the grassroots. In other settings, they can create new openings for dialogue within civil society, even when elites have already wedded themselves to inflammatory historical narratives. While it is prudent to describe their work and potential in modest terms—indeed, it is crucial in each case to assess the limits of what can be achieved—these commissions can do more than merely fill in a few blind spots in the record, as is sometimes suggested or assumed.

To better understand the rise of the historical commissions, one needs to think through several overlapping trends from the past several decades. If one asks, "Where did these commissions come from? What explains their recent proliferation?" the answer must encompass at least three factors: (1) the rise of truth and reconciliation commissions and transitional justice more generally, (2) the rise of the Internet and the twenty-four-hour news cycle, and (3) the rise of the human rights discourse.

As previously mentioned, there is an important connection between the historical commissions examined in this study and the truth and reconciliation commissions that operated in Argentina (1983–84), Chile (1990–91, 2003–5), El Salvador (1992–93), South Africa (1995–2002), Guatemala (1997–99), Peru (2001–3), the Federal Republic of Yugoslavia (2002–3), Timor-Leste (2002–5), and Morocco (2004–6).[37] These truth commissions arose in societies attempting to recover from long periods of political oppression and violence. While each commission established its own formula for defining and securing justice, all were guided by a shared belief in the importance of truth-telling for societies transitioning to democracy. These commissions appeared where there was at least some commitment to repairing the wounds of the past and restoring the fractured relationships between perpetrators and victims. Not every commission succeeded in this endeavor, and there is evidence to suggest that these commissions did not perform as effectively as their advocates have claimed. Nevertheless, all of these commissions started from a shared conviction that peace and justice are unattainable without thoroughly and directly confronting the abuses committed under the previous regime.

The truth commissions offered victims of grave human rights abuses an opportunity to tell their stories, receive recognition for their suffering, and in some cases, receive compensation for their losses. Some commissions gave amnesty to perpetrators in exchange for their cooperation and testimony, while others sought to preserve a greater space for punishment and accountability. While skeptics have questioned the link these commissions posit between truth and reconciliation, many of the victims who testified in front of them have described their experiences as being both cathartic and recuperative. In the final analysis, lack of reliable data and a dearth of comparative, longitudinal studies make it difficult to fully assess the efficacy and impact of these commissions.[38] But while it has been difficult to measure and evaluate outcomes, the demand for these kinds of truth-telling exercises in countries engaged in democratic transition speaks to their broad appeal. In any case, the increasing prevalence of truth commissions does not fully explain the advent of the historical commissions. Both truth commissions and historical commissions have influenced each other without the one completely explaining the emergence of the other.

The rise of the Internet has also aroused interest in the work of historical commissions. Whether the Internet has deepened public engagement in civic life is debatable; however, the Internet's ability to dredge up past injustices and bring forgotten histories into public view is undeniable. The structure of the World Wide Web, especially its "upstream" capabilities, has made it fertile ground for projects devoted to the recovery and recirculation of social memories, which victims (or groups who identify as such) tap into as both a source of solidarity and a platform for pushing their political demands. Cyberspace is teeming with websites whose purpose is explicitly revisionist, whether that means bringing attention to the perspective of victims, seeking exculpation for the perpetrators, or suggesting analogies and equivalencies that cloud moral judgment. An Internet connection permits rapid bouncing between the narratives of both "deserving" and "undeserving" victims and, at the same time, reveals a plethora of partisan narratives. In an increasingly wired world, one gets easy access to grievances that were confined in earlier times to library bookshelves or tucked away in archives without an outlet to collective memory. What makes this interesting (or vexing) is the web's open structure and the potential for conflict enabled by that very architecture. With a few keystrokes or clicks, one can find images featuring the severed heads of Chinese victims of the Nanking Massacre,[39] as well as sites created by Japanese groups pushing to remove all mention of these war crimes from history textbooks.[40] One can spend days browsing Holocaust remembrance sites, or one can visit the web pages set up by German expellees (i.e., ethnic Germans forcibly resettled following World War II) who have used the web to bolster their claims for compensation.[41] There is a blog, *Heroes of Serbia, Memory Eternal*, that commemorates Serbia's contributions to the Allied victory in World War I and creates "a place where Serbdom is revered, celebrated, and honored."[42] Another blog, *Remaking Rwanda: Facts and Opinions on the Ground*, heaps scorn on Western scholars who have criticized President Paul Kagame's handling of Rwanda's postgenocide reconstruction (e.g., his refusal to facilitate prosecutions of Tutsi who participated in reprisal killings against Hutu).[43] The Internet has become a global forum for the politics of history, and it has intensified the sniping that partisans previously engaged in through "traditional" media. The migration of the history wars to the realm of cyberspace has made these contests more vitriolic and reckless. New media have made past injustices and the perspectives of victims more visible, but at the same time they have created a venue where partisan narratives can be circulated cheaply and easily. Even if one cannot definitively prove it, observation and intuition strongly suggest that the Internet has helped to nourish the divisiveness to which the historical commissions have tried to respond. Still and all, the best explanation for the proliferation of the historical commissions lies elsewhere.

To understand these commissions and appreciate their full potential, we need to probe their connection to the rise of human rights in the second half of the twentieth century. By doing so, we can see how their work has mirrored key human rights instruments that aim to realize the right to truth and the right to redress for individuals and groups. The commissions take the aspirational language of the human rights discourse and give it a concrete expression. They represent an attempt to secure a brand of justice that the human rights discourse envisions but does not yet reliably secure, which is the right of a group to its history and a corresponding right to redress, where old wounds have been ignored, minimized, or insufficiently mitigated. It is obviously important not to exaggerate here. The commission model does not always succeed in bringing rivals closer together, and it can be misused to give cover to governments that have committed large-scale violations of human rights. I will have more to say about the limitations of historical commissions later on, but first I want to develop more fully the connection between historical commissions and the rise of human rights.

Historical Redress and the Right to History

Human rights and historical redress exist in tension with each other. As various scholars have noted, human rights are posited as universal ideology, whereas redress seeks to remedy specific acts of injustice suffered by particular people(s).[44] This gap between universality (rights) and particularity (redress) can appear, at first, unbridgeable. At the same time, though, redress emanates from and reinforces the human rights discourse, as it is expressed in international law, giving it a firmer basis in normal politics by taking it out of the realm of purely abstract aspiration. This move toward what is tangible and actionable marks one of the most important developments in the human rights discourse. It represents the principal distinction between human rights and earlier aspirational ideologies such as socialism and nationalism.

On the other hand, human rights do not fare particularly well where partisan histories are firmly rooted or reinforced by violence. This is especially true when the sovereignty of the state overshadows the rights of individuals and groups. In such cases, claims based in human rights are "typically elided in national and state-based narratives" and the perspective of victims is all too easily "subsumed by the state."[45] But, as this study aims to demonstrate, an important transformation is currently taking place. Increasingly, attention is being paid to the creation of mechanisms that translate abstract rights into concrete practices of justice. Dull instruments that existed for decades in the literature of the United Nations and in international law are being honed now by states and NGOs to make them more useful in specific social struggles where local conditions and agencies have made the universal ideology of human rights seem flaccid.

We can trace the connection between rights and redress back to two of the foundational documents in the human rights movement: the Universal Declaration of Human Rights (1948) and the International Covenant on Civil and Political Rights, which opened for signature in 1966 and came into force ten years later.[46] The nexus between rights and redress is further elaborated in subsequent UN instruments, which, although lesser known, are still important for understanding the genealogy of historical commissions. These include the Declaration of Basic Principles of Justice for Victims of Crime and Abuse of Power (1985); the Basic Principles and Guidelines on the Right to a Remedy and Reparation for Victims of Gross Violations of International Human Rights Law and Serious Violations of International Humanitarian Law (2005); and the Commission on Human Rights Report, "Promotion and Protection of Human Rights: Impunity" (2004/5). I briefly review each of these here with an eye toward explaining how they influenced the paradoxical, but also highly significant, relationship between human rights and historical redress.

The right of individuals and groups to their history, that is, their right to know the truth about history, emerged gradually as the principal instruments of human rights came into force. The Universal Declaration of Human Rights (UDHR), adopted in 1948, already connotes specific rights to historians (e.g., the right to freedom of expression and information in article 19) that are suggestive of a broader right to history. Although it is the nature of rights that they are inalienable and, therefore, devoid of any obligations, it is still possible to extract from the right to intellectual freedom outlined in the UDHR a corresponding set of ethical duties.[47] These would include: (1) a duty to produce expert knowledge about the past, which is linked to the right to science elaborated in article 27 of the UDHR; (2) a duty to disseminate such knowledge, which is linked to the right to information and culture articulated in articles 19 and 27; and (3) the duty to teach what historians have validated, which can be linked to the right to education in article 26.[48] If one accepts these linkages, then under the UDHR, scholars have both a right and a duty to enhance the quality of historical knowledge and to combat the influence of partisan politics on history. Originally formulated in terms of "the right to know" during the mid-1980s, this principle has emerged as "the right to truth" in subsequent UN documents.[49] Irrespective of the exact verbiage, this new rubric moved the human rights project into the realm of civil society, as well as into institutions of higher learning. Over time, this "right to truth" has heightened awareness of past injustices and encouraged demands for remediation. The rising prominence of such a right has made adjudicating past injustices a project not only for judges but also for historians;[50] and it has helped translate the abstract language of rights into the concrete duties associated with redress, particularly in the form of restorative justice and reparations. Historical knowledge, responsibly rendered, has now come to be seen as a critical step toward justice, and the suppression of such knowledge (or its absence) is now understood as the continuation and/or renewal of earlier injustices. From the perspective of the UDHR, "Knowledge of the facts of historical injustice, recent and remote alike, has a major reparatory effect *in itself*; conversely, failing to deal with historical injustice is an injustice *in itself*."[51]

Adopted in 1985, the Declaration of Basic Principles of Justice for Victims of Crime and Abuse of Power (DBPJ) helped lay additional groundwork for the right to history and for the redress movement of the 1990s and 2000s. The DBPJ is important because it recognizes that injuries caused by gross violations of human rights endure over time and may extend from the immediate victims to their family and descendants. This document also creates a framework for public inquiry and clarification, which anticipates the proliferation of both truth commissions and historical commissions. In article 4e of the DBPJ, the UN General Assembly calls on member states to acknowledge and curtail victimization by recording and publicizing the facts related to past injustices and gross violations of rights. According to the DBPJ, UN member states should endeavor "to promote disclosure of relevant information to expose official and corporate conduct to public scrutiny."[52] These disclosures may provide a basis for subsequent prosecutions (as outlined in article 4d), or they may simply help to promote "observance of codes of conduct and ethical norms" (as spelled out in article 4f). In either case, the DBPJ is intended as a "means of providing recourse for victims" (article 5d).

In the annex to the DBPJ, there are several important statements regarding access to justice. The first of these carves out an explicit space for the emergent right to historical redress. Where crimes and abuse of power have been properly documented, victims are entitled to "access to the mechanisms of justice and to prompt redress." The annex does not specify which mechanisms are best for achieving justice, but it establishes two categories for implementation: judicial and administrative. Although the declaration does not specifically mention historical commissions, it is easy to see how these might fit under its conception of justice. The annex holds that the needs of victims can be facilitated by any process that "[allows] the views and concerns of victims to be presented and considered."[53] This would obviously embody much of what the right to history entails. The annex is, therefore, a crucial statement on the desirability and ethical rectitude of such a right, if not exactly a blueprint for its application.

Adopted twenty years after the DBPJ, the Basic Principles and Guidelines on the Right to a Remedy and Reparation (2005) are even more explicit in their formulation of the right to history and redress. Invoking the UN Charter, as well as the UDHR and the two International Covenants on Human Rights (i.e., the Covenant on Civil and Political Rights and the Covenant on Economic, Social, and Cultural Rights), this document cements the right to justice for victims of gross violations of human rights. The Basic Principles and Guidelines entail no new legal obligations but instead call on UN members to "identify mechanisms, modalities, procedures and methods for the implementation of existing legal obligations."[54] This effort to complement existing obligations with new mechanisms is intended to develop what the authors of the document have called a more "victim-oriented approach" to the remediation of large-scale injustice. In regard to historical injustices, which reach farther back than the crimes that typically preoccupy transitional regimes, the UN proclamation asserts that there will be no statute of limitations on the pursuit of justice. In other words, the full realization of democratic norms requires a reckoning with past atrocities, regardless of how far back the history of abuse extends. The 2005 guidelines do not specify who can make a claim for redress, but the document states that victims are persons who "individually or collectively suffered harm." The inclusion of collective harm, in light of the UN's earlier recognition (1985) that harm to victims can be passed down to subsequent generations, appears to support demands for reparation in the case of more distant injustices. It is obviously problematic that no clear line exists to differentiate actionable injustices from older injuries that can no longer be justly remediated. One can certainly ask, "How far back does a putative right to redress extend before everything in the past is up for grabs?" So far, there has not been a definitive answer.

Antoon De Baets has argued that rights extend only to the living and not to the dead, so that the responsibility to repair injustice ends when the last victims have passed.[55] But this only rekindles the debate over the identity of victims. Who counts as a victim, and who is excluded? Why, in the context of international politics, are some victims seen as deserving, while others are told that they must accept the past as it is? In "Superseding Historic Injustice," Jeremy Waldron contends that the moral significance of the past stems primarily from "the difference it makes to the present."[56] Instead of automatically moving to return victims of past abuse to the status quo ante, Waldron asks a practical question: How are the victims faring presently? If the victims or their descendants are no longer actively suffering as a consequence of a past injustice, then, for Waldron, the right to redress no longer applies. This is, in essence, a principle of just resource allocation. If the victims of past injustice have endured long enough to replace what they lost with something comparable, then Waldron claims that the old injustice has been transcended. In other words, if the past makes no practical difference to the present, in terms of resource distribution, it ought to be relinquished as the basis of moral demands.[57] But this reduces the meaning of suffering to material deprivation, and it runs against the grain of the current human rights paradigm, which posits that the needs of victims can be not only material but also psychological and emotional. Human dignity may be difficult to calculate on a financial ledger, but human rights exist to protect against more than resource diminishment.

Staying within the human rights discourse, there is one more UN document that bolsters the right to history. In 2003, the UN Commission on Human Rights requested that the organization's secretary-general solicit an independent expert to compile a list of best practices for combating impunity. In 1997 the commission adopted a Set of Principles for the Promotion and Protection of Human Rights, but despite broad support for the initiative, difficulties arose over how to implement the core principles. Responding to this challenge, the UN secretary-general solicited Diane Orentlicher, a professor of law at American University and a highly regarded human rights scholar, to produce a report on best practices, which she submitted in February 2004.[58]

Orentlicher's report drew on a variety of sources. Prior to its submission, UN Secretary-General Kofi Annan invited member states to provide information on recently implemented measures to combat impunity. Replies came from twenty countries.[59] The UN also convened an "expert workshop," which brought together a number of NGOs.[60] The contributions of these groups ultimately converged around three principles, which, according to Orentlicher, interlink to provide a "multifaceted strategy" and a "comprehensive approach" to the problem of impunity. Above all, Orentlicher urged that member states accede to the international treaties that already comprise what we may call the human rights canon. Beyond this, she recommended that members commit themselves to three points: (1) the right to know, (2) the right to justice, and (3) the right to reparation. These three principles, Orentlicher maintained, should be utilized to "promote the broad participation of victims and other citizens."[61] Taken together, these recommendations speak directly to the historical commissions that are the subject of this study.

While much of her report related to the work of truth commissions, Orentlicher's arguments can be extended to cover the historical commissions without much difficulty. Although their methodologies differ, both commission types offer the same potential benefits, that is, to help victims cope with uncertainty, to achieve a measure of justice so that society can realize its democratic aspirations, and to explore appropriate measures for repairing past injustices. In the case of truth commissions, uncertainty might stem from the anguish individuals experience while the safety and whereabouts of their loved ones remains unclear, or it might arise from something more visceral, such as the panic that arises at the prospect of encountering one's torturer in a public setting. For the victims of historical injustice, the quality of uncertainty is different. Of course, these individuals may also have waited for decades to learn the fate of their loved ones, or they might have tried for many years to recover property that was unjustly wrested away from their families, but because the historical commissions tend to paint in broader strokes than the truth commissions (i.e., in terms of trends and general knowledge, rather than individual cases), they do not always produce the sort of knowledge that answers specific questions of this nature. One of the principal issues for the historical commissions is the difficulty they have navigating between individual life stories and the large data sets required to buttress generalized historical knowledge. Elsewhere, I have discussed this aspect of the commissions' work in terms of their ability to both "silence and un-silence" different aspects of the past.[62] Notwithstanding such tensions, the historical commissions can still offer relief against the anguish of not having one's experience publicly or officially acknowledged. In other words, the historical commissions can assuage the victims' uncertainties regarding the validity of what they hold to be true about the past and, therefore, about themselves. This obviously does not eliminate the problem of the influence of politics on historical knowledge, but it does provide a general framework for what victims of past injustice are entitled to receive. As the Inter-American Court of Human Rights (IACHR) has put it, victims of past injustice have a right "to know the full, complete, and public truth as to the events that transpired, their specific circumstances, and who participated in them."[63]

International law also strongly suggests that the right to know extends to groups as well as individuals. The IACHR has affirmed that the right to know the truth includes a collective dimension. "Society has a right to know the truth [regarding] atrocities of the past."[64] Disclosure of the truth, in some cases, might enable members of society to prevent the repetition of atrocities, but clarification, Orentlicher has argued, serves a reparative function in any case. Whether it is performed by a commission that exchanges perpetrator testimony for amnesty, or by historians who scrutinize the documentary record to contextualize the facts concerning past injustices, truth-seeking can become an important emblem of justice and reparation. By emblem, I mean something largely symbolic but not exclusively symbolic. Even if historical clarification does not lead directly to prosecutions or other retributive measures, it can still represent a kind of restorative justice. By taking an alternate route, one that eschews vengeance (even lawful vengeance) but at the same time demands accountability in the form of acknowledgment, historical commissions can supply more than what is merely second best. "[Each commission] casts its findings and conclusions not in terms of individual blame but instead in terms of what was wrong and never justifiable. In doing so, it helps frame the events in a new national narrative of acknowledgement, accountability, and civic values."[65] More than just an opportunity to clarify the facts, the historical commissions offer a chance to pronounce reasoned moral judgments, which is what academic historians have mostly shied away from until recently.

Historical commissions can also explore the past in a more nuanced manner than what normally emerges from judicial proceedings. In court, lawyers must direct their questions to particular individuals, and they are constrained by evidentiary rules concerning what is deemed admissible and relevant to the case. By contrast, a commission "can try to expose the multiple causes and conditions" that contribute to large-scale atrocities and mass violence like the Holocaust.[66] Outside the antagonistic setting of the courtroom, historical commissions can probe the influence of economic structures, long-standing intergroup hostilities, totalitarian policies and politics, military and police practices, and other processes of dehumanization that contribute to acts of genocide. They can do this, moreover, in a deliberate manner that encourages rich understandings of causality and resists the oversimplifications and stereotypes that reinforce group conflict. By amending the past and opening the record to a broader, multifaceted mode of analysis, historical commissions can offer redress in several overlapping forms: (1) they can relieve the suffering of victims by supplying official (or, anyway, public) acknowledgment for their travails; (2) they can begin a process of moral rehabilitation, by which the nation recommits to principles it claims to value but has failed to honor consistently; (3) they can supply a rich, explanatory context for past injustices that opens bridges for political reconciliation; (4) they can provide documentation to establish or reinforce a case for restitution; and (5) they can lay a foundation for new educational projects that restore dignity to the victims, apportion guilt responsibly, and create a new basis for intergroup cooperation. While the potential of these commissions is by no means unlimited, one of their main advantages is the flexibility they exhibit in terms of design and implementation. As I show through my analysis of recent Holocaust commissions, these initiatives offer one possible way to foster and uphold the principles of justice spelled out by Orentlicher.

Before we can delve into a detailed discussion of specific commissions, there is a potential contradiction that ought to be examined more closely. Throughout this chapter and elsewhere in the text, mediating history is sometimes presented in terms of negotiation and compromise. Where groups have embraced divergent accounts of the same events, the historical commission model appears to offer a way forward by opening up what could be regarded as a "middle way." But as I have stated already, the style of negotiation I describe is distinct from the plea bargaining that lawyers pursue on behalf of their clients or from the old-fashioned horse-trading that diplomats have used to broker certain peace agreements. A quid pro quo strategy may or may not be suitable, depending on how far and in what specific ways competing accounts of the past differ. Because commissions must uphold a rigorous social scientific methodology in order to rise above the level of partisan history, there will be some cases where these commissions cannot offer even modest validation to one (or any) of the contending perspectives. Scientific investigation will ratify some perspectives while invalidating others, in which case there may be little or no chance of "splitting the difference." In South Africa, Desmond Tutu, the chairman of the Truth and Reconciliation Commission (TRC) set up by the Unity Government in 1995, never wavered in his belief that prospects for postapartheid reconciliation depended on acknowledgment of guilt on both sides of the color line.[67] In Guatemala, by contrast, the Comisión para el Esclarecimiento Histórico (Historical Clarification Commission), which was convened in 1994, specifically rejected "the theory of two devils" that posited co-responsibility for the human rights abuses that took place during that country's long civil war. The Guatemalan report (1999) attributed 93 percent of the rights violations and violence during the war to the state and only 3 percent to the rebel factions.[68] Findings like these obviously restrict what can be accomplished through a process of historical mediation, although the commission model still offers possibilities for recontextualization and for historical explanation that reapportions guilt by means of careful analysis of causality (e.g., chains of command, underlying socioeconomic imbalances, etc.). Once again, mediating history should not be mistaken for the problematic notion that "everything is up for grabs." While mediation entails a distinctive way of reading the historical record, there are limits to the way(s) in which the past may be legitimately amended. Besides making a case for the peace-building potential of the historical commission model, the case studies in this volume also help delineate which aspects of the past can be negotiated and within what limits. Mediating history looks for wiggle room where ambiguities in the documentary record have become the focal point for divergent historical narratives, but there are also core principles within the discourse of individual and group rights that set absolute limits on what may be achieved through dialogue and negotiation. Certain interpretive conflicts, like partisan debates over who is/is not a "deserving" victim, will not be ameliorated unless or until rivals are willing to extend to their adversaries the same right to truth that they have claimed for themselves. And even if they do, this will likely produce new dilemmas. In chapter 4, for example, the difficulties of the Commission of the Historians of Latvia (CHL) can be traced directly to what has become a "non-negotiable" sticking point, that is, the readiness of Western scholars to put Latvia's past into a comparative framework and the determination of Latvian historians to privilege what they see as its unique attributes. Whether the two sides will be able to clear this hurdle at some point in the future remains unclear, although some of the cases presented here (e.g., France-Germany in chapter 5) suggest that their chances of doing so will be improved by having tried once already. In the end, though, it has to be said that the commission model is no guarantee for successful mediation. Even where parties have expressed "an honest desire to understand and to respect the historical memories of others," as was the case in Latvia, the actual engagement of historical data can result in an ugly clashing of perspectives. This leads to one final consideration, which is closely related to the potential for clashing but is also part of the larger argument I want to make concerning historical acknowledgment as a form of reparation.

The case of Latvia is helpful for the purposes of this study primarily because it has entailed so much disagreement about who are the victims and who are the perpetrators. Mary Poovey has argued that the Western conception of justice ultimately depends on the potential for intersubjective agreement regarding what constitutes a fact or evidence.[69] Where there is no such agreement, Poovey asserts, there can be no true justice but only the triumph of one view at the expense of another. Mediating history does not fully overcome this problem, nor do the historical commissions represent a neutral instrument for digging out the truth of the past, in the way that a paleontologist might be seen as excavating the truth of a *T. rex*. The model presented here arose from a scientific discourse that privileges observable phenomena but, at the same time, has had little to say about which facts—or whose facts—provide the most useful picture of the universe. Where historians choose between plausible interpretations of the same data, they are no longer practicing a purely scientific methodology but instead have moved into the realm of the sociopolitical. What the commissions can do about this apparent "Achilles' heel" is relatively simple and straightforward but also not very likely to satisfy those who have their understanding of the past overruled in the process of clarification.

In Norway, the Skarpnes Commission, which was appointed by the Ministry of Justice in 1996 to investigate the spoliation of Jewish property during World War II, broke into two factions when it came time to submit a report on its findings. The majority (five of seven) drafted a report that tallied

Jewish "losses" alongside Norwegian "losses" but offered no serious exploration of how these losses came about or of how they came about differently for each respective group. The majority report fails to mention that only one of these groups was targeted by the Norwegian Nazi Party (Nasjonal Samling), nor does it treat Vidkun Quisling, Norway's collaborationist head of state from February 1942 until May 1945. In the view of the majority, all Norwegians suffered profoundly as a consequence of Germany's attack in 1940, therefore "individual citizens accordingly had to accept that their postwar lives would begin with financial loss and diminished welfare."[70] The minority report, drafted by Berit Reisel and Bjarte Bruland, takes a different view. Without disputing the facts and figures proffered by the majority, the minority report enlarges the scope of the inquiry to explore questions of culpability, indemnity, and justice that the majority chose not to engage. Simply put, the majority report placed Jewish spoliation in the context of "national suffering," while the minority report treated these losses in the context of war guilt and collaboration.[71] The readiness of the commission's minority to explore Norway's history of collaboration through a complex conception of guilt and responsibility that goes beyond (or outside of) conventional legal categories speaks clearly to the innovative potential of these projects. As this point is crucial to the larger aims of the present study, I will return to this notion at various points within parts I and II and, once again, in the conclusion.

Both of the Norwegian commission's reports were sent to the Ministry of Justice and to the prime minister in 1997. Presented with two sharply divergent interpretations of the same events, Norway's minister of justice, Grad Liv Vaalla, held a press conference in which he repudiated the findings of the majority. "The loss of the Jews cannot be limited to economic calculations only," Vaalla told reporters. "The organized deportation and liquidation was mass murder, murder of a people. We cannot change what happened, but *we can set a moral standard* to remind everyone of this dark chapter in the history of Europe."[72] Norway's prime minister Thorbjorn Jagland and its foreign minister Bjorn Tore Godal supported Vaalla's view, and both issued press releases in which they stated that they would rely on the minority report for guidance in drafting specific recommendations to parliament regarding restitution and suitable commemoration.

The Norwegian example teaches several important lessons. It shows, first of all, that the commission model raises, but does not always resolve, the problems of knowledge and evidentiary standards that Poovey unpacked in her work. It also reveals that commissions are sometimes "multivocal" in spite of themselves and that this multiplication of perspectives can mimic the partisan debates over history, even where commissions have been created specifically to tame

them. Finally, it shows what historians have long known about the engulf-
ment of history by politics, even if they have not fully internalized this point.
What matters about the Norwegian case is not so much the fact that the
commission split after examining the same historical sources but that the
Norwegian government, when called upon to choose between the two, put its
weight behind the account that most clearly supported the "right to know"
claimed by the victims of the Holocaust, arguably the cardinal event in the
emergence of the human rights discourse within international law. There are
obviously legitimate ways of talking about Norwegian suffering, just as there
are legitimate ways of exploring German victimization at the end of World
War II (see chapter 5). What the rise of the historical commission model
suggests, however, is that these conversations must take place at a remove from
the genocidal violence perpetrated by the Nazi regime, its allies, and collaborators. It is a cliché to say that justice allows for healing of the victims, and,
unlike the clichés we accept because they really do seem to be accurate, the
"truth-and-reconciliation" formula has yet to be thoroughly validated. It is,
rather, one variable in a larger experiment, which aims to see what the world
might look like if both perpetrators and victims were to receive their due.
Experimental or not, this has been a pronounced feature of the human rights
discourse since the 1980s. "Who gets acknowledged?" is a critical part of the
mediation process that historical commissions can engage, but they must
always do this in the real world, where opposing sides claim to know the truth
when they see it, including the truth about history. The principal claim of this
study is not that historical commissions have a monopoly on truth or that they
represent a surefire method for bringing rivals together to settle disputes over
the past. My contention is simply that we need to account for the fact that
these disputes are being adjudicated, increasingly, through a methodology
that tries to take account of human rights and gives these rights a capacious
meaning, not just for the present but also for those who live presently in the
shadow of the past. Like every other right, the right to history invoked here is
realized where those in power grant it recognition. The commissions analyzed
in this book attest to the increasing prevalence of precisely this phenomenon.

Part I

National Holocaust Commissions

France and Switzerland

Myths of Resistance and Neutrality

Vichy France and the "Parenthesis Theory"

Until Jacques Chirac apologized for the anti-Semitic policies of the Vichy government on July 16, 1995, no French president had acknowledged France's involvement in the Holocaust. Prior to Chirac's apology, French collective memory circulated beneath an armor-plated maxim, which eschewed deep consideration of collaboration while also elevating the Resistance to mythological status: "Vichy was not France." For half a century, this formula was used to counter suggestions that anti-Semitic measures enacted after France's capitulation to the Nazis in May 1940 were in any way connected to the French nation. Although the majority of France's Jewish population (approximately 330,000 in 1940) survived the war, 76,000 French Jews were deported during the Nazi occupation, of which only 2,500 returned. "Vichy was not France" was the refrain that allowed three generations to distance themselves from the fate of those who did not return.

A new wave of historiography in the 1980s pushed France's wartime record into a more revealing light. In particular, Henry Russo's study *The Vichy Syndrome* (1987) forced readers to confront the past on less forgiving terms, though myths of resistance dating to the de Gaulle period and the "parenthesis theory," which asserted Vichy's exceptionality, remained engrained in public consciousness.[1] Only with Chirac's apology, given on the fifty-third anniversary of the Vélodrome d'Hiver deportation action, did the veil finally drop away.[2]

Emphasizing that the "Vél d'Hiv" roundup was planned by French civil servants and carried out by French police, Chirac lamented: "These black hours will stain our history forever and are an affront to our past and traditions. . . . The criminal folly of the occupiers was seconded by the French, by the French state." France, Chirac added, "land of Enlightenment and human rights, land of hospitality and asylum, on that day committed the irreparable."[3] Elsewhere in his speech, Chirac highlighted the achievements and courage of the French government-in-exile, referring to "another France" that "had never been at Vichy, [but was] alive and thriving in London."[4] Chirac's apology marked a break from the parenthesis theory, but France also gained a twin: one France was guilty, while the other maintained its honor.

Reaction to Chirac's speech was mixed. For some, the reference to London diluted the overall impact of the apology, whereas others, including Russo, commended the president for his careful attention to historical detail.[5] But despite the debate it stirred, or rather because of it, Chirac's speech marked a watershed, not only in France's public discourse on the Holocaust but also in the government's stance and policies regarding Vichy.[6] While Chirac's predecessor, François Mitterrand, endeavored to contain difficult memories of Vichy in the past, Chirac's apology opened the nation's history for critical revision and amendment.[7] As a direct consequence of his intervention, the French government launched two historical commissions whose work clarified important details related to the policies of the Vichy government, and which also led to significant programs of reparation as well as to the creation of a new foundation devoted to Holocaust commemoration and education.

Jewish Spoliation as the Preface to Genocide

At Chirac's behest, the prime minister Alain Juppé convened the Study Mission on the Spoliation of Jews in France from 1940 to 1944 (hereafter Mattéoli Commission) in February 1997. The commission was given a four-point mandate: (1) to study the conditions under which spoliation occurred, (2) to evaluate the extent of such spoliation, (3) to learn what happened to plundered assets, and (4) to make recommendations regarding appropriate reparation(s). To execute this program, the commission divided its work into five topical areas: (1) internment and spoliation, for example, the program of "frisking," which took place in detention camps outside Paris and in Loiret; (2) "Aryanization" of Jewish business; (3) spoliation of apartments and other real estate; (4) looting of artworks and appropriation of cultural assets; and (5) blocking and confiscation of financial accounts. The commission also investigated what it termed "immaterial spoliation," for example, the denial of copyright benefits to Jewish authors and composers, although this ranked as a relatively minor issue in the overall work scheme.

In addition to researching the details of spoliation, the Mattéoli Commission also reviewed the restitution programs undertaken by the government following France's liberation. Testifying in front of the U. S. House of Representatives Committee on Banking and Financial Services in 1999, Ady Steg, the commission's vice president, noted that Charles de Gaulle had contacted both the American Jewish Congress and the World Jewish Congress (WJC) in 1940 and 1941 to assure members of these organizations that property seizures undertaken by the Vichy government were regarded as "entirely invalid" by Free France and that such measures would be immediately countermanded upon (Allied) victory.[8] Steg also testified that French banks were ordered on August 30, 1944—just days after the liberation of Paris—to unblock all frozen accounts and that further efforts to return seized assets were made in subsequent months. Using archival sources to trace the fate of seized assets, the commission found that France had achieved a restitution rate of more than 90 percent in the period from 1944 to 1958.[9] Steg acknowledged that not all plundered assets had been returned, either because the owners did not return to reclaim them or because legal heirs did not know the full extent of their family's estate or because claimants failed to meet administrative deadlines. A Holocaust survivor himself, Steg pledged that France would identify and return all remaining unclaimed assets, and he assured American lawmakers that the Mattéoli Commission operated independently, despite receiving its funding from the French government. Steg told the congressional committee, "The commission's primary objective is a historical one: to establish the truth concerning spoliations."[10] To accomplish this goal, the commission recruited three historians whose areas of expertise were directly relevant to the project: Claire Andrieu, Antoine Prost, and Annette Wieviorka. The commission also retained the famed Nazi-hunter, Serge Klarsfeld. Aided by a group of young doctoral students and archivists, the Mattéoli historians reviewed a huge amount of material—the archives for the General Commissariat for Jewish Issues stretched more than a kilometer—and, in general, avoided publicity that impeded their work.[11]

In 1999 the commission's president, Jean Mattéoli, recommended that the French government create a separate body to examine individual claims for reparation. The Commission for the Compensation of Victims of Spoliation Resulting from Anti-Semitic Legislation (CIVS) was put under the direction of Pierre Drai, who was formerly the head of France's Supreme Court.[12]

Announcing new funding for Drai's commission, Lionel Jospin, the prime minister, reiterated that all unclaimed assets would go to help the victims, and he announced that a newly created public trust fund, the Foundation for the Memory of the Shoah (FMS), would receive and administer these assets.[13] The FMS also received substantial contributions from France's business sector, including major banks, where conduct during the war had been particularly detrimental to Jews and where restitution initiatives following the war had been imperfect. In his statement to the American congressional committee, Steg emphasized that the Mattéoli Commission aspired to higher ends than simple arithmetic and accounting. The main objectives, Steg asserted, were moral, historical, and pedagogical: "We have an obligation to consider the human circumstances and consequences of despoliation. This means taking into consideration the sum of the anguish, humiliation, suffering, and death that resulted from being despoiled."[14] Spoliation under Vichy, the commission determined, was more than mere plunder. It was a deliberate program to demean and dehumanize the victims and to prepare them for more coercive measures (i.e., arrest and deportation), which ultimately led to the Final Solution. As Antoine Prost, one of the commission's chief historians, explained in an interview, "Spoliation was not just to eliminate 'Jewish' influence in the national economy and to raise billions. It was also, by specific design, used to deprive the livelihood of thousands of ordinary people and make life physically impossible so as to make them literally disappear from the landscape. Thus, it was a daily persecution and a preface to genocide."[15] Working from 1997 to 2000, the Mattéoli Commission amended the history of Vichy in three significant respects. It found that the scope of Jewish spoliation was much broader than previously assumed or acknowledged. It negated the parenthesis theory ("Vichy was not France") by documenting the involvement of French officials in the planning and execution of spoliation measures and deportation actions. And finally, it linked anti-Jewish policies in France to the organized mass murder in the East. In the commission's view, France had been an active facilitator of the Holocaust.

The Mattéoli Commission submitted its final report on April 17, 2000. The commission published its findings and recommendations in twelve volumes, covering more than 3,000 pages. A summary report (205 pages) was also prepared.[16] The commission was praised by leaders of France's Jewish community for documenting the full extent of wartime plunder, which the summary report described as "stunning," and for recommending a far-reaching program of individual and communal restitution. Leaders in the French Jewish community also commended the commission's commitment to moral principles. Henri Hajdenberg, president of the Representative Council of Jewish Institutions, went so far as to say that demands for financial restitution were secondary to historical clarification and public dissemination of the facts.[17] Clearly, though, the monetary dimension was an important aspect of the commission's work, particularly for businesses and the government, which wanted reliable estimates of potential liability. Based on its archival research, the commission found that the Nazis and their French collaborators stole Jewish assets totaling not less than $1.3 billion. While the commission estimated that 90 percent of plundered assets were returned by 1958, the final report also described a complex and exhausting administrative process, which victims had to navigate in order to reclaim their property.[18] For thousands of victims, particularly those whose financial and emotional reserves had been depleted, these hurdles proved too high. The Mattéoli historians also noted the inherent limitations of archival documentation, and this led them to recommend the creation of a separate commission for vetting individual restitution claims (the CIVS or Drai Commission).

In addition to a summary of the salient financial data, the Mattéoli report supplied a detailed timeline that offered new insight into the mechanics of spoliation and an answer to long-standing questions regarding where the orders for these programs had originated. According to the commission, the first explicitly anti-Jewish measures in France were enforced directly by the German military and the Nazi regime. On September 27, 1940, less than three months after the establishment of the Vichy government, Germany ordered a census to record the identity of all Jews living in France. Three weeks later (October 18), Germany issued the first order geared explicitly toward spoliation of Jewish assets. Under this decree, business contracts made with Jews after May 23, 1940, could be canceled immediately. While credit institutions were not specifically cited, a number of prominent French banks took this as an opportunity to restrict access to accounts belonging to Jews. In other words, the Mattéoli Commission found that French bank officers entered into the confiscation process on their own initiative when vague orders from Germany made such a move possible. German decrees opened the door to large-scale expropriation, but French bankers walked themselves across the threshold.

Spoliation intensified quickly thereafter as Nazi and Vichy law became further intertwined. Following Wannsee and the arrival of Karl Oberg as head of the French SS force (May 1942), Vichy officials, including Pierre Laval, entered into negotiations with Germany to adapt and streamline the deportation process that had begun two months earlier. The first French transport, carrying more than 1,000 Jews, left for Auschwitz on March 27, 1942, and six more trains followed before even larger roundups, like the one at Vél d'Hiv, began in July.[19] Arrests in the southern "free zone," meaning the territories governed by the Vichy government, followed in August 1942. While Laval initially tried to shield French-born Jews by promising Oberg the handover of all "foreign" Jews, by 1943 he was prepared to meet Germany's growing deportation quotas in exchange for "some kind of political security" in the event of a Nazi victory over the Allies.[20] Although Jews in France's southern cities could avoid deportation in some cases, provided they had sufficient resources to buy protection, a direct Nazi presence in the Vichy territory after November 1942 greatly increased the threat they faced there. Also, whereas Vichy officials initially authorized only the transport of adults, by late summer 1942 they had modified their policies to allow for the deportation of children. By autumn 1942, 42,000 Jews had passed through the Drancy internment camp on their way to the labor camps and extermination centers in Nazi-occupied Poland. While some scholars have emphasized that the majority of Jews deported from France were "foreign" (i.e., Jewish refugees who had fled Nazi invasions earlier and elsewhere),[21] the Mattéoli Commission found that 76,000 Jews (i.e., 25 percent of France's total Jewish population) were deported from France between 1942 and 1944.[22]

The most striking aspect of the Mattéoli report was the direct connection its authors made between spoliation and deportation in the context of a highly organized and premeditated genocide. Loss of wealth and property not only struck a psychological and financial blow against the victims, but it also funneled Jews in France toward the liquidation centers in a more literal sense. As Steg explained, "Not only had [Jews] lost their possessions, but they were also made far more vulnerable; they were easier to hunt down, arrest, and, ultimately, deport."[23] According to the commission's report, the archival record included clear evidence of "crushing responsibility" on the part of the Vichy government and its bureaucratic underlings. Instigated by Germany, spoliation and deportation were "organized and carried out" by Petain, Laval, René Bousquet (the secretary-general of the French police), and the rest of Vichy, reaching down to ordinary citizens, like the French bank officers who seized Jewish assets when the opportunity arose, ignoring or downplaying—or not yet comprehending—how their actions facilitated mass murder.

The Mattéoli report also included some mitigating evidence for the Vichy period. While spoliation gained momentum after 1941, other anti-Jewish measures were less effective in France, and some that succeeded at first became less onerous over time as a consequence of lax enforcement. For example, faced with a strong public backlash, Vichy did not impose the yellow star on Jews in the southern zone, while Jews in the occupied north were required to display the badge beginning on June 7, 1942.[24] There is also evidence that Vichy officials and French civilians in the financial sector blocked or ignored certain German directives when they felt they could do so safely. When the Allies showed signs of recovery and stabilization in 1942–43 and victory over the Axis began to seem not just possible but even likely, some French bankers adopted tactics of "passive resistance" against new Nazi orders.[25] Emboldened bank officers tried not to answer German queries, or they dragged out the process of implementation, sometimes for half a year, before enacting new orders. While these episodes provide important context, obviously they do not transform the French banks into a white-collar Resistance cell. As Claire Andrieu pointed out, the harshest spoliation measures had already been applied by this time, and most of the measures imposed earlier were enforced straight through until July 1944.

The Mattéoli Commission did not attempt to explain Vichy policies by delving into the interwar period. The commission's report does not explore the 1920s and 1930s when pacifist movements on both the Right and the Left enjoyed widespread popular support. France's Socialist Party (PS, Parti Socialiste) included a pacifist wing, which sought to shrink the standing army and reduce the period of military service, even after German troops had reoccupied the Rhineland in 1936. On the Right, pacifism mixed with traditional European anti-Semitism and spawned cynical (not to mention unfounded) claims that Jewish politicians with links to the occult hoped to provoke Germany into launching a strike on France. A different but related sentiment existed on the Left. René Gérin, a decorated World War I hero, lycée professor, and the leader of the International League of Fighters for Peace, who was twice imprisoned as a conscientious objector in the 1930s, also felt that the most serious threat of war came from within France, especially from inside parliament, where a Jewish influence, he claimed, had set the country on a collision course with Germany.[26] Arguments in favor of Franco-German understanding and détente came from both ends of the political spectrum, and these spawned a variety of initiatives aimed at fostering reconciliation between the two countries.[27] When Germany invaded Poland in September 1939, many French citizens preferred a negotiated settlement with Germany to a protracted military conflict. Vichy, it could be argued, did not represent a sudden collapse of morality as much as a continuation of the dread of war that suffused France (and much of Europe) throughout the interwar period. Notwithstanding such evidence, the Mattéoli Commission insisted that their project aimed at moral rehabilitation in addition to historical clarification. That meant limiting the scope of the inquiry to exclude anything that hinted at moral relativism or exculpation. Instead, the commission stuck deliberately to the period of the occupation and to the files generated by France's postwar restitution services. By 1999, the commission had examined 67,000 different accounts and checked property records across more than 460 separate dates to ascertain what was taken and when, and also where these looted assets ended up, if they were not returned. Claire Andrieu described this work plan, which ignored the interwar period, as a "doctrine of action."[28]

Reparations and the Right to History

When France's parenthesis theory collapsed in 1995, politicians framed the issue of restitution and repair in terms of rights and responsibilities. Elaborating on his Vél d'Hiv apology, Chirac emphasized that reparations were not only a question for the Jewish community but should be seen as a "grande cause nationale."[29] Lionel Jospin offered that the government's commitment to payback sprang from fundamental human rights, including the right of victims to public acknowledgment of their historical experience. The creation of the Mattéoli Commission was intended to both engage and overcome the politics of deciphering that truth. Jospin insisted that no amount of material compensation could ever fully repay the debt that France owed to the victims: "It is normal that the victims of this unprecedented tragedy should demand their rights. Given the dimension of these events, however, we know that no reparation can every truly repair [the damage], for what happened is irreparable. Nonetheless, it is just and right that those who were despoiled should demand and obtain reparation."[30] One could say that Jospin's platitudes were simply another tactic aimed at limiting France's legal exposure and avoiding the possibility of a costly class-action suit. The point I want to make, however, is that these moral invocations are not completely free or painless for those who make them. Once the historical discourse shifts onto moral and ethical grounds, the consequences for both perpetrators and victims can be profound. Historical inquiry subsequently moves along two parallel tracks. One asks, "What exactly happened?" while the other wonders, "Who owes what to whom?"

From its inception, the Mattéoli Commission benefitted from the cooperation of major French banks. Again, this ought to be read, at least in part, as the outcome of strictly pragmatic calculations. On the other hand, it is important to note—because it signals so much about the moral sea change that occurred in France at that time—that the commission had no legal power to subpoena documents, but instead received a special "derogation" that provided access to information (e.g., archives and account information), which otherwise would have remained confidential. Banks that could have left the Mattéoli researchers to flounder in their corporate archives instead helped the historians locate the most revealing documents. In March 1999, a spokesperson for the French Bankers Association announced that its members (106 institutions) would enact sweeping measures to return dormant assets to Holocaust victims and their heirs.[31] The banks pledged to (1) intensify their efforts to achieve full restitution, (2) cooperate with the commission's investigation, (3) circulate internal documents identifying dormant assets, (4) relinquish unclaimed assets to the Foundation for the Memory of the Shoah, (5) disclose procedures related to the handling of dormant accounts, and (6) make a supplemental contribution to the FMS within twelve weeks of the publication of the commission's final report. Through their association, the banks admitted to having been "cogs in the terrible machine of confiscation of Jewish assets."[32] In a carefully crafted statement aimed at both the French public and the foreign jurisdictions, like the United States, where class-action suits were moving toward the courts, the banks cited a "duty of reparation toward the victims" but also deflected some degree of responsibility by implicating a "terrible machine," which transformed into "cogs" the (previously) human beings who determined official bank policies.[33] By contrast, the Mattéoli Commission found that Jewish spoliation enjoyed unambiguous support from French civil servants and bank officers (i.e., from real people rather than cogs). The commission noted strong external pressures to conform to Nazi law, but ultimately they rejected explanations that undercut the moral agency of individual French citizens and the institutions they served. Andrieu characterized the relationship between Nazi Germany and Vichy as being one of lord to vassal, and she argued that Jewish spoliation in France reflected a condition of "subordination within collaboration." Vichy officials did not exercise full sovereignty, but the limits to their power became obvious within the context of their collaboration. While French banks emphasized institutional failings that made guilt diffuse and impersonal, the commission, without always "naming names," highlighted personal responsibility and individual moral transgressions. It is significant, given the absence of a direct legal requirement, that the French banks accommodated the commission's inquiry and cooperated in organizing and combing through the archives, but their willingness to participate in the investigation was, of course, never entirely altruistic. The banks managed to avoid legal sanctions abroad only by entering into the commission's domestic inquiry as compliant partners. On January 18, 2001, the governments of the United States and France signed an executive agreement that indemnified French banks against further class-action suits, and three ongoing suits were subsequently dismissed on March 27, 2001.[34] These agreements and the protections they afforded to French corporate interests highlight the potential of commissioned history to support a larger process of negotiated justice. Here, the victims received back their assets and saw their historical claims recognized by an official body, while banks got relief against legal uncertainty and a chance to resume their operations with a freshly scrubbed moral slate. While skeptics sometimes claim that these quid pro quo admissions allow perpetrators to escape the harsher sanctions they deserve and avoid taking responsibility for other unjust acts, the reactions of Jewish groups in France and across the Atlantic tell us something important about the benefits for victims.

Founded in Geneva in 1936 and currently headquartered in New York City, the WJC was initially critical of the Mattéoli Commission, calling their inquiry an exercise in "juvenile statistics work" and saying that the researchers could not speak for all Holocaust victims.[35] Over time, however, the WJC warmed to the idea of an official commission, despite lingering concerns that Jews in France did not have sufficient political clout to ensure a fair outcome. Speaking for the WJC in 2000, Elan Steinberg offered lukewarm support for the Mattéoli Commission's final report: "We have no reason to believe that this has been anything but an honest undertaking."[36] By that time, criticism from the WJC had helped convince the French government to create a separate commission, the CIVS, to deal directly with individual restitution claims. Pressure from the WJC, in the form of a threat to boycott all French banks, convinced the officers of these institutions to cooperate with both of the French Holocaust commissions and submit their records for external review. While Jewish leaders in France resented these tactics and called on the WJC to quit meddling in what they considered a local affair,[37] it is also hard to imagine that close scrutiny from a large international organization with proven political influence made the outcome of the Mattéoli inquiry less favorable to victims. In any event, the WJC took a clear step back when France and the United States signed the executive agreement (2001) that released French banks from further liability in exchange for providing $22.5 million toward individual restitution payments and €100 million for the FMS's commemorative and educational programs.[38] Notwithstanding the tensions between the WJC and France's local Jewish communities regarding who may legitimately speak for victims, the WJC's involvement raises an important point concerning the politics of restitution. While skeptics may argue that these sorts of tactics and negotiations demean the memory of the victims or feed a sentimental politics that gives cover to governments and corporations who want to avoid more expensive claims, the insistence of victims that official apologies like Chirac's are incomplete until they are backed by a substantive program of restitution highlights their importance. If these negotiations were conducted as cynically as their critics have suggested, we would not expect to see jousting over who represents the victims (the biggest "players" would always take the lead), nor would there be readiness on the part of some perpetrators to pay back their victims above and beyond what can be documented through archival research.

Distinguishing Between Material Restitution and Moral Reparation

In their final report, the Mattéoli historians described the extent of Jewish spoliation in France as "stunning." Although other groups were deprived of their property during the Vichy period, the commission viewed the circumstances surrounding Jewish despoilment as uniquely unjust. Pressed by the French government to provide an estimate of the sum total losses for the purpose of gauging potential indemnification, the Mattéoli Commission was able to show that no less than $1.3 billion in total assets was looted from France's Jewish communities. According to the commission, however, the vast majority of registered assets (90 percent) were returned to the victims or their heirs in the decade following France's liberation (1944–54). Simple arithmetic would peg the unreturned remainder at approximately $130 million, yet France's government and big banks paid out more than two and half times that amount just to the FMS.[39] Moreover, the CIVS (Drai Commission), which was established to evaluate and settle individual restitution claims, reviewed 32,913 claimant files (as of April 2013) and paid out approximately $639.2 million.[40] The Mattéoli Commission estimated that French interests retained just 10 percent of all looted assets ($130 million) after 1954, and yet by 2013, France's government and banks had paid out close to $1 billion in compensation.

There are several possible explanations for this apparent discrepancy: (1) the Mattéoli estimate for total looted assets ($1.3 billion) was too low, (2) the estimate for postwar restitution (90 percent) was too high, or (3) the French government and French corporations paid out considerably more than was technically owed. As a reminder, the figures above do not include supplemental funds (approximately 2.4 billion francs) that the government and banks voluntarily contributed to the FMS (i.e., unconnected to specific claims or historical research). How should we regard what seems to be, on its surface, a massive overpayment? What, if anything, can be said for the relationship between the Mattéoli Commission's estimates and the total French payout (still growing) to victims and the groups that represent them?

There are two things to consider, if we are to make sense of the apparent discrepancy between estimated losses and total payments. The first issue is technical. The Mattéoli estimates for total looted assets and total postwar restitution were never more than rough estimates, which the commission calculated on the basis of incomplete archival records. Not all records from the Vichy period survived intact, and of course many individual losses and seizures were never recorded in the first place. Also, many of the compensatory measures applied by the CIVS were developed "on the fly," as it were. For example, there was no agreed-upon standard for assessing property values, and no clear formula existed for reviewing the small, often poorly documented claims that victims brought to the CIVS. If an individual recalled being separated from a modest sum of money during the "frisking" procedures at the Drancy internment camp, how might his loss be verified or repaid? What could that money have purchased had it remained in the hands of its owner? Would repayment be made in the original amount or with interest applied? If the latter, how much exactly? The limitations of archival materials and the improvisational nature of the exercise meant that solutions to these problems had to be created ex nihilo. In a sense, what the Mattéoli inquiry provided was a macroscopic overview of Jewish spoliation. Despite more than three years of meticulous work, the methodology employed by the Mattéoli Commission was inadequate for assessing individual losses and compensation claims in a detailed manner. The Mattéoli work plan was neither designed nor intended to see down to the granular level, where individual histories and specific experiences of loss and victimization are documented (or not). It is problematic, for this reason, to link the Mattéoli estimates to actual payouts made by the CIVS or to any of the specific compensation measures made in the wake of the Mattéoli report. In one respect, the CIVS was intended as a continuation and extension of the Mattéoli inquiry. In another respect, the CIVS was made to start from scratch by virtue of its interest in individual microhistories.

The second consideration for properly evaluating the payouts of France's two Holocaust commissions is moral. In her statement to the Committee on Financial Services, Claire Andrieu explained that the Mattéoli Commission saw its work as a measure of justice, which encompassed both material and moral components. She regretted that it was sometimes necessary to speak about the Vichy period in a cold "scientific mode" (i.e., using dates, figures, percentages, and financial jargon) when a "more sensitive discourse" would have been appropriate.[41] Andrieu also described how the commission implemented a conceptual plan comprised of three columns. In the first two columns, the commission tallied total assets restituted against total assets not yet restituted. The compilation of these figures required a huge commitment to archival research, but it was relatively straightforward work in terms of its technical requirements. The third column, Andrieu said, was reserved for what the commission termed "moral reparation." This is where the commission made its recommendations for additional compensation to support the rising "Holocaust consciousness" in France that Chirac's apology helped to nurture. In other words, the commission's intention was never to reproduce in column 3 (recommendations for reparation) the total documented in column 2 (un-returned assets). There was always an understanding within the commission and inside the government that justice would require more than financial correction and that payback could not consist only of neat, arithmetic calculation. Andrieu was unequivocal in describing the third column as "clearly more important" than the second.[42] Beyond financial restitution, which the commission defined as compensation based on verifiable losses, the commission's chief objectives always included reparation, that is, an enduring expression of France's inestimable moral guilt in terms both real and symbolic. Given that the injustice was, as Chirac had put it, "irreparable," the Mattéoli Commission attempted to describe not only what the country ought to have done (meaning its failure to protect and preserve republican virtues), but also how the government intended to conduct its affairs in the future. Moral reparation signaled France's recommitment to liberal-democratic principles and to the human rights norms, which it still wished to embrace, despite having failed to do so in the past.

The Mattéoli Commission's rejection of the parenthesis theory proved crucial in this. Although the commission used explanatory formulas, which at times recalled the moral evasions of the past, ultimately its work documented a record of collaboration that included room for moral choice and individual initiative. For the period between 1940 and 1944, Andrieu stated, "the main sovereign of continental France [was] Nazi Germany." At the same time, Vichy held "a secondary sovereignty," which Andrieu described as a "vassal dictatorship." The power of that dictatorship was sufficient to allow Vichy officials to take two important steps against Jews on their own. These measures defined the status of Jews in France (October 3, 1940) and called for the internment of foreign-born Jews (October 4, 1940). After this time, all major decisions undertaken by the Vichy government were "inspired by the Germans and ancillary to discussions with them." Again, Andrieu characterized this state of affairs as "subordination within collaboration."

The significance of Andrieu's formula is twofold. First, it preserves a place for national responsibility and accountability by placing the experience of coercion (subordination) within a larger framework of moral choice (collaboration). Second, by insisting on the importance and preservation of moral agency, this formula undercuts the "Vichy was not France" doctrine, which clung to previous narratives for this period. On the other hand, Andrieu noted the determination of de Gaulle and Free France to right the injustices that

French Jews endured under Vichy's "vassal dictatorship." The "tri-partition of sovereignty" (Germany, Vichy, and Free France), she argued, "led to results that, although terrifying and shameful forever, [were] less terrible than in most other occupied countries." With the exception of Italy (20 percent), France deported fewer of its Jews (25 percent) than any other Nazi-occupied country. As Serge Klarsfeld put it, one-quarter of French Jews were deported with the complicity of Vichy, whereas three-quarters were saved.[43] While Klarsfeld's statement evokes elements of the Resistance myth, it also validates the Jewish perspective by highlighting France's ultimate moral responsibility for those who were deported and killed. If Jews fared better in France than most other places, the commission also affirmed that Vichy's decision makers and bureaucrats, many of whom were aligned with the Third Republic prior to the war, had facilitated the Holocaust when they might have done otherwise. Rejecting the description of Vichy as a "puppet state," the Mattéoli Commission divided sovereignty among three levels, leaving ample room for immoral action within a government that still represented the French nation. In the commission's final analysis, Vichy officials made choices in the country's name for which restitution and reparation were seen as the necessary and appropriate countermeasures.

Human Rights as an Adjudicating Authority

The work of the Mattéoli Commission was never simple, even if it entailed a certain amount of dry reading and number crunching. Throughout the inquiry, commission members attempted to focus on "the barbarity [sic] at the root of it all."[44] In 1999, with the project still going full bore, Andrieu asked the U.S. Congress for more time to investigate and clarify the facts. This was a highly sensitive issue, as a handful of class-action lawsuits filed in the United States had put pressure on French banks to begin compensating victims in the form of a legal settlement. Andrieu countered, "Our conviction is that any premature global settlement would hamper the bringing to light of the truth, and hinder the consciousness currently rising."[45] For members of the commission, historical truth and public consciousness of past injustice were equally important to material compensation, and redress would be deemed insufficient if the banks were allowed to pay their way out of full disclosure. The same attitude helps to explain why the commission was so eager to work with the banks, rather than against them (e.g., through the enforcement of their special derogation). For the commission, clarification had to be a cooperative endeavor rather than a coercive assertion of power. If French banks were forced to turn over their records under threat of legal punishment, they would be doing only what authority required, which is precisely how many Vichy officials defended themselves when pressed to account for their actions. By partnering with the banks in a cooperative inquiry, the commission maintained, "a new consciousness arises that plays the role of Holocaust education."[46]

While the commission's concern over the effects of coercive power seem somewhat overblown, it speaks to the question of political continuity, and it bolsters France's commitment to Holocaust education. The French government has made Holocaust education a compulsory subject in public school curricula, beginning in primary school and continuing through high school. Since 2000, one of the major initiatives of the FMS has been curriculum revision to reflect the shift toward public acknowledgment of France's role in the Holocaust and to present the findings of the Mattéoli Commission to a broader audience. This reflects the commission's conviction that "nothing enduring can be established without public recognition of facts."[47]

One can also argue that the Mattéoli Commission has made an impact on French foreign relations, specifically its bilateral relations with Israel. In 2005 the respective heads of state signed an agreement to create a new partnership, the France-Israel Foundation, which aims to promote mutual understanding and closer ties between the two countries in the areas of education, culture, science, and business. The foundation sponsors a range of collaborative projects: from research on neurodegenerative disease to avant-garde film festivals to supper clubs, where guests can hear lectures by midlevel diplomats speaking on topics of bilateral interest. Since 2010 the foundation has sponsored a program, "Just Memories," devoted specifically to Holocaust commemoration. This initiative provides travel stipends to the grandchildren of French rescuers—the "righteous gentiles" who risked their lives to help Jews during the Vichy era—so that they can visit Yad Vashem in Israel and meet with Holocaust survivors, whose lives in some cases were saved by these visitors' own relatives.[48] While civic initiatives of this kind take place a long way from the diplomatic forums where the policies governing bi-state relations are formulated, the France-Israel Foundation has consciously aimed to utilize the past as a tool for fostering bilateral cooperation and mutual understanding.

Finally, the French government received a very important endorsement in 2009, when the European Court of Human Rights (ECHR) ruled that France's reparations program had provided full and fair compensation, both morally and materially, to victims of anti-Semitic policies enacted during the Vichy period.[49] When descendants of Jewish deportees brought a case to The Hague, claiming that the French government and the national railway system should be held liable for transporting their relatives to the Nazi death camps, justices for the ECHR ruled that while France was clearly responsible for the deportations, the claimants' losses had already been compensated "to the greatest possible extent." The ECHR also determined, as France's Supreme Court had earlier, that French reparations were in line with other European states whose authorities had "committed similar actions." The ECHR's seven justices ruled unanimously in favor of the French government, and they highlighted "the financial and non-financial means of compensation" that had already been provided to victims. The judges especially applauded France's "formal recognition of the role of the State," and even suggested that this was a standard other countries might want to apply. In other words, the ECHR used its powers to promote the Mattéoli Commission as an outstanding model for achieving historical justice. The Mattéoli Commission not only removed the parenthesis from around Vichy but also dealt with the consequences of French collaboration by applying a standard of justice that the ECHR deemed exemplary.

Switzerland: Neutrality and the Question of Depiction

In Switzerland, the analogue to the Vichy parenthesis theory is the myth of neutrality. When World War II ended, Swiss leaders and ordinary citizens embraced an idealized narrative built on the twin planks of national survival in the face of pan-European destruction and the deterrent effect of the Swiss military. Unlike other countries, which had been drowned in the rising tide of Nazism or had stayed afloat through moral compromise, Switzerland, according to the neutrality myth, staved off German aggression without compromising its highest principles. When the Allies pressed Switzerland in 1945–46 to return plundered assets, which had entered the country via Germany or some other intermediary, Swiss politicians denied that such debts existed. One member of the Federal Council, a right-wing Catholic Conservative, stated, "Switzerland has nothing to make amends for either to the victims of Nazi persecution or to Jewish or other organizations."[50] Another council member, a Social Democrat, echoed this assessment, explaining, "Actually, Switzerland has nothing to make amends for, and [foreign] countries are not entitled to make any claims."[51] This perspective was bolstered by Edgar Bonjour, who wrote a multivolume history of Swiss neutrality based on research conducted in the 1960s in which he managed to incorporate and minimize "new findings" suggestive of collaboration within a heroic narrative that highlighted Switzerland's special status as an enduring "Alpine Republic."[52] Cold

War politics also lent support to Switzerland's neutrality myth. In the United States, Allen Dulles, who served as head of the Central Intelligence Agency from 1953 to 1961 and had held a key intelligence post in Bern during the war, described Switzerland's wartime policy as "benevolent neutrality" in 1966.[53] While there were short-lived and relatively mild debates within Switzerland during the 1960s and 1970s that challenged specific aspects of the neutrality myth,[54] broader questions concerning a national policy of complicity were avoided in the public discourse until the mid-1990s when the Nazi Gold controversy forced a reappraisal of the record.[55]

Yet, even as evidence of collaboration with the Nazis mounted in the 1990s, both in terms of Switzerland's economic cooperation with Berlin and the creation of anti-Semitic policies that forced Jewish refugees back into the hands of the German SS, Swiss politicians resisted a straightforward admission of culpability. In a speech given to commemorate the fiftieth anniversary of Armistice Day, President Kaspar Villiger acknowledged that Switzerland developed a needlessly restrictive refugee policy during the war, which amounted to a death sentence for thousands of Jews, but he maintained that Swiss officials did everything possible, within the limits of national security, to protect these victims. Villiger's comments reflect the ambivalence of Swiss memory, and they suggest a past without the possibility of different choices:[56]

> Our country was spared the Second World War. That should fill us with gratitude. Other countries liberated Europe, saved European culture and permitted us, too, to share in a free future. Our country, placed in an extremely menacing position, did all that was humanly possible to preserve its independence, its values and its integrity . . . but Switzerland did not act in all it did, as its ideals might have required. That should make us think a bit. Switzerland was in fact guilty regarding its attitude to the refugees. We are talking about all the Jews who, refused entry into Switzerland, were thereby assured of certain death. Was the lifeboat really full? . . . Have we always done everything possible vis-à-vis those who were being tracked down and deprived of their rights? As far as I am concerned, beyond all doubt we are guilty of having supported that policy towards the persecuted Jews. But it would be wrong to blame the Swiss authorities in charge at that time. All those in positions of responsibility for the country then acted solely for its wellbeing, according to their lights. Therefore to nail them to the pillory today would be quite unjust.[57]

Villiger was the first government official to recognize and apologize for Switzerland's humanitarian failures, and there is a marked difference between his remarks here and the official statements from the late 1980s. At the same time,

Villiger's speech has a timid and even defensive quality, particularly in comparison to other political apologies for similar policies (e.g., Chirac's apology for the Vél d'Hiv roundup). Referring to Alfred Häsler's widely read book, *Das Boot ist voll*, Villiger asks, but does not clearly answer, whether "the boat was full," meaning, was Switzerland unable to accommodate all of the Jewish refugees who sought asylum there, as was claimed in 1942, when the government closed its borders to Jews seeking asylum?[58] Villiger concedes that Switzerland "supported a policy" that facilitated Jewish persecution,[59] but he also deflects moral guilt as an immediate consequence by adding that Swiss officials acted properly by putting national survival above the plight of refugees and that Switzerland could not give aid to Jewish refugees without inviting catastrophic consequences. While he notes that Germany's policy of stamping the passports of its Jewish citizens with a *J* was undertaken at the request of Swiss officials in 1938, he does not fully explore the significance of this mark, which Swiss immigration officers argued would help make the process of reviewing asylum applications more efficient.[60] Because asylum, under Swiss law, could not be granted on the basis of racial persecution, but only on political grounds, some argued that the *J* stamp was simply a tool for properly handling a flood of claims. Yet no other religious community was made to register or identify itself in the same manner. Other countries, of course, including Great Britain and the United States, also maintained restrictive immigration policies during this period and used quotas to limit the number of Jewish immigrants they admitted. Should Switzerland be held to a different standard? Should location count as a consideration? Switzerland's proximity to Germany made it the easiest country to reach for the Reich's Jewish refugees. Can the facts find a place in a narrative aimed at explanation rather than accusation or exculpation?

Independent Commission of Experts (Bergier Commission), 1996–2001

Stung by the Nazi Gold scandal and facing negative publicity abroad over policies adopted in the 1930s and 1940s, Switzerland broke decisively from the myth of neutrality in December 1996. In response to pointed criticism that Switzerland had maintained a close and mutually enriching relationship with the Nazi government throughout World War II, the Swiss parliament established the Independent Commission of Experts (ICE) on December 12, 1996, under the direction of Jean-François Bergier.[61] The commission was funded for five years and given a broad mandate to explore a range of topics: (1) Swiss banking practices, including gold trading and foreign currency transactions; (2) the movement and fate of other assets, including insurance policies and cultural properties; (3) benefits derived from the "Aryanization" measures applied elsewhere; (4) the exploitation of forced labor; (5) Swiss refugee policy and its connection to Nazi war objectives; (6) the relationship between Swiss industrial and commercial firms and the German war economy, and (7) the extent of Switzerland's postwar restitution programs. While the ICE pursued all of these projects—the commission's sizeable budget (20 million Swiss francs) helped pay for a large research staff—the most important outcomes related to refugees, banking, and restitution. The commission established research centers throughout Switzerland, and it also attempted to develop an international orientation that would account for the transnational scope of Nazi criminality. While the ICE had no direct ties to the Swiss government beyond the budget it received, the commission was granted special legal powers to ensure the compliance of Swiss business firms and to protect private archives against tampering or destruction. Critics argued that the commission was created to validate the government's truth, but members of the commission insisted they were able to pursue their work with "full academic autonomy."[62] As with the Mattéoli Commission in France, members of the ICE worked in their own names and did not always reach a consensus. There were convergences around key issues, however, on which the ICE elaborated in March 2002 in its final report.

Prior to releasing the final report, the Swiss commission had already published many of its preliminary findings. Working individually and also in small groups, ICE members and their research staff authored twenty-five separate volumes, covering more than 11,000 pages.[63] Some of these studies were narrow in scope, for example, volume 2, which dealt with I. G. Farben and its role in the Swiss economy, and volume 5, which examined Switzerland's electricity exports to Germany. Other volumes addressed broader topics, for example, volume 13 on the role of Swiss banks in the German economy between 1931 and 1946. The final report (597 pages), which was published in four languages, provided a synthesis of the commission's research and a summary of its key findings. Although Bergier lamented that the final report had been rushed, he also felt that the commission succeeded in promoting a "genuine dialogue" on important topics, all of which were drenched in "highly charged and conflicting emotions."[64]

Despite what Bergier referred to as "instances of minor incongruity," where members of the commission reached different conclusions on the same subject, the ICE's final report provides a coherent and integrated appraisal of Switzerland's wartime record. Bergier stressed that the commission's work was not intended to provide a comprehensive account of the Swiss war experience, but rather that the inquiry was guided by the issues and questions set forth in the original mandate. "Our task," Bergier explained, "was to shed light upon certain controversial or insufficiently analyzed aspects of this history, aspects in which it appeared that Switzerland, that is to say its political authorities and economic decision-makers, had perhaps been derelict in assuming their responsibilities."[65] The final report, therefore, highlighted three areas of "egregious failure."

First, with respect to refugees, which Bergier called the "the most delicate area" of the commission's work, the ICE found that Switzerland had applied a restrictive policy under which individuals facing grave danger were unnecessarily turned away at the border. The report provides no specific figure for the number refused entry and notes that the source material only allows for speculation, although the ICE accepted that the number was undoubtedly "large."[66] Jewish asylum seekers who did gain entry, the commission found, were poorly treated and subject to conditions that violated their dignity. In his introduction to the final report, Bergier observes: "The courage of certain citizens along with their sense of justice, plus the selfless commitment of large segments of the population succeeded in toning down the official policy. But they were unable to bend it. Yet the authorities knew the fate that was in store for the victims. They also knew that a more flexible and magnanimous attitude would not have generated consequences of an unbearable nature either for the country's sovereignty or for its inhabitants' living standard, however precarious it might have been at the time."[67] One of the claims here—that Swiss officials knew the likely outcome of their refusal to permit entry to Jewish refugees—appears to be unassailable, at least for the period after 1941. The ICE located a memo from July 1942 written by the deputy chief of the Ministry of Justice and Police, in which the author notes the "awful" conditions in the East, which he says makes the "desperation" of the refugees understandable.[68]

The second claim—that Swiss authorities knew they could loosen their refugee policy without inviting reprisals from Germany or compromising living conditions for their own citizens—was harder to substantiate, though by no means impossible. Despite the inflexibility of its official policy, Switzerland managed to accommodate "several thousand" refugees in the second half of 1942.[69] That the Swiss did so without triggering a humanitarian crisis (e.g., concerns had been raised over a shrinking food supply) suggests that the "boat" was not yet full, and the absence of any German retaliation, ipso facto, can be taken as evidence that the risk to Switzerland was not as dire as some claimed. In any case, the ICE report emphasizes that Swiss authorities could not have doubted the fate awaiting those who were turned away.[70] Although the number of Jews who were denied asylum has remained a topic of debate, in the final report, overreliance on two weak claims ("the boat was full," and Germany would punish Swiss leniency) points to undeniable moral failure.[71]

Regarding Switzerland's economic ties to the Axis, the ICE judged that these had been necessary for the country's survival but also went "too far." On the one hand, cooperation with Nazi Germany has been construed as "an element of resistance," since these concessions helped Switzerland stave off military aggression. On the other hand, the ICE found that authorities in Bern and executives in some companies did not take full advantage of the "leeway" given by Berlin to manage their financial affairs independently. Switzerland's economic planners gave first priority to national survival, but there were other factors at work too. According to the final report, "Significant parts of the economic elite were instead thinking further ahead and focusing on longer-term postwar prospects. Irrespective of the outcome of the military trial of strength, these groups were working to keep the export economy competitive and to gear it towards promising markets and corporate structures."[72] In the aluminum industry, for example, Swiss exports after 1940 went exclusively to the Axis, where high demand supported favorable pricing. This arrangement continued even after aluminum supplies at home started to dwindle; vendors sold to Germany, while refusing to fill orders from the Swiss military and other sectors of the Swiss economy.[73] Taking a broader view, total exports to the Allies declined sharply between July 1940 and July 1944, while exports to the Axis nearly quintupled over the same period.[74] In general, though, Switzerland's trade balance with the Axis during this period ran at a deficit, meaning the Swiss imported from Germany more than they exported. "Before 1942, and again in 1944, far more goods came into Switzerland than were exported. Economic relations with Germany went far beyond the relative levels of ordinary foreign trade structures and could no longer be described as [standard practice]."[75] This level of cooperation, Bergier noted, "was not consonant with the strict respect of Swiss neutrality."[76] At the same time, the close economic relationship between Switzerland and Germany, according to the ICE, was never ideologically motivated: "Parts of the Swiss economic elite showed ideological affinities to the love of order and the anti-Communist attitudes of Nazi Germany, but such sympathies were not expressed through the intensity of economic exchange."[77] This points to a rather dramatic explanation for Switzerland's economic entanglements with Germany. According to Bergier: "The recurrent theme that runs like a red thread through the thousands of pages of analysis is, indeed, that of a 'business logic first' attitude. The consequence was at best myopia, but more often blindness, with respect to the rights of the [victims] of the Nazi regime."[78] Switzerland's failures in the economic arena were, according to the ICE, more bureaucratic in nature and subtler in terms of their consequences than what transpired under its patently immoral refugee policy. Driven by an instinct for profit, Switzerland's business leaders used logic that made the victims of Nazi racial policy virtually invisible. In the upper reaches of government, Switzerland's Council of Ministers were "out of touch" with the political forces operating throughout the rest of Europe. There was, in the words of the ICE, "a peculiar absence at the top," which ensured that business goals overshadowed moral concerns. In other words, the ICE faulted Switzerland's leaders more for what they failed to do than for their concrete decisions: "Within changing interest constellations and power situations, the Swiss authorities conducted negotiations during the war which were aimed primarily at ensuring that the country was adequately supplied. It was precisely this approach which also met German requirements and was able to take into account the profit calculations of Swiss companies."[79]

The third area of failure covered by the ICE pertained to Switzerland's postwar restitution policies. As in the case of Switzerland's economic alignments, the commission focused on "responsibilities that were inadequately discharged" rather than on malfeasance stemming from anti-Semitic beliefs. The fact that so many different groups failed to take adequate steps toward restitution in the postwar era—the commission examined the government, heavy industry, banks, insurance companies, art galleries, and museums—did not suggest maliciousness in the view of the ICE as much as "non-recognition of [the] problem."[80] In cases where plundered assets were brought to the attention of the Swiss authorities, these individuals applied long-standing principles, for example, banking policies aimed at maintaining discretion and the withholding of "privileged" information, which impeded justice and prolonged the suffering of victims. The ICE explored a host of questions related to restitution, ranging from how Swiss banks and insurance companies approached the concept of property rights to how "authority, law, and the economy interact[ed] as regards *Wiedergutmachung* [i.e., reparation]."[81]

The commission's overall assessment of Swiss reparations and restitution is strongly influenced by its findings regarding public perceptions of these issues at the end of the war. Among Swiss, the ICE found, the perception of injustice at the end of the war was "only slight." Political leaders rejected any suggestion that Switzerland had profited from the war or had instituted policies that violated its neutrality. Modest restitution payments made under the Washington Agreement (1946) sparked criticism and anti-Semitic clichés from ordinary Swiss citizens, and Swiss bankers accused groups negotiating on behalf of Holocaust victims of greedily pursuing assets for themselves with no intention of returning them to their rightful heirs. In 1952, the head of the Swiss Bankers Association, Jakob Diggelmann, argued that Holocaust survivors were at risk of having their lost assets re-plundered, this time by groups claiming to represent them, and that the reluctance of banks to enter into hastily drawn up restitution programs reflected a strong desire to protect the victims against further theft. Diggelmann asserted: "The Federation of Jewish Communities is not concerned with transferring heirless assets to possible claimants, but is endeavoring to establish such heirless property in a special procedure so as to benefit by taking possession of it. The actions of the opposing party therefore constitute a veritable raid on assets lying in Switzerland."[82] According to this perspective, Swiss banks required additional time to trace the provenance of dormant accounts so that the eventual restitution of these assets would not produce new injustices. That the deposit of these funds into Swiss accounts *already* represented an injustice did not seem to register with Diggelmann or other members of the banking association. According to the ICE, external pressure led to belated attempts to speed the pace of reparations in the 1960s, but again, these initiatives did little to change the perception of Swiss authorities and business leaders that they were under no obligation to make any repayment.[83] While Jewish communities in Switzerland favored the introduction of more efficient restitution measures, these groups were too small to effectively influence official policy. In general, "victims and their organizations were not in a position to make their voices heard to any great extent," and this remained the case until the mid-1990s when the silence about the past was finally broken.[84] "Whilst human rights began to play an ever more important role in international relations, the end of the Cold War brought a relaxation of firmly entrenched ideological fronts."[85] In essence, the collapse of Communism changed the ground rules regarding the politics of history, and this shift triggered a global reexamination of assets linked to the Holocaust, with Switzerland at the epicenter. Switzerland, according to the ICE, failed to live up to its own high standards for humanitarian assistance, but at the same time, other countries had also behaved poorly and Swiss guilt was by no means unique.[86]

The Significance of Unanswered Questions

When Bergier announced the commission's findings, he emphasized that the final report should be seen as an overture to future discussions and study, rather than as the last word on Switzerland's wartime history. This is an important point. The primary function of these bodies is to clarify and demythologize darkened and taboo corners of national self-understanding so that nonpartisan and transnational understandings of the past can gain traction. In other words, these commissions aim to generate answers that can effectively mediate the past. But it is equally important that historical commissions commit themselves to good questions, even when these cannot be immediately answered in a national context. To effectively amend the past, Bergier has said, commissioned history must "point toward new horizons for further discussion."[87] This means that commissions must define their work as open-ended, even when their mandates expire after a fixed interval. Otherwise, if these commissions attempt to give a definitive account of past events, or if there is a suggestion that the duty to understand the failures of the past has been fully discharged, then their reports are likely to reinforce rather than dampen the rancor of the partisan discourse. Even when a commission raises new questions and leaves the door open for future work, as the ICE clearly tried to do, there is no guarantee that their work will overcome the pull of ordinary political bickering. While the commission's final report received little criticism from academic historians, others asserted that the inquiry failed to give an objective account and dwelled too much on Switzerland's (supposed) failures. Markus Somm, the editor of the *Basler Zeitung*, felt that the ICE allowed the darker side of Swiss history to overshadow the positive aspects of Switzerland's wartime conduct.[88] Why do the failures of a few, Somm complained, eclipse the good conduct of the many? What about Henri Guisan, the commander of the Swiss military, whose defensive mobilization at the start of the war, some have argued, staved off a German invasion? What about the Swiss who helped to rescue and hide Jews, in spite of the risks this entailed (Yad Vashem names forty-five Swiss on its honor roll of Righteous Gentiles)?

In fact, the ICE dealt directly with Guisan in a section of the final report titled "Awareness, Knowledge, and Power," in which the general received a mostly favorable assessment, but which also placed him at the periphery of the economic structure and parliamentary councils where critical decisions were made.[89] Also, in contrast to what Somm contended, the ICE reported at length on the assistance provided to refugees before and during the war. For example, the final report notes that Switzerland accepted close to 300,000 refugees by the end of the war, a figure that far surpasses the highest estimates for Jews who were refused entry. But, as the ICE observed, this comparison occludes what the commission was charged with investigating in the first place, that is, whether there had been a more restrictive policy in place for Jews as compared to others.[90] If immigration officials had only been "confused and under pressure," as earlier narratives suggested, then the total number of admitted refugees would almost certainly have been lower and the high proportion of Jews among those refused entry would not have been so pronounced. The substantive issue is not whether the ICE ignored important counterevidence—the commission very clearly addressed what Somm claimed had been overlooked—but whether the commission developed appropriate comparisons around the available evidence.

The ICE devoted a long section of its final report to the question of "context and comparison," specifically as these related to the Swiss refugee policy. The commission felt strongly that historical understanding was not possible without thorough contextualization, that is, without taking into account European and global trends at the time, and this line of thinking is evident throughout the report. As an example, the ICE punctuated its findings regarding anti-Semitism in Switzerland with a qualifier—that xenophobia and anti-Semitism had been widespread in Europe (and elsewhere) for decades prior to the inception of the Nazi regime in Germany—and that these trends had a negative effect on international efforts to address the refugee problem during the interwar period.[91] Against this backdrop, instances of anti-Semitism in Switzerland only showed that the Swiss were like many other countries at that time, not that they were more bigoted, or less tolerant, than the global norm. This is an important clue for evaluating specific Swiss refugee policies. It points to an international failure to uphold liberal democratic norms of the age, for example, in the framework set up by the League of Nations,[92] and it normalizes, or at any rate relativizes, what some readers of the final report will understand as an outrageous assault against human decency. As the commission noted, thirty-one other countries besides Switzerland were invited to the Evian Conference in 1938, and all but one, the Dominican Republic, refused to increase their quotas for Jewish immigrants. Switzerland, from this perspective, acted no worse than Great Britain, France, or the United States, who had called for the meeting. But these kinds of comparisons can quickly lead to irresponsible history. For example, Markus Somm claimed that the ICE did a poor job of documenting the many cases in which Swiss citizens sheltered Jews in their own homes or helped them find safety elsewhere. Indeed, the final report makes no mention of the "righteous" Swiss recognized at Yad Vashem.[93] But what if we contextualize this data by placing the Swiss numbers alongside those of other countries? There are more Swiss (45) enshrined at Yad Vashem than there are Britons (19) or Americans (3). So, why single out Switzerland? Judging from these numbers, Switzerland appears to have been more positively oriented toward Jewish refugees than either Great Britain or the United States, despite the role these countries played in "the defense of democracy against dictatorship." On the other hand, Poland (6,339) is more heavily represented on the Yad Vashem list than any other nation, and not by any small margin. If Somm wants to use the stories of Swiss rescuers to undercut the ICE narrative of moral failure, then it stands to reason that Switzerland (with the United States and Britain) must bear a greater responsibility for the Holocaust than Poland. If the work of rescuers in Switzerland allows Somm to minimize the controversies concerning Nazi Gold, slave labor, refugee policy, Swiss economic ties to Germany, and the failure to locate and return "dormant" assets, then the work of many more rescuers in Poland should offset what historians have learned about Polish involvement in the mass killings of Jews. But, of course, trade-offs likes these make no positive contributions to our understanding of the Holocaust. Critics of Holocaust commissions sometimes complain that these initiatives feed postmodern relativism by broadening guilt to non-Germans (thereby diluting it) and by blurring the lines between perpetrators, bystanders (i.e., those who could have done more to protect victims but chose not to), and the plainly innocent (i.e., those who simply endured what was foisted on them). The commissions analyzed here can certainly be read to support a narrative in which guilt and responsibility for the Holocaust are radically diffused, even to the point of making these categories meaningless. While the transnational aspect of Holocaust crimes enhances understanding of the subject, there is no legitimate way of talking about the Shoah without giving special consideration to German perpetrators. Even if the Holocaust has sometimes been seen, in retrospect, as a foundational event for a "postnational" Europe, Germany, of course, must bear ultimate responsibility for the fate of Jewish victims. Holocaust commissions like the ICE have attempted to balance these two approaches, but the tension between them is something partisans have seized on to undercut their work and politicize the debates over responsibility. The point I wish to emphasize is that these commissions, despite certain limitations, can offer nuanced conceptions of guilt and/or responsibility that go beyond, or outside of, the traditional legal categories that require either/or adjudication. Unlike criminal tribunals, which consider the question of guilt within a relatively narrow legal framework—one is either guilty, or not, of breaching the law—commissioned history allows for subtle gradations of guilt that go well beyond the "degrees" of guilt familiar to conventional (e.g., American) legal systems and penal codes. Beyond the questions of intentionality and premeditation, the historical commissions can get at the various processual forces—social, political, cultural, and economic—that create the environments in which large-scale human rights abuses and mass violence become possible.

Teaching the Holocaust in Switzerland

Despite the strong endorsement that the ICE's final report received from the Swiss government, Switzerland's war record continued to spark public debate, largely due to the influence of national politics and the jockeying of certain parties. In particular, the growth and influence of the conservative Swiss People's Party in the 1990s lent support to those who sought to minimize Switzerland's responsibility.[94] For instance, one People's Party MP (member of parliament) published and distributed pamphlets in which he accused the ICE of intentionally sullying Switzerland's reputation abroad, while another offered that the members of the ICE "ought to be given a proper beating."[95] At the same time, center and center-left parties in the ruling coalition apologized for Switzerland's moral failures during the war and applauded the ICE for its work. The conflict of memory in Switzerland at the level of political parties was not replicated in the community of Swiss historians, who, by 1997, shared mostly the same view on the key issues. This convergence of opinion among scholars helped to spawn a new school textbook, which was published in 2006.

The book, *Hinschauen und Nachfragen: Die Schweitz und die Zeit des Nationalsozialismus im Licht aktueller Fragen* (Looking Closely and Inquiring: Switzerland in the Period of National Socialism in Light of Current Questions), jointly written by two scholars in the field of history education and two former ICE researchers, was approved for use in the country's largest canton, Zürich, though teachers there were not required to adopt it.[96] When members of the Swiss People's Party attempted to block the textbook's implementation, the canton created an advisory board, which included four individuals representing the ICE, to facilitate its publication. The board also recruited one conservative MP to accommodate the perspective of those who had lived through the war and experienced it directly.

Hinschauen und Nachfragen's five chapters deal with the Holocaust from different perspectives. The authors emphasize methodological questions throughout the text, and they claim to resist "ready-made answers." The main objective of the textbook, according to its authors, is to cultivate "intellectual autonomy" by helping students construct their own responsible narratives and critique the partisan narratives to which they have been exposed. However, as Bernhard Schär and Vera Sperisen noted in their analysis of *Hinschauen und Nachfragen*, the textbook's skepticism extends only so far.[97] While students are encouraged to question received knowledge and are led through exercises designed to highlight the constructed nature of historical knowledge, these sections of the textbook ultimately lead to chapter 4 in which the findings of the ICE are presented as authoritative. As Schär and Sperisen put it: "[The textbook] pretends to help readers grapple with a supposedly open, uninterpreted history . . . while surreptitiously delivering a diluted version of the experts' interpretations of this history."[98] In chapter 5, which rehearses the justifications given in defense of Switzerland's refugee policy, the authors wrap up their discussion by presenting the ICE's interpretation, that is, that the policy was "needlessly restrictive" and sacrificed Jewish lives when "the boat" was not yet full. On the one hand, the ICE's explanation is presented as merely one possibility among others. On the other hand, the ICE perspective supplies the last word on the most sensitive issue within the larger debate, and the authors present the commission's findings as a kind of trump card. Given this approach, the key question is whether (or to what extent) this textbook should be considered a tool of political indoctrination. If it only proclaims the truth of the (current) political majority and fails to seriously weigh the interpretations of the conservative minority (while pretending to do so), then how does the textbook—or, going further, the ICE's twenty-five volumes of published research—mitigate the effects of ideology?

Schär and Sperisen defend the textbook against the charge of propaganda, while also acknowledging that it is clearly imprinted by the politics of its authors. Ultimately, they argue, the textbook achieves "relative autonomy," which is the best possible scenario where the social sciences are concerned. The authors of the textbook adhere to disciplinary conventions, take up and analyze countervailing viewpoints, provide evidence for their conclusions, and in the end, "they promote a version of collective memory, values, and national identity that is shared by a majority within state power."[99] In other words, Schär and Sperisen view the alignment between the textbook and state power as the aftereffect of an untainted investigation. This does not mean that the project included no political agenda. The textbook, after all, asks and answers the same questions that the government proposed in the mandate given to the ICE in 1996. Like the commission's investigation, the textbook is concerned primarily with assessing the military threat that Switzerland faced following France's surrender in June 1940 and with understanding the moral challenges that Swiss officials confronted in their dealings with a hostile and criminal regime. While the preface asks readers "whether" Swiss officials and businesses were complicit in the crimes of the Nazi regime, the rest of the text documents the ways in which they were indeed complicit. This slippage makes the book somewhat heavy-handed, but one could also argue that it signals the authors' attempt at mediation, that is, their effort to "incorporate, but also transcend" the main points of the partisan debate.

It is difficult to assess whether *Hinschauen und Nachfragen* achieves its stated learning objectives. Schär and Sperisen have pointed out that there is a profound lack of empirical research on "the practical usage" of school textbooks. We know little about the ways teachers employ these materials (e.g., the degree to which they reinforce or resist the authors' goals) and even less about the ways students are influenced (or not) by the strategies employed by their instructors. It seems safe to say that good textbooks are useless without good teachers, but there is little agreement, in any case, about what qualities make for a "good" textbook or, for that matter, what outcomes are most desirable for history education. By asserting the "relative autonomy" of a narrative that implicates Switzerland in the Holocaust to a far greater degree than was accepted in the past, *Hinschauen und Nachfragen* attempts to reconfigure Swiss memory and reconfirm Switzerland's European identity through official condemnation of a past injustice. The dissemination of the ICE narrative in (some) Swiss schools signals at least some degree of commitment to the discourse of human rights and to the moral and legal norms associated with "civilized" society.

Daniel Levy and Natan Sznaider have argued that the Holocaust now serves as a litmus test for nations wishing to assert their credentials as members of civilized society.[100] Levy and Sznaider present this development as part of a larger process of globalization and the consolidation of what they call "cosmopolitan memory." Old categories and boundaries may blur as new collective memories of the Holocaust take shape, but strong identification with the crime, its unique features, and the unprecedented moral damage it did, not only to German perpetrators but to other groups besides, has emerged as a fixed point in Europe's liberal democratic discourse. Tony Judt put this point succinctly in *Postwar*, writing that Holocaust recognition has become "the price of admission to Europe."[101] But regardless of how one describes the new standard, the upshot remains the same in terms of what it means for Holocaust historiography and for the commissions that have investigated this period. Nonetheless, the primary significance of these commissions is not what they reveal about the Holocaust. While some commissions have made important discoveries in previously unexplored archives, most have not produced startling revelations. In the case of the ICE, the commission's findings did not depart significantly from what individual scholars had written earlier, nor did they cut against the grain of scholarly consensus.[102] Bergier acknowledged as much when he presented the final report in 2002. Instead, what is important about these commissions is the shift they signal away from national, territorialized memory and toward a globalized collective memory, which regards guilt differently (oftentimes, more broadly) and extracts new ethical obligations from it. These obligations form the backbone of a liberal democratic discourse based on the universal rights of individuals and groups to equal treatment, nondiscrimination, and truthful representation of the past (i.e., the right to history), a subject I return to later in this study.

A Final Assessment

The rise of historical commissions in the 1990s and 2000s has sometimes been attributed to a paradigm shift, which brought new attention to the moral responsibilities of bystanders and minor perpetrators (i.e., those who implemented, rather than engineered, the criminal policies of the regime) during—and after—episodes of genocidal violence. According to this perspective, the new attention to morality was mirrored by the rise of the human rights discourse and by a heightened desire within the international community to make multicultural tolerance a pillar of social policy. This could certainly apply to Switzerland and the ICE, although there were also significant external pressures brought to bear. One of these, clearly, was the impact of class-action lawsuits brought in the U.S. courts. It is also true that Switzerland's Jewish communities asserted themselves more strongly in the 1990s than in previous decades. This study argues inter alia that the proliferation of Holocaust commissions reflects an emergent norm based on the "right to history" and that the mediated histories produced by successful commissions can deepen democratic commitment where liberal states have failed to abide by such principles in the past or have allowed partisan interpretations of the past to undermine the right to truth. Perhaps this does not emerge clearly from looking only at the ICE, which could be characterized, more soberly, as an example of historians playing the role of "political troubleshooters."[103] But I would argue that the full significance of the ICE, or, for that matter, any of the other Holocaust commissions, only becomes clear from a comparative perspective. Events in Switzerland suggest that the public impact of commissioned history is not always deep or long lasting. Historical clarification initiatives like the ICE might simply represent a transitory moment in the political oscillation between polarized perspectives. In a statement written in 2013 to mark International Holocaust Remembrance Day (January 27), Swiss president Ueli Maurer asserted that Switzerland had been a safe haven for many persecuted people during the Nazi era and "a country of freedom and law" throughout the war.[104] Representatives for Switzerland's Jewish communities chastised Maurer for failing to mention "the refugees who were turned back to a certain death" and for minimizing the insights of the ICE.[105] Academic historians and members of the political Left also expressed concern. Maurer, who is a member of the conservative Swiss People's Party and one of the architects of the party's aggressive populist platform, assumed the presidency on January 1, 2013, but his reputation as an outspoken critic of European multiculturalism was already well established.[106] A decade after the ICE final report first grabbed headlines, Maurer's ascendency and the rise of the Swiss Right more generally represent a setback in the trend toward acknowledgment and contrition, at least at the official level. Among a certain set of intellectuals and with broad segments of the youth, the main points of the ICE narrative appear to have taken root, but as of 2013 the Swiss government takes cover once again under the myth of a friendly but determined neutral country "standing aside" during a period of global conflict and protecting itself against foreign aggression. Perhaps the lesson for academic historians is that their insights do not hold up against determined ideological opposition, unless there is willingness on the part of mediating voices to enter the political debate and defend historical interpretation on the basis of both its scholarly integrity and moral substance. Reflecting on the politics of history in Switzerland and the role of historians in public debates over the past, Georg Kreis has urged a separation between academic historiography, which seeks a scientific basis in "methodically reflected analysis" and sociopolitical historiography, which, he says, "wants to express and promote writings which deal mainly with principles and commitments."[107] Watching the ICE report lose ground to the debunked perspective of the Swiss People's Party, one must ask whether this boundary is morally tenable. Kreis describes "shyness" among Swiss academic historians about provoking public debate(s) over the past, particularly when these revolve around their own work or that of their close colleagues.[108] In a small country like Switzerland, where academics often know each other well and depend on one another for career advancement, there is, Kreis says, "a great reluctance to thrash out differences of opinion" in public. But this mollifying tendency cedes ground to other individuals and interests whose treatment of the past is less responsible. The right to historical truth makes clear demands on those scholars who cannot discharge their moral duties simply by pointing interested parties to the library stacks where their best work quietly resides. Instead, thoroughgoing confrontation with the past requires historians who embrace a role in the public debates and understand the political stakes inherent to the conflicts that manifest as historical controversies.

2

Poles and Jews

Mediating
the Jedwabne Conflict

The fall of communism in 1989 produced a sharp increase in
dialogue and cooperation between Poles and Jews, but
the two groups share a grim history that makes deep reconciliation difficult to
achieve. The past can be a meeting ground for groups who want to understand
each other, but it can also work as a wedge when painful histories coalesce
around divergent memories. The debates that erupted in Poland following the
publication of Jan Gross's *Neighbors* help illustrate how history threatens group
identity as well as the possibilities for mediating between partisan perspectives.

Ritualized Forgetting and
Accusatory Narratives

Originally published as *Sąsiedzi* (2000), Gross's study of
Polish-Jewish relations during World War II appeared in English one year later
as *Neighbors: The Destruction of the Jewish Community in Jedwabne, Poland.*[1]
Located in northeastern Poland, Jedwabne was seized by the Soviet Union at
the beginning of the war and was overrun again by German troops near the
end of June 1941, following the launch of Hitler's eastern offensive. *Neighbors*
explores one particular episode from this period, which took place on July 10,
1941, when, according to Gross, the Polish half of this small "East European"
town murdered the Jewish half—approximately 1,600 men, women, and

children—by clubbing, hacking, drowning, and burning them. Gross contends that many of the Jewish victims knew their killers intimately and that the Polish perpetrators, rather than being forced into these acts, as some have claimed, eagerly carried out the killings without any outside prompting or assistance.[2] Even though German Gestapo were present on the day of the massacre, Gross presents the testimony of eyewitnesses, who state that Polish authorities proposed the mass killing themselves and then insisted, when the Germans tried to dissuade them, that no Jews should be spared. Gross's interpretation of the massacre sparked a furious debate over Poland's role in the Holocaust and over the reworking of Holocaust memory more broadly. A similar, though less vitriolic, debate had waxed and waned in the decades following World War II; however, by the time Gross's book appeared, there was little interest (in Poland, at any rate) in exploring this aspect of history. *Neighbors* not only dredged up a repressed past, but it also shone a light on the mechanisms that had been used to expunge the Holocaust from Poland's public consciousness.

The debate over Poland's role in the Holocaust began immediately after World War II when the Stalinist narrative of "The Great Patriotic War" and the working-class anti-Fascist front began to coalesce. Discussions about the war were framed in the official discourse so as not to bring attention to the millions of Jewish victims or to the anti-Semitic character of the Nazi extermination program. One can see this marginalization of Jewish victims and Jewish memory in Nathan Rapoport's Warsaw Ghetto (Heroes) Monument, which was unveiled in 1948.[3] Depicting a group of "mytho-proletarian" resistance fighters standing in front of two civilians,[4] the relief casts the insurgents in a heroic but also unemotional pose, which elides their Jewish identity and glosses over both the horror of their experience and the question of who bears responsibility for their plight.[5] Instead of collective remembrance, the memorial has become a site of ritual forgetting.[6] This amnesia coincided with a wider prohibition regarding any questioning of Polish behavior during the war or the subject of Polish-Jewish relations more generally.[7] Even in the literary and intellectual circles where there was some interest in exploring dark periods of Polish history, officials enforced a strict silence on these subjects beginning in 1948.

Under Władysłav Gomułka, the Polish United Workers' Party (PZPR, Polska Zjednoczona Partia Robotnicza) continued to manipulate the memory of the Holocaust in the second half of the 1950s and throughout the next decade. According to Antony Polonsky and Joanna Michlic, this was part of "the gradual process of ethno-nationalization of communism," and it reflected a general "resurfacing" of the Jewish question within the Worker's Party.[8] Under this rubric, Holocaust victims were stripped of their Jewish identity and were counted as deracinated members of the international anti-Fascist collective or as members of an undifferentiated workers' nation. At the Auschwitz-Birkenau Memorial Museum, which was renovated in 1955 to reflect the new political current, exhibits recorded losses by nationality, but the word "Jew" was scarcely mentioned. This also was true at other camp memorials. Jews who were killed for "racial" reasons were submerged in a broader story of national martyrdom by means of sweeping statements that ignored the context of particular acts of violence, for example, the six million Poles killed during the war. This helped entrench a "parallel fates" narrative, in which Jewish and Polish deaths were described as numerically equivalent while crucial distinctions in the manner of death and motive for killing were either deliberately blurred or left unarticulated. "If negative Polish behavior was mentioned at all, . . . this was presented as a marginal social problem, limited to a small and unrepresentative group, a phenomenon that was paralleled in other European countries."[9] In fact, the parallel fates narrative was not an original creation of PZPR but was something the party appropriated from the anticommunist opposition. After hearing of anti-Semitic outbursts involving Poles living under the Nazi occupation, the government-in-exile began to downplay these incidents as early as 1943 by suggesting they were isolated events, which did not reflect the true Polish nation.[10]

Within the PZPR, a faction linked to the prewar National Democratic Party (Endecja) continued to manipulate the memory of the Holocaust during the mid-1960s by launching an anti-Semitic campaign that culminated in the anti-Zionist purge of 1968.[11] Taking the parallel fates narrative a step farther, the leaders of this faction equated the fates of Jews and Poles by emphasizing that both groups endured similar persecution and suffered equivalent losses. This could be considered the inaugural moment in the competition for victimhood, which Jan Gross's book helped rekindle more than thirty years later. Using an exaggerated version of an already tendentious argument regarding the "equal fates" of the two groups, the apologists attempted to wipe the slate clean by claiming that any wrongs Poles had done to Jews after June 1941 were matched (or even outweighed) by the wrongs that Jews had done to Poles earlier (i.e., following the Hitler-Stalin pact). This helped spawn a closely related theme within the debate over Poland's role in the Holocaust, that is, the influence of so-called "Jewish anti-Polonism" in postwar politics. When critical remarks about Polish behavior appeared in Western accounts of the war, apologists used "anti-Polonism" or "Polonophobia" to discredit any damaging reappraisals of the past and thus highlight what they saw as a deliberate and prejudicial downplaying of Polish sacrifices and suffering.

These tensions help explain how and why Polish and Jewish memories of the Holocaust diverged so widely in the postwar era, and they also help make sense of (without validating) the reckless statements that participants in the Jedwabne debates have sometimes made. For example, when President Alexander Kwasniewski begged forgiveness for the massacre on behalf of the nation in July 2001, Poles were bitterly divided over the content and appropriateness of the official apology. A Catholic priest in the Jedwabne parish, Father Edward Orlowski, not only skipped the memorial service where Kwasniewski made his statement, but he also challenged the entire premise of Polish guilt. "These are all lies," Orlowski told reporters. "Germans are responsible, so why should we apologize?"[12] On another occasion, Orlowski spoke even more candidly in terms that left little room for compromise: "The Jews have their memory, and we have ours."[13]

In his work on Jedwabne, Gross directly addresses allegations—the "current stereotype," he calls it—that Jews in Poland "enjoyed a privileged relationship with the Soviet occupiers," which made them obvious targets of Polish retaliation once Nazi forces dislodged the Soviet occupation.[14] Gross writes, "Of course there were 'collaborators' or NKVD agents among the Jews, but as we know very well, not exclusively among the Jews, and in Jedwabne . . . *not even primarily* among the Jews."[15] Rather than something that Jews brought on themselves through political treachery, the massacre in Jedwabne was, according to Gross, the product of widespread and deeply rooted Polish anti-Semitism. This anti-Semitism, Gross contends, "was embedded in the experience of war." At the same time, he argues, "it predated any Communist attempts to take power in Poland, because it was firmly rooted in medieval prejudice about ritual murder."[16] In making this statement, Gross aligns himself with those who have been most critical of Polish behavior during the war. For example, he stands with Emanuel Ringelblum, the Polish-Jewish historian and politician, who, in 1944, characterized events in Poland this way: "The Polish people and the Government of the Republic of Poland were incapable of deflecting the Nazi steamroller from its anti-Jewish course. But the question is permissible whether the attitude of the Polish people befitted the enormity of the calamities that befell the country's citizens. Was it inevitable that the Jews, looking their last on this world as they rode in the death trains . . . should have had to witness indifference or even joy on the faces of their neighbors?"[17] Gross is similarly ambivalent on the question of Polish agency. He concedes that the Poles were a captive people unable to control their own destiny, but he also maintains that Poles directly targeted Jews with violence when they clearly did not have to. For the Poles who participated in the massacre, Gross contends, the torture and slaying of Jedwabne's Jews represented the realization of a collective impulse rooted in long-standing Catholic prejudice. Where did this "explosive potential" come from? Gross offers: "We must remember that in the background of anti-Jewish violence there *always* lurked a suspicion of ritual murder, a conviction that Jews use for the preparation of Passover matzoh the fresh blood of innocent children. It was a deeply ingrained belief among many Polish Catholics, and not simply among residents of the boondocks."[18] The "always" here is significant. It suggests a universality that leads Gross to the following conclusion: "The Shoah has been portrayed in scholarly literature as a phenomenon rooted in modernity. We know very well that in order to kill millions of people, an efficient bureaucracy is necessary, along with a (relatively) advanced technology. But the murder of Jedwabne Jews reveals yet another, deeper, more archaic layer of this enterprise. I am referring not only to the motivations of the murderers . . . but also to primitive, ancient methods and murder weapons: stones, wooden clubs, iron bars, fire, and water; as well as the absence of organization."[19] Even as he claims to represent the Shoah as something "heterogeneous," Gross treats the Jedwabne massacre as a microcosm— a "deeper layer," he calls it—of the Holocaust. Given the evidence he engages, the pogrom in Jedwabne becomes something incontrovertible for Gross, not only in the fact of its occurrence but, even more importantly, in his explanation of the killers' motives that recalls the "eternal anti-Semites" arguments that PZPR apparatchiks cited as evidence of "Jewish anti-Polonism" in the 1960s. At its core, then, Gross's account is an accusatory narrative. It is written to document the guilt of the perpetrators, and at the same time it serves as a moral indictment of the Polish collective, even as it also acknowledges some degree of Polish suffering.[20] The transgressions of individuals are inscribed on the nation, so that the Polish people emerge, in Gross's final analysis, as both "victims and victimizers." This is an attempt to strike a balance between the spurious arguments that cast Poles as "eternal anti-Semites" and the plainly ideological (and patently anti-Semitic) "equal fates" narrative that asks whether Jews deserved to suffer or whether they suffered at all in comparison to the Poles. Despite this balancing act, *Neighbors* falls into a trap that Gross had hoped to avoid, that is, the substitution of the universal for the particular. The "always," which Gross uses to link the Jedwabne perpetrators to a "deeper, more archaic" wellspring of anti-Semitic violence, encourages readers to think they can comprehend the totality of the Holocaust by entering the thoughts of individual Poles who, at one particular moment, forfeited some of their humanity. The methodology Gross employs is straightforward, but his aspirations are, perhaps, too high. The substitution of deep and partial understandings seems to happen despite Gross's determination to avoid that outcome.

Polish Backlash against *Neighbors*

The blurring of lines that takes place in *Neighbors*, that is, the representation of Poles as both victims and victimizers, makes Gross's account of the killings highly contentious, not only for historians who wish to dispute his findings (e.g., the role of the Gestapo and the total number of victims) but also for Poles who wish to commemorate their own group's losses, emphasize the ways in which their autonomy was eroded during the war, and document acts of resistance that would challenge Gross's claims regarding collaboration and endogenous anti-Semitism. In his introduction, Gross asserts that *Neighbors* is an unconventional study that reveals the fuzziness of well-worn categories such as perpetrators, victims, and bystanders. His interest in the slipperiness of these terms makes the book highly engaging but also threatening to those who wish to maintain the categories that keep guilt and responsibility neatly compartmentalized. This effect is especially pronounced among Poles who were steeped in the official histories of the 1960s and 1970s.[21]

In 2004, when a Holocaust documentary aired in Canada with multiple references to "Polish concentration camps," Poland's foreign minister, Włodzimierz Cimoszewicz, penned a furious op-ed piece excoriating the film's producers and the television executives who permitted its broadcast. Arguing that "the perception of human rights and a sense of justice associated with the sensitivity for historical truth" must play a fundamental role in relations between states, Cimoszewicz insisted that the Nazi extermination camps that operated on Polish soil could not be validly referred to as "Polish camps" (since they were constructed and operated by Germans), and that any reference to the killing centers in this manner was an attack against both the Polish nation and the memory of Jews who perished at these sites. "There cannot be any other reaction to such a slander and ignorance," Cimoszewicz surmised, "than the demand of unconditional regret of the broadcaster in front of the same TV viewers who were exposed to this obvious insult harming not only the Poles of today but the victims of the Holocaust as well."[22]

Neighbors provoked similar criticism among academics. In a special issue of *Slavic Review*, Wojciech Roszkowski, a prominent Polish economist and politician, challenged the credibility of *Neighbors* on two levels. Roszkowski argued that Gross's thesis remained unproven in the absence of more direct evidence. The court records that Gross utilized—fifteen Poles were arrested and brought to trial in January 1949 on charges they had participated in the killings—comprised fractured and sometimes contradictory testimonies, which, according to Roszkowski, failed to accurately reconstruct the events in Jedwabne. Moreover, he argued, the testimony of eyewitnesses provided no actual insight regarding the motive(s) of the killers or their psychological states during the massacre. This is a dubious argument—we do not know that they did it, but if they did, who knows why—that nevertheless points to some of the problems in Gross's book. *Neighbors* connects the Jedwabne perpetrators to a more general climate of anti-Semitism through speculation and inference.[23] Despite the horrible scenes recounted in the court's papers—one witness recalls seeing a man knifed and then left to die but only after his attackers had plucked out his eyes and cut off his tongue—these depositions were given by individuals whose perspectives were limited (like every perspective) and whose external vantage precluded deep, historical understanding. In his introduction, Gross argues that the Holocaust defies full comprehension: "I do not see the possibility of attaining closure here. . . . I could not say to myself when I got to the last page, 'Well, I understand now,' and I doubt my readers will be able to either."[24] Regardless, Roszkowski makes this the focus of his critique. While the main thrust of Roszkowski's argument comes close to denying the validity of all historical inquiry, he dissects Gross's methodology primarily to suggest that there are universal standards in the social sciences regarding, for example, methodology and rules of evidence, which make the interpretive forays in *Neighbors* empirically unsound and ideologically suspect. Although this is not my own position (my own response is delineated in the next section), it is still instructive for what it reveals about the politics of history.

The controversy over Jedwabne was not limited to specialized academic journals. *Neighbors* ignited fierce public debates regarding who knew what about the pogrom (and when), and for a time Jedwabne moved to the center of Poland's national conversation. Major newspapers and periodicals ran long pieces responding to Gross's book, and readers contributed their own emotionally charged letters. Writing in *Gazeta Wyborcza*, Joanna Tokarska-Bakir alleged that *Neighbors* could have been written only by a scholar who, like Gross, lived outside Poland. At home, she felt, "obsession with innocence" made Gross's project untenable. She continued, "If we can talk about the responsibilities of Polish historians for what Poles *do not know* about the Holocaust, we can do it only in terms of the sin of relinquishment. This is often the result of the innate caution of historians, which drives them away from certain subjects."[25] But what begins as "innate caution" soon moves toward moral evasion, which Tokarska-Bakir describes (in ironic disparagement) as "the right to look the other way." She links this to the "mass neurosis" of Polish anti-Semitism, which manifests itself as "escape from the problem."[26] Poland will remain trapped in this "illness" (elsewhere she refers to a "dangerous illusion") while the attitude among Poles regarding Gross's source material is characterized by doubt and skepticism rather than empathy and affirmation. Source verification remains a necessary epistemological exercise, but for an anthropologist like Tokarska-Bakir, insight into "the facts" must also account for what people say about these facts. As in the psychoanalytic dynamic, the strongest denials of responsibility are the ones that require the most intensive probing.

In the pages of *Rzeczpospolita* the historian Tomasz Strzembosz, a specialist in the period from 1939 to 1954, asserted that Gross was wrong, not about the identity of the Jedwabne killers but about the context in which the violence occurred.[27] Gross, he argued, overlooked or misunderstood the "circumstances," which included strong Jewish support for the Soviet occupation in 1939 and the active collaboration of Jews in "tortures" inflicted on the local Polish population by the Soviet secret police. According to Strzembosz, "Jews committed acts of revolt against the Polish state, taking over towns and setting up revolutionary committees there, arresting and shooting representatives of the Polish state authorities, attacking smaller or even fairly large units of the Polish Army. It was an armed collaboration, taking the side of the enemy, betrayal in the days of defeat."[28] What Strzembosz puts at the center of his account, Gross regards as an ugly and indefensible stereotype, a propaganda plank that can easily be dismantled through careful consideration of the evidence. As Gross writes, collaboration with the Soviets was something both Jews and Poles undertook, and Polish memory has overstated the primacy of Jewish collaboration. Gross cites a questionnaire that the Historical Bureau of the Polish Army circulated to record the experience of Poles in the Łomża region during the Soviet occupations. He points out that only sixteen surveys out of 125 make any mention of Jews having been especially active or vociferous in support of the occupation. Strzembosz privileges other sources, pointing to "thousands of testimonies" that, he says, illuminate the "actual role" of the Jewish population at the time of the Soviet takeover.[29] According to Strzembosz, these include Polish, Jewish, and Soviet documents, although the bulk of his argument is based around Polish sources, mainly the testimony of Polish underground fighters.[30]

Jacek Żakowski, a well-known and highly regarded Polish journalist, raised probably the most controversial criticism against *Neighbors*. (I do not include the predictable responses of the Catholic-nationalist press here.) In a long article that ran in *Gazeta Wyborcza* under the title "Every Neighbor Had a Name," Żakowski charges Gross with giving an account of the massacre that relies on "the language of ethnic war and genocide," by which he seems to mean injudicious deference to group identity.[31] According to Żakowski, the "large-scale quantifiers" that appear throughout *Neighbors*, that is, Gross's references to "the Poles" and "the Jews," as if these groups were monolithic entities, reproduces a tribal logic that "runs the risk of causing or contributing to further misfortune." Zakowski never says who might be at risk in future episodes of violence or who might commit such acts, but he cites Bosnia and Rwanda as examples of reckless language and cynical manipulation of history creating the conditions for mass violence. For Zakowski, the idea seems to be that Gross falls into the same speech patterns that nationalist demagogues used in the run-up to the genocides of the 1990s. While his claim is far-fetched, Zakowski is right to be suspicious of a narrative that attributes the mass killing in Jedwabne to "society" (this is the term that appeared in Gross's original Polish text), rather than to individuals who work (at times) as a collective. "I have the impression," Zakowski writes, "that Gross accepts too easily the view that the crime [in Jedwabne] was the work of the whole town." Even if large numbers failed to intervene on behalf of the victims—none of the literature describes even token resistance among Poles—this is not the same as saying that all of the Polish residents participated in the killings. Zakowski calls this the central thesis of *Neighbors*, which he labels "a lie," rather than an interpretative error. Zakowski refuses to accept even the loosest notion of collective guilt or national responsibility. "There is no responsibility for grandfathers and great-grandfathers," he insists, "because those not yet born had no way of restraining them. . . . Jan Tomasz Gross is responsible for himself, and I am responsible for myself. Neither of us has the right to complain to the other about his countrymen or forebears."[32]

Zakowski is right to see in *Neighbors* a tendency to generalize criminal culpability and an overreliance on broad categories that cloud historical understanding, but his conception of responsibility (or lack thereof) is problematic if history is to become a source of reconciliation. Dawid Warszawski picks up on this point in an essay he wrote in response to Zakowski and the concerns expressed by the latter over Gross's use of "ethnic language."[33] Warszawski calls the charges put forth by Zakowski "empty" but also "serious." The seriousness stems from Zakowski's narrow conception of responsibility, which, Warszawski argues, has to be accepted as "a package deal." If Zakowski wishes to claim a Polish identity, which is precisely what he does in "Every Neighbor Has a Name," then, according to Warszawski, he must also live with the "quantifiers" Gross uses and the implication of responsibility that these connote.[34] When we identify with an ethnonational collective, Warszawski writes, we choose to be responsible for whatever acts that collective has undertaken in our name. This requires us to accept responsibility for both the good acts and the bad, in the past as well as in the present. Guilt for the most serious transgressions must trickle down to subsequent generations, even if this risks reinforcing the group categories on which past ethnic violence was based. Why is this so? Warszawski argues that "without the use of this language of 'large-scale' quantifiers, it is as Zakowski correctly notes, impossible to incite hatred—but it is also impossible to lay it to rest." In other words, only by taking on the burden of the past and the crimes of our forebears can the past be overcome as an obstacle to reconciliation.

Of course, context and "circumstances" matter deeply in the pursuit of historical understanding, even where attempts at clarification lead to serious disagreement. Gross's determination to question the apologists' treatment of Jewish testimonies also matters. To foster peace, victims must be allowed to have a voice in the way history is recorded, and it is in keeping with the "right to history," described in the introduction to this study, that they be afforded that opportunity. Given the relative dearth of survivors' testimonies, these sources should be treated generously, as Gross has suggested, by accepting what we read as true unless persuasive accounts to the contrary can be located.[35] It is not unreasonable to provide this space to the victims where the pressure to look away, or to qualify and excuse, is intense. But space must be provided on the other side of the divide as well. Where evidence points to grievous misconduct, the victimizers, or their descendants, must also be part of the conversation so that guilt can be explored productively, which means characterized in terms that are not only historically accurate but also useful in terms of fostering a sense of responsibility. Guilt that excruciates to the point of triggering denial is useful neither to the victims, who wish to have the claims acknowledged and their wounds redressed, nor to the perpetrators, who wish to preserve the positive aspects of their shared identity and protect themselves against improper claims regarding their collective moral turpitude. Accusations that prompt one side to withdraw from the dialogue are similarly imprudent. A guilt-laden narrative does not productively clarify the past, if the individuals and groups whom it implicates reject it out of hand. These accounts merely reinforce the rift that exists where memories of the same event(s) have already diverged. Within the limits of disciplinary standards, bringing a measure of agreement to the two sides is the overarching goal of mediating history. Whether this can be accomplished—sometimes it cannot—depends on the particular qualities of the mediating narrative, and it requires that there be clear incentives for abiding by such a narrative. In cases where two groups each see themselves as the principal victims, common ground may be lacking. In such cases, the goal of mediation reverts to broad contextualization and to developing a conversation over which facts and which interpretations might be acceptable—even if not fully satisfying—to both sides.

Poland's Institute of National Remembrance

Poland's Instytut Pamięci Narodowej (IPN, Institute of National Remembrance) is not technically a historical commission, and IPN personnel have been reluctant to categorize their organization in that way. However, as the IPN launched its operations at the same time the debate over *Neighbors* was sending shockwaves throughout Polish society, there has been considerable attention paid to the Jedwabne documentation project that the IPN organized in the early 2000s. While the institute's director has called the IPN a "hybrid institution" that combines the investigatory approach associated with historical commissions with the archival administration of a memory institute,[36] I take it up here on the premise that the IPN has produced an effective mediating narrative for Jedwabne, which, I argue, ought to be seen as the hallmark of a successful historical commission.

The IPN was established by parliamentary decree in 1998 to encourage Poles to deal openly with the totalitarian past and the "difficult legacy of crime, hypocrisy, and distorted history" that the National Socialist and Soviet regimes left in their wakes. Although support for the IPN was at first shaky (President Alexander Kwasniewski tried to veto the legislation that created it), the IPN now has eleven branch offices (with headquarters in Warsaw) and employs more than 2,100 people. The institute's annual budget for 2009 was approximately $70 million.[37]

The IPN's mandate encompasses four core missions: (1) archival preservation and stewardship, (2) research and education, (3) prosecutorial investigations, and (4) lustration and vetting. Although the IPN is a state-funded institution (its staff are government employees), it operates with substantial independence. This is an important departure from the Main Commission of 1944–98, which investigated and prosecuted totalitarian crimes committed against Poles under the auspices of Poland's Ministry of Justice. The IPN chairman, who is elected by the Polish parliament and subject to the approval of an eleven-member executive council (the collegium), handles strategic planning for each of the institute's core missions and is responsible only to parliament. Each chair serves a five-year term and is given far-reaching authority to direct the institute's work.

The IPN's research and education programs are concentrated on twentieth-century Polish history and are subject to annual review by the collegium. Since its launch, the IPN's Office of Public Education has published more than 450 books, in addition to three regularly appearing journals and a monthly organizational bulletin. While the IPN has sponsored dozens of local and national history initiatives, most of its research relates to three major themes: (1) the

Stalinist repressions that took place from 1944 to 1956; (2) the period of martial law after 1981 and the Solidarity movement, which ultimately brought down the dictatorship; and (3) the Holocaust and its impact on Polish-Jewish relations, as well as World War II–era violence in the borderlands and the antagonisms among minority groups more generally. In this study, I am concerned primarily with the work carried out under the last theme. Given the intensity of the debates over this subject matter at home and the complications it has presented for Polish diplomacy vis-à-vis Israel, the Jewish Diaspora, and its neighbors in Europe, this is where the IPN has performed, arguably, its most interesting and innovative work.

The IPN has undertaken two separate research projects on Jedwabne. The first fell under the institute's criminal investigations and prosecutions unit and was, consequently, governed by Poland's code of criminal procedure. The second project, which is what I will deal with here, was supervised by historians in the IPN's Office of Public Education. This included historians recruited from the Polish Academy of Sciences and from universities in Warsaw and Białystok. The findings from this study were published in November 2002 as a two-volume set titled *Wokół Jedwabnego* (*The Jedwabne Case*).[38] Although these volumes do not represent an official commission report, the research they contain is instructive for anyone wishing to assess the potential role of history in conflict management. Volume 1 consists of nine chapters arranged in chronological order, running from the prewar era to the postwar trials at which some of the Jedwabne killers were prosecuted. Volume 2 reproduces 440 key documents from Polish, German, Belarusian, and Israeli archives.

When we compare the IPN's findings to *Neighbors*, it becomes clear that the IPN consciously attempted to construct a history that could engage, but also overcome, Gross's accusatory narrative. The IPN study aims at broad contextualization, and it avoids the "large quantifiers" that exacerbate ethnonational tensions in Gross's work. As the IPN's director, Krzysztof Persak, has noted, "[The task] is not only to re-create the course of events in Jedwabne on that terrible day, but also to understand the broader historical context and explain the mechanisms that led to the crime."[39] Questions of criminal and moral guilt, when they are raised in the IPN's work, are explored on an individual basis, which leads to measured conclusions about the overall climate in which the killings took place. The IPN does not use moral and legal verdicts to make sweeping pronouncements about Polish society or the moral character of Poles as a single, homogenous collective. Society, the monolithic entity that Gross places onto the scales of justice, scarcely features in the IPN report, and sober explanations take the place of damning accusations. This is not to say, however, that the IPN narrative is wholly exculpatory.

The IPN takes up Jedwabne as part of a long and complex history of Polish-Jewish relations in the Białystok region. Instead of leading with the most appalling details of the massacre, as Gross does, the IPN study begins with an overview of prewar Białystok. A subsequent chapter traces the region's history back to the nineteenth century. There seems to be, at first, some hesitancy to engage the massacre directly, as if the IPN's researchers were reluctant to unsettle the national conscience further after a difficult period of soul-searching. This cautiousness, it turns out, does a great deal to dampen the partisan tone that characterized the Jedwabne debates after the appearance of Gross's *Neighbors*. There is a notable absence in these early chapters of the thick descriptions that Gross uses to communicate the depravity of the killings. Whereas the first pages of *Neighbors* press readers to confront appalling scenes of violence—for example, "Krawicki they knifed and then plucked his eyes and cut off his tongue"[40]—the IPN begins its study with a comparatively tame discussion of demographics and attitudes regarding anti-Semitism in the Łomża Catholic diocese. It is the kind of "dry" history that tends to discourage casual readers, but it serves a purpose. By placing Jedwabne alongside other episodes of violence that took place at roughly the same time in other towns throughout Białystok, the IPN breaks down the formula that Gross developed to indict Polish "society" as a whole. Guilt is preserved without being generalized to the whole of "society," and details from Jedwabne are compared against other killings and pogroms in order to highlight the similarities and differences. By doing so, the IPN ensures that Jedwabne does not become an emblem for other episodes of violence that emerged through different channels and produced different results. The IPN's study marks a historical point in the purest sense: not every pogrom was the same in terms of its mechanics and meaning(s), and contemplation of Jedwabne does not automatically unlock a full understanding of anti-Semitism in Poland.

The avoidance of thick description as a strategy for negotiating the past requires a few additional comments. To begin with, the IPN's success with this strategy does not mean that historians must avoid including graphic details in their writing in deference to those who might take offense, and it should not be taken as a suggestion that all emotionally charged writing is inherently partial or unfairly manipulative. Reconciliation requires acknowledgment of the victims' experience; therefore mediating history cannot soft-pedal the details of their suffering. Likewise, perpetrators might not be willing to "confront the past" or question the ideological narratives they have been fed if the exercise does not in some way disturb or challenge their self-image. One could even argue that the inclusion of provocative thick description is a requirement of morally compelling historiography. Organizations like Amnesty International and Human Rights Watch publish rigorous studies of contemporary abridgements of international law, but they also develop their analyses through the inclusion of graphic victim testimonies that bring to life the moral stakes of these stories. On the other hand, it is worth remembering that historical commissions have different goals as compared to those of NGOs. Unlike Amnesty and Human Rights Watch, which circulate their materials in order to boost activism, encourage intervention, and generate financial contributions, the historical commissions aim at nuanced understanding, and in the most ambitious cases, at mediation and reconciliation as well. While the historical commissions must engage the public in order to achieve these goals, they also have to be careful not to release the emotional tripwires that reinforce hostility and increase polarization. To dampen partisan rhetoric and cultivate sober contemplation of complex events that resist convenient notions of causality and responsibility, the historical commissions will need to rely on sedate prose and unadventurous narrative style. As these commissions do not normally put victims and perpetrators into direct physical confrontation, like some of the truth and reconciliation commissions (TRC), their effect is less performative on the whole, and less cathartic, too. Then again, the historical commissions can deliberately modulate the tone and tenor of their reports, whereas the TRC have not always managed to control the emotional temperature of their public proceedings. While the role of emotion in narratives geared toward historical mediation is clearly of great importance, there is no clear-cut path on which to proceed. Rather, the historical commissions must learn how to calibrate their reports through critical assessment, which is one of the aims of this study. A tepid narrative, which a general readership finds boring, cannot be relied upon to engage partisan groups who are accustomed to discussing the past in sweeping and often hyperbolic terms. On the other hand, an emotionally wrenching narrative, which emphasizes the inhumanity of the perpetrators and depicts their violence in all of its gruesomeness without explaining it beyond a vague conception of ethnic essentialism (e.g., "congenital anti-Semitism"), is not likely to foster intergroup dialogue, let alone mutual understanding.

Attention to historical background in the early sections of the IPN study paves the way for subsequent chapters in which the researchers (1) delve into the persecution of Poles during 1939–41, the period of Soviet occupation; (2) explore the details of several different pogroms and massacres, including Jedwabne, in which Jews were specifically targeted; (3) discuss the presence of German military and police personnel in northeastern Poland at the time of the massacres and the effects of their presence on the Polish population; and

(4) present details from the trials of individuals who participated in the killings. While Gross also takes up these issues in *Neighbors*, it is important to see how the same evidence is marshaled differently in the two accounts. For example, in a chapter covering the period from 1939 to 1941, Gross concludes that the Soviet occupation was difficult for all Polish citizens and that Jews were subject to the same class-based discrimination and violence that the Catholic majority endured. The IPN, on the other hand, concludes that Poles were antagonized and persecuted from several directions during this period, so that attacks against Jews, even if they were fueled by hostile stereotypes and bigotry, might still be understood in a context of desperate self-defense. Poles faced deportation to the Soviet Union, execution at the hands of the NKVD (Narodnyĭ Kommissariat Vnutrennikh Del, People's Commissariat of Internal Affairs), attacks from Ukrainians in Volyn and Eastern Galicia, and enslavement or death at the hands of German military and police squads.[41] These factors, of course, do not excuse the violent attacks that were committed against Jewish communities in Poland, but for the IPN, they must be considered to gain a thorough historical understanding of those events. Faced with violent partition and ideological and ethnic attacks, all of which suggested the possibility of their annihilation, some Poles committed mass violence against their Jewish neighbors, who had been marked in traditional anti-Semitic discourse as a foreign and hostile element within the nation. This explanation, however, does not cover all of the violence studied by the IPN.

Compared to *Neighbors*, the IPN also reached a different conclusion regarding the role and influence of German occupation forces. Gross asserts that Germans in Jedwabne were passive onlookers (bystanders) who took pictures, while Poles slaughtered Jews without external encouragement or assistance. Gross notes that the Białystok region had a history of anti-Semitic pogroms that stretched back several centuries, but he fails to show that the peasant mobs responsible for those pogroms had genocidal intentions. Earlier attacks, like those that took place in the context of Poland's seventeenth-century wars, never approached the scale of Jedwabne and were more limited in terms of the selection of targets. Gross's suggestion that Jedwabne can be understood as the end result of a long tradition of anti-Semitic violence is problematic, even if it contains a kernel of truth. Where other attacks in 1941, such as those in Kaunas and Lwów (L'viv), resulted in death on a comparable scale to Jedwabne in terms of the overall number of victims, it was primarily adult males who were targeted, and those who were killed represented a fraction of the overall Jewish population.[42] In Jedwabne, the killers spared neither women nor children, and the pogrom resulted in the total destruction of the Jewish population. If genocidal intention was unique to Jedwabne (insofar as Polish perpetrators are concerned) "not only as a practice, but as an imaginable option," then the role of Germans is more difficult to dismiss than Gross indicates.[43]

The IPN's study is revealing in this respect. *Wokół Jedwabnego* makes no attempt to shift responsibility away from Polish residents, but there is a strong interest in probing the influence that the arrival of Germans to Białystok had on the massacre's brutal efficiency.[44] Edmund Dmitrov's chapter in volume 1 of the IPN study focuses on German units operating in Łomża and Białystok at the time of the Jedwabne massacre, and volume 2 includes documents that detail the operations of German Security Police and Gestapo in both locations. These sources show that the Jedwabne massacre occurred at the same time that German units began the systematic killing of Jews elsewhere in occupied Poland and throughout Eastern Europe. Other documents show that German units had orders to encourage Poles in Białystok to undertake "self-cleansings" and that German involvement in these operations was to be concealed whenever possible.[45] According to the historian Dariusz Stola, "These orders came in response to Himmler's complaint, in late June 1941, that [spontaneous] pogroms had not yet broken out in the Białystok region."[46] Gross chose not to pursue these threads in *Neighbors*, but the IPN used German source materials to broaden the context of the killings. This maneuver opened possibilities for new dialogue, but it also invited certain problems. Reading the IPN study, one sees that the role of the Germans and their influence on the massacre in Jedwabne enters the narrative as more of a question than a conclusion. One could argue that it is a leading question, which undermines the integrity of the project, but there is little doubt as to whether it emerges from credible sources. Whether (or not) one accepts the legitimacy of such open-ended questions, this element of the IPN narrative is helpful for understanding what mediating history offers and entails. It demonstrates, ultimately, that the ability of mediating history to defuse partisan rancor hinges on what role empiricism will play in historical inquiries. The aspirations of social science are clear in this regard, but we can still ask: To what extent, or at what point, does strict empiricism prevent a mediating history from addressing conflicts, if standards of evidence are conceived in a way that makes fierce political contestation inevitable and insurmountable? We know that absence of proof does not count as proof of absence, but in cases of rancorous disagreement, what should we make of ambiguous sources that do not suggest easy or straightforward interpretation? Can we feel around the edges of these materials, as the IPN's historians seem to, while still maintaining a commitment to objectivity? I contend that the best historical commissions can and do. To the extent that legitimate historical interpretation remains partly an art, historical commissions might use this freedom to their advantage. This relates directly to the debate over the role of Germans in Jedwabne.

Gross employs eyewitness testimonies to "prove" that Germans played no decisive role in the Jedwabne massacre. Nothing in the accounts he reviews suggests that Germans led the way; therefore Poles, he reasons, must have organized the violence independently. Others can claim with some justification that these testimonies are useless in terms of helping to understand what the Germans actually did in Jedwabne.[47] There are certainly other good explanations as to why Poles would deny the involvement of Germans. Dariusz Stola, for example, asserts that Poles who were questioned in postwar trials may have chosen to deny German participation because an admission on this point would have cast them as Nazi collaborators.[48] The perpetrators, he argues, were more willing to accept full responsibility for the murders than to incriminate themselves on charges of collaboration, since punishment for the latter would have been more severe. The IPN narrative leaves this door open, whereas Gross attempts (not entirely convincingly) to slam it shut. Clarification in the IPN study is conceived in modest terms rather than through categories that make collective guilt inexpugnable. Some will object that this approach to history entails an excessive emphasis on explanation, which risks excusing perpetrators for crimes that can never be forgiven. It could be argued, though, that the IPN narrative, far from being an attempt to whitewash the past, is instead an attempt to describe the events in Jedwabne in the appropriate shades of gray. The anti-Semitic character of the massacre is neither denied nor downplayed, but the circumstances that led to the killings are opened up to further questioning.

This effort to broaden the context of the massacre will likely strike some readers as a move toward relativism. If the atrocities are framed in a way that makes them understandable, or to some extent logical, then Jedwabne begins to blend with other instances of mass violence. As the number of comparable cases increases, there may be a tendency to view them through the same lens. All killing becomes a sad testament to the unavoidable collapse of decency under extreme circumstances. This trope will be uncomfortable (if not objectionable) for those who regard the Holocaust as a singular event, and it will be patently offensive to survivors who have built their identities around these events. These individuals see themselves (or their forebears) as the specific targets of particular acts of violence, which, of course, they were. By challenging Gross's contention that Polish society, as a whole, was responsible for the killings, the IPN might be seen as attempting to revive the old narrative that blames Germans first, and only afterwards accepts that Poland's "dregs" may also have played a part. One could argue that the IPN narrative is another attempt to give primacy to Polish suffering or that it helps to validate those who still wish to assert their "right" to look away from Polish crimes. We should remember, too, that the bulk of the IPN's research concerns the "Stalinist crimes" that were committed against Poles *after* the country had been largely cleansed of its minorities. Considered in this light, the IPN's Jedwabne study begins to resemble the "double-victim" narratives that nationalists in East Central Europe used throughout the postwar era as a shield against criticism that placed their countries in a less than favorable light. Is the IPN study merely another partisan history? Are we looking at the reverse side of Gross's coin?

I contend that the IPN has separated itself from the partisan discourse by laying the foundation for a "shared narrative," which can bridge the divide between Poles and Jews and, at the same time, support the cultivation of democratic values in Poland.[49] The IPN narrative provides an account of the massacre that forgoes the "tenacity of the exclusivist ethno-nationalist legacy of the past" and moves the debate closer to the victims' perspective, which Gross privileges.[50] It also stands as an important rejoinder to the generalizations and the fiercely determined, but never entirely convincing, conclusions that make *Neighbors* an accusatory tract. Instead of competing assertions over who suffered more gravely, the IPN study renders the history of Jedwabne in terms that both sides of the debate can accept with only minor qualification. The IPN insists on treating the massacre as a "local phenomenon" from which larger generalizations cannot readily be deduced, yet in the final analysis the killings are carried out by Polish perpetrators, who (might have) let themselves be influenced by German actions being conducted nearby. Guilt appears as something concrete here, but it is also circumscribed, since the IPN rejects the formula that connects the killers in Jedwabne to the Polish nation as a whole. It is a fine line that the IPN attempts to walk here, but it creates important distinctions that open new routes to understanding. Take, for example, this paraphrase of the study by one of its principal authors: "The anti-Jewish violence by Poles *happened at a specific time and place.* Before World War II, the Łomża region was an area where the Stronnoictwo Narodowe (National Party) was especially strong. This was a nationalist party with anti-Semitic tendencies. In the 1930s, the Łomża region was especially notorious for its anti-Semitic excesses. One of the largest pogroms in the area took place in 1933 in Radziłów. Anti-Semitism was widespread there and was reinforced by the clergy of the Łomża diocese, most of whom supported the Stronnoictwo Narodowe."[51] Here, the IPN highlights what many Poles still deny: a deep and long-standing tradition of Catholic anti-Semitism and a documented history of anti-Semitic violence in northeastern Poland. At the same time, these forces are depicted in a way that keeps them fixed within a specific regional and political subculture. What *Neighbors* ascribes to the level of the national collective is more thoroughly contextualized and historicized here. Polish clerics in Łomża helped to stoke the flames in which Jedwabne's Jewish residents perished, but the narrative does not extrapolate anything more from this point. The IPN identifies and condemns Polish perpetrators; it accepts that their violence was homegrown, yet these concessions do not implicate the Polish nation in the deep, shaming manner that Gross attempts to. There is a clear principle of responsibility in the IPN's narrative, but the authors do not propose collective guilt. The essential point is not that the genocidal attacks took place without the help of some Poles, but rather that the pogroms "cannot be reduced to a single scenario."[52] In some instances, Germans encouraged and incited Poles to initiate "self-cleansing actions." In others, Polish perpetrators were forcibly coerced into committing violence, for example, made to murder Jews while they themselves were threatened with death or extreme punishment. In still other cases, the pogroms occurred spontaneously without any German participation or presence. The scale and scope of these outbursts also varied. In some places the intent was genocidal; in others the motives appear to have been more limited. The number of victims also varied significantly. Images and memories of mass graves, which reappear throughout the Holocaust literature, may or may not be valid, depending on the location of a particular event. What Gross develops as a metaphor that encapsulates the Holocaust's larger meaning, the IPN treats as a historical particularity. While the term "negotiation" suggests too much in the way of bargaining and compromise, the IPN's study represents a powerful antidote to what Piotr Wrobel has called the problem of "double memory."[53]

These possibilities for convergence exist for other contested elements within the larger debate over Jedwabne. For example, the IPN study casts doubt over the highest estimates for total number of deaths. While witnesses who testified at the 1949 trial claimed that all but a handful of Jedwabne's 1,600 Jews were murdered, the IPN cites public records and demographic studies that suggest a total of perhaps half that figure.[54] An archeological study of the massacre site, which revealed two mass graves, was made in May 2001. The results of this dig suggest that the remains of 400 to 450 victims are present there.[55] There are also Soviet documents, including population surveys from 1940, that suggest Gross's estimate may be too high by a factor of three.[56] Accounting for these discrepancies between the number of victims identified in the mass graves and the census records that point to a higher number of Jewish residents is hardly straightforward, although forced migration and internment have been suggested as possible explanations.[57] Gross has said that the archaeological surveys made at Jedwabne were conducted hastily and sloppily, to the point that these "findings" should be disregarded completely.[58] Given the importance of the numbers, particularly for victims and their heirs, scholars need to take extra care here. In the end, both "sides" will probably have to accept some degree of uncertainty. The IPN's study requires concessions from both the Polish and Jewish sides. Jews can see their core beliefs validated in the IPN report—the massacre that many Poles repressed or refused to acknowledge is clearly incorporated into Poland's history—but at the same time they are asked to revise downward their estimates for the total number of victims. They are also encouraged to contemplate a new context for the killings, one that suggests different patterns of violence in different places and the possibility of external influence, even where some claim to remember (or have attempted to document) Poles acting alone. On the other side, Poles see the blanket label of congenital anti-Semitism lifted in the IPN narrative, but they are also pressed to accept two difficult points: first, that some of the anti-Semitic violence in 1941 was the product of homegrown bigotry, and second, that Poles who killed Jews were not always coerced into doing so, nor were they lashing out against traitors, even if they adamantly believed that to be the case. The IPN study also shows that nothing in the record can substantiate the "Zydokommunism" (Jew-communism) myth that ethnonationalist partisans conjured after the war to bracket responsibility for the pogroms and downplay their significance.

Finally, the IPN's Jedwabne project is noteworthy because it directly addresses the political maneuvers through which the massacre was purged from public memory. The IPN's research shows that the trial of Jedwabne perpetrators in 1949 was one of more than sixty similar legal proceedings.[59] Of course, these trials are critical for understanding the events of July 1941. To begin with, they attest to the fact that the 1941 pogroms did once garner public recognition. These were public trials, involving hundreds of individuals summoned to court to face charges ranging from robbery to homicide. The records from these cases also strongly suggest that there were many more Poles who participated in the pogroms, even if they were never investigated or indicted. During the Jedwabne trial, at which ten of the twenty-two defendants were eventually found guilty and sentenced, both witnesses and suspects named several dozen other individuals, alleging that they also had participated in the massacre, yet none of these individuals ever faced questioning from the authorities. Persak, the IPN's chief historian for the Jedwabne project, has noted: "At other trials, the situation was much the same. Community solidarity and the desire to protect its members were other common elements. Although many in court may have claimed the accused were innocent, no one denied that Poles participated in the pogroms—and that more, often mentioned by name, had taken part as well."[60] Sentences handed down at these trials ranged from two and a half years to life in prison, but judges often commuted sentences, citing "exceptional" circumstances, which really meant coercive pressure.[61] While four cases ended with death sentences, only one of these was actually carried out. Persak notes that the pogroms, which were never kept secret, were well known among local residents in the Łomża District and Białystok region in the years immediately after the war. The truth of these events, he says, was forgotten gradually, until Gross recovered many of the grimmest details almost sixty years later. As much as the actual massacres, this process of erasure and forgetting was also a moral failure for which the Poles are now atoning. Whether the IPN's mediating narrative can elicit deep reconciliation between Poles and Jews is a different matter.

Reconciliation is a notoriously slippery concept, one that scholars have struggled to measure or quantify. Some see it as the lynchpin of transitional justice following periods of political oppression and violent conflict.[62] Others view it as a vague expression of idealism, which can easily derail the process of democratization by creating unrealistic expectations in communities still riven by suspicion and mistrust.[63] In any event, reconciliation requires significant emotional adjustments on the part of both victims and perpetrators, and even where these difficult transformations are achieved, they do not necessarily endure.[64] Vamik Volkan has likened the process of reconciliation to the opening and closing of an accordion.[65] The two sides move toward each other as the music swoons, but then withdraw quickly, often on a discordant note that hangs over the next phrase. This alternating current between rapprochement and enmity, Volkan has stressed, can run through multiple cycles, sometimes over the course of several generations. This "accordion effect" offers periodic opportunities for dialogue that mediators must learn to recognize and exploit if the cycle is ever to be broken.

Judging from the public debates and partisan histories it spawned, Gross's *Neighbors* seems to have put Poles and Jews through one of these cycles. The IPN's Jedwabne project represents a successful attempt to broker a negotiated history in the wake of that controversy. I do not argue here that Gross's work is wholly invalid or even methodologically unsound, but rather that his use of "large-scale qualifiers" and his structural conceptualization of the massacre are unhelpful if using the past to ameliorate conflict is seen as a priority. Gross ought to be commended for recovering the perspective of Jewish victims and changing the assumptions regarding their testimony from doubt to belief. His principal mistake consists of producing a narrative that takes inadequate account of the perspective of its villains. As the first to retrieve these events and bring them back into the public consciousness, Gross was likely to become the enemy of mainstream perception in any case, but this point does not protect him against every criticism either. My criticism of his work in no way suggests any sympathy for the perspective of his opponents. Rather, I am asserting only what is obvious already, which is that *Neighbors* highlights the place of interpretation in the construction of historical knowledge. Facts do not suggest their own meaning, and there is no way to reconstruct the past without some degree of subjectivity. So the mark against Gross here is not simply "incomplete objectivity" (of which all historians are guilty) but rather of having authored a study that fails on a formalist level if the criteria for success are understood to include conflict mediation and intergroup reconciliation. It is not my contention that the IPN has eclipsed Gross in terms of fact-finding, but that the IPN's handling of the facts allows for possibilities, in both historical and political terms, that *Neighbors* does not. At the end of the day, this can be a compelling reason to give the IPN primacy over Gross.

On the other hand, if we compare their work in literary terms, the IPN study will undoubtedly strike some readers (in places) as dry, unwieldy, and uninteresting. Whereas *Neighbors* became an international sensation and sold brilliantly in Polish, English, French, German, Dutch, Spanish, and Italian, the IPN's study has been less well read, to put it charitably. In the WorldCat database, *Wokół Jedwabnego* shows up in forty-two libraries, while *Neighbors* has taken a place on the shelves of more than 1,600 institutions.[66] There is no question as to which narrative style sells better or excites more attention among readers of history, and this is something that proponents of mediating history will need to address. For some readers, responsible history will always seem inaccessible and uninviting. It is full of qualifications—it includes words and phrases such as *perhaps, possibly, could have*, and *might have been*—which make it seem watery in places, particularly to lay readers. On the other hand, Gross's account of the massacre teems with details that invite psychological speculation and empathic identification; this is both a reason for its huge success and for its unsuitability as a mediating account of the massacre. The IPN study is more tentative, more questioning, more measured, and less definitive. So, how can a mediating history engage a general audience—there being no chance of ameliorating conflict without capturing the interest of nonspecialists—without resorting to the conceptualizations of history that privilege dramatic presentation and ironclad conclusions over mutual understanding? If mediating history represents a centrist approach to the past, how can it raise itself above the shrill voices that tend to resonate at the extreme ends of the political spectrum?

One answer is that mediating history must strive to "teach the debates" that it attempts to defuse. To navigate between the most polarized Polish and Jewish perspectives, a mediating history of Jedwabne must scrutinize not only the massacre but also the rhetorical and political tropes through which the event has been represented. A mediating history will incorporate the politics of history (i.e., the ideological premises that support competing interpretations of the same event) while it seeks to transcend them at the same time. The IPN has made marked headway in this area. Its programs and strategies complement and counterbalance one another in terms of the burden they place on the Polish conscience, but at the same time the scholarship is serious in that it does not dodge the question of national responsibility or capitulate to the demands of nationalist apologists. Among historians and also in the public eye, the IPN is regarded as an impartial investigator, able to confront Polish history in a rigorous and methodologically sound manner while aiming at larger problems of conflict mediation.

Austria and Italy

The Reich and Its Allies

Austria's "Life Lie":
Confronting the Victim Theory

In an essay from 1987, Hermann Langbein (1912–95), a Viennese antifascist partisan who fought in the Spanish Civil War and was later interned at Dachau and Auschwitz, asks whether one is permitted to forget the past if it produces intense discomfort.[1] Langbein, who also wrote about resistance cells in the Nazi concentration camps, posed the question not with respect to his own personal history but in the context of Austria's larger struggles with the past and, in particular, with the unpleasantness surrounding the so-called Waldheim affair. The "affair" refers to the controversy that erupted in Austria in 1985–86 after it was revealed that Kurt Waldheim, the former secretary-general of the United Nations and a candidate for the Austrian presidency, had understated or possibly covered up his involvement with the German Wehrmacht during World War II. For many, Waldheim's evasions came to embody Austria's "national syndrome," meaning the tendency of (some) Austrians to reject responsibility for the nation's failings and to dwell on their own victimization rather than contemplate the suffering of others. Waldheim won the presidency, but controversy over his wartime record escalated to the point that several countries, including the United States, refused to issue him travel visas needed to attend major diplomatic and political conferences.[2] The negative publicity surrounding Waldheim turned Austria into a virtual pariah state.[3]

Austria's memory syndrome has been described in a variety of ways. Historians have described and debated Austria's "victim thesis" at length.[4]

Langbein called it Austria's "life lie" (*die Östereichische Lebenslüge*).[5] Regardless of the rhetoric, most of these debates have circled back to the Moscow Declaration (October 1943), in which members of the Grand Alliance designated Austria as the first victim of Nazi aggression.[6] Austria, according to this principle, ceased to exist as a state after the March 1938 Anschluss that incorporated the Alpine Republic into the German Reich. The Moscow Declaration allowed Austrians to cultivate a national myth that portrayed the Anschluss as "the rape of Austria" and ignored the groundswell of support for Hitler in Vienna and Austria's own encouragement of Nazism.[7] As in the case of France, the Austrian myth celebrated and overstated acts of resistance, and omitted crucial evidence of Austria's complicity with the Nazi regime at both the official and unofficial levels. Violence and atrocities driven by homegrown anti-Semitism disappeared under the veil of this myth, along with other instances of "biological" cleansing (e.g., against the Roma and homosexuals). Instead, the myth preserved the memory of political persecutions that targeted left-wing Austrians and the efforts made by some within the Austrian Catholic Church to shelter the Reich's racial enemies and help them find safe passage overseas. In 1945, Karl Renner and the new Provisional Government espoused the victim thesis in an effort to gain flexibility against American and Soviet demands, and to preserve the new economic order that Austrians created via large-scale property expropriations after 1938 and the "wild Aryanization" of Jewish property that resulted from the Kristallnacht pogrom.[8] Where talk of these abuses emerged (e.g., when American occupation forces pushed for strict restitution laws for Jewish property), the victim thesis was applied to tamp down political pressure. According to the myth, Austria did not exist when these crimes took place, therefore Austrians could not be responsible for implementing potential remedies.

The Waldheim affair heightened pressure in Austria to reexamine this chapter of the past, and it spurred a paradigm shift in the attitudes of both elite and ordinary Austrians regarding the Nazi period. This shift occurred quickly, beginning in 1991, when Chancellor Franz Vranitzky, in a speech to parliament, acknowledged the responsibility of private Austrian citizens for the crimes and abuses that unfolded immediately prior to and during World War II. In 1993, while traveling in Israel, Vranitzky expanded this concept of responsibility to include the Austrian state.[9] Speaking at Hebrew University in Jerusalem, Vranitzky ventured, "We have felt and still feel [that] the connotation of collective guilt does not apply to Austria, but we do acknowledge collective responsibility. We share a moral responsibility because many Austrians welcomed the Anschluss supported by the Nazi regime and helped it to function. We have to live up to this side of our history."[10] Vranitzky laid a wreath at the Yad Vashem memorial, where he pledged that the Austrian government would do more to help Holocaust survivors. A year and a half later, Austria's president, Thomas Klestil, went before the Israeli Knesset and apologized for Austria's role in the Holocaust. Stressing a desire to normalize bilateral relations between the two countries, Klestil told reporters at a state dinner held in his honor, "When people are able to live together and accept the lessons of history, they are able to move towards the future."[11] In his address to the Knesset, Klestil made brief and noncommittal comments regarding reparations for Holocaust victims, but he acknowledged, "We know full well that all too often we have spoken of Austria as the first state to lose its freedom and independence to National Socialism and far too seldom of the fact that many of the worst henchmen in the Nazi dictatorship were Austrians. . . . On behalf of the Republic of Austria, I bow my head with deep respect and profound emotion in front of the victims."[12]

Klestil's rhetoric flies high here, although some media outlets in Israel felt that his statement fell short of a full-fledged apology. Setting aside the rhetorical minutiae, Klestil's speech reflected a deliberate strategy on the part of the Austrian government to improve relations with Israel by revisiting the history of the Holocaust, and it mirrored a change in the general attitude of ordinary Austrians with respect to the past.[13] For ten years beginning in 1994, more and more Austrians came to accept a sentiment that had existed earlier only among certain intellectuals, in a handful of political leaders, and with a certain segment of the youth, namely, that the crimes committed in Austria during the Nazi period created a moral obligation for the contemporary Austrian nation and its citizens. The rise of Jörg Haider in the second half of the 1990s created acute embarrassment and a new diplomatic crisis for Klestil and Vranitzky as they attempted to consolidate a forward-thinking approach to the past. Nonetheless, it should be remembered that roughly three-quarters of Austrians rejected Haider's Freiheitliche Partei Österreichs (FPÖ, Freedom Party of Austria) and never warmed to the mixture of nostalgia, revisionism, and denial that was peddled by (and to) the Far Right in Austria as the twentieth century came to a close.[14] While the self-pitying reflex continued to appear in a certain set of Austrians, particularly after 2000, when the European Union threatened to impose sanctions against Austria as a punishment for the FPÖ's antiliberal rhetoric, the majority of Austrians were ready to embrace the government's new program of moral responsibility. In an opinion poll conducted in February 2000, 69 percent of Austrians indicated that they would support compensation for the victims of the Nazi slave-labor program; 20 percent opposed the proposition.[15] By that time, the federal government had already launched a historical commission to reexamine Austria's record between 1938 and 1945 (when, according to the victim's thesis, the Austrian state had ceased to exist), as well as the period after 1945, when the postwar government first faced questions regarding responsibility for injustices committed in the preceding era.

The Jabloner Commission: Mandate and Methods

Austria's Historikerkommission (Jabloner Commission) was first convened in November 1998, after having been established in October by a joint decree of the executive and legislative branches. While the commission received its budget from the Austrian government, the chancellor, vice-chancellor, national assembly speaker, and deputy national assembly speaker all expressed a desire to ensure its independence and autonomy. Clemens Jabloner, a legal scholar who had held a number of positions within the federal government dating back to the 1970s, was appointed to chair the commission, and Lorenz Mikoletzky, the director-general of the Austrian state archive, was also tapped for the project. A slate of candidates was quickly drawn up to fill out four other seats, including three to be held by Austrian scholars and one reserved for a "foreign expert."[16] Officially, the commission's task was "to investigate and report on the whole complex of expropriations in Austria during the Nazi era and on restitution and/or compensation . . . after 1945."[17] Jabloner described the work a bit less awkwardly in 2002, when he said that the commission understood its role as "making some difficult and sensitive problems of recent Austrian history comprehensible to as many people as possible."[18] He also characterized the commission as a scholarly response to Austria's need for "complete purification."[19]

Jabloner stated that the commission owed its existence to more than Austria's inner paradigm shift and that the government took action when external pressures began to threaten Austria's standing in the international community. Besides the imbroglio surrounding Haider and the FPÖ, Jabloner cited pressures stemming from class-action lawsuits filed in the United States and the examples of neighboring states, most notably Switzerland, which had launched their own inquiries, despite internal opposition and the prospect of huge financial liability. In addition, there was the matter of looted and stolen artworks.[20] Jabloner also credited a change in the attitude of the victims themselves, including not only Austrian Jews, many of whom were now a generation or two removed from any direct memory of the Holocaust, but also Roma/Sinti and homosexuals, who no longer felt intimidated by the prospect of cultural backlash.[21] Furthermore, according to Jabloner, progress in research on contemporary history and fresh access to source materials in the former Soviet bloc made 1998 the right moment for Austria to reexamine the past and probe the international dimensions of Nazi-era crimes.[22]

The work plan and methodology of the Jabloner Commission are interesting in comparison to the other projects examined in this study. While the Jabloner Commission took on a huge amount of work, virtually all of its published studies focused on "the economic aspects of the National Socialism in Austria."[23] Although other commissions pursued similar inquiries, that is, questions concentrating on the sale and seizure of Jewish properties, the costs of professional exclusions made on the basis of race, and the many documented instances of outright plunder, the decision of the commission to examine the Nazi era through a strictly economic-legal lens imparted a depersonalized and sterile quality to the work. Jabloner insisted that the commission followed a "multi-disciplinary approach," but this is not evident in the summary report.[24] This could be a result of the commission's main limitation; unlike some of the other commissions treated in this study (e.g., Switzerland's ICE), the Jabloner Commission was given no magisterial powers, and consequently its members had to rely on the cooperation and goodwill of the organizations and institutions whose records it wished to examine. This need for cooperation helps explain the monotonous quality of its reports. On the other hand, France's Mattéoli Commission (see chap. 1) also worked on a cooperative basis with the organizations it investigated, and Claire Andrieu touted this principle as one of the fundamental reasons for its success. To force businesses into handing over their records under threat of legal punishment, Andrieu argued, re-created the structure of coercion that underlay the crimes of the Vichy era (1940–44). Whether one accepts this assessment or not, it pushes back against the claim that commissions, which lack legal authority to enforce compliance, will tend to achieve underwhelming results.

In keeping with its overall approach of treading lightly, the Jabloner Commission also shied away from making direct recommendations for legal or political action. Instead, the commission hewed closely to its mandate and focused its energies on historical clarification. Jabloner explained the commission's reluctance to contemplate the question of remedy as an appropriate response to the government's carefully worded mandate, although other national commissions, which were also provided with strict mandates (once again, France's Mattéoli Commission provides a good comparison), nevertheless sought to highlight the moral and legal obligations arising from their economic and legal analyses.[25] The Jabloner Commission attempted to explain the motives that shaped the policies aimed at expropriation, but it mostly avoided any deeper questions concerning Austria's responsibilities to the victims of the

Holocaust and the responsibility of ordinary Austrians to commemorate and make good Jewish losses. Reflecting on the commission's work, Jabloner accepted that Austria's victim thesis was "inadmissible . . . in terms of morality"; moral contemplation, however, is largely absent from the reports that were published by the commission between 1998 and 2003.[26] To some extent, it seems that the full significance of the commission's work—its importance for developing a bulwark against racist, xenophobic, and anti-Semitic sentiments still extant in the twenty-first century—dawned on Jabloner only after the commission had completed its work. While the project was active, Jabloner's influence imparted a bureaucratic dryness that diminished the commission's overall impact.

The arid and impersonal quality of the commission's reports also owes something to the decision to outsource large portions of the project to outside scholars whose work intersected with the scope of the mandate. While this approach might have seemed prudent, given the huge amount of source material, it also crowded the commission's deliberations. In the initial application round, the commission received three hundred applications for research contracts from nine different countries, of which forty-five projects were funded. By 2003, when the commission released its final report, 160 researchers had contributed forty-seven studies. This multiplication of labor and perspectives (six commission members supervising the 160 scholars) generated a veritable mountain of fresh research, but it also produced disjointed results. Further complicating matters, the commission incorporated the work of several independent commissions, which were established in the private sector to assess the involvement of individual companies and business interests in the Nazi-era expropriation of Jewish assets.[27] Once again, the input of the private sector enlarged what the Jabloner Commission was able share with the public. The commission published fifty-four volumes with more than 14,000 pages of analysis and documentation. Discussing these results at a press conference in 2003, Jabloner expressed his hope that people would study each of the fifty-four reports in detail, rather than just skimming the summary.[28] However, in a lecture he gave in 2009, Jabloner allowed that the final report had been "perhaps not very readable."[29] He went on to describe the need for integrating the commission's findings in school curricula, which he described as a task for Austria's Ministry of Education. The point of rehearsing all this is to show how unwieldy these projects can become, even when the mandate is relatively constrained. The desire to engage the work of previous commissions, together with the decision to outsource the majority of the investigative work and, most significantly, the reluctance of the commission to expand the inquiry beyond the bounds of strictly economic and legal considerations, combined to dilute the impact of the initiative, although some of the commission's findings, as we shall see, were truly significant.

Major Findings

Jabloner has said that the commission made an effort to get moving quickly and purposefully following its first meeting in late 1998. The commission gave first priority to the issue of slave labor, according to Jabloner, because of the advanced age of ex-slaves and because lawsuits and diplomatic pressure from the United States and other countries had created a rising crisis for Austria's leaders and lawmakers, not to mention its business interests.[30] By giving priority to slave labor, the commission opened itself up to the charge of foot-dragging from other groups seeking justice and accountability. However, Jabloner has stated—and the commission's subsequent work record supports him here—that this was merely a matter of setting priorities and developing a conscientious work plan, as opposed to shirking work that might reveal even darker episodes from Austria's past. The commission published a preliminary report in February 2000 on the plight of foreign workers who were brought to Austria to support the Nazi war effort. According to the report, nearly one million non-Germans (most of them conscripted in the East) were made to work in Austria from 1939 to 1945, typically under dehumanizing conditions that sometimes resembled plantation slavery. While the commission worked to finish its report, the Austrian government appointed an official negotiator to lead discussions between groups representing the ex-slaves and the Austrian companies that exploited their labor. In the press, Jabloner emphasized that the commission was interested only in researching the facts, and that the question of compensation was entirely in the hands of the government's chief negotiator.[31] He also remarked that the advanced age of the remaining ex-slaves led the commission "to act as quickly as possible," although he did not elaborate on how exactly the commission's report constituted a form of action, nor did he explain why one set of aging victims warranted attention before others, who also had reached an advanced age. In any event, the commission's research showed that of the 992,900 laborers who were brought to Austria during the war, 239,000 were still alive in 2000. The *Financial Times* reported in March 2000 that the number of survivors, together with the outcome of German negotiations on the same issue, suggested that Austrian companies might be liable for repayments totaling 25 billion shillings (approximately $2.4 billion). This figure did not take in or project any of the costs associated with Jewish spoliation (i.e., Aryanization), which the Jabloner Commission had not yet tabulated or reported at that stage of its work. Regarding the slave-labor report, Jabloner said simply, "It is too late in some ways, but better we do it now rather than in ten years, or never."[32]

Following the release of the slave-labor report in 2000, the Jabloner Commission turned to the issues of Jewish spoliation and postwar restitution. Over the next three years the commission released a handful of interim reports, detailing progress and findings related to these issues. The commission's bulky final report was submitted on January 24, 2003, and consisted of two main parts, one on expropriation and another on restitution.

By far, the most important finding in the final report is the link that the commission identified between economic damage stemming from Aryanization and the program of genocide that the Nazi regime pursued during the course of the war. By presenting this connection at the beginning of its report, the commission highlighted Austria's complicity in the Holocaust and undercut the basic premise of the victimization theory. The summary report begins: "The economic damage done to Jews—bans on employment and training, expropriation of moveable and immovable property—destroyed their social and individual existence. This destruction was associated with [their] expulsion and was also—in retrospect—a preliminary stage in the deportation and annihilation of those Jews who stayed within the areas of Nazi rule."[33] While the insertion of "in retrospect" limits responsibility, the linkage between Aryanization and the program of annihilation is presented clearly and in a manner that obviously departs from the postwar discourse built around the Moscow Declaration and the presentation of Austria as "the first victim" of Nazi aggression.

The final report also described "complex motives" for the "unprecedented" expropriation of Jewish property.[34] The commission found that spoliation was linked to individual, group, and state interests. In addition to traditional anti-Semitism and racism, property expropriations were motivated by the lure of immediate enrichment, sociopolitical considerations (e.g., the provision of housing), and an array of "economic interests," which included everything from the hostile takeover of rival businesses to capital accumulation to the pursuit of monopolistic dominance in a particular business area to procurement of funds to maintain the war effort. Regardless of the motive, the commission found that these expropriations supported an explicit program of forced emigration and deportation. Prior to the war, Austria's Jewish population, mostly concentrated in Vienna, stood between 201,000 and 214,000. The report stressed the heterogeneity of the prewar Jewish population, since the anti-Semitic propaganda of the Nazi era (and the rhetoric of the neo-Nazi movement) helped create a myth regarding the pervasive wealth and influence of the Jewish "race." While the final report notes the presence of "an established upper-middle-class and middle-class stratum," there were also "relatively poor Jews," including many who emigrated from the eastern end of the Habsburg empire in the fin-de-siècle era and during World War I. The Jabloner report also described increasingly limited opportunities for emigration beginning in 1941, particularly after the passage of the Reich Citizens Act (*Reichsbürgergesetz*) on November 25, under which Jews who remained in the Reich territory effectively forfeited whatever property they had left. After this time, Jews in Austria were subject to deportation and consignment to the ghettoes that served as delivery points to the extermination camps. While the majority of Austria's Jews emigrated between 1938 and 1940—those who did were subject to a punitive tax (*Reichsfluchtsteuer*) equal to 20–25 percent of total assets— approximately 50,000 Jews were deported either to the ghettoes in the East or to the camp at Theresienstadt (Terezín) located in what is now the Czech Republic. By November 1942, Austria's Jewish population had declined to approximately 7,000, with most either in hiding or married to non-Jews.[35]

The Jabloner report includes detailed information on the wave of Aryanization that followed shortly after the Anschluss (March 12, 1938). Aryanization of real estate was completed by a variety of means, including questionable and forced contracts of sale. The proceeds from these sales were normally deposited to a blocked account to which the Jewish "sellers" had no access.[36] Jewish renters were driven from their apartments in what the report describes as a frenzied outburst of "wild Aryanization." The report describes these as "spontaneous actions" but also notes the presence of Nazi officials: "All the reports of those affected tell of looting and violent break-ins, usually by armed Nazi party members but also by neighbors in the same house."[37] On May 10, 1939, the Law on Tenancies with Jews legalized the eviction of Jewish tenants by Aryan landlords, but the commission report also notes that 44,000 apartments in Vienna had already been Aryanized prior to that time. Jews who were evicted were reassigned to new and generally inferior quarters, which they typically shared with several other families. Later, those who had not escaped or emigrated were sent to "holding camps" before their final transit to the east. Aryanization of apartments continued until April 1945, and the commission documented a total of 59,000 expropriations in all.[38]

As with the expropriation of real estate, the looting and seizure of moveable properties began immediately following the Anschluss, often with violent assaults against the owners. Initially, these seizures took place without any official decree to regulate the takeover; the commission notes, however, that Nazi officials participated alongside "sections of the local population." In July 1938, Austria's State Police were authorized to conduct auctions for the moveable properties seized from Jews in the preceding months. High-value items (jewelry, artworks, and fine furniture) were normally offered through one of Vienna's established auction houses, though ordinary household goods also appeared in some lots. Various groups, including high-ranking members of the Austrian Deutsche Nationalsozialistische Arbeiterpartei (DNSAP, German National Socialist Workers Party), siphoned the profits generated by these auctions, and a cut was also reserved for the auction houses and the antique dealers who helped run them. In some cases, the most valuable items were reserved for public museums or academic institutions, such as the University of Vienna, while other properties, including rare books and liturgical manuscripts, were directed to the National Library. "Numerous private individuals were also able to buy things particularly cheaply . . . because of their connections to the Gestapo or to influential Nazi officials."[39]

The Jabloner Commission investigated several other aspects of Jewish spoliation and economic discrimination. The final report presents data on employment bans (and other damages to professional life), the refusal to redeem life insurance policies purchased by Holocaust victims, the special taxes and levies to which Jews were subject, and the seizure of securities and foreign currency. The report also explores the exclusion and removal of Jewish students from Austria's state-funded educational institutions.

The commission endeavored to calculate the estimated value of all seized and looted assets, but this presented huge difficulties. In a report filed on February 1, 1939, on the process of "de-Jewing" Austria (*Entjudung in der Ostmark*), Walter Rafelsberger, the state commissar in the private sector, estimated the total value of registered Jewish assets at approximately 2.042 billion reichsmarks (RM). The commission's review of registration documents from 1938 yielded an estimate of between 1.842 billion and 2.9 billion reichsmarks. "The difference," according to the commission report, "results from the—ultimately unknowable—uncertainty about how many Jews were obliged to register and how many were actually present in April 1938."[40] The report also raised several issues that could widen the margin of error in these calculations, ranging from undeclared and improperly valued assets to the difficulty of assessing the integrity and completeness of key archives.

As to other calculations, which could reveal further damages to the Jewish community in Austria, the commission noted a variety of impediments. For example, the commission found no comprehensive records that would allow for a precise count of the total number of Jewish-owned business in 1938. Research on this topic has produced estimates ranging from 25,000 to 36,000. The official records of the Nazi party identify 25,440 Austrian businesses as being Jewish-owned, out of which 18,800 (approximately 75 percent) are recorded as having been liquidated by 1940. Jewish banking houses were also closed and liquidated during this time, but again, the commission's research does not offer a precise estimate of the scale and scope of these expropriations.

Moveable properties presented an even bigger challenge in terms of accurate valuation. According to the Jabloner report, these items cannot be quantified "even approximately." There are some records that allow for a rough tally of auction proceeds; for example, Gestapo files show an intake of 13–14 million reichsmarks. Other kinds of damages, however, such as lost wages resulting from employment bans and professional decertification, have proven impossible to calculate.[41] Moreover, there are damages that no financial calculation can fully represent. For example, the Jabloner report analyzes data on glass breakage and unpaid insurance claims stemming from the Kristallnacht pogrom (November 9–10, 1938) without any exploration of the psychological trauma these events produced in the Jewish collective consciousness. Whereas Marion Kaplan, in her exceptional study of the everyday life of Jews in Nazi Germany, *Between Dignity and Despair*, manages to reconstruct from diaries and private letters a sharp increase in the suicide rates among German Jews following the pogrom and the "public degradation ritual" it entailed, the Jabloner report goes no further than a superficial analysis of shattered glass panes and their insured value.[42] This clinical and detached aspect of the Jabloner report, which must be regarded as its chief shortcoming, is something I return to in the evaluation section in this chapter. In the years since the commission submitted its final report, Jabloner has started to explore the subject of expropriation in more engaging terms. In an essay from 2007, Jabloner called Jewish spoliation in Austria "a harrowing picture of a huge enterprise of what today one would call 'organized crime.'"[43] The process of plunder, he wrote, ranged from "clever takeovers" to "pure acts of unadulterated force."

The second half of the Jabloner report covered restitution and compensation programs after 1945. This was an exceedingly technical component of the overall project with a highly complex chronology, owing to several false starts, multiple interventions from external actors (e.g., the Allied occupation forces), and a frustrating delay between two principal waves of restitution (1945–55 and 1958–2001). While the pressure to create an investigatory commission in 1998 included the judgment of experts who "denounced [Austria] for its lack of generosity toward Jewish victims" and the repeated charge that Austrian restitution programs in the postwar period had been "halfhearted and grudging," the final report (2003) takes a more moderate position. As Jabloner asserted, the commission's findings effectively debunked the two extreme positions that animated the controversy surrounding restitution and compensation. According to Jabloner, "it is not true that Austria restituted everything stolen and compensated all who had been exploited. But it is alike not true, as has been repeatedly alleged, that Austria avoided any and all responsibility. . . . A system of restitution was built up, but hesitatingly, slow-moving, full of gaps and traps."[44]

The final report criticized Austria for resisting Jewish restitution immediately after the war, and it described the eventual process of compensation as "labyrinthian and expensive." Under Karl Renner, the provisional government in 1945 began the process of documenting property expropriations for the period between 1938 and 1945. An Assets Confiscation Registration Decree, passed in autumn 1946, formalized the process, but there was no clear plan for how to return stolen properties or even whether the new government should bear the costs of restitution. Social Democrats (SPÖ, Sozialdemokratische Partei Österreichs) and communists who participated in the governing coalition suggested the creation of an official restitution fund, but this money was to be used only to support "needy victims" of Nazi persecution, including non-Jews within their own ranks; the plan made no provisions at all for returning stolen properties to their rightful owners. In general, Jewish restitution was stymied in the years immediately following the war by what the commission described as Austria's "refusal to accept any (co-) responsibility for Nazi crimes and their consequences."[45] Instead, Austrian leaders as well as ordinary citizens used the Moscow Declaration (1943) and the victim thesis to push the responsibility for restitution back onto Germany.[46]

Despite these obstructions, Austria passed seven restitution acts between 1946 and 1949, but these were limited in various ways. The first act, passed in July 1946, covered only those properties that ended up in the hands of the state, and together the seven measures created what the Jabloner Commission called "a confusing and partly contradictory web . . . made up of numerous laws and regulations, of the conflicting interests of political parties, economic associations, victims' organizations, and the Allies."[47] A decision was made early in 1946 to apply a principle of restitution-in-kind, which meant that the government paid no indemnification for properties that had been destroyed, modified, or removed. Instead, the government returned only those properties that had remained intact and undisturbed since the Anschluss, although claimants still had to contend with a host of restrictions. This principle remained in place until 1955, when the Vienna State Treaty was signed and Austria's sovereignty was formally restored. There were also political challenges to the restitution acts, which limited and slowed their application. Following the passage of the Third Restitution Act in February 1947, business interests appealed to the government to limit the scope of restitution, arguing that such measures introduced uncertainty into the economy and threatened Austria's recovery.[48] According to the Jabloner report, it was the Allies, particularly the United

States, who pushed the Austrian government to follow through on their restitution pledge.

Based on the results of its investigation, the Jabloner Commission determined that Austria's restitution acts "did largely fulfill the intended objective [which was] the restitution of expropriated property." However, the commission also found that there were significant difficulties for applicants seeking the return of their property and that loopholes in the seven acts created imposing obstacles for victims, which required "both financial and mental strength" to surmount. By the early 1950s, a series of court decisions had made for a complex and difficult process, one marked by an increasingly restrictive attitude toward the victims of Nazi crimes. In general, the commission found, for Jews who were robbed and brutalized by the Nazi regime, its many supporters, or simply by the apolitical bystanders who used the Anschluss as an opportunity to enrich themselves, it was easier to reclaim lost and stolen assets in the Federal Republic of Germany than it was in Austria.[49] Ambiguities in the laws were generally interpreted in the government's favor, and lack of oversight made it hard for victims to appeal problematic rulings.

In its report, the commission admitted to difficulty piecing together the history of Austrian restitution, in large part because a collection of files from Vienna's Provincial Court, pertaining to 1947–55, was destroyed in the second half of the 1980s. Analysis of the remaining files gave only a partial picture of the process because the majority of cases were adjudicated in the period covered by the missing files. Despite this gap in the record, the commission judged that there had been no "general tendency on the part of the Restitution Commissions to drag cases out or to deny legal rights."[50] On the other hand, documents showed that restitution proceedings were time-consuming and that Austria's Restitution Commissions enforced strict application deadlines that excluded many Jewish victims from the process. Claimants typically had no more than three years to file a case, while, according to the commission, the Austrian Civil Code normally allows thirty years as the ethical time frame in which one may contest illegal and disputed contracts.[51]

While many claimants were disqualified on the basis of these strict deadlines, the commission's research showed that the vast majority of accepted cases (77 percent) were settled in the claimant's favor, while the courts rejected only 15.5 percent of the claims they received. A small percentage of applications (7.5 percent) were withdrawn or transferred. Though these numbers support a mostly favorable assessment of the restitution process (if one overlooks the legitimate claims that were never registered or were filed too late), the commission also reported: "It can be said that the files show the Vienna FLD (Provincial Financial Directorate) to have shown mistrust toward Jewish restitution applicants."[52] This mirrors the language and application of the 1947 Victims Welfare Act that favored individuals who had participated in the political resistance over victims of racial persecution.[53]

Finally, the Jabloner Commission paid close attention to the State Treaty of Vienna (1955) and the obligations imposed by this document regarding restitution, compensation, and the victims of gross human rights violations more generally. Article 26 in the treaty describes specific restitution obligations toward victims of Nazi persecution; however, the commission's analysis of the government's record after 1955 indicates "non-fulfillment" stemming from inadequate implementation of key provisions. Pushed through by Social Democrats and Christian Democrats in the ruling coalition, Austria's parliament passed the Kriegs-und Verfolgungssachschädengesetz (KVSG, War and Persecution Material Damages Act) in June 1958, specifically to fulfill the requirements of Article 26. The KVSG paid state compensation for damages stemming from political persecution between 1933 and 1938 and between 1938 and 1945, but the act placed an upper limit on compensation (10,800 Austrian shillings [ATS], or approximately $1,023) and disqualified any victim who was earning more than ATS 72,000. Actual damages, in other words, were "only partly compensated for, or not compensated at all."[54] Facing continued pressure from the Allies, Austria passed the Settlement Fund Act in 1961, which offered compensation for monetary damages incurred during the Nazi period (e.g., seized bank accounts, stolen cash, stock seizures, and the imposition of punitive taxes). The law, however, offered no clear criteria for payment and capped the fund at $6 million, which the Jabloner Commission judged "not sufficient to cover all damage." Again, rough estimates for total Jewish losses, based on partial data for registered assets only, run easily into the hundreds of millions and quite possibly into the billions.[55] In 1996, the Austrian government disgorged a collection of looted artworks, which it put up for auction. Proceeds ($14 million) were transferred to a fund that then made more than 6,800 payments to Jewish victims from Austria.[56]

Only in 2000, as the Jabloner Commission prepared to release its preliminary report on expropriation, did the Austrian government make a concerted effort to compensate the victims of Nazi persecution. Between 2000 and 2007, Austria's National Fund for Victims of Nazi Persecution, which was negotiated as part of the broader Washington Agreement, paid out approximately $142 million in modest lump sum payments ($7,000) to survivors who had lost real estate.[57] From 2000 to 2003, also under the terms of the Washington Agreement, Austria paid out another $210 million through what was termed the General Settlement Fund (GSF). This covered "liquidated" and otherwise transformed properties as well as properties that had been transferred to a new owner who was unaware of its origins. In this way, the government provided compensation to many of the victims who lost property through other means besides the formal Aryanization laws.[58] In total, the Washington Agreement compelled Austria to pay approximately $480 million in compensation. A fund to repay the victims of Nazi slave-labor programs in Austria provided an additional $420 million. Former inmates who had been interned at one of Austria's concentration camps received a separate compensation package of DM 10 billion through Germany's Remembrance, Responsibility, and the Future Fund (Stiftung EVZ).[59] The Conference on Jewish Material Claims Against Germany (Claims Conference) has assembled detailed information for all of these funds and compensation programs on its website.[60]

Evaluation

Although our picture of these commissions can be distorted if we lean too heavily on the analyses provided by their own members, their comments oftentimes do provide important insights. In the case of Austria, Clemens Jabloner has been careful to depict his commission's research as a partial reckoning with the past. While this might seem unnecessarily defensive, given that the commission's published reports exceeded 14,000 pages, Jabloner has insisted that the commission's inquiry represents merely a "starting point for further scholarly work."[61] In the course of its five-year study, the commission faced many difficulties while mining the available source materials, and Jabloner has reflected on the commission's inability to pursue certain questions (let alone suggest reliable answers) in light of such challenges. Many pertinent facts were never recorded (e.g., assets pilfered without registration), and some that were recorded have been lost or have not been recovered. In a number of cases, the commission was faced with missing or destroyed files, while elsewhere their researchers "made surprising finds in forgotten archives and dusty cellars."[62] As Jabloner has observed, academic research "can always go further," and no investigation, no matter how broad, can claim universal insight. In the years since the commission released its final report, research on spoliation and restitution has intensified, as Jabloner put it, "as it should."[63]

More troubling than the difficulties of working with limited and compromised source materials was Jabloner's assertion in 2002 that the facts in the commission's reports "speak for themselves."[64] We can understand this, on the one hand, as Jabloner's determination to raise the commission's inquiry above the level of politics. On the other hand, this was also an implicit defense of the commission's refusal to make legal recommendations regarding reparation. In either case, we can push back against Jabloner's contention that these reports represent an assembly of pure facts. To begin with, we can invoke the postmodernist critique of history, which posits that representation of the past is always a political enterprise. The commission's mandate already made a distinction regarding which victims were (potentially) deserving of compensation and which victims were not. Moreover, the selection of source materials defined and constrained what the commission reported. The decision to sort through property records and insurance documents following the Kristallnacht pogrom but not the intimate letters and diaries in which victims of these attacks described their despair, their sense of isolation, and their concerns for the well-being of their families already had imposed a moral structure onto the commission's findings. In the commission's narrative, expropriation of real estate and certain moveable properties amounts to compensable crime, but terrorizing Jewish families in an open display of hatred—to the point that many Jews contemplated or committed suicide—does not. Both of these scenarios are documented in the historical record, although the visceral experiences of the victims are largely excluded from the commission's report, but data from relevant property registries is presented in extraordinary detail and is combed through in the most exhaustive manner. Not only do the facts in these reports not speak for themselves—they speak for the historians who have chosen to examine this history through a particular lens—they also occupy a space where other facts might have produced a different understanding, one more closely aligned to the experiences of victims. This is, again, the most significant shortcoming of the commission's overall effort.

Reading the Jabloner report, one notes a preoccupation with quantitative analysis and forensic accounting. The crimes of the Nazi era are almost always approached and analyzed in terms of the economic damage they produced. As mentioned earlier, Kristallnacht is presented as an event that destroyed x square meters of insured glass, y number of sacred manuscripts, z number of synagogues and community centers, and so on. Material quantities are matters of intense concern, as are the discrepancies between the declared value of seized properties and the total number and value of subsequent compensation payments. These calculations are rehearsed in detail, even as the authors acknowledge their insufficiency. The final report states, "The amount of assets confiscated cannot be enumerated. Nor can the sum of restitution and compensation be given even an approximately accurate monetary value." Yet this is the dominant trope throughout the final report. Even Jabloner himself admitted dissatisfaction with this approach and the results it produced. In closing the final report, Jabloner hints at what the commission's study failed to recover and the ways in which the moral framework of the project might be responsible for these omissions: "Drawing up a balance sheet is sometimes linked to the idea that Austria might achieve 'closure' in respect [to] restitution and compensation or even [regarding] National Socialism itself. For many reasons, this idea is mistaken. Last [but] not least there is the serious objection to recent developments in the restitution debate which arise from the concern that the monetarisation of history, the conversion of guilt into debts, however justified it is to enable the victims of Nazi crimes to receive compensation, may itself ultimately involve deflecting guilt and attempting to draw a line under the issue."[65]

This is a potent self-criticism. Even though the crimes of the Nazi era are impossible to comprehend without some consideration of the monetary damages they produced, an inquiry limited to a review of financial costs overlooks the deep moral guilt implied by the term "historical injustice." Karl Jaspers explored this scenario in his landmark essay "The Question of German Guilt" (1961). Where the concept of guilt is criminal and political, thoughts turn naturally to questions of punishment and liability. But in the process, Jaspers felt, deeper moral and metaphysical questions are often evaded, particularly by those who took no direct part in the events under investigation. While it is an affront to liberal-democratic norms to charge an entire group with the crimes of specific individuals, the evasion of moral and metaphysical questions at the group level removes any possibility for what Jaspers termed "penance and renewal" and "a transformation of human self-consciousness before God."[66] This helps pinpoint the limitations of the Jabloner initiative. The evidence that the commission presented—the facts that supposedly speak for themselves—yielded a degree of liability, which could be paid back via restitution; the commission's findings did not, however, encourage penance, which Jaspers saw as "an inner development" stemming from moral reflection. It is debatable whether the commission's inquiry encouraged any serious reappraisal of national pride and identity. The final report allowed readers to believe that where others from a previous generation had sunk to criminal depths, contemporary Austrians, who came of age after the fact, have been unfairly made to carry the burden of guilt.[67] The report reinforces a national identity for Austrians, which can be worn proudly at moments of shared achievement but also shrugged aside wherever the question of historical guilt arises.

Since 2009, Jabloner has tried to inject a stronger moral component into the problematic concept of guilt embedded in the commission's work. Looking back on the project, and especially at the way Austrians in the postwar era invoked the Anschluss to deny culpability for Nazi-era crimes, Jabloner has written that these legalistic arguments were advanced specifically to shield Austria from any kind of moral reckoning or accountability: "As purposive as the juridical construction was in foreign policy, it [is] inadmissible in terms of domestic policy and, more important, in terms of morality."[68] Had this sentiment been applied more systematically during the commission's inquiry, the content of the report would likely have been different. As it stands, the commission's work touched only on what Jaspers described as the most superficial and easily remediated concepts of guilt.

The Jabloner Commission report leaves open the possibility that further exploration of Austrian guilt might still take place. "In the future," Jabloner writes, "it will be the task of politicians, other authorities, researchers, teachers, journalists, and others to transmit the results to a wider audience."[69] Observing that "property deprivation also includes lost education," Jabloner has urged more work on "the fate of persecuted, murdered, or exiled students at Austrian universities." He has also asked scholars to pursue new work on "the devastation of intellectual life."[70] Despite the fact that the commission's published reports are massive, Jabloner clearly views the work as incomplete. This could be an acknowledgment that the commission's investigation skewed the results in problematic ways. Or it might not be. Whatever the case, it is worth reiterating that the commission's work did lead to some substantive initiatives aimed at material compensation, even though the commission made no explicit recommendations along these lines. As the commission was still conducting its research, the Austrian chancellery used one of the interim reports (2000) to push through a "Reconciliation Fund Act," which disbursed restitution payments in excess of €350 million to former labor slaves.[71] Unclaimed money from this initiative was rolled into a "future fund" earmarked for "projects that serve the interests of commemoration of the victims of the National Socialist regime, as a reminder of the threat of totalitarian systems and despotism."[72] Austria also signed the Washington Agreement (January 2001), under which its government achieved legal peace (e.g., against new class-action suits filed abroad) in exchange for their passage of an additional compensation act and the creation of a General Settlement Fund ($210 million) aimed at a "comprehensive resolution of open questions."[73] This included restitution in kind for seized properties still in the possession of the government, lump sum payments for individuals who lost tenancy rights to their properties following the Anschluss, and funding for the renovation of derelict Jewish cemeteries.

In addition to these commemorative and reparative measures, Austria's "future fund" also stipulated that the government would lend its support to new projects geared toward promotion and respect for human rights and tolerance.[74] This was a significant feature of the deal inasmuch as Austria, like several other European nations, experienced a resurgence of right-wing populism in the 1990s and early 2000s. The rise of Jörg Haider and the FPÖ in the

1990s—the Freedom Party went from single-digit obscurity in the mid-1980s to capturing almost 27 percent of the national vote in 1999—introduced to Austrian politics an ideology that "combines pan-German traditions with Austrian patriotism, mixes opposition rhetoric with an appeal to xenophobic resentments, and plays with Nazi revisionism and Holocaust denial."[75] As governor of Carinthia, Haider lavished praise on the Third Reich for its spectacular employment record. In 1995, while out stumping for the FPÖ, Haider spoke enthusiastically about the glories of Germany's Waffen SS and Wehrmacht, and at an annual meeting of former SS officers, he congratulated these "people of good character" for "stick[ing] to their convictions, despite the greatest opposition."[76]

While members of the Historikerkommission never raised the specter of the FPÖ directly, Haider's quasi-fascist ramblings and the difficulties these presented in terms of protecting Austria's international image played an important role in the government's decision to launch this initiative. Jabloner commented in 2009 that the commission gave encouragement to those who wanted to promote liberal democratic values. Reflecting on the commission's work, he wrote, "Although, according to international surveys, Austria is not worse than many other countries in this respect [i.e., prevalence of anti-Semitism], we must stay vigilant and continue to strengthen our efforts, particularly at a time when economic crises and political events such as those in the Middle East threaten to increase racist, xenophobic, and anti-Semitic attitudes all over Europe."[77] Jabloner came to see the commission's work as a contribution to the taming of right-wing movements throughout Europe. Without mentioning specific names, Jabloner invoked not only developments in Austria but also the rise of right-wing demagoguery throughout the rest of Europe (e.g., Christoph Blocher and the People's Party in Switzerland, Istvan Csurka's Truth and Life Party in Hungary, Marie Le Pen in France, etc.). To what extent, if any, the Jabloner Commission—or any other commission presented here—will be an effective prophylaxis against right-wing extremism remains, for now, unclear.

Italy:
Divided Memory and the *Brava Gente*

Most visitors to Yad Vashem will encounter the Garden of the Righteous during their tour of the memorial. On the Wall of Honor, under Italy, eighty-nine names appear, including that of Giovanni Palatucci. Once dubbed "the Italian Schindler," Palatucci was born in the southern province of Avellino on May 31, 1909. He became a police officer in 1937, and following a stint in Genoa he was sent to the city of Fiume (now Rijek in Croatia). Assigned to the office for foreigners, Palatucci is described in the Yad Vashem database as having been "gentle and reliable in his relations with local Jews."[78] The memorial credits him with having personally saved five Jews, although widely circulated stories present a much larger number. In these accounts, when Germany invaded Italy in 1943, Palatucci prevented the mass deportation of Jews from Fiume by destroying their files and providing forged documents and even cash to some. Prior to this, Palatucci is said to have shielded Jews from more severe persecution by preemptively transferring them to the internment camp at Campagna, where his contacts guaranteed benign treatment. In some accounts, Palatucci is credited with having saved as many as five thousand Jews.[79]

Palatucci's heroism has been widely commemorated. In Israel, the city of Ramat Gan named a street in honor of Palatucci in 1953, while in Italy, there are public squares and streets dedicated to his memory in Milan, Salerno, Turin, Trieste, and Rome. In New York, the Anti-Defamation League honored Palatucci posthumously—he died in the Nazi concentration camp at Dachau in February 1945—with the Courage to Care Award on May 18, 2005, which the city's mayor, Michael Bloomberg, officially designated as "Giovanni Palatucci Courage to Care Day." In 2002, John Paul II's vicar in Rome, Father Gianfranco Zuncheddo, began to collect evidence and testimony to make a case for Palatucci's beatification. Working from documents located at the Ministry of the Interior in Rome, Zuncheddo commented that Palatucci's record revealed "[an interest] in marginalized people, political refugees, Jews, everyone."[80] One Holocaust survivor, after hearing that he had rescued thousands of Jews, wrote a letter in support of Palatucci, in which she claimed, "[he] went beyond command: he loved his neighbor more than himself."[81] For a short time, the USHMM included Palatucci in an exhibition devoted to understanding the ordinary people who collaborated with the Nazi regime, as well as others, like Palatucci, who "[made] the choice to help."[82]

Given the depth and breadth of such accolades and the powerful way that his story reinforces the Italian self-image of a *brava gente* (a good and decent people), subsequent developments in the case of Palatucci may come as a surprise. In June 2013, after receiving a letter from the Centro Primo Levi (CPL, at the Center for Jewish History in New York), the USHMM scrubbed Palatucci from its digital exhibition and began work to remove him from its museum displays. Sent by a group of scholars who spent six years researching the role of Fiume in the consolidation of the Repubblica Sociale Italiana (RSI, Italian Social Republic),[83] the letter described Palatucci as an enthusiastic

Nazi collaborator and "a willing executor of [Italy's] racial legislation."[84] After completing a review of nearly seven hundred documents, many of them previously unstudied, the CPL researchers concluded that while he might have assisted a small number of Jews, possibly on the order of his superiors, Palatucci did much more to enforce the racial laws, which Italy implemented in 1938, and to facilitate the deportation of Jews from Italy.[85] The CPL study paints Palatucci as a diligent bureaucrat, whose work was crucial to the implementation of Italy's persecutory laws. The "good deeds" that have been attributed to him, the researchers showed, were undertaken within the official system, rather than against it. While some of the beneficiaries of his "rescue" efforts believed that he had risked a great deal by intervening on their behalf (a number of these "witnesses" gave their testimony in his favor fifty years after the fact), the CPL concluded that Palatucci offered assistance only in a small number of cases, where his superiors were inclined to do the same or where he could safely provide help to privileged individuals (e.g., by supplying Jews with false papers identifying them as Catholics). Palatucci's death in a Nazi concentration camp, the researchers found, stemmed from German accusations of embezzlement and treason rather than from any assistance he gave to Jews in Italy. The CPL report also noted that more than half of Palatucci's personnel file in Rome was comprised of requests made by family members to recover his pension (which Italy's postwar government initially withheld), and unsubstantiated materials, collected after his death, outlining plans to celebrate Palatucci's life as a savior of Jews. The adulatory literature surrounding Palatucci, the CPL concluded, is based almost entirely on a series of official proclamations made between 1950 and 1953, when both the Italian government and the Catholic Church were working to repair their images and distance themselves from the fascist era. In reality, the CPL's research showed that Palatucci's work consisted mostly of compiling and updating an official census of Fiume's Jews, which was subsequently used to strip them of their civil rights and citizenship, facilitate their spoliation, secure their internment, and eventually organize their deportation to Nazi death camps. In short, the CPL dismantled the "Italian Schindler" and replaced him with an ambitious, middle-ranking bureaucrat who pledged an oath of loyalty to Mussolini's RSI in 1943, remained in Fiume when others left, and actively persecuted antifascist partisans while simultaneously assisting the Nazi Judeocide. Regarding his reputation as a rescuer and the case for his sainthood, the CPL report states: "Records show unequivocally that the two main claims of mass rescue attributed to Giovanni Palatucci and his uncle . . . have no historical basis."[86] The authors conceded that direct evidence of Palatucci's role in Jewish rescue operations is unlikely to appear in official archives, as any such plans would have been pursued secretly, but they hastened to add that no trace of his assistance appears in the documents of his purported beneficiaries, that is, the Jews he is said to have rescued.[87] Although both the Giovanni Palatucci Association (Rome) and the Vatican rejected the CPL's report, the latter describing it as the result of shoddy research driven by an ideological desire to smear the Church,[88] a representative for Yad Vashem stated that the museum would carefully examine all of the available evidence.[89] Like so much of the history connected to Italy's fascist era, the memory surrounding Palatucci is now deeply divided.

While the unraveling of Palatucci's story could be seen as a minor development, the political ramifications and symbolism are worthy of further exploration. On the one hand, the impact of the Holocaust on Italy was limited in terms of numbers. Compared to other European countries, Italy had a small Jewish population prior to World War II (approximately 50,000 in 1933). Millions of Jews were liquidated in the East beginning in 1941, but Jews were not deported en masse from Italy until autumn 1943 and then only in relatively small numbers (approximately 8,000). As a percentage of the prewar Jewish population, no other combatant country had a higher survival rate (or lower death rate) than Italy.[90] Even before the war, Italian Jews were shielded from many of the abuses they faced in the Reich. Overt expressions of anti-Semitism were rare in Mussolini's Italy, and Jews were able to join the Fascist Party right up until September 1938, when Mussolini introduced a package of racial laws (*leggi razziali*) resembling those promulgated by Hitler three years earlier.[91] These decrees defined who was Jewish, banned "mixed" marriages, and forced the removal of Jews from most government jobs, from military service, and from positions of prominence in the media. They also called for the expulsion of foreign-born Jews living in Italy as well as all Italian Jews who gained citizenship after 1919, two tasks for which Palatucci's census data proved extremely useful. Recent research shows that Italy's racial laws were zealously, if unevenly, enforced by Italian bureaucrats, although there was little work on this aspect of the Holocaust prior to the late 1980s. This helps explain how a "parenthesis theory," similar to the one circulated in France after Vichy, gained traction in Italy as the war wound down and Italians prepared for a new political order. Liberals, in particular, relished a narrative for the Mussolini era that transformed fascism into something decidedly un-Italian, a "foreign, imported phenomenon" with "no lasting effect on Italian society."[92] This effort to distance the population from a regime that held sway for more than twenty years fit with a corresponding Resistance myth, which provided a positive self-image for Italians as they faced the immediate challenges of rebuilding and an uncertain future. The idea that Italians had waged a unified struggle against the Salò Republic (1943–45), as opposed to a Civil War fought on the basis of class, region, and ideology, depended on the willingness of Italians to equate the fascist regime with a "foreign, usurping enemy, the Nazi."[93] To those who wished to consolidate the republic, it scarcely mattered that this brand of unity never existed. Instead, the Resistance myth and the parenthesis theory reinforced each other and discouraged serious historical contemplation for more than a decade (1945–61). When partisans finally captured and executed Mussolini in Mezzegra on April 25, 1945, Italy was faced with a massive loss of life (450,000), widespread physical devastation, and appalling conditions of deprivation. Amplified by the political pressures of the nascent Cold War, these conditions discouraged critical thinking about the recent past. For the most part, ordinary Italians wanted to put the war behind them, which meant that atrocities committed at home would not be seriously investigated or even contemplated. Except for brief interludes when the past resurfaced unexpectedly, the desire to forget (or to misremember, as the case of Palatucci shows) prevailed in Italy from the late 1940s through the end of the 1950s.

While Italians distanced themselves from fascism after the war and avoided confronting the violence that Mussolini's regime perpetrated, the 1960s brought these issues back into view. On one level, the centennial celebration (1961) of Italy's unification fed a patriotic avoidance of the darkest episodes connected to the Mussolini era; on another level, this wave of pride piqued curiosity (at both ends of the political spectrum) in the history of both fascism and antifascism. Calls for a critical reengagement with the fascist era were augmented by the global media attention that surrounded the trial of Adolf Eichmann in Jerusalem in 1961. As the 1960s proceeded, the rise of a left-leaning youth culture helped break the taboo on questions regarding responsibility for the Holocaust; at the same time, the outbreak of the Arab-Israeli War in 1967 raised new questions concerning Jewish settlement and survival in the Middle East. Among Italians, and in Europe more generally, awareness of the Holocaust deepened again in the 1970s and 1980s thanks to a rising presence in the popular culture and several well-publicized debates over the interpretation of Holocaust history and "the limits of representation." In Italy, the fiftieth anniversary (1988) of the *leggi razziali* sparked new interest in the question of responsibility, and the 1990s and early 2000s brought Holocaust consciousness to a peak, as the end of the Cold War presented new possibilities for inquiry, and Hollywood released a string of Holocaust films embraced by critics and popular audiences alike. However, even as the Holocaust became more prominent in the public consciousness, a rift developed in Italian collective memory. As the 2000s unfolded, left-leaning Italians began to acknowledge the role that Italy played in the genocide, and, on the Right, attachment to the *brava gente* myth mixed with various strains of revisionism that clouded the issue of responsibility.

This ambivalence could be seen clearly in 2001 in the politics that surrounded the launch of *Il giorno della memoria*, Italy's first official Holocaust memorial day. Observed on the anniversary of the liberation of Auschwitz (January 27), the Day of Memory demonstrates how Italians have tried to digest the legacies of fascism, and it reveals how the Shoah still acts "as a filter for issues of national and collective memory and identity."[94] *Il giorno della memoria* gained official status thanks to a law (Legge no. 211) that passed Italy's parliament, unanimously, in July 2000. But even though the law's passage showed broad "moral respect" for the Holocaust among Italian lawmakers, the measure was "shot through with subtle, indirect tensions and revisionist ideological positioning."[95] As Robert Gordon has observed, there are several elements of law no. 211 that seem to "de-Italianize" the Holocaust, even though the law explicitly refers to the racial persecution of Italian Jews.[96] For example, it avoids invoking the Shoah directly, instead relying on neutral language, which pushes the work of commemoration beyond Italy's national borders.[97] In fact, the January 27 date of observance refers to an event in Poland, not the anti-Semitic violence that took place in Italy. Furio Colombo, the bill's principal sponsor and a member of the Democratic Left, initially proposed October 16 as a way to commemorate the roundup and deportation of 1,000 Jews in Rome in 1943, but strong opposition from conservative MPs forced him to abandon this plan. Crucially, law no. 211 makes no direct reference to fascism or fascists. Where it alludes to fascists, it does so in positive terms, by recalling "those, *with differing positions and allegiances*, who opposed the extermination project."[98] That same law also fails to mention the concentration and deportation camps that operated within Italy (e.g., Campo di Fossoli), encouraging Italians to think instead of "what befell the Jewish people and the Italian military and political deportees *in the Nazi camps*."[99] In general, the Day of Memory emphasizes the concept of victimhood, without giving much thought to the identity of the perpetrators or to the question of responsibility. It sets Jewish victims alongside Italian political prisoners and deportees without differentiating between the experiences of these groups, and it highlights the transnational European character of the Holocaust without exploring Italy's contribution.[100] While Furio Colombo emphasized that the Shoah must be regarded as an "Italian crime," others have used the Day of Memory to highlight what Italian Gentiles suffered at the hands of the Nazi SS.[101]

Il giorno della memoria is not the only example of the way that Holocaust memory in Italy has shaded toward evasion. Even where anti-Semitism and the Holocaust have moved to the center of Italy's official history, political roadblocks still occasionally recall the old trope of denial. Perhaps the best example is the (as of yet unopened) Museo della Shoah, slated to be Italy's first official Holocaust museum. The plan for the museum calls for new construction at the site of the Villa Torlonia, Mussolini's main residence in Rome from 1925 to 1943; the plan received approval in 2005, but no ground has been broken as of early 2015, and there are doubts as to whether the project will ever get on track. The president of the museum's planning committee has attributed the delay to financial constraints, but politics have also come into play. Gianni Alemanno, the mayor of Rome (2008–13), helped shepherd the project through city council, but he also sided with historians and fellow politicians who argued that fascism could not be judged an absolute evil, even if Italy's racial laws had been unjust.[102] At times, Alemanno, a former member of the "postfascist" National Alliance, appeared to stand with conservatives, who called on the museum to give "parallel acknowledgement" to Italian victims of Communism in order to "balance out" the harms inflicted by the totalitarian regimes of the twentieth century.[103] It remains to be seen what the museum will be like, but wrangling over content and presentation has already led one of the museum's backers to resign from its board of directors. Even with a museum whose explicit mission is to document the links between fascism and anti-Semitic violence, political obstacles have prevented a full admission of Italian culpability.

This defensiveness has been internalized by some of the museum's supporters: delays have repeatedly pushed back construction, while plans for future exhibitions and research have been outlined by a steering committee headed by one of Italy's leading Holocaust scholars, Marco Pezzetti. Pezzetti has stated that the Museo will present the Holocaust not only in an Italian context but also in a broader European context, which is consistent with the transnational character of the Holocaust. Unfortunately, tension between these two approaches can easily be seen as relativizing or downplaying the impact of the Holocaust in Italy. Discussing the overall aim of the museum in early 2013, Pezzetti highlighted the limited scale of Italian deportations in comparison to those that occurred in Eastern Europe.[104] Even though there were roundups in Italy, Pezzetti noted, "by the time that the first Italian Jews were deported from Rome in October 1943, three-quarters of East European Jews had already been killed."[105] This is, on the one hand, an empirically valid statement. Compared to Jews in Poland, Latvia, Lithuania, Ukraine, Belarus, Hungary, Romania, Greece, Czechoslovakia, Austria, France, Belgium, Holland, and Germany, Jewish communities in the Italian territories were relatively safe, particularly in the first four years of the war. In fact, many Jews saw Italy as a kind of safe harbor during this period. Despite a formal alliance with Germany,

Italy resisted Nazi demands to round up and deport Jews from Italian-held territories (such as those in Yugoslavia, Greece, and France), and the Italian military generally did not participate in either deportations or mass killings of Jews.[106] While this was a reflection of a specific military strategy, rather than a case of philo-Semitism, Italians have cited these facts, together with the data on Jewish survival rates, to bolster the myth of the *brava gente* and minimize their responsibility for the Holocaust. These arguments and comparisons are, however, morally dubious, even if they are valid, strictly speaking. Not only did Italy cooperate with Germany from 1936 to 1939 and fight alongside the Reich from 1940 to 1943, but the Italian regime contributed directly to the Holocaust, first through the passage of laws that eroded Jewish rights, and later through administrative assistance and military/police involvement. Attempts to "balance out" the suffering of Jews by focusing on the suffering of Gentiles, or by showing how the outcome had been worse elsewhere, reflect an indifference to moral reckoning. This does not mean, of course, that the experience of a minority group automatically overrides the suffering of the majority or that Italian Jews are owed something more than Italian Gentiles. It means only that divided histories, like Italy's, cannot be mediated without a certain amount of anxiety arising on both sides. A maneuver that deliberately ignores, downplays, or attenuates the suffering of others is not only morally repugnant but also illegitimate in terms of its impact on historical interpretation. Some of the commissions analyzed in this volume have indeed managed to bridge (or at least narrow) the memory gaps that make Holocaust history difficult and painful for some in Europe, but it is true as well that new initiatives, like the Museo della Shoah, can accentuate the bad feelings they hope to overcome. When a project is delayed for years and years, and local politicians speak about their desire to see the project finished without ever taking concrete steps to secure the funding that would get it started, then we have to say that the past has become an impediment to self-understanding for Italian society.

We can see this impediment once more by delving into the Italian historiography on fascism and the Holocaust. Tracing the literature from the mid-1940s to the present, one sees three distinct phases of (dis)engagement.[107] Initially, Italians were reluctant to explore these subjects, except through the lens of a "parenthesis theory," which downplayed their importance. According to this line of thought, fascism had been a "foreign, imported phenomenon" and a departure from Italy's otherwise liberal-democratic trajectory.[108] Italy's Resistance myth quickly solidified during the years 1945 to 1949, as evidenced by the large number of Resistance monuments constructed at the time.[109] This framework was not seriously challenged until the 1960s, when students and other members of the New Left began to ask pointed questions about the persistence of a fascist mentality and what they saw as a "cultural continuity," which linked postwar Italian society to the era of Blackshirts and one-party rule.[110] With interest in the Holocaust already rising due to the centennial celebration of Italian unification and the capture and trial of Eichmann, Italian culture and politics entered a strongly antifascist phase. This second phase, during the 1960s and 1970s, coincided with the opening of the archives of the National Fascist Party and was characterized by repeated attempts by the Italian Communist Party to leverage the memory of fascism for political gain. The 1970s also brought fierce contestation of the past into the public sphere and introduced a new wave of criticism aimed at historical representation(s) that reinforced the *brava gente* concept.[111] Not surprisingly, in the 1980s, there was a strong backlash against this kind of criticism, which dovetailed with the conservative politics of that decade. The third phase, a period of *anti*-antifascism, accelerated in the 1990s at precisely the moment that Holocaust consciousness was peaking throughout the rest of Europe.[112] Proponents of the new approach, most notably Renzo De Felice and Emilio Gentile, claimed to bring a "new objectivity" to the study of fascism, while their critics accused them of fashioning an apologia for fascism. In his seven-volume biography of Mussolini, De Felice distinguished fascism from Nazism, arguing that Italy bore no responsibility for Auschwitz.[113] Moving in a similar direction, Gentile sought to understand fascism "on its own terms," rather than as a blood relative of the other totalitarian regimes. While he understood fascism to be a unique entity, Gentile perceived some overlap with other radical authoritarian systems, which he associated with "the sacralization of politics in the modern age."[114] In other words, while they shared certain structural traits, fascism, Nazism, and Stalinism each aspired to be totalitarian in their own unique ways.[115]

The Anselmi Commission

Considered together, these items—the case of Palatucci, the politics of *Il giorno della memoria*, the long-delayed Museo della Shoah, and the rise of anti-antifascism in Italian historiography—help frame the work carried out by Italy's principal Holocaust commission. The Anselmi Commission, as it came to be called, was established by executive decree (signed by Prime Minister Massimo D'Alema) on December 1, 1998.[116] Tina Anselmi, a Christian Democrat and a member of Italy's Chamber of Deputies (1968–87), chaired the commission. Anselmi, who joined the Resistance at the age of seventeen, had already established a reputation for herself as the head of a Parliamentary Commission of Inquiry charged with investigating the P2

Masonic Lodge crime syndicate in the early 1980s and as a long-time proponent of equal opportunity and equal rights legislation.

Initially comprised of thirteen members and later expanded to fourteen, the Anselmi Commission enlisted personnel from a variety of backgrounds: ministry officials, members of the Italian Jewish community, executives from the banking and insurance industries, and a handful of scholars, including three historians and two archivists. The commission also hired a cadre of research assistants who contributed significantly to the project.

Despite rising interest in the fascist era and Italy's role in the Holocaust, the Anselmi Commission was given a narrow mandate aimed at "reconstructing the events concerning the acquisition of Jewish assets by both public and private bodies."[117] The investigation covered a limited time span, from September 1938 (the enactment of the *leggi razziali*) to April 25, 1945 (Italy's liberation). This periodization and the mandate's emphasis on crimes against property proved to be limiting, as the commission did not pursue other important questions, such as examples of physical violence unrelated to property seizures or spoliation. The wording of the mandate also meant that the commission was given no opportunity to make recommendations concerning additional reparations. Tasked with making a detailed inventory of all property seizures and subsequent restitution, the commission had no latitude to explore how uncompensated losses might be addressed. Despite the narrowness of the mandate, the six-month deadline set out in the original decree proved unrealistic, and the commission was granted three separate extensions before submitting a final report in April 2001. In the end, the commission operated for approximately twenty-eight months, although there was pressure throughout this interval to bring the project to a quick conclusion. Starting later than similar commissions in Switzerland, France, and Austria, the Anselmi Commission nevertheless ended its work more quickly than the rest. Deeply informed by the commissions that preceded it, the Italian project operated in what one of its research assistants has called "a spirit of imitation."[118]

Even though its members put a significant amount of energy into the project, the Anselmi Commission achieved underwhelming results, which did little to overcome Italian indifference to Jewish losses. Presented with the commission's final report, Italy's prime minister, Giuliano Amato, stated that Italy should not retain ill-gotten properties, but he offered no specific plan for how such holdings might be identified and returned. His successors also avoided taking action, and Italy, with one minor exception, has not pursued any uniform program of restitution since the 1960s.[119] In general, the commission's research showed widespread persecution of Jews in Italy between 1938 and 1945 and pervasive spoliation of Jewish property; however, the consistent emphasis of the final report on the difficulties of proper accounting—as opposed to the consequences of deportation—did little to harmonize the memories of Jews and Gentiles. In this regard, the Anselmi Commission closely resembled the Jabloner Commission. Michele Sarfatti, one of the commission's three historians, described the huge troves of data that were reviewed in the course of the investigation and the way these sources encouraged an increasingly microscopic analysis: "We examined thousands and thousands of records, containing endless information on clothes shops belonging to Jews, on toothbrushes belonging to Jews, on Jews barred from sitting on the board of joint-stock committees, and Jews barred from hawking pins."[120] Sarfatti has said that these documents allowed the commission to work up "a general outline of the historical events," but this outline is also swamped with details and particularities, which distract from the bigger picture. The report rehearses a set of uncontroversial facts and arranges these in an orthodox manner characterized by a clinical detachment.

Of course, historical explanation always endeavors to balance specific data with general conclusions. Responsible interpretation depends on an inductive methodology, which assembles data into viable patterns, and a deductive follow-up, which draws out the broader implications. Looking at the final report, one sees that the Anselmi Commission was deeply committed to the inductive side of this process. Readers can learn a great deal about Italy's racial laws and the economic effects these had on Jews. For example, the report documents how Jews rushed to sell their assets soon after the enactment of the racial laws, often at a steep loss, in order to avoid their outright seizure later on.[121] Some companies stopped hiring Jews at this time, and many Jews saw the collapse of their own businesses. Jewish-owned firms with government contracts saw these rescinded, and Jewish merchants who sold products under a state-issued license lost permission to do so.[122] Jews were barred from all public employment, and foreign Jews were expelled from the country and lost the majority of their assets in the process. Under the racial laws, Jews who owned large homes or land tracts were required to sell them to the government (at considerably less than market value), although this measure affected less than 10 percent of Jewish property owners and, in any case, "was implemented very slowly."[123] A clear pattern of persecution emerges in the final report, which brings the huge scale of the economic damage into focus. Again, all of these policies were implemented in 1938, prior to the war and before the German invasion when nobody had yet heard of the Salò Republic. During the next seven years, "virtually everything was taken."[124] If the Anselmi Commission had continued in this direction, the final report could have been a profound and revealing piece of historical writing. Unfortunately, the commission's attention to easily quantified data, rather than to the lived experience of the victims, transformed the project into a dry recitation of facts.

The commission's first meeting focused on defining some of the key terms cited in the mandate. There were, for example, lengthy discussions and debates concerning the appropriate meaning of "Jewish citizens," and even something as basic as the meaning of "Italy" became a point of contention. Given that its members came from different professional backgrounds, the commission worked not only to identify areas of mutual interest but also to develop a coherent work plan. In the process, the commission arrived at three overarching objectives: (1) to provide an analysis of the legal norms and regulations that governed official policy in the period under review; (2) to make a comprehensive assessment of the expropriations that took place in that interval, that is, scope, victims, and mechanisms, and to tabulate the total estimated value of all seized property; and (3) to review and document the scope and scale of all postwar restitution programs. To streamline the process, the commission established an internal steering committee responsible for shaping the basic framework of the final report. This group met approximately fifteen times before being pared down once more to complete the actual drafting of the report.

The commission's official status assured access to a large number of public and private archives not previously studied. Working from these sources, the commission created a database of 6,100 confiscation decrees for the period between 1938 and 1945. The commission also received correspondence from individuals and organizations, offering tips, petitioning for the return of specific properties, seeking compensation, and inquiring about looted artworks. These letters were dutifully answered despite there being no requirement in the mandate that the commission do so. In some cases, the letters prompted the commission to make specific inquiries, which led to the return of one-of-a-kind cultural properties. The commission also claimed to have seriously contemplated the content of these letters and their "weighty moral implications," although it is unclear from their own reports how such implications factored into the work. Researchers endeavored to collect materials from different regions throughout the country, but the commission was unable to evaluate everything of potential importance, given the time constraints. Where source material was thin or the record was unclear, the commission simply moved on to other tasks with the recommendation that further study be conducted in the future. This emerged as an idée fixe in the final report, referring back to the call for "further in-depth historical study."

Although the commission reached out to a long list of organizations for help in locating documentation, questions remained at the end of the project as to whether the most salient materials had been identified. Of course, every historian faces this challenge. With the historical commissions, however, choices regarding source material are shaped by the mandate, and the general contours of the investigation are prescribed in advance of the inquiry. On the other hand, commissions sometimes choose to look beyond the constraints of their mandate. This was the case for the Anselmi Commission, for example, where unpaid insurance claims and the question of slave labor came to the fore. Concerning the former, the commission engaged several of the major insurance companies in Italy, as well as officials from Italy's regulatory body for the insurance industry, to review documentation related to unpaid claims written for Holocaust victims.[125] Separately, these firms cooperated with the International Commission for Holocaust-Era Insurance Claims (ICHEIC) to negotiate a settlement in excess of $100 million.[126] With respect to slave labor, the Anselmi Commission cooperated with the International Organization for Migration (IOM, Rome) and with German diplomats in Italy to review data on the number of Italians who were deported to the Reich for slave labor. As in the case of the unpaid insurance policies, a settlement for former slave laborers was negotiated separately by an external agency.

The significance of these departures from the official mandate is twofold. They reveal, first of all, that commissions can assert themselves where outside pressure raises questions that threaten the government or fail to pique official interest. At the same time, these departures show how the Anselmi Commission reflected, or at least fed, certain nativist sentiments regarding who was considered a victim. In the case of insurance claims and slave labor, while these "problem areas" were handled separately by other bodies seeking historical justice, the Anselmi Commission ultimately decided that it would not be possible to give a full account of the Holocaust in Italy without exploring the details. The commission pursued these two issues, despite their not falling under the mandate, in part because these topics helped define the context of the period under investigation but also because external pressures (e.g., class-action lawsuits in foreign jurisdictions and the attention of the United States and the European Union) necessitated a response. The final report strongly hints that the commission took an interest in these items because they offered an opportunity for political action, but this only serves to underscore the fact that the commission was not empowered to make direct policy recommendations.[127] These sections of the report signal that the commission was positively oriented toward a program of reparations without being able to enact one unilaterally, which helps explain the ultimate failure of the Anselmi Commission in terms of its inability to effectively fuse history and political advocacy. It also shows how (and why) the project remained incomplete. Summing up his thoughts on the commission's inquiry and impact, Michele Sarfatti wrote in

2002: "As one can see, virtually everything was taken, and a great deal has obviously been returned. In my opinion, the State and the various state and private bodies should now complete the historical inquiry and see to it that the assets are returned, or that compensation is paid for them."[128] Sarfatti recommended the creation of a separate commission to handle individual compensation and a memorial foundation, which could use restitution funds to seed worthy educational and commemorative programs. In effect, Sarfatti suggested that Italy should take the same steps that France did when it launched the CIVS and the Foundation for the Memory of the Shoah.[129] Although the Anselmi Commission cannot be blamed for the fact that the Italian government ignored its recommendations, it is a useful reminder that the governments that establish these commissions are also in a position to bury their findings and ignore their suggestions. Hoping to overcome the "amnesia and indifference" that characterized the main current within Italy's Holocaust memory,[130] the Anselmi Commission was mostly relegated to the role of spectator while other organizations, whose authority did not depend on the government, extracted settlements from the Italian firms that benefitted from the Holocaust and the fascist war of aggression.

The commission's decision to pursue the question of forced labor in Germany has added significance, insofar as the vast majority of Italians conscripted into these programs were not Jewish. Prior to the passage of the racial laws, Italy's Jewish population numbered approximately 50,000. Following Mussolini's (first) downfall in 1943 and the invasion of the northern half of the country by Nazi troops, German authorities began to round up Jews in Rome, Milan, Genoa, Florence, Trieste, and other urban centers. The majority of Italian Jews managed to elude capture, although little has been uncovered concerning their strategies for survival. By the end of the war, Germany deported 8,564 Jews from Italy and the Italian-held territories along the Mediterranean. In August 2000, when Germany established a multibillion-dollar fund to compensate the victims of forced and slave labor during the Nazi period, the IOM in Rome undertook to identify potential claimants in Italy. The IOM submitted a list of 44,000 possible beneficiaries, which dwarfed the total number of Jewish deportees. Most of the Italians on the list were either political prisoners who fought for the Resistance or interned soldiers, both of which groups were ineligible for compensation through the Conference on Jewish Material Claims Against Germany. Sensing that Germany might try to limit compensation to Jewish victims but also aware that the Remembrance, Responsibility, and the Future settlement was intended to assist all victims of Germany's slave-labor program, whether Jewish or not, the Italian government sent officials from the Ministry of Foreign Affairs to Berlin in November 2000 to advocate on behalf of non-Jewish deportees, particularly Italy's interned military personnel, who represented the largest category within the list of those 44,000 claimants. By 2006, the German Future Fund had paid €386 million to the IOM, which then disbursed individual payments to settle 90,000 claims in and around the Mediterranean. While the vast majority of these payments went to non-Jewish victims, the Anselmi Commission worked with the IOM to make sure that Italy's list was accurate. Given the identity of the claimants, most of this work had no direct relation to the question of Jewish spoliation; however, the commission departed from its formal mandate to support the documentation process because domestic politics demanded an inquiry that would benefit the national majority. While the Anselmi Commission could not persuade the Italian government to complete the process of Jewish restitution, the Ministry of Foreign Affairs used the commission's work to secure compensation for non-Jewish victims of Germany's slave-labor program. This is an important example of the way that governments can employ the work of historical commissions selectively to support what is politically expedient. Italian politicians embraced the commission's peripheral findings on slave labor since these revelations reinforced Italy's record of antifascist resistance, whereas the report's primary focus, that of spoliation, failed to persuade lawmakers that further action was required on behalf of Jewish victims.

Another revealing section of the Anselmi report deals with the problem of terminology, specifically the commission's discomfort with some of the terms that appeared in government records following the passage of Italy's racial laws. Commission members sought to distance themselves from terms like "Jewish citizens" or "the Jewish race," since these were viewed as "incompatible with the general principles of our legal system and therefore unacceptable."[131] The commission also argued for the individual's right to a private life and for a concept of citizenship without ethnonational baggage. While these were not controversial points, it is still peculiar that the commission felt a need to disavow discriminatory language, which clearly belonged to and arose from a specific historical context. One might see this as signaling a reluctance on the commission's part to engage a chapter of Italy's history during which the fundamental values of liberal-democracy (e.g., group-neutral citizenship) were not merely absent but in fact attacked and dismantled in the name of quasi-Darwinian pseudoscience. This same defensiveness can be seen elsewhere in the final report. Before launching into a difficult and potentially painful discussion of the illiberal policies promoted by the Italian government for more than twenty years, the commission first insisted on the fact of Italy's moral rehabilitation. Section 2.1 of the summary report on racial terminology and usage of the term "Jewish" ends triumphantly with a note on the abrogation of the racial laws on January 20, 1944, and the transitional government's decision to regard them as nonexistent. Concerning the racial politics of the Mussolini era, the commission seemed to say, Italy must be regarded as already cleansed and repaired.

Other examples of deflection appear later in the report. Section 5, "Organizations Consulted and Methodology," shows the vast scope of the project and the huge number of investigative leads that were pursued. The commission contacted an assortment of organizations, looking for assistance and information: state archives and documentation centers, a variety of bureaucratic agencies, government ministries, police precincts, historical institutes, cultural organizations, business associations, military tribunals, Jewish unions, and so on. There are several telling comments in the report regarding what kinds of information the commission sought from these organizations and what kinds of documentation these inquiries procured. For instance, the commission contacted the Military Advocate General in 1999 seeking documentation related to Italy's postwar tribunals. Among the responses they received, the Military Advocate of Turin sent documents related to Jewish spoliation in northern Italy, including records from the trial of Karl Friedrich Titho, who served as commander at the Fossoli concentration camp. Titho was investigated for murder of "enemy" individuals, for violent mistreatment of POWs, and for the deaths of sixty-seven noncombatants.[132] While Titho was never brought to trial in Italy, the files of the tribunal included copious evidence of the crimes for which he was eventually prosecuted in the Netherlands. The Anselmi Commission report cited documents that "shed light on heinous crimes committed in [Fossoli], by German military personnel, against Italian prisoners" and mentioned "the shooting of two Jewish [prisoners] for trivial motives." Another tribunal document detailed crimes "carried out individually or jointly by German troops and troops of the Italian Social Republic." These statements reveal a great deal about the political context in which the commission operated since they deal with events that directly reinforce the myth that Italians played no role in the camps or in the anti-Semitic violence perpetrated there. By focusing on crimes committed by members of the Nazi SS in 1944–45, the commission also diminished the impact of the previous period, (1938–43), during which Italian officials enforced the *leggi razzilai* and spoliation of Jewish property proceeded without significant German involvement. To be fair, most of the Anselmi report is devoted to events the military tribunals did not engage, in other words, the period prior to the German invasion. So it is inaccurate and unfair to say that the commission refused to entertain any notion of Italian guilt. Nevertheless, the commission's exploration of German guilt has the effect of relativizing Italian responsibility for crimes committed against Jews prior to 1943. Next to the example of criminals like Titho, Italian anti-Semitism appears less severe. If German war crimes are seen as the standard of absolute evil, then Italian crimes migrate to a less offensive category. Even though the tribunals were important in terms of developing a broad understanding of the Holocaust, the commission's interest in German war criminals created a hierarchy of responsibility, which shielded Italians from the kind of blame reserved for German perpetrators. In the final analysis, this might be a valid assessment, but it also undermines the possibilities, and perhaps even the purpose, of taking a full moral inventory of the Italian past. The question here is whether we should be at all surprised if the Anselmi Commission, which was created for the purpose of reconstructing events related to Jewish spoliation in Italy, worked within a moral framework that consistently attributed fascist-era injustices to Germans in Berlin. Even if the Italian government, by creating this commission, acknowledged ipso facto that the rights of Jews had been infringed on Italian soil, the mandate began from the premise that fascism was a foreign ideology and that Germans bore responsibility for the worst crimes. With respect to Jewish restitution, the Italian government treated the Anselmi findings as a closed chapter, whereas fresh evidence of German war crimes has led Italy, on several occasions, to reopen legal proceedings against former Nazis.[133]

Among the dozens of Holocaust commissions launched in Europe during the 1990s, the Anselmi Commission was one of the last to get started (December 1998). Compared to Switzerland, France, and Austria, the Italian initiative also had the shortest working life. To pursue its work, the commission sought assistance from a range of actors, and many organizations cooperated wholeheartedly. The commission queried 851 banks regarding Jewish assets and met with representatives of twenty-four financial institutions to discuss the best methods for identifying and returning stolen properties. In their final report, the commission noted both the huge scale of the expropriations and the increasing severity of these measures over time. According to the report: "No one was spared: neither rich nor poor, shopkeeper nor industrialist, shareholder nor the possessor of a modest bank account. The confiscation orders listed everything: not only silverware, real estate, land, works of art and valuable carpets, but also humble household objects and personal effects."[134] While the Mussolini government generally refused to deport its Jewish citizens prior to November 1943 and even shielded Jews who resided in or migrated to Italian-occupied territories during the war, expropriations between 1938 and 1943 exposed Jews to severe hardships, which made them highly vulnerable to the "new provisions" and "grim measures" introduced in 1944. The Anselmi report highlights this connection between property rights and human dignity/life,

and the commission clearly sought to balance the financial and legal considerations of the investigation, that is, the technical aspects of spoliation, with
larger questions of emotional and moral significance. As Tina Anselmi wrote
in her introduction to the report, "More than a question of money, seizure
was part of a policy of persecution whose final aim was moral extinction followed by extermination. No historical reconstruction can do full justice to the
anxiety, humiliation, and misery to which men and women were subject, day
after day."[135] This reflected the conviction of the commission's leadership that
historical clarification hinged not only on quantitative verification but also on
intensive engagement with the "qualitative aspect of spoliation."[136] We can
draw a comparison here to France, where the Mattéoli Commission insisted
on a need for both material restitution and moral reparation.

However, despite the declaration of its chair regarding history and moral
striving, the Anselmi Commission failed to realize its hopes for the future.
The responsibility for this belongs primarily to the Italian government, which
launched the project at the last possible moment (and only when the costs of
ignoring Jewish claims threatened to become unbearable), and then failed to
implement the commission's recommendations for further action. But the
commission also bears some responsibility. Generally speaking, the shortcomings of the Anselmi initiative fall under two categories. The first and most
basic was the commission's inability to secure restitution for victims who had
not yet been compensated. Assessing Italy's postwar restitution program was
one of the commission's top priorities.[137] While limitations in the source
material and time pressures made this difficult, the commission managed to
give a fairly comprehensive presentation of Italy's postwar restitution legislation.
Although Italy's postwar government passed restitution measures relatively
quickly, complex procedural requirements and difficulties locating certain
properties and their heirs excluded many potential claimants from receiving
compensation. Victims also found that they received varying degrees of
assistance depending on what branch of government they petitioned. While
antifascist MPs generally supported Jewish restitution programs, victims encountered greater resistance in the judiciary, where little was done to purge
fascist-era appointees. Overall, the Anselmi Commission offered a "positive
judgment" on the scope and scale of Italy's postwar restitution programs.
Where Holocaust survivors returned to Italy and put their claims through the
proper channels, these individuals typically received back their property. On
the other hand, victims experienced greater difficulty when properties were
plundered (i.e., unofficially robbed), lost, or destroyed. Heirless properties
and properties unknown to surviving relatives also posed problems. These blind
spots in Italy's postwar restitution program led the Anselmi Commission to

recommend a follow-up study to locate unreturned assets. The commission also recommended that a new investigative body be created to expedite the return of such assets. The final report urged the Italian government to take immediate action to compensate victims of confiscation and theft and to redress losses resulting from anti-Semitic persecution. Anselmi pointed specifically to France and to the work of the CIVS as a potential model for coupling historical clarification and restitution. Crucially, Anselmi understood the need for further compensation as arising from a moral debt incurred by Italy as a result of racial injustices that specifically targeted Jews. "The sufferings of any war leaves a debt that must be paid," she noted. "However, in our case, that suffering was caused through the deliberate implementation of discriminatory laws and regulations that brutally isolated part of our population simply because of their birth."[138] Anselmi's use of "our" suggests acknowledgment of Italian (as opposed to German) responsibility, while her reference to discrimination based on birth distinguishes Holocaust victims from other Italians who suffered under the Nazi occupation. This is a stark contrast to Italy's Day of Memory, which treats Jewish and non-Jewish victims alike as the recipients of similarly unjust treatment under the German occupation. In terms of developing a factually informed, historically nuanced, and morally reflective account of Jewish spoliation, this section of the Anselmi report performs as competently as any of the other commission reports examined in this volume. Unfortunately, Italy's political climate discouraged implementation of the commission's recommendations for action. Shortly after the commission presented its report to Prime Minister Giuliano Amato, the Italian government fell. Amato was replaced by Silvo Berlusconi, who showed no interest in exploring Italy's role in the Holocaust or in accepting any responsibility for anti-Semitic crimes. Confronted with this power shift, Jewish groups in Italy did little to press for further action. But even if political instability led the Anselmi initiative into a dead end, this does not relieve the commission of all responsibility for its failure either.

From a distance, the Anselmi Commission appears to have done everything it could to elicit official acknowledgment. The final report characterized Jewish spoliation as a sweeping crime against property and lives that was committed by Italians (and others) as part of a larger program of anti-Semitic persecution geared toward extermination. The commission documented a range of postwar restitution measures, but it also revealed that these programs failed to deliver justice to all victims, who were not always well positioned (or even alive) to navigate the claims process successfully. The report recommended that the government set up a program to make additional payments to victims who were passed over or denied a full hearing based on a technicality. At the same time, the Anselmi report hinted at some of its own limitations, and it raised concerns, which the authors conceded they had not been able to fully overcome. There are a multitude of digressions throughout the document about the various holes in the source material and the impossibility of drawing firm conclusions based on spotty evidence, but the most important self-criticism, by far, related to the difficulty of deriving universal historical understanding from individual case studies. As Anselmi stated in her introduction, the commission was established to conduct "a general investigation of dispossession," but historical inquiry requires in-depth engagement with particular data points that do not always lend themselves to generalization. In other words, there is a tension between the quantitative data that the commission was called upon to tabulate and the meaning of individual life-experiences recorded in the archives. Readers of the report cannot assess the full effects of anti-Jewish legislation without delving into what Anselmi termed "the merits and resolution of individual requests," yet there is an epistemological gulf separating each particular instance of injustice from the commission's broader retelling of a historical injustice. The failure of the Anselmi Commission to secure restitution for uncompensated victims of spoliation stems most directly from the meanness and instability of Italian politics, but at the same time something in the commission's basic approach seems to have weakened the imperative to act. I am referring to the difficulty of fully registering the individuality of the victims and the meaning of their losses against the backdrop of a general history of spoliation. Even if historians require "large-scale quantifiers" (i.e., not only collective terms such as "the Italians" or "Italy's Jews" but also the arithmetic sums that commissions use to calculate the extent and effects of spoliation) to consolidate the experiences of disparate individuals and preserve a possibility for intergroup reconciliation, these cognitive structures diminish the pathos of individual historical experience. This could be described as "losing the trees for the forest."

Members of the Anselmi Commission wrestled with how to navigate between "the quantitative and qualitative aspect[s] of spoliation." The conclusion to the final report begins with comments on the "limited sufficiency" of historical analysis for representing "the dimensions and extent of the damage."[139] In her introduction, Anselmi laments the impossibility of achieving "comprehensive knowledge of everything," and she acknowledges the limitations of the commission's historical reconstruction: "I think it must be accepted that quite a number of aspects can never be clarified in full."[140] These are not exactly profound insights, but they do signal the commission's trepidation over what others have referred to as "the limits of representation." Commission members clearly worried over how their report would be received and whether it could satisfy multiple audiences. But where other scholars have given serious thought to the kinds of proof that underpin historical knowledge and to the impact their methodological choices have on the reception of history,[141] the Anselmi Commission, confronted with a mountain of source material, charged headlong into their work and drafted a report that leaned heavily on brief encapsulation of diverse facts. Aware of the importance of qualitative analysis and the ways in which attacks on particular properties presaged attacks on particular lives, the commission nevertheless launched into a series of quantitative exercises aimed at summarization. Perhaps the best example of this is the section of the final report that treats the expropriation of Jewish property between 1943 and 1945. As this is the period in which Italy's anti-Semitic decrees directly facilitated the Nazi genocide, there would seem to be an urgent need for deep, qualitative analysis here. Yet readers learn almost nothing about the fates of individual victims, except possibly indirectly, for example where the seizure and sale of their property is recorded. The report states that Italian officials in the Ministry of the Interior targeted warehouses in the northern town of Maderno where Jewish wholesalers stored their wares. On December 1, 1943, less than ten weeks after the establishment of the Salò Republic, Italian officials raided these locations, where they seized 26,846 pairs of stocking and 1,900 pairs of gloves, together worth 1 million lire.[142] These items were auctioned off with the proceeds given to families of regime loyalists who were killed in political attacks orchestrated by the Resistance. Thus, this section of the report provides a detailed picture of spoliation, and it lists specific offices and individuals responsible for seizing particular properties. With respect to the perpetrators, then, the Anselmi Commission did move beyond "large-scale quantifiers" to discuss the criminal misbehavior of specific individuals.

Other commissions (e.g., Austria), in their narration of similar episodes, elected not to "name names," and it is worth asking which of these strategies does more to encourage national responsibility for historical injustice. Even more revealing, though, was the Anselmi Commission's strategy with respect to victims, which was the exact opposite of that used for perpetrators (i.e., no individual identification). It is telling that the Anselmi report neither provides the names of the merchants whose inventory was seized in Maderno nor mentions what happened to these individuals after their warehouse was raided. While the report shows that somewhere between 7,700 and 7,900 persons classified as members of "the Jewish race" were arrested in Italy during this period "and then deported or killed," not one of these individuals is identified by name. The report states that 6,720 deportees have been positively identified (of which 5,896 were killed), but again, the victims are counted as a group rather than individually. In the end, readers know more about the items that were stolen—those 1,900 pairs of gloves, mixed by style, size, and gender—than they do about the human beings who were despoiled, arrested, then hastened toward their death either in the Italian camps or in the extermination centers farther away. We learn a few details about what was in their hands and pockets at the moment they were apprehended, but there is nothing that tells us who the victims really were, what kind of lives they led, how they related to each other or to their non-Jewish neighbors prior to their becoming racial enemies of the state. Missing entirely from this account are the memories and the voices of the victims themselves. The Anselmi Commission worked intensively with the archival traces of "prelinguistic phenomena" (e.g., inventory lists, bank ledgers, currency exchange receipts, etc.),[143] but their analysis of these documents produced only quotidian meaning. While there is obviously no chance of collecting the memories of everyone involved in executing the *leggi razziali*, and certainly no way of collecting the memories of everyone who suffered under them, the commission's presentation of a quantitative history built solely around seemingly objective facts filtered through large-group categories lessens the moral impact of the work. The Anselmi report comes very close to being a formless history, which is to say, a perfunctory rehearsal of facts without sustained reflection on the way these events were experienced by the victims or the way these experiences currently figure into the memories of survivors. This brand of history becomes possible where a government insists that the impact of the Holocaust was limited and where the perspective of victims is not well represented in the political mainstream. It is for this reason that international Jewish organizations have been so insistent on having a role in the negotiation of Holocaust restitution and reparations. Afforded an opportunity to learn from other commissions that began their work earlier, the Anselmi Commission instead repeated the mistakes of the least compelling examples.

4

Lithuania and Latvia

The Limits of "Double Genocide"

ike Poland (see chap. 2), the Baltic states found themselves overrun three times during World War II. The Molotov-Ribbentrop Pact led to a Soviet takeover in June 1940. The launch of Germany's eastern offensive, Operation Barbarossa, then paved the way for a period of German occupation (1941–44). A renewed Soviet offensive dislodged the German forces in 1944–45 and led to the annexation of these territories by Soviet Russia. While Jewish communities throughout the Baltics were ruthlessly persecuted and nearly eliminated by war's end,[1] the ethnic majorities also suffered devastating losses.[2] At the conclusion of the Cold War, when the Baltic states regained their independence, the historical discourse surrounding World War II evolved to include new discussions of previously taboo subjects. New questions arose concerning the periods of Soviet and Nazi rule, and the experiences of ethnic majorities and minorities under both regimes. Even as they faced pressure from Western governments and Jewish victims' organizations to confront the history of the Holocaust, ethnic majorities in the Baltic states were more concerned with commemorating their own losses. A "double genocide" narrative emerged, which acknowledged, but also downplayed, Jewish losses at the hands of the Germans, while it highlighted national losses (i.e., those suffered by the ethnic majority) at the hands of the Soviets.[3] The Baltic populations showed little interest in exploring what Jewish groups remembered, which was a wave of anti-Semitic violence characterized by widespread collaboration between the local population(s) and the Nazi forces (complicity), as well as other assaults in which local populations acted independently (self-initiative). The "double genocide" narrative that took hold in the Baltics resembled the "parallel fates" narrative that emerged in Poland during the 1960s and 1970s.[4]

Facing external pressures, and eager to secure membership in NATO and the European Union, Lithuania, Latvia, and Estonia established investigatory commissions in 1998 to deal with this contested period in their history. This chapter focuses on two of these commissions (Lithuania and Latvia) because their structure was better suited for promoting bilateral dialogue—if not always in practice then at least in principle—and because the size of the prewar Jewish populations in these countries was much higher than in Estonia. In terms of overall impact, the Latvian commission was arguably more successful than its Lithuanian counterpart.[5] However, there were problems in both cases in terms of translating political support for the commissions into effective historical mediation and winning public support. It is doubtful whether these commissions generated a significant degree of Baltic-Jewish reconciliation, although their work left certain positive legacies worth considering.

Lithuania:
The Jaeger Report
and the Question of Collaboration

In its Annual Report (2010) on the Worldwide Investigation and Prosecution of Nazi War Criminals, the Simon Wiesenthal Center put Lithuania at the bottom of its rankings for willingness to bring Nazi-era war criminals to justice. Along with several regional neighbors (Estonia, Ukraine, and Hungary), Lithuania received a grade of F for its failure to investigate and prosecute suspected Nazi war criminals despite the absence of any legal obstacles to doing so.[6] Leonidas Donskis, a Lithuanian representative in the European Parliament, echoed the Wiesenthal Center's assessment, calling his country's record of impunity a "disgrace." Donskis reckoned, "It will be impossible for Lithuania to come to terms with its history . . . until the country's elite admits that the provisional government of Lithuania in 1941 collaborated with the Nazis and acted against Lithuanian [Jews]."[7]

Prior to World War II, Lithuania's Jewish population was approximately 160,000 (7 percent of the total population). By 1941, following an influx of refugees from the west, the Jewish population in Lithuania had swelled to approximately 250,000 (10 percent of the population). At the end of the war, an estimated 94 percent of these individuals—the highest extermination percentage in occupied Europe—had been killed, either at the hands of the invading Nazi forces or at the hands of Lithuanians who conducted their own pogroms. Many of the killings, as the archival record clearly shows, were overseen by a combination of German and Lithuanian forces. The extent to which Lithuanian collaborators participated freely in the killings, or whether they were coerced by the occupying forces, has been much debated, although evidence from the archives suggests that the former scenario (i.e., voluntary collaboration) was at least sometimes the case.[8]

In one of the most studied documents of Holocaust history, the so-called Jaeger Report, SS Colonel Karl Jaeger, the commanding officer for one of the Nazi killing units (Einsatzkommando 3) that operated around Vilnius in the second half of 1941, refers to the "essential" help his troops received from the local population.[9] Writing from Kovno on December 1, 1941, Jaeger noted that the goal of "clearing Lithuania of Jews," an operation he described as "virtually completed," was made possible chiefly through his arrangements with another SS officer, Joachim Hamann, who had "ensure[d] the cooperation of the Lithuanian Partisans and Civil Authority."[10] By his own accounting, Jaeger's unit was responsible for killing more than 137,000 Jews in Lithuania between July 2 and November 25, 1941.

Jaeger's report emerged as a crucial piece of evidence in the United States' criminal case against Jonas Stelmokas, a Lithuanian army officer alleged to have assisted the German occupation and to have participated in the extermination operations against Lithuanian Jews. While the government's lawyers argued that Stelmokas served as a "voluntary" member of a Lithuanian unit (Schutzmannschaft) that "advocated, assisted, participated, and acquiesced in the murder and persecution of Jews and other unarmed civilians in Lithuania," judges for the Court of Appeals (3rd circuit) ruled that Stelmokas's membership in a Lithuanian unit was not sufficient to connect him to specific crimes against humanity. However, although no evidence linked Stelmokas individually to the murder of Jewish civilians, the court's reading of the Jaeger Report affirmed that Lithuanian partisans had played an essential role in the cleansing actions that decimated Lithuania's Jewish population. Even though Stelmokas withstood (some of) the charges against him, the fact of broad and voluntary collaboration on the part of Lithuanian units with the Nazi occupation was repeatedly highlighted in the court's judgment.[11] The government's case did not clarify the exact number of Lithuanians who participated in the genocidal actions against Jews, but a comparison of written records, including the report made by Jaeger and the testimony of noted Holocaust historian Raul Hilberg, suggests a figure between eighty and five hundred participants for the actions in and around Kaunas (September and October 1941). How many Lithuanians volunteered for actions elsewhere, or how many participated spontaneously, did not emerge from the evidence presented against Stelmokas.

The ambiguities and uncertainties of this case, together with the tension between partisan perspectives on the larger question of collaboration, made Lithuania an excellent candidate for historical clarification. In September 1998, President Valdas Adamkus announced that Lithuania would convene a historical commission to foster reconciliation among nations based on a clearer understanding of the past, and a better accounting of the crimes and injustices perpetrated during the Soviet and Nazi occupations. The International Commission for the Evaluation of the Crimes of the Nazi and Soviet Occupation Regimes in Lithuania (ICL) met for the first time on November 17, 1998, and was chaired by Emanuelis Zingeris, a scholar specializing in Lithuania's Jewish history and an MP who played a prominent role in the pro-independence Sąjūdis movement during the late Soviet era.[12] Among Zingeris's first acts as chair was his decision to divide the commission into two sub-committees, one devoted to investigating crimes of the Soviet occupation and the other to examining crimes of the Nazi occupation. It was Zingeris's firm belief that the crimes committed by each regime ought to be treated separately so as "to avoid superficial analogies" that might color or distort the commission's evaluation.[13] It was also a strategy Zingeris deliberately employed to undercut the double-genocide narrative. A secretariat was created in 1999 to coordinate the commission's work and to raise the profile of the commission at home and abroad. The secretariat was also tasked with organizing conferences, workshops, and symposia related to the commission's work. In 2007 the ICL suspended its work, following the so-called Arad affair in which a government prosecutor investigated a prominent Lithuanian Jew and Holocaust survivor, Yitzhak Arad, on charges he had committed war crimes against Lithuanian civilians while fighting as a member of the Soviet partisan forces during the war. As Arad was also a member of the ICL (and a former director of Yad Vashem), this was obviously a major complication for the commission's work, and, ultimately, it was an obstacle that could not be overcome.[14] Before it collapsed, however, the ICL published a three-volume study of the Nazi period, which included one volume devoted solely to the question of Lithuanian collaboration and the recorded instances of "self-initiated" attacks against Jews. The commission also helped to seed an impressive teacher-training program, which created sixty-two tolerance education centers throughout the country.

The ICL listed four major goals in its mission statement: (1) to pursue research that fills existing gaps in Lithuania's modern history; (2) to stimulate a process aimed at understanding the crimes of the Nazi and Soviet occupations, and promoting historical justice in cooperation with available partners; (3) to educate Lithuanians of all ages about crimes that took place during

World War II and to pose "sensitive questions" about these events so as to remove obstacles and barriers to democratization; and (4) to work with policy makers in Lithuania to formulate an "objective official position" on historical issues connected to the commission's work. In its outreach materials and working papers, the commission emphasized both the right of its citizens to know what happened in their country during the war and the duty of all Lithuanians not to cover up, conceal, or distort what responsible scholarship recognizes about the past. Open engagement with the past, no matter how potentially distressing, was thus conceived of by the commission as a crucial test of democratic commitment as well as a foundational exercise to establish respect for human rights and to strengthen civil society. The ICL mission statement also outlined plans for the dissemination of its research findings. New educational materials for Lithuanian students were specifically mentioned, along with public seminars aimed at promoting general education and civic engagement. Finally, the mission statement highlighted the commission's interest in calculating moral and material damages stemming from the three periods of occupation, though the document did not specifically state whether (or how or from whom) monetary reparations might be sought. The ICL's conception of historical justice emphasized what the human rights discourse has framed as "the right to know," and the main thrust of its work focused on the reparative effects of truth rather than on addressing the material losses associated with historical injustices. This point was received differently among diverse segments of the Jewish community, where there exists no uniform opinion regarding how the crimes of the Holocaust can best be repaid or whether they can be repaid at all. Still, it is significant that the ICL linked its fact-finding and educational missions to larger questions of justice and democratic values.

The ICL published energetically during its ten years of operation. Other commissions, for example the Latvian commission, which published twenty-five volumes (including eight on the Nazi era), may have outperformed the ICL in this area, but the quality and scope of the Lithuanian research is impressive nonetheless. In addition to the more than twenty reports and essays, which its members and research staff prepared and which have been archived in the commission's research database, the ICL published eight longer volumes, including three that dealt exclusively with the Nazi occupation: volume 1, *Preconditions for the Holocaust: Anti-Semitism in Lithuania* (2004); volume 2, *Murders of Prisoners of War and of the Civilian Population in Lithuania, 1941–1944* (2005); and the most controversial (because of the role played by ethnic Lithuanians), volume 3, *The Persecution and Mass Murder of Lithuanian Jews during Summer and Fall 1941* (2006). Together, these three volumes provide a richly documented history of Jewish life in Lithuania prior to World War II—volume 1 traces the history of anti-Semitic prejudice in Lithuania back to the late nineteenth century—and a detailed analysis of the presence of Lithuanian anti-Semitism in everyday life. These studies emphasize the relative security that Jews in Lithuania enjoyed in the interwar period as compared to Jews in Poland, Romania, Hungary, and Russia. The ICL does finally conclude, however, that Jews in Lithuania were "essentially treated as second-class citizens" following the coup d'état in 1926, which brought Antanas Smetona back to the presidency and set the stage for a long period of authoritarian rule (1927–40).

The ICL also delved into the origins and persistence of nationalist myths, including the equation drawn between Jews and Communists, which the Nazis used as a fixed point in their propaganda campaigns. With respect to World War II, the commission highlighted the interval from 1940 to 1941, suggesting that the experience of two harsh occupations radicalized anti-Semitic sentiments and created an atmosphere in which latent hostilities assumed a new brutality, and thus new possibilities for violence arose on a previously unthinkable scale. In the crucible of war, the ICL asserted, Lithuanians were moved to murderous acts of violence, whereas they had previously been committed (or at least resolved) to coexistence with their Jewish neighbors. The overarching narrative presented by the ICL is one in which a young, unsteady democracy finds itself hijacked by two violent regimes whose influence corrupted the moral core of the Lithuanian nation to the point that its members carried out genocidal killings for which there was no historical precedent. Traditional anti-Semitism became something more monstrous in the context of the nation's existential crisis. Even if Lithuanian citizens participated in the near-extermination of the Jewish population, which the commission confirmed, they did so at a moment of profound disorientation when they were under assault from external forces whose brutality they felt compelled to mimic.

Rules and Procedures: Explanation or Exculpation?

Prior to releasing any reports, the ICL drafted detailed procedures to regulate its work.[15] In order to advance the project, Zingeris and co-chair Liudas Truska implemented an interesting procedure for managing the workflow. Individual historians were recruited (on the basis of their expertise) to complete research papers on specific topics relevant to the commission's mandate. These papers were then submitted to a panel of experts (typically four to six scholars) who each authored a short review of the original report, which they then forwarded to the full commission for a vetting process based on discussion, debate, and deliberation. At the end of this peer-review process, members of the commission drafted a summary, which was then put to a vote and either approved by the majority, in which case the document became an "official" finding, or rejected as invalid, in which case a new study might be requested from a different author. Members who chose not to support conclusions adopted by the majority were invited to express their views in a separate minority opinion, which also became part of the commission's official record. Although this mechanism suggests a strong commitment to multiperspectival history, in fact there are no examples of any dissenting views in the commission's online database.[16] While this does not invalidate the overall exercise, it represents a missed opportunity in light of the difficulties the commission encountered in the aftermath of the Arad affair. It is also worth noting that the online database includes several unapproved research reports, which the commission never managed to move through the full vetting process.

The online database provides a good glimpse into how the commission prioritized its research, even though the project was never completed. Of the fifty-five topics that the ICL identified for further study, thirteen relate to the Holocaust and the period of Nazi occupation (1941–44) and forty-two pertain to the two periods of Soviet occupation (1940–41 and 1944–90). One possible conclusion is that the experience of Soviet occupation represents a more significant psychological wound for the Lithuanian nation as a whole.[17] Not only did the second Soviet occupation last longer than the Nazi occupation (four and a half decades as opposed to three and a half years), but the terror imposed by the Soviets also impacted more Lithuanians than the Nazi genocide (tens of millions versus hundreds of thousands).[18] In other words, it is understandable that the ICL concentrated its efforts where popular opinion and collective memory were most deeply invested. On the other hand, the ICL devoted three of its eight major studies to the period of Nazi occupation. This reinforces the importance its members attached to the injustices perpetrated during this period. Even if the general public has been more concerned with the crimes that took place during the "last occupation" (i.e., 1944–90), the ICL made it clear that reckoning with the Holocaust entailed not only a moral obligation for the Lithuanian nation but also a necessary step toward political transition (democratization) and European integration. In this regard, it is highly significant that the commission's first chair, Emanuelis Zingeris, was the only Jewish member of Lithuania's parliament. It is also important to take stock of the liberal pedigree of the president (Valdas Adamkus) who created the commission.[19]

Adamkus and Zingeris undoubtedly recognized that an investigation of the Holocaust would provoke controversy on the domestic front. While a majority of surveyed Lithuanians (67 percent) expressed a desire to know an objective national history instead of a "prettified version" in polling conducted in September 2002, conservatives deeply resented the idea that their nation should feel guilty about some aspects of the past. When Algirdas Brauzauskas, Lithuania's first post-Soviet president, apologized in the Israeli Knesset in 1995 for the role that Lithuanians played in the Holocaust, public protests erupted at home. In the press, Brauzauskas was excoriated for having "humiliated himself unnecessarily."[20] It did not help matters that Brauzauskas also promised to revoke the blanket pardon that Lithuania's prosecutor-general extended in 1991 to Lithuanians accused of involvement in Nazi-era crimes. In his memoir, Brauzauskas recalled the apology and the controversy it spawned: "I did not want to keep to the ostrich policy while in the West the legal, moral, and economic issues of the Holocaust [were] solved."[21] His comment articulated the twin concerns of the moment (not just in Lithuania but across Eastern Europe), such as how to make amends for a repressed record of collaboration and how to perform penance publicly so as to secure an alignment with the liberal democratic West.

As talk of the presidential apology mixed with other issues related to Lithuania's Holocaust history,[22] a string of anti-Semitic editorials appeared in one of the nation's major newspapers (*Lietuvos Aidas*), prompting a lawsuit from the president's office, which charged the paper's publishers with inciting ethnic hatred.[23] While political elites strove to confront Lithuania's role in the Holocaust, broad segments of the population held fast to a narrative of victimization, causing consternation in the international community, where there was already a sense that the president's apology in 1995 did not have the support of Lithuanian society as a whole. Alfonsas Eidintas, a historian and intellectual who served diplomatic stints as Lithuania's ambassador to the United States and Israel, wrote of this divide between the elite and grassroots perspectives: "Lithuanians thought they [were] defending the honor of the assaulted motherland. . . . While politicians started to act in a determined way to erase a 'white spot' of history, it became clear that the wider society, alas, [was] still incapable of learning the facts about the Holocaust in Lithuania, to understand them and to feel the moral guilt of sorts for the deeds of the killers."[24] This rift became a permanent feature of the nation's public discourse, which the ICL, despite its best efforts, never managed to fully repair. On the one side, Westerners have been reluctant (or at least slow) to acknowledge the painful legacies of Lithuania's experience under Soviet rule. On the other side, the Lithuanian government has been so eager to bring attention to these crimes that they have sometimes missed opportunities to acknowledge the role that Lithuanians played in the Holocaust and in the mass shootings of Jews, for example, in the Ponary Forest near Vilnius.[25] This bifurcation of historical memory created and reflected a political impasse, which resulted in the de facto suspension of the ICL's work in 2007.

The Arad Affair

At the age of sixteen, a few days before Nazi troops liquidated the Jewish population in his village, Yitzhak Arad fled to the forest and joined the Soviet-led resistance in Lithuania. Unlike the vast majority of Lithuanian Jews, Arad survived the Holocaust and even fought the Nazi forces directly while fighting on the Soviet side. Following the war, Arad immigrated to Israel, where he completed his doctoral studies in history. His memoir, *The Partisan: From the Valley of Death to Mount Zion*, appeared in English in 1979 to great acclaim. On the basis of his academic achievements, Arad served from 1972 to 1993 as the director of Yad Vashem, Israel's official memorial to the Jewish victims of the Holocaust. Arad was not one of the ICL's original members, but he was recruited by Zingeris to boost the commission's profile abroad and to make sure that the perspective of Jewish victims would be fairly represented. He joined the commission as the official representative of Yad Vashem and participated until September 2007, when he suspended his membership amid allegations that he had committed war crimes against Lithuanian civilians while fighting with the Soviets in 1944.

The "affair" itself erupted when Lithuania's chief war crimes prosecutor, Rimvydas Valentukevicius, announced that his office would investigate Arad for crimes allegedly committed sixty-three years earlier in the course of fighting described in Arad's memoir. During what Arad described as a "punitive action," he and other Soviet-backed forest fighters burned Lithuanian civilians out of their homes in a reprisal attack aimed at punishing Nazi collaborators who had previously killed two of their comrades.[26] Valentukevicius, according to one report, used Arad's memoir to help build a case against the historian, just as he used other memoirs in subsequent investigations of Holocaust survivors.[27]

Until Valentukevicius began his investigation, Arad had participated on the ICL in the same capacity as its other members. The case against Arad took shape only after the ICL published an interim report in 2006 that provided a stark account of the role Lithuanians had played in the mass murder of Jews. Portions of Arad's memoir were reprinted in April 2006 in *Respublika* (Lithuania's second-largest daily paper) along with denunciations of him as a war criminal and murderer. Valentukevicius's investigation of Arad officially opened the following month. When asked whether the investigation owed anything to the media campaign against Arad, Rytas Narvydas, head of special investigations at the government research center charged with documenting war crimes and acts of genocide, acknowledged that the *Respublika* article had indeed been a factor. Asked whether anti-Semitic elements had attempted to manipulate the war crimes prosecutor's office, Narvydas admitted, "It does happen from time to time."[28] Malicious or not, the investigation led to Arad's withdrawal from the ICL (Sir Martin Gilbert also resigned in solidarity), and the affair, perhaps as intended, led the ICL to suspend its activities. Arad denied all of the prosecutor's allegations, saying the investigation was politically motivated. In an interview with *Rzeczpospolita*, Arad maintained, "I have never killed a civilian. It could have happened during battle, but I have never killed a civilian or a prisoner of war in cold blood."[29] Valentukevicius countered: "We have many documents which allow us to think Arad participated in criminal activities."[30]

Of course, there is always some latitude in what a person may reasonably think about the past, but Valentukevicius's determination to bring charges against Arad appears to be another attempt at conjuring the "parallel fates" narrative. In this case, Valentukevicius's tactics proved to be extremely damaging to Lithuania's global image. Lithuania's foreign affairs secretary, Oskaras Jusys, conceded as much in 2009, when he stated that the prosecutor's office had let itself be pushed around by "outside" elements and that there had been no basis for an investigation of Arad. "Their mistake was to go ahead without clear evidence," Jusys lamented.[31] He added that the case "created so much damage" for Lithuania, a reference to the statements of condemnation that poured in from the United States, the European Union, Israel, and the international Jewish community. In a letter copied to Secretary of State Hillary Clinton, five members of the U.S. House of Representatives wrote directly to Andrius Kubilius, Lithuania's prime minister, to express their concern over the attacks against Arad and other Lithuanian Holocaust survivors. "Investigations into Jewish resistance fighters under the accusation of war crimes charges," the letter read, "serve to discredit heroic Jewish resistance fighters, and create an imbalance in the public discourse over this painful era in a manner that diverts attention from efforts to bring those responsible for atrocities against Lithuanian Jews to justice."[32] The letter also raised "serious concerns about anti-Jewish sentiment in national media." Although the American lawmakers stopped short of a threat of sanctions, asking only for "assistance in helping us understand the sudden energetic pursuit of investigations into the activities of Jewish partisans," Jusys must have understood the implications.

After appealing to the prosecutor to drop the case against Arad (the case was closed in 2008 without any charges filed), Jusys expressed more frustration when other high-profile investigations were launched by the same office a short time later: "We have been able to clean one mess, and now other things are happening."[33] Jusys's comments show how the right to history has established itself as an emergent political norm. In an earlier era, Jusys could have responded with an argument based around national sovereignty. Judging the Lithuanian past would have been seen as an internal matter of absolutely no concern to outsiders, who could not appropriately judge the significance of events they did not experience. But the fact that Jusys recognized these historical debates as "a mess" signals that Lithuanian elites already accepted that the discourse of rights had globalized these conflicts and brought new actors into the conversation. To be sure, the right to history makes stonewalling and diversionary theater into matters of public record and global concern.

Gauging the ICL's Achievements

Like the IPN in Poland, the ICL was created to explore the legacies of three periods of totalitarian violence. But while Lithuanians were more interested in discovering the facts related to crimes of the two Soviet periods, Westerners were more concerned with the Nazi period and the history of the Holocaust. The involvement of outsiders necessitated a balancing act, which unfortunately led nationalist partisans back to the narrative of "double genocide" that the ICL was eager to dispel. Investigating Nazi and Soviet crimes helped the ICL establish partnerships with well-resourced research organizations, and it enabled Zingeris to stifle accusations of one-sidedness. But this division of labor also fed the relativism of Lithuania's apologists, who wanted to evade responsibility for past injustices against Jews and accentuate the suffering of their co-nationals. On the one hand, the ICL used a balanced approach to its advantage to probe highly controversial subjects, such as the role of Lithuanian mass media during the peak of anti-Jewish extermination efforts (summer and fall of 1941).[34] On the other hand, it proved difficult for the ICL to invoke Jewish suffering (or Lithuanian complicity) without provoking a backlash from partisans who rejected anything that tarnished the nation's image. This put the commission in an unwinnable position despite its well-intentioned effort to promote the right to historical knowledge alongside an obligation not to ignore or distort difficult chapters of history.

To the credit of its members, the ICL never shied away from the question of Lithuanian collaboration, which represented the main focus of its research on the Nazi period.[35] From the outset, its members and staff recognized that the biggest test of legitimacy would be the results of investigation into the events of the summer and fall of 1941. Speaking at Yad Vashem in 2002, Markas Zingeris, lead researcher for this part of the project, asked, "Will the Lithuanian public be prepared to accept the results of [our] work?" The Lithuanian media had become more educated on the subject since the presidential apology in 1995, but opinions in the street proved more stubborn. Zingeris remarked, "In view of this, the Commission's Secretariat has to invest a lot of energy into an educational effort, starting with the key thing: the education of educators."[36] To achieve this, the ICL sent Lithuanian teachers to the United States, where they worked with the New Jersey Commission on Holocaust Education.[37] These teachers were encouraged to continue their training through sponsored visits to Yad Vashem. Because Soviet-era censorship had instilled widespread ignorance on subjects related to Jewish history, the ICL also worked with publishers, nongovernmental organizations, and Holocaust and Jewish Studies programs at several Lithuanian universities to encourage new scholarship on topics related to the history of Lithuanian Judaica (including issues outside the scope of the Holocaust). Translations of foreign-language materials were commissioned to ensure that rigorous scholarship, as well as classic texts like *The Diary of Anne Frank*, would be available to students in the primary and secondary schools. The ICL also reached agreements with Lithuania's Ministry of Education and Science to make sure that teaching materials with notable omissions and mistakes were replaced with updated works. New textbooks and curricula, a new generation of teachers, and time—so very crucial in a country still influenced by Soviet-educated gerontocrats—were the commission's antidotes to the memory gaps and prejudices that permeated Lithuanian society. Unfortunately, economic uncertainty and social dislocation, which all of the postcommunist countries faced to different degrees during their transitions to democracy, offered fertile ground to right-wing groups eager to capitalize on the politicization of the past.

It is tempting to see the work of the ICL in a cynical light, given the pressure that countries in the former Soviet bloc faced following the collapse of communism. To perform a ritual of repentance and fall in line with the discourse of apology that their coveted allies in the West already embraced must have seemed a politically expedient course in 1998, even to the most fervent nationalist. From inside the ICL, the view was more idealistic. In 2002, Markas Zingeris emphasized that the ICL was not created to flatter diplomats in Brussels who held the keys to NATO and the European Union. Holocaust research and education, Zingeris stated, are not "like the bow-ties . . . required on formal occasions," but rather, are "an integral part of the education of modern citizenry."[38] The ICL could at least prove that Lithuanian society was not monolithic and that a change in mentality was possible, even if that change represented, for the time being, only a minority view. According to Zingeris, a nascent movement at home could bring Lithuanians at all levels of society over to the culture of contrition and inspire the collective soul-searching that Karl Jaspers and Theodor Adorno understood (in the German context) as fundamental to the achievement of historical justice and democracy. Unfortunately, the Arad affair cut the legs out from under that prospect. What I would emphasize, though, is the recognition, not only on the part of Zingeris but also in the upper echelons of political officialdom, that silence in the face of questions regarding Holocaust complicity was no longer a viable option, and that Lithuanian-Jewish relations had moved to the center of a larger discussion of Lithuania's international standing and democratic credentials. In other words, historical commissions do not necessarily have to succeed in an absolute sense for us to appreciate their significance as the bellwethers of a new politics.

But what should we make of the polarization between Lithuania's elites, who were committed to clarification and contrition, and the popular mainstream, where stereotypes and prejudices have continued to restrict critical thinking and moral judgment? Why has so little understanding trickled down to the grass roots? We can rehearse some of the ICL's conclusions here, since these are specific points of contention in the ongoing debates over Lithuania's past.

As previously stated, the ICL determined that Lithuania had a tradition of anti-Semitic prejudice, which extended back to the nineteenth century and found its basis of support in perceptions of deepening economic competition between the Jewish and non-Jewish communities.[39] The commission concluded that anti-Semitic prejudice in Lithuania took on a more virulent character in the interwar period as a result of deteriorating economic conditions caused by global economic downturn and the policies of Antanas Smetona's authoritarian government, which aided Lithuanian merchants who were happy to see their Jewish competitors reduced to insolvency. Despite rising tensions associated with anti-Semitic incidents from this era, the ICL found no evidence of any deaths stemming from pogroms prior to World War II. Relations between Lithuanians and Jews, according to the ICL, took a decisive and fateful turn in the first period of Soviet occupation (1940–41) as a new image of Jews as "the traitors of Lithuania" and "collaborators with the occupiers" permeated mainstream society. In this period, the ICL noted, the word "Jew" became synonymous with "Communist" despite the fact that "the number of Jewish members in the Communist Party was very insignificant compared to the total membership of the Lithuanian Jewish community."[40] As the ICL showed, membership in the Communist Party never rose above 0.28 percent of the total Jewish population in Lithuania, and the proportion of Jews among total party membership never exceeded 16.2 percent.[41] To put this into perspective, Jewish membership in the Communist Party during this period never exceeded 593 persons, while 99.72 percent of Lithuania's Jews chose not to join the party. Yet the myth of a Jewish-Communist nexus persists in Lithuania, as the Arad affair revealed. This says something potentially detrimental about the effectiveness of the historical commissions and their ability to overcome popular memory by means of truth-seeking and clarification. At the same time, based on the ICL's work until 2007, it is a mistake to say that there is no prospect of a mediating history here.

It may simply be too early to judge the outcome and ultimate effectiveness of the ICL's work. Zingeris has asked whether "five decades of Hitlerite indoctrination, suffocating Soviet silence, fact manipulation, [and] absence of open discussions" can be overcome in just one generation.[42] Referring to Czesław Miłosz's seminal book, Zingeris has written that educational advances in Lithuania are still thwarted at times by a "captive mind" syndrome. On the other hand, we risk making the Lithuanians into an exotic "other" if we persist in seeing them as unable to overcome habits of mind that make rational discourse persuasive. The facts on the ground are stark, but they can also be over-inflated. Zingeris has written of "dozens of anti-Semitic articles" published in the daily newspaper *Lietuvos Aidas* as new details from the Holocaust have come to light, and he has denounced the former mayor of Kaunas for a string of anti-Semitic outbursts he made in the run-up to his election in 1999.[43] Zingeris has also reported on public opinion polls that show Jews ranked at the bottom (with the Roma) on a list of nineteen ethnic groups in terms of public attitudes and perceptions.[44] Given such views, it is not surprising that the ICL failed to fully bridge the gap between public opinion in Lithuania and in the Western mainstream, where Holocaust denial and revisionism are regarded as outrageous, irresponsible, and even criminal. One can point to vandalized Holocaust monuments in Lithuania as evidence of deep-seated anti-Semitism—in July 2011, vandals spray-painted "Hitler was right" on a stone laid to honor the 72,000 Jews who were murdered in the Ponary forest near Vilnius—but events like this occur everywhere, including the West, where history, some would argue, has been confronted more openly. The ambiguity of these occurrences, their being simultaneously "isolated events" and the "tip of a much larger iceberg," is precisely what makes the historical commissions important. These commissions provide a forum in which national histories can be responsibly investigated without giving credence to the large-scale "ethnic identifiers" that deepen intergroup conflicts. The ICL has made it possible to trace the history of the Holocaust in Lithuania without reinforcing narratives that overstate the magnitude of Lithuanian complicity or take evidence of such collaboration as proof that Lithuanians orchestrated their own Holocaust, apart from Wannsee and the Nazis' Final Solution. As in other cases where Holocaust commissions have engaged the question of collaboration, complicity, and self-cleansing (e.g., Poland), the ICL has managed to show how local populations worked in support of the Nazi genocide without their being indistinguishable from or identical to the Nazi ideologues who laid the foundation for the killing and who mobilized the resources for it.

Partisan history continues to exert a strong hold in Lithuania. At the site of the Ninth Fort outside Kaunas, where approximately 9,000 Jews (half of whom were children) were shot and killed over the course of two days (October 28–29, 1941), a double memorial has been placed to commemorate both Nazi- and Soviet-era crimes.[45] The equation drawn between these two episodes and the notion that a "double genocide" unfolded in Lithuania both hinge upon the erasure of Lithuanian participation in the Holocaust. Without any direct reference to the role that Lithuanians played in the murder of Jews, the Ninth Fort memorial plaque identifies the killers only as Nazis and their assistants.[46] The plaque makes no mention of the five police companies that SS Colonel Jaeger assembled by drawing on the "reliable" elements among Lithuania's anti-Soviet partisans, nor does it provide details on the specific actions in which these Lithuanian units participated, events that Jaeger likened to "shooting in a parade."[47]

Even where the intention is not malicious, double genocides, as one writer has noted, rarely stay double for very long.[48] At the Museum of Genocide Victims in Vilnius, the entire exhibition space and all four of the museum's major collections are devoted to documenting "the physical and spiritual genocide of the Lithuanian people" during the fifty-year period of Soviet occupation. The Holocaust is not treated at all, not even as a wave of violence at the hands of German perpetrators. The museum is housed in a building once occupied by the KGB, so the focus on Soviet-era repressions is understandable to some degree, but the Holocaust's invisibility is disconcerting.[49] One of the preserved prison cells at the museum site features carved inscriptions made by individuals held there between 1941 and 1944 when the Gestapo used the building as a headquarters for its operations. The museum's curators refer to this interval as "one of the most dramatic" in the history of Lithuania, and while there is a brief mention in the museum's literature of the 200,000 Jews killed in Lithuania during the German occupation, there are no details regarding the circumstances under which these people were persecuted and killed, and no responsibility for the violence is designated. Instead, the Holocaust in

Lithuania is presented through the passive voice: "about 200,000 Jews were killed."[50]

To be fair, there is also a museum in Vilnius devoted to the history of Lithuanian Jewry and Judaica. The Vilna Gaon Jewish State Museum, established by order of the Lithuania Ministry of Culture in 1989, features permanent exhibitions on the history of Jewish life in Lithuania, the experience of the Holocaust, and the commemoration of Lithuanian rescuers, who risked their lives to save Jews. Currently under the direction of Markas Zingeris, the museum also speaks directly to the issue of "Lithuanian partisans" and the role these individuals played in the genocide. In an exhibit titled "Katastrofa" (Catastrophe), which treats the rise and annihilation of Litvak civilization, placards assert that Holocaust victims in Lithuania were murdered "by their neighbors, . . . their schoolmates, coworkers, or patients."[51] The museum also deals with the delicate issue of Jewish-Soviet cooperation. Because some Jews considered the Soviet regime to be the "lesser of two evils" and because the Soviets allowed Jews a place in their bureaucratic structure (a role the Lithuanian state did not offer them at that time), an unspecified number of Lithuanian Jews, according to the museum's literature, aligned themselves with the Soviet order. The result, according to the museum's literature, was an intensification of the bias against Jews among Gentiles who were "already negatively predisposed toward them."[52] The Catastrophe exhibit goes on to explain that the first anti-Jewish pogroms took place in Lithuania before the arrival of German forces and that these episodes were typically perpetrated by "local thugs and fascists," many of whom were subsequently recruited by the Nazis as they strove to accelerate the extermination of Jews and other "undesirable elements." In Kaunas, in the largely Jewish suburb of Slobodka, the museum's organizers use German testimonies to document the unprovoked slaughter of 1,500 Jewish residents (June 25, 1941) at the hands of their neighbors, noting that the homes of victims were systematically plundered at the conclusion of the killing.[53] In short, the Jewish State Museum documents indigenous anti-Semitism and genocidal violence, all of which are consistent with the reports produced by the ICL. However, while the museum appears to be a public outreach effort on the part of the commission, there are several things to consider here that put the museum in a clearer light.

First, many of the museum's exhibition materials were created by Holocaust survivors themselves rather than by a professional curatorial staff. Maps, memoirs, and book excerpts have been combined in a decidedly "low-tech" approach to historical representation that strives for authenticity over slick stylization. This approach has been consciously fostered in order to encourage visitors to confront the individual dimensions of the tragedy. The museum's exhibits are meant to stand as a testament to the survival of the few and as testimony to the annihilation of the many. One of the museum's cofounders and a principal creator of its exhibition materials, Dr. Rachel Margolis, was awarded a certificate of appreciation in 2005 by Lithuania's prime minister Algirdas Brauzauskas for her contributions to the anti-Nazi struggle during World War II. Despite receiving this award, Lithuanian police in 2007 questioned Margolis, whose entire family was killed in the Holocaust, as a potential witness in the war crimes case that state prosecutors were pursuing at the time against Yitzhak Arad.[54] Margolis eventually left Lithuania for Israel, citing fear of media and police harassment. Her name is listed (with Arad and Fania Brantsovsky) in the letter that U.S. congressional representatives sent to Vilnius in 2009 to protest investigations into the wartime activities of Jewish partisans and the "imbalance in public discourse" over atrocities and war crimes committed during the Nazi and Soviet occupations.[55] Lauded by the prime minister in 2005 for the role she played in the anti-Nazi Resistance, by 2008 Margolis no longer felt safe enough to continue living in Lithuania and, given her age, will likely spend the remainder or her life in exile. As with Arad, her own memoir was used by the state prosecutor to build a case against her.[56] Margolis and Arad are now the symbols of Lithuania's contested history and the political vicissitudes of historical clarification. Distortion and minimization of Nazi-era collaboration on the part of some Lithuanians has created an atmosphere in which national heroes can be investigated for treason and the desecration of Jewish monuments is made to seem trivial or even natural. While the ICL can be credited with having initiated an important dialogue on the past, one that perhaps opens the door to the possibility of Jewish-Lithuanian reconciliation at some point in the future, we should be realistic regarding the commission's record of translating empirical gains into public understanding.

Following the desecration of two important sites of Jewish memory and mourning in Lithuania in 2011, the Yale historian Timothy Snyder wondered why these attacks did not produce an international scandal like the theft of the *Arbeit macht frei* sign from the gates of Auschwitz had in 2009. The answer would tell us a great deal about the absence of an effective mediating history in the former case. It would also serve as a reminder that the right to history asserts itself as both universal and indivisible. We ask a great deal from Lithuanians when we press them to confront the history of the Holocaust more openly, while, at the same time, Russians at both the elite and grass-roots levels continue to describe in terms of "liberation" what the Lithuanians experienced as "occupation" and "genocide." Westerners looking for more historical openness from Lithuanians would do well to remember the locales in Lithuania where more people were killed after VE day than during World War II.[57]

While this fact does not eliminate the responsibility of the Lithuanian government to more fully engage the history of the Holocaust and to seek justice on behalf of its victims, it does explain, at least in part, the difficulties that Lithuanians have had in doing so.

Latvia and the Desire for a "European Discourse"

The Commission of the Historians of Latvia (CHL) was established on November 13, 1998, at the behest of President Guntis Ulmanis.[58] Ulmanis convened the CHL in response to international pressure over Latvia's perceived unwillingness to openly confront the past and the Holocaust in particular.[59] Originally comprised of eleven historians from various state and local institutions, the CHL grew to include twenty-four members, including twelve who were recruited from outside the country. The principal task of the commission was to investigate crimes against humanity committed during the Soviet and Nazi occupations. The CHL chose not to adopt formal rules of procedure like the Lithuanian commission had, but it organized its work along similar lines.[60] The CHL broke itself into four subgroups working under the following categories: (1) Soviet Occupation, 1940–41; (2) German Occupation, 1941–45; (3) The Holocaust in the Territory of Latvia, 1941–45; and (4) The Soviet Occupation from 1944/45–91.[61] When the commission's initial term expired in 2001, President Vaira Vike-Freiberga granted an extension, which she renewed twice more in 2004 and in 2007. In 2009, under significant pressure to stabilize the nation's economy, the Latvian government cut off funding for the CHL, resulting in the cessation of its major activities.[62] From 1998 to 2009, the CHL published twenty-five volumes and hosted several international conferences aimed at fostering a multilateral discourse on Latvian history and the wartime experience, the "time of troubles." Although these exchanges did not always succeed in harmonizing the perspectives of Latvian and international scholars, the CHL brought to light a variety of new archival materials and can be credited with significant fact-finding.[63] As with the ICL in Lithuania, the legacy of the CHL appears to be mixed. The commission explored the issue of Latvian collaboration with the Nazi regime and the role of Latvians in the mass killings of Jews in a mostly productive (though not always consistent) manner, and Westerners who participated in the project were better able to appreciate the depth and scope of the Soviet-era atrocities suffered by the Latvian people. But the CHL also fell short of its ultimate goal of taming disagreements over the past and stemming conflicts over the details and meaning of recent historical events. At the conclusion of its work, there was still a sense among Westerners that Latvian scholars were unwilling to acknowledge the full extent to which their countrymen cooperated in the Nazi genocide, and relations between Latvia and Russia were unsettled by the refusal in Moscow to accept the Latvian perspective on the Soviet period. Disagreements within the Latvian commission on crucial questions of context and responsibility led its members to sidestep the kinds of debates that mediating history must engage unflinchingly in order to ameliorate intergroup conflict. With the CHL, we get a narrative that is multivocal but also cacophonous and contradictory. Normally considered one of the virtues of truth-seeking commissions, the desire to bring together disparate voices and perspectives resulted in the CHL losing momentum and winding down its work in 2009 with more of a whimper than a bang.

Two events, in particular, provide a gauge of the overall significance of the CHL's work. The first of these was the publication of the CHL's fourteenth symposium volume in 2005.[64] Compiled by the members of the commission and introduced by Valters Nollendorfs and Erwin Oberländer, volume 14 was significant, first of all, because it attempted to summarize all of the commission's work up to that point. It also revealed the ways in which lack of internal consensus and consistency undermined the overarching goals of the commission. The second key event for understanding the CHL's mixed legacy was the international scholars' conference, which the CHL hosted in 2009 on the subject of "Occupation, Collaboration, Resistance: History and Perception." According to Oberländer, the conference was an attempt to bring together three separate memories of World War II: the Western memory, which emphasized Nazi aggression and the Holocaust; the Russian memory, built on a narrative touting victory and liberation; and the Eastern European/Baltic memory, which revolved around the experience of "double genocide" and dual dictatorship.[65] Although the conference attempted to consolidate these memories, the "honest desire to understand" on the part of its participants did not translate into effective mediation.

The CHL published volume 14 under the title *The Hidden and Forbidden History of Latvia under Soviet and Nazi Occupations 1940–1991* in 2005.[66] This was an attempt by the commission to encapsulate its prior findings and present them to an English-speaking audience. Nollendorfs and Oberländer, the volume's editors, stated that the primary objective for this study was "to start developing a historical discourse that accounts for the real victims and the actual perpetrators of both occupations."[67] The idea was to foster an exchange on key topics related to the "time of troubles," that is, the 1940s, when Latvians experienced intense social disorientation and brutal violence. These topics included the illegality of the Soviet occupation in 1940; the Holocaust in Latvia and the role of local populations; the participation of Latvians in the German military (e.g., interpreting source materials concerning the creation of the so-called Latvian SS); the mass deportation of Latvian nationals during the Soviet occupation and the question of whether these amounted to genocide; and the more general problem of defining and characterizing acts of resistance and collaboration under foreign occupation and domination. The editors expressed hope that their project would be viewed as an effort to "set the historical record straight after so much deliberate concealment and manipulation of historical facts," but they also noted that "the opinions expressed and the conclusions reached by the individual authors are their own."[68]

This last line sounds like tired "legalese" in the ears of Westerners. It is the kind of thing one expects to hear when tuning in for a controversial radio broadcast or at the outset of certain cable-access shows, wherein the host wants to have a lively exchange of viewpoints, but the station carrying the broadcast does not wish to have any legal responsibility for the actual content. For a commission aiming at historical mediation, this kind of distancing maneuver is unfortunate. It allows the commission to disavow the work and findings of its members, when doing so would be politically advantageous or helpful for avoiding the fallout generated by specific interpretations. Certainly, disagreement can have a useful role within the historical commission framework. In the bilateral commissions that are examined in part II of this study, agreeing to disagree can sometimes be the only practical way forward and the only way to keep the project from exacerbating the conflicts these commissions aim to ameliorate. Disagreement and contradiction become more problematic, however, when commissions allow these discursive breakdowns to occupy the center of their work, which unfortunately is what happened in the case of the CHL, as a close reading of volume 14 reveals.

In an introductory chapter contributed by commission member Alfred Erich Senn, titled "Baltic Battleground," the author endeavors to provide an overview of the Baltic experience from 1940 to 1991. He also focuses on specific questions and issues, including the belief, still common among Latvians today, that Jews in Latvia were closely aligned with the first Soviet occupation and that their actions in 1940–41 represented an overt attempt to destroy the Latvian nation. Senn writes that Jews, particularly young males, were overrepresented in the Soviet apparatus that took control of Latvia after June 1940 and that Jews who supported the new regime—many did not, as Senn also points out—gained "an unprecedented prominence in public life in all three [Baltic] Soviet republics."[69] It is for this reason, Senn continues, that Latvians in the summer of 1941 attacked civilians, including Jews, who were thought to have supported the Soviets during the preceding year. "In all three republics," Senn writes, "local activists attacked retreating Soviet troops, and the violence also targeted civilians identified with the Soviet regime. *This demand for vengeance quickly led to a wave of mass killings of Jews regardless of age or sex.*"[70] Here, Senn lays out essentially the same narrative that Jan Gross tried to dispel in *Neighbors*, his exploration of the Jedwabne massacre (1941) in Poland.[71] For Senn, violence perpetrated by local populations in the East is understandable (though still abhorrent) given the realities of Jewish cooperation with the Soviets. Senn never says that the national majorities in Latvia (or elsewhere in the region) were right to defend themselves in this way, but he asserts that the violence they committed against Jewish civilians is understandable in light of specific events that unfolded earlier. Senn quotes Azreal Schochat on the history of Lithuania: "The special ferocity which the population demonstrated toward Lithuanian Jews during the Holocaust was undoubtedly the outcome of the very complex political situation created by the Soviet occupation in 1940 and 1941." He then generalizes this principle to explain attacks against Jews elsewhere in the region: "The Soviets had disrupted the old social order and had raised the level and expectations of violence in all three Baltic republics."[72]

Although this is controversial, given its resemblance to the "Jewish-Communist Nexus" myths that took hold in the Baltic states and Eastern Europe, Senn's narrative is not immediately problematic insofar as the legitimacy and authority of the CHL are concerned. One might quibble over the numbers he cites to prove Jewish enthusiasm for the Bolshevik takeover, but his arguments spring from legitimate sources and his interpretations, even if they are limited in their scope, still fall within the realm of rationality. But if Senn's argument passes muster on its own, there is still reason to be concerned with the way it compares to statements made by other members of the CHL.

In a subsequent chapter in the same collection (vol. 14), Aivars Stranga, who chaired the CHL's subcommittee on the Holocaust in Latvia, arrives at a starkly different conclusion regarding the same historical episode. While Stranga acknowledges that the Holocaust represents "the gravest crime in the modern history of Latvia," he also asserts that Latvians undertook no spontaneous (i.e., self-initiated) actions against Jews.[73] In fact, Stranga maintains that no pogroms took place during the interregnum (the stretch of days or weeks, depending on location, between the first Soviet occupation and the installation of the German regime) and that there were no mass killings of Jews conducted by Latvians in this period.[74] Stranga records occurrences of "brutal humiliation" and looting of Jewish properties, but he contends there were no genocidal campaigns and "no spontaneous terror" at that time.[75] When genocidal killing began a short time later, Stranga says, these were "initiated and administered by the Germans, though they tried to make it look like a local enterprise."[76] Stranga focuses on the role played by Einsatz-gruppe A of the German security apparatus SD (Sicherheitsdienst), the organization that, in his view, was directly responsible for "the implementation of the Holocaust in the Baltic."[77]

This instance of contradiction, that is, Senn and Stranga taking mutually opposed and irreconcilable stances on the same events, compromises the efficacy of the CHL's project. To be clear, Stranga does not deny that Latvians participated in the mass killing of Jews. He explains in detail how Latvian Self-Defense Units (Selbstschutz) and Auxiliary Police Units (Hilfspolizei) took part in executions that claimed tens of thousands of Jewish victims.[78] He also describes how Latvian auxiliary SD forces, including the notorious Arājs Commando, cooperated with German units in some of the worst instances of violence.[79] But according to Stranga, these were not the Latvian partisans who had earlier formed their own paramilitary units. Those units, he writes, "never took part in the annihilation of the Jews," having been disarmed by the Germans upon their arrival in July 1941. Stranga never discusses whether the same individuals from these paramilitaries later ended up in the units that participated in the killing of Jews, since this is extraneous to the point he wants to make: that Latvian units, which played a role in the Holocaust, were "formed and controlled by the Germans."[80] This is a starkly different account compared to what Senn offers on the period of interregnum: "Anti-Soviet emotions exploded in a bloodlust intensified by Nazi-inspired images of frightened 'Jewish-Bolsheviks' running to escape popular retribution."[81] One can fall back here on the editors' disclaimer that opinions expressed in the CHL's report are merely those of the individual authors and do not represent the commission's official view, but this forfeits any possibility for a mediating history that engages but also overcomes ideological differences that produce different interpretations of the same events. In their introduction, the editors point out how the Holocaust had become a "zone of disagreement and turbulence" for the members of their commission, and they describe how the persistence of mythologies from the Nazi and Soviet periods have proven resilient to the mediating exercises they hoped to encourage.[82] They point out, rightly, that historical mediation requires time and commitment, and that the contradictions embodied in the current report, which was published in 2005, might be regarded as a useful starting point for future discussion. "Once [the] ideological causes are understood, it should be possible to start developing a historical discourse that accounts for the real victims and the actual perpetrators of both occupations. This, we hope, is only the beginning of such a discourse."[83] Unfortunately, when we look ahead to the projects that the CHL undertook in the next phase of its work (2005–9), we see that the debate over Holocaust history in Latvia remains deeply polarized and that conflicts over the "time of troubles" have hardly abated and, in some cases, have even intensified.

In her review (2007) of the CHL's summary report, Eva-Clarita Pettai comments that the Latvian commission "speaks with many voices."[84] She does not say whether this represents one of its virtues or one of its shortcomings, although she does ask whether the commission needs to achieve "a unified version of the past" in order to succeed. The lesson here is that "multivocality" cuts two ways. While there can be benefits to a narrative that speaks with many voices, contravening memories can also harden over time. When they do, prospects for a mediating history are greatly diminished. If ambiguities in the source material make it difficult for commissions to support a definitive position, these need to be aired fully and probed in a spirit of good faith (in other words, teach the debate). But where commission members remain divided over how to interpret the same events and source materials, there does need to be some principle of adjudication. This highlights the importance of having clear procedural guidelines, like those adopted by the ICL in Lithuania. Although "proceduralism" may be used as a strategy for avoiding or obscuring controversy, it is essential that mediating history does not dive into an epistemological abyss, where nothing can be said with confidence and every claim about the past is equally valid. In cases where the attempt at clarification leaves the commission deadlocked, and mutually exclusive interpretations of the same events remain on the table, majority and minority perspectives will need to be spelled out and a decision made at the level of officialdom (e.g., at the executive or parliamentary level).[85] The force of history ultimately depends on the belief that social scientific methodologies can be applied in ways that limit subjectivity and offer us something true. As nothing can be both itself and not itself at the same time, intellectual discrepancies like the one between Senn and Stranga need to be resolved; otherwise, history will be regarded as merely a branch of literature. Of course, commissions must guard against the formulations that reinforce stereotypes and ideologically driven myths. But pulling punches, as the CHL appeared to when its project leaders claimed no official adherence to the conclusions of its members—is not consistent with successful mediation. Just as it is possible to be "almost too politically contentious," which is how Pettai characterizes the CHL's summary report, it is also possible to be overly capacious.[86] Historical commissions can stumble into both errors at the same time. Whether this requires that commissions put specific issues to a vote and apply the principle of "majority rules" or postpone the publication of an official report until their members are closer to reaching some consensus, a mediating history cannot emerge where there is merely repetition of the same fixed and divergent points. Before budget cuts and concerns over the consequences of a stalemate forced its suspension in 2009, this is the kind of holding pattern in which the CHL found itself.

One of the last undertakings for the CHL before it dissolved was an international conference on "Occupation, Collaboration, and Resistance."[87] As they had for previous events, the organizers stressed a desire for dialogue between Latvian scholars and researchers traveling to Riga from other countries. Erwin Oberländer, one of the organizers, hoped that the event would foster a "broad multilateral discourse marked by an honest desire to understand and to respect the historical memories of others and thus prevent them from being exploited and used to spread new political disagreements and conflicts among nations."[88] Notwithstanding this admirable statement of purpose, the conference produced a far less noble outcome.[89] Discussions that began on a sober note escalated into emotional debates, often as the result of some inflammatory question or comment from the audience, and attempts at calm explanation devolved into accusations of either naïve or willful misunderstanding. As one conference participant put it: "It seemed like a dialogue of the deaf: Western scholars were eager to step beyond the historical details of particular events and developments to draw comparative conclusions from Western and Eastern European experiences with totalitarian occupation, while Latvian historians continued to stress (and defend) the historical uniqueness of their country's experience and refuse[d] to engage in comparative efforts. Moreover, they more or less openly implied a lack of historical understanding or even a deliberate ignorance of the Latvian experience on the part of their non-Latvian colleagues."[90] What makes this description so disheartening is the resemblance it bears to the "irresponsible history" described in the introduction to this study.[91] With the CHL, the problem is not so much an explicit intention to deceive as it is a question of negligence, that is, the Latvian and non-Latvian sides neglecting to consider the harmful effects of their own recalcitrance. Where historical accounts have been carefully researched and written and there is a commitment to methodological integrity, there is also a responsibility to enter into dialogue on a good-faith basis. In the historical discourse, the moral duty to be honest is mirrored by the duty to take seriously the experiences and memories of others. This does not simply mean that we must try to put ourselves in the other person's shoes (although empathy matters a great deal). It means that there is a way to disagree over the meaning of facts that strikes a balance between the needs and values of the parties who are at odds. Of course, historians must honor the core commitments of their discipline, so there is no chance of our arriving at the dangerous conclusion that "anything goes." But I assert that it is possible, given enough time and the proper framework for negotiation, for these dialogues to lead gradually to new ways of seeing the past. This is what makes the historical commission model potentially so useful. One can emphasize the importance of the process where the results have been disappointing, but this is also convenient rhetoric for commission members who have let their hard work overshadow the necessity of further refining the process of mediation.[92] Where they exist, even momentarily, possibilities for reconciliation need to be exploited. Although intergroup conflicts may take generations to resolve, false starts toward reconciliation and new exchanges of the same old accusations can be more damaging than quiet biding of time.

Part II

Bilateral and International Commissions

5

Germany and
Its Neighbors

Despite not having a single, comprehensive policy to regulate its relations with neighboring states, Germany has made reconciliation a major plank in its post–World War II foreign policy. While soldiers and civilians often sought to avoid public discussions of war guilt in the immediate aftermath of VE Day, the government of the Federal Republic quickly developed a policy aimed at reconciliation with former adversaries following Germany's partition in 1949. Since then, Germany's reconciliation plans have sometimes aimed at purely pragmatic ends, as in the case of the Schuman Plan (1950) and the creation of the European Coal and Steel Community. In other instances, most notably the decision to pay restitution to Israel, German reconciliation appeared to encompass both pragmatic and idealistic aspirations. In Germany and Western Europe more generally, the lowering of the Iron Curtain played a crucial role in fostering cooperation among neighbors, but at the same time there was a deeper realization, dating back to the interwar period, that Europe's future prospects depended on taming the imperial ambitions and political ideologies that spawned two horrific wars in a single generation. Over the course of the next fifty years, rising Franco-German reconciliation (and the project of European integration that it enabled) became the example par excellence of modern nation-states putting aside their past differences and steering away from a cycle of conflict for the sake of future generations, but Germany also built important bridges to the East, particularly with respect to Poland and the Czech Republic. Rapprochement at times flowed from the highest levels of executive power. Konrad Adenauer, West Germany's first chancellor, worked directly with Charles de Gaulle to broker the Élysée Treaty in 1963, which set up regular summits between the two countries for the purposes of bolstering joint security and fostering economic and cultural development. Two decades later, Helmut Kohl and François Mitterrand joined hands on the Verdun battlefield in 1984 to commemorate the losses suffered there on both sides during World War I. Perhaps the most famous example of a head of state promoting reconciliation, however, was Willy Brandt's kneeling gesture at the Warsaw Ghetto in 1970 to ask forgiveness from the Poles for Germany's occupation crimes. While it oversimplifies the postwar era to put it so plainly, there is some truth to the notion that today's European Union stands on these kinds of gestures and diplomatic initiatives. They are the expressions and the building blocks of what some have called "Europe's common DNA."[1]

Below the executive level and farther away from state power, other initiatives have also contributed positively to reconciliation between Germany and its neighbors. Since the 1970s, and especially during the past ten years, German historians and history educators have participated in a number of bilateral textbook commissions, which have engaged some of the most contentious legacies of World War I. While these bodies are obviously not the same (in terms of their structure, mission, and output) as the government-appointed commissions analyzed in chapters 1–4, both share a common idea that the past can be utilized for peace. In this chapter I take up three examples of bilateral historical commissions that emerged through nongovernmental channels but still opened the way for important discussions of reconciliation at the national level.

Germany and France:
From Hereditary Enemies to Partners

At war three times between 1870 and 1940, and pitted against each other in the third instance in what was commonly understood as an epic battle between the forces of civilization and barbarism, Germany and France, for most of the nineteenth and early twentieth centuries, seemed locked in a permanent battle for supremacy. The Franco-German rivalry, in fact, stretched back much farther than 1870, to the dissolution of Charlemagne's empire in the Middle Ages and to the ancient feuds fought between pre-Roman tribes. By the 1900s, this tradition of hostility led many to see the modern states of France and Germany as "hereditary enemies." Owing to its brutality and unprecedented scale, World War I led broad swaths of the French and German populations to favor a reset of relations, but even as many millions in the 1920s took up the cry of "No more war!" and statesmen attempted to create a framework of treaties geared toward stabilizing post-Versailles Europe, by the early 1930s circumstances had undermined the efforts to secure peace. In the span of seven years, France and Germany went from cosponsoring the Kellogg-Briand Pact (1928), which renounced war as an instrument of state policy, to contemplation of and preparation for yet another war, following Germany's withdrawal from the League of Nations (1933) and Hitler's decision to nullify the Treaty of Versailles (1935). By 1939–40, the two "hereditary enemies" were once again on a war footing.

As Europeans prepared for war following Germany's invasion of Poland, it is doubtful whether anyone could have imagined the ways in which the coming conflict would, ultimately, drive Europe toward integration or the degree to which the continent would be politically and economically interconnected before the end of the century. In May 1945, with fifty to sixty million dead, mountains of rubble in the place of beloved cultural monuments, armies of occupation arrayed across the continent, and hunger pressing down on the civilian population, the idea of a Franco-German friendship treaty would have seemed absurd to most, and it would have been pointless (or offensive) to talk about history as an instrument for nurturing cooperation and understanding. Just six years later, however, historians and teachers from both France and Germany drafted a diplomatic document based on a shared history of their mutual rivalry and a deeply held belief that scholastic history instruction must overcome the national perspectives that had made social memory a source of conflict for previous generations.[2] This moment in 1951 had its own history, and it provided a foundation for a more recent bilateral textbook project geared toward cultural negotiation of the past.

In 2003, at a Youth Congress held in Berlin to celebrate the fiftieth anniversary of the Élysée Treaty, 550 high school students from France and Germany drafted a set of resolutions aimed at deepening reconciliation between their countries. Among their recommendations was a proposal for a jointly written history course book, which French and German pupils would study in their own languages, but whose content would be the same otherwise. Such a project, the students felt, would help to expose and overcome the negative preconceptions and stereotypes that the two populations still held regarding each other. Unique in its concrete aspects and envisioned outcome, if not necessarily in its overarching sentiment, the students' proposal was quickly endorsed by President Jacques Chirac and Chancellor Gerhard Schröder. Within six months of drafting the resolution, a Franco-German project team was assembled, and publishers were secured in both countries to produce a three-volume history of Europe, spanning from antiquity to the present. The team was comprised of seventeen authors, seven French and ten German. Guillam Le Quinrec

(France) and Peter Geiss (Germany) directed the work and oversaw the writing. Working in French-German pairs, team members started with the most recent history, which they organized in a separate volume (2006) covering 1945 to the present. Next, the team worked through what was considered the most contentious material, the history of the modern period, from 1815 (the Congress of Vienna) to 1945. This volume (2008) covered not only the two world wars but also the Franco-Prussian War (1870–71), which many saw as paving the way to the Great War in 1914, and the aftermath of the Napoleonic Wars, which some viewed as the catalyst for the rise of aggressive nationalism during the next one hundred years. The team concluded the project in 2011 with a study of Europe from antiquity to 1814, a long span they saw as being less politically charged than the rest of the work. Described by one reviewer as "the world's most adventurous history textbook project" and as a pedagogical tool that produced an important shift "from nation-centered history education to international understanding and reconciliation,"[3] the joint textbook series appeared under the title *Histoire/Geschichte* and captured significant media attention when the first volume appeared in May 2006.[4]

Volume 3 (Europe after 1945) was the first in print and was greeted with high praise by the two governments, whose leaders hailed the work as "symbolically sealing Franco-German reconciliation."[5] In media interviews that touched on the mechanics of the writing process, the authors described a series of free-flowing discussions, which only occasionally became heated and in which individual word choices often became the subject of lively debate. At the end of these discussions, the two sides normally arrived at a single formula, which they considered to be a "balanced" narrative. Where their divergences could not be mediated, the authors agreed to highlight these differences and discuss them directly in the text. For example, in their treatment of the role of the United States in postwar Europe, the German authors found their French counterparts to be unjustifiably "anti-American," while the French writers saw too much enthusiasm for the Americans on the German side and uncritical acceptance of American policies. This difference of perspective is noted in both editions of the course book without any attempt to adjudicate between the two.[6] Instead, the subject is presented as opening the way to a legitimate debate, which can bring into view the political prejudices and assumptions of the students who engage it. Students are encouraged to use these materials for the purpose of sharpening their critical thinking skills.

There are also some noteworthy discrepancies between the French and German editions, despite the original intention of publishing identical textbooks. One analysis suggests that 80 percent of the content of volume 3 is shared in the French and German editions.[7] The remaining sections either treat different subject matter (e.g., the German edition has a detailed section on the German Democratic Republic [GDR], which is sharply abbreviated in the French edition), or they treat the same topics in different ways. For example, where the authors deal with the victims of Nazi racial persecution and the Holocaust, the German edition cites six million Jewish victims and 500,000 Gypsy victims. In the corresponding section, the French version provides significantly lower figures: five million Jewish victims and 200,000 Gypsy victims.[8] Unlike other discrepancies, which are highlighted for further discussion, this potentially "teachable moment" receives no further comment. The authors do not to expand on the difficulties of making precise estimates based on ambiguous source materials or on the political pressures Germany faces to accept the highest estimates. Despite these occasional incongruities, however, the two sides were optimistic about their work and its potential impact in the classroom. Government officials also described the project in highly favorable terms. Speaking at the textbook's release party, which took place at a World War I museum near Somme, France's education minister emphasized the potential to transform international relations by contemplating the past through a shared lens: "The great lesson of this story is that nothing is set in stone; antagonisms that we believe are inscribed in marble are not eternal."[9] Except for a small number of especially contentious items, like the role of the United States in European affairs, the authors of *Histoire/Geschichte* found it relatively easy to overcome the partisan perspectives that characterized the "nation-centered" textbooks already available in the scholastic market. Where the two sides differed, their disagreements usually centered on questions of methodology or on how to balance different approaches to history (i.e., social, diplomatic, economic, cultural, etc.). In the few cases where there was sharp disagreement over specific content or how to address specific questions (e.g., regarding historical causality and responsibility for conflict), the authors understood these as particularly valuable opportunities for intellectual exploration. As Peter Geiss, the chief writer for the German side, explained: "You always have two views, at least two views, and that allows pupils to develop their own standpoint, their own image of history. . . . That's very useful within democratic and liberal teaching of history. One needs to know others' points of view and think of the history of one's [own] nation in that way."[10] Geiss's statement encapsulates the raison d'être of the larger project. His comments reveal the authors' firm belief that twenty-first-century citizenship requires self-interrogation, empathic identification with out-groups (as construed by the nation-centered perspective), and a willingness to examine one's own conclusions within a larger framework of interpretative possibilities. Geiss's statement also reflects the team's belief that historical clarity can arise only where groups accept their role and responsibility for past injustices. As one of the French writers put it, "It is only when each national side has the courage to reveal the dark sides of its own national history, as it happened, that work on the joint history textbook becomes possible."[11]

Notwithstanding Geiss's enthusiasm for the inclusion of multiple "points of view," the joint textbook presents some difficult questions regarding the limits of historical interpretation and the subjectivity of historical sources. Even as the publishers of *Histoire/Geschichte* touted their project as helping to launch a revolution in educational policy and history pedagogy, others criticized the project and its authors for undermining the epistemological framework of the social sciences and encouraging postmodern relativism. The second volume, in particular, which covers the long nineteenth century and the two world wars, provoked criticism from some reviewers who felt that excessive attention to methodological questions would lead students into a nihilistic black hole, where the authority of well-vetted evidence is never fully accepted and reasoned argument is regarded as little more than isolated opinion. In an extended review of volumes 1 and 2, which appears on the website for the European Association of History Educators, Wojciech Roszkowski disparaged the authors of *Histoire/Geschichte* for "mak[ing] the student think that reaching the truth is harder than it really is."[12] According to Roszkowski, the joint textbook promotes independent thinking without giving students the necessary grounding in the facts, and it leads to overly general conclusions that do not reflect all of the available evidence. Coverage of interwar politics, Roszkowski contends, fails to consider "the most basic differences between authoritarian and totalitarian systems." Volume 2 depicts the retreat from democracy during the interwar period as a pan-European scourge, but the authors do not indicate how this trend manifested differently in different settings. As a result, students have no way to differentiate between (to take one example) the politics of Józef Piłsudski in Poland and the rise of Hitlerism in Germany. These two countries are presented as having gone down similar, if not identical, paths, whereas nothing, Roszkowski insists, could be farther from the truth. For Roszkowski, this is not simply a mistake of degrees but rather a willful misconstrual of the facts, which results from the authors' desire to delegitimate and blot out national differences. According to Roszkowski, there is a "leftist ideological tone" throughout *Histoire/Geschichte*, which improperly suppresses national feelings and discourages what he calls "natural and valuable attachment to one's own . . . community."[13] Instead of an objective account in which each conclusion is firmly grounded in fact, "the intention of creating common Franco-German memory has become all the world to the authors."[14] Political correctness, Roszkowski concludes, has driven the authors to give a lopsided presentation in which their own political predilections overshadow historical truth. Regarding the changing role of women in society, Roszkowski asks, why not also give some space to the "negative results"? And on religious life, which Roszkowski equates with the rise of "aggressive atheism," what about examples like Italy and Poland, which challenge the authors' contention that "secularization is inevitable and irreversible."

It would be easy to dismiss Roszkowski as a conservative crank and read his review of *Histoire/Geschichte* as one more salvo in the long-running "culture war," but he is correct (to a degree) about the intrusion of politics into history. This obviously does not validate his claim regarding the "negative effects" of feminism, nor does it support his contention that *Histoire/Geschichte* suffers from "scandalous deficiencies." But even if we regard his review as a clumsy attempt at political usurpation, Roszkowski's rhetoric should alert us to the danger of reactivating the partisan perspectives that mediating history seeks to overcome. By entering into the political fray, historical commissions can unintentionally amplify the discontents of globalization. Historical commissions will not be able to perform their mediating role effectively if their interventions are viewed, across the board, as detrimental to the advancement of knowledge. Even if the authors of *Histoire/Geschichte* would like to shrug off Roszkowski's criticisms as an example of the outmoded thinking their project seeks to replace, they ought to be concerned to read elsewhere, for example in an article that is sympathetic to their enterprise, that their discussions of methodology encourage readers to believe "there is hardly any objectivity in history writing and interpretation."[15] On the one hand, supporters of the Franco-German textbook have applauded its attempt to "harmonize the teaching of . . . national histories and create a common vocabulary consistent with contemporary European ideals and ideas."[16] On the other hand, some of the same positive reviews of *Histoire/Geschichte* have also raised concerns regarding how these projects draw a line between fostering empathy for differing viewpoints and feeding a sense of ambivalence that obscures essential differences (e.g., between the *Parti Populaire Français* and National Socialism in Germany) and clouds moral judgment. It is one thing to say that *Histoire/Geschichte* has created "a pedagogy for peace where a huge mental divide had to be bridged."[17] It is something else to document convincingly how the jointly written textbook has transformed student thinking from a nation-centered view to "a new social and transnational footing," or whether it has done so at all. While voices like Roszkowski's may not be influential in decisions to adopt the Franco-German textbook, his critique signals a recalcitrance on the Right regarding the value of a common historical consciousness for Europe. Certainly, in France, where the 2005 referendum to adopt the European Constitution failed by a wide margin (45.3 percent in favor; 54.7 percent opposed),[18] there is an attachment to the nation as a *grande cause* and to a particular identity that resists the homogenizing conclusions *Histoire/Geschichte* makes about recent European history. Of course, it remains to be seen whether political integration has reached a limit in Europe, but push-back against the Franco-German textbook, even if it represents only a marginal view among educators and academics, already tells us something about the limits of cosmopolitanism.

For those who worry about the potential of history to deepen prejudice and promote conflict, the good news is that *Histoire/Geschichte* has enjoyed considerable success in terms of its sales and adoption. Both France's Ministry of Education and the sixteen separate education ministries for the German Länder have approved the three-volume set for their history curricula (this approval allows schools and teachers to decide for themselves if they would like to use the textbook), and there has been solid demand on both sides of the Rhine. Volume 3 (post-1945) sold 80,000 copies in the first two years after its release, and the joint textbook project has been presented (favorably) at several academic conferences, leading to some interesting discussions regarding the transferability of the Franco-German model to other conflicts, and the possibility of creating a common history textbook for all twenty-seven countries in the European Union.[19] And although a few countries (e.g., Denmark, Britain, and Poland) have voiced their objections to such a plan, the fact that this possibility is raised in serious discussion already says something about the perceived success of *Histoire/Geschichte*.

It is difficult to imagine such a positive reaction in the absence of a broader trend toward Franco-German reconciliation. *Histoire/Geschichte* builds on more than seventy-five years of bilateral textbook initiatives and emerges from a history of reconciliation, which stretches back to the immediate postwar period. Even as Germany and France were still faced with the damaging effects of World War I, the international community was already encouraging rapprochement through unconventional means. In 1925, the League of Nations launched the International Commission for Intellectual Cooperation, which gave member states a chance to raise objections over the content of history books published in other countries. The following year (1926), the French Teachers Union (Syndicat national des instituteurs) launched a campaign to halt the production of "bellicose" textbooks and to develop a new history curriculum that would be "resolutely pacifist."[20] Germany's national teachers union (Deutscher Lehrerverein) held a meeting in 1929 to discuss, among other things, the need for "textbook reform in light of reconciliation."[21] These conversations reflected the optimism of the second half of the 1920s, and they mirrored the key diplomatic initiatives of the period, for example the Treaty of Locarno (1925) and the Kellogg-Briand Pact (1928). Even as a trend toward hypernationalism was taking shape, particularly in countries that felt aggrieved by the outcome of World War I, historians and schoolteachers convened the International Conference for the Teaching of History (1932), which its organizers hoped would "[blow] a current of international air into the teaching of history."[22] This conference led to a new bilateral initiative, the Franco-German Historians Meeting, in November 1935. Delegates met for a week in Paris in an attempt to reach consensus on thirty-nine specific issues that had cast a shadow over the shared history of their two countries. These included the history of contested borderlands (e.g., Alsace-Lorraine), responsibility for the war between France and Prussia in 1870, and thirteen items specifically related to the origins of World War I. On some points, the delegates managed to reach an agreement fairly easily, whereas other items, particularly those that touched on the most recent events (such as the "war guilt" and reparations clauses that France inserted into the Treaty of Versailles), led the two sides into long, unproductive arguments "over small semantic differences that seemed to harbor much broader cultural meaning."[23] Though delegates from both sides, some of whom had fought in World War I, shared the ideal of a common history, they also "carried the weight of personal memories as well as national myth[s]." Because of this baggage, the meeting failed to live up to the expectations of its organizers, and much of the positive energy that delegates brought to Paris dissipated before the project was completed. International affairs also intruded. By the time the two sides managed to publish their findings in 1937, Nazi officials had forced Germany's delegates to break off contact with their French counterparts.[24]

While the first Franco-German Historians Meeting revealed the difficulties of disentangling social memory from experimental pedagogy and scholarship, it also laid the groundwork for a second attempt at bilateral cooperation following World War II. In 1948, while American authorities were still conducting trials of lesser-known war criminals and pushing for a sweeping program of denazification, Germany's director of public education, Raymond Schmittlein, established the Institute of European History "to pave the way for Franco-German rapprochement" and "[to] promote the study of the history of Europe in its unity."[25] At about the same time, the United Nations Educational, Scientific, and Cultural Organization (UNESCO) organized a series of international history textbook discussions, which revisited many of the themes of the first Franco-German Historians Meeting. The momentum generated by these initiatives, and the launch of the International Schoolbook Institute (under the direction of Georg Eckert) in 1951, led Schmittlein to organize a second meeting of the Franco-German Historians Commission. Unlike the first meeting, which fizzled thanks to a combination of psychological issues (i.e., the inability of its delegates to fully detach from core elements of their respective national myths) and political circumstances (i.e., Germany's rapid shift toward one-party dictatorship), the second meeting in May 1951 produced a different outcome, which we can link directly to the *Histoire/Geschichte* project fifty years later.

Participants came to the second meeting with many of the same convictions of their predecessors regarding the toxicity of nation-based narratives and the need for a shared perspective on the past. This time, however, the meeting achieved the consensus that failed to develop in 1935. After some initial stumbling, Pierre Renouvin (France) and Gerhard Ritter (Germany) took control of the meeting, and it is largely due to their influence that the endeavor concluded with a joint agreement consisting of forty resolutions. Both men insisted that the work should unfold in strict accordance to documentary evidence and that the meeting should be conducted in a scientific spirit. These principles proved to be helpful, and the two sides reached a number of agreements that had eluded their predecessors. For example, Resolution 18 stated that France and Germany shared equal responsibility for the outbreak of World War I and that neither side had conducted its affairs in 1914 according to a "premeditated desire for war." Other topics proved to be more resistant to compromise. Both sides observed that French and German textbooks remained far apart in their estimates of Germany's reparations payments following World War I. Resolution 35 held that these differences should be openly acknowledged in future textbooks and also that there should be no expectation of convergence, since "[it] appears impossible to reach agreement on the exact numbers."[26] Where the evidence allowed for multiple interpretations or did not support a firm conclusion, Renouvin and Ritter shifted toward cultural diplomacy, emphasizing the historian's responsibility to future generations not to dwell on differences but to look for common ground instead. As the project reached its conclusion, Renouvin and Ritter allowed a place for "prescriptive forgetting in the interest of reconciliation." In letters they exchanged after these meetings, the two men contemplated the role of compromise in social scientific inquiry, and they discussed how and under what conditions the subjectivity of historians might be legitimately introduced into such compromises. Ritter, in particular, saw the intrusion of politics into history as something unavoidable, especially while a profound political transformation was taking place in Germany, and he defended the project of Franco-German reconciliation against less charitable viewpoints. "I would very much like to emphasize that I don't consider our agreements . . . as a 'foul compromise' that one signs without conviction," Ritter wrote. "There is a good chance I will have to endure political attacks after the publication of the [Agreement], but I shall not be deterred by that—especially not at this moment when the European peoples are so apparently taking a big step forward."[27] With Europe already moving toward integration (e.g., NATO and the Schuman Plan), Ritter felt that a way had been cleared for a new approach to the past. The Franco-German Historians Agreement thus fit with the other examples of reconciliation taking place in Europe at the time.

It is important not to exaggerate the impact of the 1951 agreement. Conference delegates gave minimal attention to the most recent conflict between Germany and France, and where they did, this provoked intense debate. Of the forty resolutions contained in the agreement, only one (the last) addressed the Nazi regime, and Ritter and Renouvin went around in long circles before deciding there was no common ground on this point. Resolution 40 held that "most" adults in Germany failed to comprehend the essence of Nazism when Hitler rose to the chancellorship in 1933. Germans who voted for the National-sozialistische Deutsche Arbeiterpartei (NSDAP, National Socialist German Workers' Party), according to this perspective, did not realize that by doing so they were effectively dissolving their democratic state. Given their ignorance, the German masses could not be held morally accountable for the regime's subsequent criminality. Among the French delegates, this formula was viewed as both historically incorrect and improperly exculpatory, but Renouvin relented after failing to persuade Ritter that a more probing statement, one that implicated more Germans or excused fewer, would better promote reconciliation. In the final document, Resolution 40 read as follows: "Most of [Hitler's] electors—who expected him to establish an authoritarian regime—recognized too late, or underestimated, the danger of his taking advantage of his regime to establish a tyranny without limits and to destroy the constitutional state."[28] The resolution mentioned nothing about the effects of Nazi tyranny, either for the German people or for European Jews, and there is no mention of the Holocaust anywhere in the agreement. Ritter did acknowledge that there was no way to prove the contention made in Resolution 40, since the historical record provided no documentation that could reveal the mind-set of all those who had voted for Hitler in 1932 and 1933.[29] He insisted, though, that his was a "safe historical judgment," which reflected the popular sentiment in Germany at the beginning of the Nazi era.

Siegel and Harjes note that the Franco-German agreement generated "little controversy" when the resolutions were published in 1952.[30] We could infer from this that the historical interpretations contained in the document enjoyed broad support, but it is also possible that weariness of the past (and the early signs of economic recovery in Western Europe) more clearly explained the absence of opposition. History textbooks in West Germany and France moved away from the nation-centered model that the delegates wanted to replace in 1951, but whether this was a direct result of the Historians Agreement remains unclear.[31] Textbooks in Germany already seemed to be moving in this direction prior to 1951, as the Historians Agreement lent added legitimacy to the trend. Textbook revisions in the early postwar period appear to owe something to the Franco-German conference, but one also needs to consider what one of the participants in 1951 called "the spirit of the times." There is a riddle to explore here, which is easy to relate but difficult to solve convincingly. It applies not only to the Franco-German case but also to others like it that entail the challenges of overcoming divergent views of the past and the need for citizens to divest themselves of their strong attachments to the nation. The riddle goes: "Which comes first, negotiated history or reconciliation?" But wait for the trick. The answer, it turns out, is "neither."

Germany and Poland:
Rapprochement and Joint Textbook Revision

Just as the Élysée Treaty (1963) became a pivotal moment in the history of Franco-German reconciliation, the Treaty of Warsaw (1970) produced a major reset in the relations between (West) Germany and Poland. A core component of Willy Brandt's Ostpolitik, the treaty provided a framework for normalization by acknowledging Poland as "the first victim" of Nazi aggression and by accepting the permanency of the Oder-Neisse line (i.e., the postwar German-Polish border). Many still remember Brandt's spontaneous gesture at the Warsaw Ghetto monument, his kneeling and head-bowing expression of respect and sorrow, which occurred on the same day the treaty was signed. Along with U.S.-Soviet missile reduction talks (e.g., SALT I) and the Helsinki Treaty (1977), Brandt's apology to the Poles stands as one of the signposts and high points of the period of détente. If we consider the events that led to the treaty and analyze its consequences, not only for diplomatic relations between Poland and Germany but also for the way this instrument rekindled a historical dialogue between the two nations, there is a close resemblance to the Franco-German trajectory described earlier. In the same way that formal acknowledgment of past grievances allowed France and Germany to start down a new path together, Brandt's symbolic apology, and the treaty that framed it, helped clear a way forward for Germany and Poland, whose history entailed so much bitterness and enmity.

One of the tangible, though lesser known, results of the Warsaw Treaty was the creation of the Joint Polish-German Commission of Historians and Geographers for the Revision of School Textbooks in 1972 (hereafter Polish-German Historians Commission). Organized and funded by UNESCO, this initiative brought together historians from Poland and the Federal Republic of Germany for a series of meetings aimed at reestablishing scholarly dialogue and removing the past as an obstacle to peaceful relations. Even though the early meetings produced no major breakthroughs, the commission became a forum for intellectual exchange at a time when Moscow still strongly discouraged outward displays of "ideological cooperation" with the West. Over the course of more than two dozen meetings and conferences, the participants created a collaborative environment for historical mediation, which represented an "alternative culture" to the official narratives that structured the two countries' entangled history during the early postwar period.[32] Although Germany and Poland nurtured this dialogue through a variety of channels, the Historians Commission allowed the two sides to capitalize on the broader processes of rapprochement by engaging scholars on a regular basis and by moving gradually toward the most sensitive topics.

The Polish-German Commission began in 1972 from "an extremely low level of cross-national communication."[33] Historical dialogue had been largely frozen during the interwar period, as both sides cultivated an ethnic perspective on the past that fueled border revisionism. Following World War II, the politics of the Cold War required that Poland and East Germany cultivate an official friendship, which implied a ban on the most sensitive topics in the history of their bilateral relations. At the same time, in the West German state, anti-Communism melded with traditional anti-Polonism, and historians working on the East (Ostforschung) typically did so through the lens of German cultural achievement and ethnic settlement. Intellectually speaking and in terms of its academic treatment, Poland remained a part of Germany, just as it had been in the geopolitical sense until 1919. The Treaty of Warsaw changed this dynamic at the level of officialdom, but signs of reconciliation were already rising from below. In November 1965, Polish bishops sent a "Pastoral Letter" to their counterparts in Germany, inviting their Catholic brethren to participate in the millennial celebration of Polish Christianity, slated to take place the following year. In their letter, the Polish clerics recalled the historical events that fed hostility between the two countries, and they expressed their hope that mutual understanding might one day take the place of mutual resentment. The letter's key passage described the Poles' explicit wish that that the two nations would be able to build a bridge by letting go of their historical grievances: "We forgive and ask forgiveness."[34] Although the letter was repudiated by Poland's Communist Party leader, Władysław Gomułka, who previously had designated West Germany as Poland's primary enemy, it created an opening for political dialogue and new discussions at the level of civil society. As Gomułka's influence waned, the Treaty of Warsaw was negotiated through this opening, and the Historians Commission attempted to give scholarly support to the sentiments that the bishops had described in spiritual terms.

The commission's early meetings focused on accepting historical outcomes and steering away from self-referential, nation-centered narratives (e.g., the German habit of seeing the East without its Slavic culture). Participants set lofty goals at these early meetings, as most of the discussions related to safe and relatively distant topics, which few nonacademics considered interesting or important to their identity. A noteworthy exception was the conference in 1977, which focused on German and Polish resistance movements during World War II. Besides being a topic from the recent past, that is, one still (mis)informed by living memory, and one that, quite literally, touched on questions of life and death, this conference proved to be important for the "critical comparative assessment" that the participants attempted to develop and for their willingness to pursue a common theme in two very different political and historical contexts.[35] While other conferences during this period treated less charged subjects (e.g., 1848 and the Vormärz period), the conference in 1977 demonstrated that some members of the commission were prepared to tackle the most polarizing and deeply politicized topics. In terms of both shared questions and methodology, the commission's work during this period offered strong evidence of a shifting tide in Polish-German historiography and, more generally, in their bilateral relations.[36]

Encouraged by their early success, the Polish-German Historians Commission organized a landmark conference in 1986 that dealt with World War II, the Holocaust, and the history of ethnic expulsions in the German-Polish borderlands. While both countries had produced scholarship that touched on these subjects obliquely, the 1986 conference marked a breakthrough in terms of directly engaging hotly contested issues and arriving at (or at least contemplating) a consensual formula for mutual understanding. The most remarkable thing about this conference was the extent to which members of the commission had already, almost a decade earlier, anticipated and addressed the arguments that ethnically oriented organizations like the Bund der Vertriebenen (Germany's Federation of Expellees) would later make regarding the immoral treatment of German civilians in the last phases of the war, and the degree to which these noncombatants had been unjustly victimized under postwar policies authorized by the Allies. While groups representing the expellees criticized the commission following the 1986 conference for failing to give the expulsions a more prominent place on the agenda and for putting Polish-German bilateral relations above historical truth, in fact the commission had already issued a statement on the resettlement of Volksdeutsche in the recommendations for textbook revision, which they published in 1976/77.[37] Although the word "expulsion" was deliberately avoided, Article 22 of the recommendations cited the "demographic transfers" that took place in the months prior to Germany's surrender and during the next several years. Those who fled ahead of the Red Army or were evacuated after Germany's surrender, the commission concluded, "suffer[ed] great losses."[38] Of course, without further amplification, this statement fell short of the acknowledgment sought by the expellees. The quality and character of German suffering received no real attention—the term "losses" evoked primarily material deprivation—and the question of responsibility was scarcely raised at all. The commission noted only that these transfers were undertaken "on the basis of inter-allied agreements." But even if the first recommendations for textbook revision did not adequately represent the experience of the German expellees or seriously engage questions of morality and responsibility, it is significant that Polish and German historians, after decades of ethnic polarization, managed to produce a "largely convergent" interpretation of the origins and consequences of World War II at a conference in 1986, when millions of veterans and survivors of the war were still alive in both countries. That the expulsions generated so little controversy at the conference in 1986 says a great deal more about the scope of consensus among Polish and German experts than it does (as the Bund der Vertriebenen tried to suggest) about the constraints that left-wing political correctness places on historical debate. By 1986, little or no debate existed among mainstream scholars in either country regarding the fact of the expulsions or the abundant evidence that German expellees had suffered grievous harms, up to and including death, as a consequence of their forced transfer. More recently, however, the politics of history have centered on how to properly contextualize the expulsions and give them meaning within a larger narrative that preserves German guilt and does not relativize the victimhood of those who suffered under the Nazi occupational regime. As the Polish-German Historians Commission demonstrated in 1986, this does not necessarily entail the creation of a hierarchy of victims so much as it requires rigorous analysis of a multitude of perspectives and a commitment to open dialogue.

It is important to note how the conference in 1986 impacted subsequent historiography. In Poland, the shift to a postnationalist framework was especially pronounced. Younger Polish historians such as Włodzimierz Borodziej (who served as the commission's Polish secretary during the 1980s) produced new works that strove to foster an international dialogue free from the conventions and constraints of Soviet-era narratives. Whereas early in his career Borodziej had prepared a doctoral thesis (1983) on Nazi responses to resistance in occupied Poland, which cast Poles in their Soviet role as both victims and antifascist partisans, his work after the 1986 conference showed the remarkable extent to which members of the commission were determined to think outside of the traditional nationalist framework. In 2000 Borodziej coedited a volume on the plight of the German expellees, which was largely sympathetic to the German side and explored their losses in detail along several axes (e.g., material losses, psychological impact, etc.).[39] Prior to 1986, Polish involvement in a project of this nature would have been virtually unthinkable.

Following the collapse of Communism in East Central Europe in 1989 and the reunification of Germany in 1990, the Polish-German Historians Commission continued to build on its accomplishments. Over the years, but especially after 1986, members of the commission developed a reliable method for fostering historical dialogue, which entailed (1) sincere and determined engagement with divisive questions, (2) measured responses to partisan perspectives instead of rejecting them out of hand, and (3) the pursuit of consensus without demanding the removal of divergent viewpoints. Through its annual conferences and jointly edited publications the commission established a professional language and a shared value system, which deepened the possibilities for "cross-national communication" and created a civil atmosphere for historical debate open to controversial interpretations. While the two sides did not always arrive at a common view of the past, they allowed that divergent views could be valid and beneficial to the pursuit of an enriched understanding of the past. As members of the commission moved on to pursue their own projects, the joint negotiations in which they participated appeared to leave a lasting imprint on their work. Increasingly after 1989, historians from both countries undertook studies that aimed to "deconstruct national narratives" and ensure that debates over national history remained "pluralistic."[40] Such work strongly suggests that these commissions can both exercise and help propagate democratic values.

Perhaps the most compelling thing about the Polish-German Historians Commission is the way its work has been championed by government officials looking to jump-start bilateral negotiations when relations have appeared shaky. The years between 1989 and 1997 saw a "spiral of rapprochement, trust-building, and reconciliation" between the two sides, but the following decade was fraught with difficulties, to the point that some observers began referring to this interval (1998–2007) as another "ice-age."[41] Poland and Germany were at odds almost constantly in the first decade of the twenty-first century over geopolitical considerations (e.g., Poland's support for the U.S.-led war in Iraq), economic initiatives (e.g., the Nord Stream gas pipeline), and bureaucratic considerations connected to the European Union's institutional overhaul. The thorniest issue, however, stemmed from Poland's accession to the European Union in 2004 and led to fears in Poland that German expellees were preparing to make legal claims on their lost properties.[42] The relationship reached a low point in the fall of 2003 when *Wprost*, one of Poland's largest news weeklies, used a cover image featuring Erika Steinbach, the head of the German Expellees' Federation, outfitted in an SS uniform and riding atop Germany's chancellor (Schroeder), who was depicted as her submissive and obedient steed. The cover appeared at a time when Steinbach was loudly pushing for the creation of a new cultural resource in Berlin, a Center for the Expelled, which she described as a memorial to the twelve million Germans who were expelled from Eastern Europe after the Allies drew up their postwar settlement plan.

As tensions escalated, diplomats used the example of the Polish-German Historians Commission to restore confidence among those seeking rapprochement and to highlight prospects for reconciliation. Speaking in June 2002, the Polish ambassador to Germany, Jerzy Kranz, praised the commission as an example of international cooperation that rises above the difficulties of the past: "The Poles envy the Czech car manufacturer Skoda, which is now a subsidiary of Volkswagen, as a showpiece of good cooperation with the Germans, but the Czechs envy the Poles [for] the German-Polish Textbook Commission."[43] With the question of the German-Polish border permanently resolved in 1990 under the terms of the Two Plus Four Agreement, the Polish-German Historians Commission worked with a renewed sense of purpose. No longer faced with the prospect of partition, Polish historians began to think more seriously about the cultural legacies of the German past in the western territories. German historians, meanwhile, worked to promote the commission's model for joint inquiry in the former GDR. German reunification prompted the commission to expand its membership, and beginning in 1992 the commission's next ten conferences were held at sites in the former East Germany. No longer the only forum for cross-national dialogue, the commission also began to focus more of its energy on scholastic pedagogy and the development of new school curricula.

In 2001, the commission released a new bilateral teacher's manual, which replaced the recommendations for textbook revision developed in 1976/77. Published as *Germany and Poland in the Twentieth Century*, the new manual ran to 432 pages (the previous recommendations came in at eighteen pages) and built on the commission's thirty-year record of achievement. Whereas textbooks created according to the earlier recommendations aimed at eliminating stereotypes that encouraged Polish and German students to see their counterparts either as marauding enemies (the Polish view of Germans) or as victims to be pitied (the German view of Poles), the 2001 manual sought to overcome all objectification by focusing on the history of Polish-German interrelations. Taking a thematic rather than a chronological approach, the 2001 manual attempted to illuminate general historical and sociological trends by delving into particular aspects of the Polish-German relationship. Each topic was presented in a separate chapter prepared by a mixed team of German and Polish scholars. Specific areas of investigation included borderlands, minorities, expulsion, traditional enemies, gender issues, and Communist rule.[44] In addition to the conveyance of certain historical facts, the manual was designed to deepen historical consciousness and spark curiosity by raising questions regarding the constructed nature of historical knowledge and by analyzing the considerations that historians weigh when deciding whether a particular event is worthy of inclusion in the curriculum. The manual does not suggest a specific teaching style but instead provides raw material to enable German and Polish teachers to develop a common instructional plan. Not only did the new guidelines embrace the delicate topics that older textbooks avoided or examined through the lens of nationalist mythologies, but they were also specifically intended to provoke readers and to stimulate debate. In a few places, where members of the commission disagreed over specific material—for example, some Polish members were reluctant to include documents that showed homegrown anti-Semitism because they felt these would feed stereotypes and reinforce old resentments—the two sides negotiated creative solutions. In such cases, the authors inserted a sidebar commentary that explicated these fears and suggested different possibilities for how the sources might be contextualized. According to Robert Maier, the project director, "thousands of teachers" ordered the guide in the first year of its release.[45] Not surprisingly, Maier has described the significance of the manual in effusive terms: "The guide explodes a historical presentation based on national history, which asserts the full homogeneity of [one's] own society and differentiates itself from the outside with a latent hostility. [It] defends as well a common European construction of the future on the basis of universal values."[46]

Whether the manual achieves what Maier claims, it has nonetheless made a significant impact on the relationship between Germany and Poland. While one former member, Gerard Labuda, derided the commission's work after 1990 as stale and ineffective, politicians found new ways to praise the manual in the decade after its release.[47] In 2007, following a visit from his Polish counterpart, Germany's foreign minister, Frank Walter Steinmeier, discussed the need to open a new chapter in Polish-German relations and the possibility of using "symbols" to facilitate this process. Promising to visit Warsaw more regularly, Steinmeier pledged German assistance to reconstruct a church in Gubin and raised the possibility of building a dedicated German-Polish meeting center for future diplomatic summits. He also expressed strong support for a new German-Polish history textbook, like the *Histoire/Geschichte* series created with France, which would be based on the commission's 2001 guidelines for developing cross-national histories in a European mold. During the next year, the importance of shared history to rebuild Polish-German relations became a regular talking point with Steinmeier, as Poles continued to express their concerns over the Center Against Expulsions planned for Berlin. While Gerhard Schröder maintained that his government would not support the compensation and restitution claims of the expellees, many Poles still objected to the center on the grounds that it equated German suffering with the experiences of other groups who were targeted by the Nazis. Steinmeier, who acknowledged the center as "one of the most delicate matters" affecting Polish-German relations, accepted that Germany had opened itself to charges of manipulating history by promoting the center in a way victims of Nazism found profoundly offensive. He urged caution, both in terms of future plans for the center and with respect to the appointment of its senior staff, and over the next several months he continued to push for the creation of a joint Polish-German history textbook. Michael Müller, the co-chair of the Polish-German Historians Commission, also expressed enthusiasm for a textbook project, saying that the question of the expulsions had been settled and no longer posed a problem, at least in terms of reaching a scholarly consensus. In comments to the Polish media, Müller signaled that the joint textbook project would go forward easily if both governments agreed to support it. "Both Polish and German experts," he stated, "feel it is out of the question for history to be portrayed in the way Erika Steinbach promotes."[48] One diplomat suggested that a shared perspective on the recent past could help Poland and Germany sort out other controversial issues, including the conflict over construction and profit sharing for Nord Stream, the northern gas pipeline.[49] Steinmeier "wants to make Polish-German relations one of the most important elements in his foreign policy," the diplomat told journalists, which helped to explain why the foreign minister had taken every recent opportunity to push for a joint history textbook.

Berlin's desire for a breakthrough with Warsaw and Steinmeier's strategy of pursuing this, at least in part, through the promotion of a jointly written history textbook suggest an important point regarding the potential of history for mediating conflict. In the literature on historical commissions and joint textbook projects, there is a marked skepticism regarding the capacity of nego-tiated history to shape international politics. This has emerged as a running debate among those who study the politics of history in contemporary society. The same debate runs through the current scholarship on truth commissions, where authors often take for granted what is still only a tentative hypothesis: the idea that a full and accurate account of past injustices will help settle inter-group conflicts rather than inflame them. One side in these debates holds that international affairs are governed, as they have always been, by a principle of realism, according to which the strong do what they can and the weak endure what they must. Since the nineteenth century, this perspective has been ex-pressed through a principle of realpolitik. States act according to their interests, while justice, morality, and compassion come into play only if these can be leveraged for political advantage. The realist perspective allows that historical dialogue is an interesting lens through which to consider international relations, but it also rates these negotiations as epiphenomenal, meaning that their impact is determined by political processes and considerations. Even among those who have participated on historical commissions and, therefore, have an investment in the claim that they can support peace and cooperation, there is a habit of including long qualifiers and disclaimers in the discussions of their impact. As one member of the Polish-German Historians Commission has observed, these joint textbook projects tend to succeed where there is already "a favorable general political surrounding."[50] In the absence of a positive mutual disposition where, for example, adversaries do not yet accept the outcome of past conflicts or do not believe that the other side has accepted responsibility for past transgressions, these initiatives often struggle to gain traction. The realist camp, in other words, which includes many who ascribe real value to these commissions, maintains what appears to be a bedrock truth: "On the whole . . . bilateral textbook initiatives among former enemy states . . . need a certain political climate. They cannot initiate or replace a general politics of reconciliation and détente, but have to be a part of it."[51] From this perspective, the Polish-German Historians Commission has flourished because of the "Pastoral Letter" and the Treaty of Warsaw, both of which preceded it. Like-wise, *Histoire/Geschichte* has gained a foothold (despite criticisms against it) because of the Élysée Treaty, the coal and steel interests (which laid the groundwork for the European Union), the strong desire for a common defense strategy, and because both Germany and France have separately engaged with questions regarding the Nazi past, responsibility for the Holocaust, and so forth. Seen in this light, the textbook initiatives appear to be an outward sign of a deeper reconciliation framework established by other means.

It would be foolish to doubt primacy of concrete interests, including economics and geopolitics, when making an assessment of the new relationship between Germany and Poland. Michael Müller and others connected to the Polish-German Historians Commission are correct to point out that bilateral relations cannot be reduced to a simple question of historical dialogue. But even so, Müller's commission provides an important example of the way that history can enter politics—here a history of conflict was deliberately engaged by a high-ranking government official (Steinmeier), who could have side-stepped the issue, as others had—and drive diplomacy toward improved bilateral relations. This lends credence to a second camp in the debate over the political efficacy of historical commissions, whom we might call the idealists. In contrast to the realists, who see the commissions as a by-product of warming relations, the idealists claim (and here I am portraying them, a bit unfairly, as more starry-eyed and naïve than they actually are) that reconciliation requires historical accounting and settlement, and that the commissions offer an exceptionally good model for working through the past. While the idealists usually do not pin all hope for reconciliation on historical commissions, they nevertheless understand these initiatives as powerful agents of reconciliation. In some cases, the idealists have worked directly for the commissions whose powers they tout as being transformative. In other cases, the idealist position has been espoused by outsiders who have examined a single commission or case study and come away with a positive impression, which they project onto other commissions whose work they know less well. Often, these assessments come from historians, who want to make their field of study politically relevant or simply wish to deliver what they see as good news for practitioners in the field of conflict resolution. In general, though, the idealists have been sophisticated thinkers, who eschew the cynicism endemic to certain academic fields. What a political scientist might take to be sentimental and unimportant to the way international politics are conducted (i.e., the notion that former enemies might like to understand each other better), the idealist embraces as a possibility for making historical knowledge useful.

This study attempts to take in a range of case studies specifically so as to avoid the "enthusiasm trap" into which some of the idealists have fallen. It sets out from what is, admittedly, a less than original proposition: that the debate between realists and idealists presents a false dilemma. As models for historical negotiation and conflict mediation, the commissions analyzed here cannot be grasped fully through either lens. Instead, I want to suggest that the historical commissions are interesting and important—and sometimes useful—because of the way they combine the realist and idealist perspectives. If reconciliation represents a long-term process of fostering peace and cooperation between former enemies through a combination of shared historical understanding and concrete bilateral projects, then commissions like the Polish-German example can contribute to both aspects of this dynamic. Lily Gardner Feldman has put this succinctly in her work on Polish-German reconciliation where she writes that reconciliation "involves both ethical and emotional dimensions and practical and material aspects."[52] While historical commissions are concerned with facts and the interpretation thereof, their work is also symbolic. Historical commissions do not have the same direct impact on bilateral relations that a friendship treaty or a billion-dollar trade package do. But the fact that these commissions have sometimes been supported and utilized by the same people who negotiate such agreements speaks to their relevance for high-level diplomacy. There are even some cases (e.g., Czech-German) where historical commissions have been included as specific commitments within major treaties aimed at solidifying bilateral relations. Bilateral commissions and joint textbook projects have emerged as new diplomatic tools because of their capacity to satisfy strong moral demands, such as historical clarity, acknowledgment, contrition, and the like, while also supporting pragmatic interests (e.g., convincing a neighbor to accommodate a gas pipeline).

Steinmeier's push for a Polish-German history textbook is more than just an interesting sideshow outside the tent of international affairs. Jointly written histories do not erase centuries of strife, and they can increase tensions where a strong attachment to national history still exists and attempts to build empathy with outsiders who are regarded as "too multicultural." The historical commissions are far from being a cure-all remedy. But narratives that break down the intellectual barriers created by national histories are more than just window dressing for officials who want to give a friendlier appearance to old-style realpolitik. It took less than two years for Steinmeier's proposal for a joint history textbook to develop into a concrete plan for action. In January 2008, the Polish-German Historians Commission received authorization from the two respective governments to begin working on a joint publication. Preliminary discussions began in May 2008 and concluded in December 2010, when the commission presented a new set of recommendations for the development of a shared textbook.[53] The new proposal called for a multivolume work that would cover five periods, spanning from the ancient world to the early twenty-first century. The planning committee recommended that the new series treat the past from a German-Polish perspective and that the portrayal of each period incorporate the experiences of both countries so as to "expand the academic debate surrounding historical themes."[54]

The project was put under the direction of the Georg Eckert Institute for International Textbook Research (GEI, in Braunschweig, Germany). In May 2012, the GEI secured publishers for the textbook in both Germany and Poland. The writing was given over to a binational panel of experts, who formed working groups to produce individual chapters, which they then submitted for approval (or revision) to a bilateral steering committee. In 2011, the commission released a 135-page project outline, which emphasized the authors' desire to move away from "national creation stories" in order to focus on "sub- or supranational communities."[55] Michael Müller, who served as project director on the German side, spoke optimistically when asked whether the process would be contentious, saying that he expected a fruitful conversation and many fresh perspectives: "Of course historians will always disagree. But they no longer disagree along the same frontlines as conflicts between nations. What divides them instead are, for example, methodological schools, and these are frontlines that run right through our national delegation."[56] Robert Traba, who chaired the Polish contingent, emphasized that cross-national history negotiations do not require that the two sides accept a tepid compromise. "European history arises out of different memories," Traba told reporters. "An attempt to come up with some sort of middle position between the differing perspectives would [be] doomed to failure." This statement shows the commission's commitment to multivocality rather than consensus rooted in compromise. Traba insists that any possibility for transcending historical conflict depends on the willingness of adversaries, not simply to hear out the other side but to preserve a space for their rival's memories, especially where these run counter to their own. To recall Charles Maier's formula, mediation depends on "rigorous analysis of presuppositions from all contending points of view."[57] Ultimately, joint history must allow for divergent interpretations of the same facts, but it also requires basic agreement on what constitutes a fact, which facts ought to be considered as primary, and what can be fairly deduced from a given set of facts. Mediated history demands that memory should capitulate to verified facts, but it does not require rivals to keep the same memories. Rather, a negotiated history asks that groups seriously examine the record, read it holistically rather than selectively, and draw careful conclusions that lend meaning to the past, while accepting that others may attach a different meaning to the same event(s).

The first volume in the Polish-German joint history series is anticipated for 2015.[58] Until it appears, one can only wonder, "What if the other side is wrong?" In other words, what if one side persists in seeing the past in ways that contravene the available evidence and/or are threatening to the other side's group identity? If Poles, for example, understand themselves as a devoutly Christian people who have honored and lived the Gospel for more than one thousand years, and yet others see the Polish nation—or, at least, what they take to be a representative sample thereof—as being responsible for terrible acts of vengeance, vicious ethnic killings, and despoliations, which exceeded all established moral norms, can such a rift be mediated? At some point, are we not compelled to choose between competing versions of the past?

Unless they want to be consigned to the political fringes, Poles may not deny that the vast majority of their German neighbors were forcefully removed from their homes beginning in 1944, although they may choose to see these "resettlements" as an understandable policy in light of what the Nazi occupation wrought on their country. Germans may prod Poles to accept their preferred term for these events (i.e., expulsion), since it communicates the violent, disorienting, and, in some cases, lethal effects these policies had on German civilians who were subjected to them, including a disproportionate number of children.[59] Germans who wish to participate in the dialogue may not deny that the military and police forces mobilized in their name killed approximately three million Poles in the six years leading up to the expulsions, or that their elected leader, prior to launching a war of aggression, signed a pact with the Soviet Union that effectively wiped Poland from the map and encouraged the physical liquidation of the Polish people or their deracination under Marxist doctrine. These things cannot be reasonably contested, even if not all Poles and Germans accept the evidence that supports them. As stated previously, mediating the past does imply that "anything goes." It is also worth repeating that no member of the Polish-German Historians Commission has called these facts into question, and this is a testament to their professional integrity and the social scientific standards to which they adhere. Of course, the real debate—at times the conflict has seemed intractable—is centered elsewhere. Many Poles today understand the resettlement to have been both warranted and just, while many Germans, including some in positions of political power, consider these expulsions to have been criminal acts for which the victims and their families are entitled to compensation. Legally speaking, the expellees' organizations have run out of room in their search for a remedy.[60] Politically, their representatives have so far failed to bring the German government around to their side, as most of the policymakers in Berlin either do not accept the core of their argument or do not attach sufficient pragmatic value to their cause. Historically, a great deal still remains up for grabs. The Polish-German Historians Commission has adopted a minimalist position to this point. In 1976/77, following tense negotiations, the commission published joint recommendations for textbook revision in which the "demographic transfers" were acknowledged, and Germans west of the Oder-Neisse were described as having "suffer[ed] great losses." By 1986, members of the commission had reached congruency in this matter, such that they no longer regarded it as a pressing topic, even at a conference devoted to World War II, the Holocaust, and the "expulsion complex." Politics have rolled onward in the meantime, and the expellees have not only built up their ranks but have also placed their representatives high up in the government. The debate currently focuses less on textbook depictions and more on future plans for the Center Against Expulsions. That debate has risen sharply in intensity. In 2011, Germany's parliament, spearheaded by support from Angela Merkel's Christian Democratic Union (CDU) and by its coalition partner, the Free Democrats, passed a proposal to establish an official day of commemoration for German expellees. The passage of this measure provoked a letter of condemnation signed by sixty-eight historians from Germany and the rest of Europe.[61] In particular, signatories condemned the MPs who voted in favor of the bill for scheduling the commemoration on August 5, which is the anniversary of the "Charter of German Expellees" (1950). That document, which renounces "revenge or retribution," has been criticized for failing to place the expulsions into an appropriate historical context, that is, one that takes account of Nazi aggression and racial violence. According to the historians who signed the protest letter in 2011, "There is no word [in the charter] about the cause of war, about the mass crimes of the National Socialists, about the murder of the Jews, Poles, Roma and Sinti, Soviet prisoners of war, and other persecuted groups." Depending on how one translates it, the charter declares either that the German expellees "were most affected by the agonies of the period" or that they "suffered most from the hardship of [the] time." In response to the bill's passage, a spokesman for the Polish Foreign Ministry simply observed: "The document does not serve the interests of Polish-German reconciliation."[62]

This episode can be read in several ways. Given that Merkel's CDU was facing tough regional elections, it is easy to imagine that the proposal for an official day of commemoration was simply a political ploy, designed to rile up sympathetic voters and guarantee strong turnout. Perhaps the German government understood that the proposal would "ruffle feathers" in Warsaw but felt that Germany had sufficient leverage over the Poles in their most sensitive dealings. Or maybe passage of this measure points to a rift within the German Right, between pragmatists, who are loathe to do anything that threatens diplomatic relations with Poland, and hard-liners, who will not accept any representation of the past in which the expellees "got what they deserved" or were relocated for the greater good. The way forward is hard to decipher, but the Polish-German Historians Commission seems to be moving on a potentially productive track. As one of the historians who signed the letter of protest in 2011 put it, "There are possibilities to remember the victims of expulsions. But I don't see any justification to focus exclusively on Germans because of the danger of losing sight of the context."[63] It will be interesting, to say the least, to see whether the Polish-German history textbook employs this kind of approach when it is eventually released for publication.

Germany and the Czech Republic: The Manifestations of "Mutual Support"

If Steinmeier's support for a Polish-German history textbook shows how politics and historical dialogue can sometimes mesh, the Czech-German case shows that blended approaches to the past—equally attentive to morality and the practical concerns of the state—are not yet universal. Whereas Poland and Germany have recently attempted to use history for the purpose of strengthening reconciliation, the Germans and Czechs have repeatedly allowed disputes over the past to disturb their bilateral relations. When representatives of the Sudetenlandern (Germans expelled from Czechoslovakia at the end of World War II) proposed a "reconciliatory commission of truth" in 2008 to clarify the breadth and impact of the postwar expulsions, the Czech Foreign Ministry curtly refused to engage. A spokesperson for the ministry commented, "There are enough discussion platforms that deal with the resettlement, and another one is not necessary."[64] While Czech and German historians have worked together on the question of the expulsions in several settings since the early 1990s, including a joint textbook project, these efforts have not delivered the benefits (in terms of bolstering cooperation) that one would hope to see.

Czech-German relations have waxed and waned since 1989, but most setbacks and periods of friction can be traced to a common theme: the question of the Beneš decrees and the expulsion of the Sudeten Germans between 1945 and 1947. These decrees, which were drafted by the Czechoslovak government-in-exile while World War II was still being fought and ratified (retroactively) by the Interim National Assembly of Czechoslovakia in March 1946, called for the involuntary "transfer" of 2.5 million ethnic Germans as well as 500,000 Hungarians out of the Czechoslovak territories at the end of the war. While these forced resettlements were conducted under the supervision of the International Red Cross and with the auxiliary support of the Allied command under the terms of the Potsdam Agreement, witnesses reported brutal mistreatment and appalling acts of violence, including summary execution, rape, scalping, and dismemberment. One expellee suggested that the excesses he witnessed after liberation made his earlier detention in a Nazi concentration camp look "like a holiday."[65] Estimates regarding the number of Germans who died as a result of the expulsions vary widely, from 30,000 (on the Czech side) to 250,000 (on the German side).[66] Václav Havel, the former Czech president, denounced the expulsions as "deeply immoral," but he also insisted that the outcome of these expulsions, including the expropriation of private property, could not be reversed. Much as "Aryanized" properties were given or sold to Germans after 1933, assets seized under the Beneš decrees were redistributed to Czechs and Slovaks prior to being nationalized after 1948. The fall of Communism in 1989 and the Czech program of privatization and restitution once again called the legal status of these properties into question. In Hungary, Austria, and Germany, expellees and their families pressed to reclaim assets taken from them in the course of their removal. Since 1989, the Beneš decrees have been a constant thorn in the side of Czechs and Germans working to foster reconciliation between the two countries. The politicization of the expulsions has been an obstacle whenever plans to improve bilateral relations have emerged, and efforts to conjure a mediating history, while noteworthy, have not succeeded in putting the conflict to rest.

One of the most memorable examples of the way that the Beneš decrees have complicated the Czech-German relationship and unsettled European affairs occurred in 2002, when both countries were preparing for national elections and a small handful of Eastern European countries, including the Czech Republic, were in the process of negotiating their accession to the European Union. In a radio interview clearly intended to improve his standing with conservative voters, the Czech prime minister Miloš Zeman was asked to comment on property claims put forward by Sudeten Germans and on the legality of the Beneš decrees more generally. Describing the expellees as Nazi sympathizers and calling them "Hitler's fifth column," Zeman responded that the Sudetenlandern were "traitors" and that Beneš had done them a favor by sending them to Germany. In a follow-up interview, Zeman hypothesized that mass executions might have been warranted, and he suggested that the expellees were lucky to have been treated humanely (which they were not). While these comments may have scored points with Czech nationalists, they also set off a firestorm in the international arena, which Zeman and others struggled to contain.

Setting aside any political calculations behind these provocative comments, it is important to understand that Zeman's remarks did not come out of thin air. For weeks prior to these interviews, Jörg Haider, the head of Austria's right-wing FPÖ, had been goading Zeman and the Czech government to nullify the Beneš decrees and clear the way for the return of properties seized from the Sudeten Germans. Haider's needling brought to the fore what Czech and German officials had previously tried to push into the background. While the expulsions had been a stumbling block in the early 1990s, when the Czech Republic worked out a flawed policy for post-Communist property restitution, the debate over the Beneš decrees appeared to be quelled in 1997, when Germany and the Czech Republic signed a "Declaration on Mutual Relations and Their Future Development."[67] The purpose of this accord was twofold: (1) it acknowledged that Czechs and Germans shared a common cultural heritage, which included a difficult legacy of historical conflict; and (2) it sought to close the books on the question of restitution for Sudeten expellees by substituting mutual statements of regret for legal sanctions and the return of seized properties. Intended as a first step toward balancing the historical ledger, the declaration urged remembrance, vigilance, and reconciliation. Paying tribute to "the victims of National Socialist tyranny and to those who resisted it," the German side accepted responsibility for "a historical development which led to the 1938 Munich Agreement." In turn, the Czech side expressed regret for the "expulsion and forced resettlement of Sudeten Germans" and, in acknowledgment of the fact that guilt had been attributed to the expellees collectively, for "the excesses which were contrary to elementary humanitarian principles as well as legal norms existing at the time." Both parties pledged not to "burden their [mutual] relations with political and legal issues which stem[med] from the past."[68]

The exchange between Zeman and Haider in 2002 showed that these "issues" were still far from settled and that social memory continued to exert a dangerous hold on international politics. Zeman's remarks triggered an international crisis that ultimately involved all of the countries in the region and very nearly torpedoed plans for the enlargement of the European Union. Within a week of Zeman's initial comments, Hungary's prime minister Viktor Orban joined Haider in the call to revoke the Beneš decrees; in Germany, Edmund Stoiber, Bavaria's minister-president and Gerhard Schröder's chief opposition in the upcoming general election, began to align himself more with the hard-line Sudeten, who comprised a significant bloc within his constituency. By demanding an apology from Zeman, who refused to give one, Stoiber (Christian Democrat) was able to paint his rival, Schröder (Social Democrat), as "soft" on the expellee question and, therefore, on foreign affairs more generally. Meanwhile, hoping to appease the nationalist clique at home and the Sudetenlandern, in particular, Schröder postponed his scheduled visit to Prague. A political summit scheduled to include the four "front-runners" for European Union accession was also cancelled when the Czech delegation angrily withdrew. The crisis reached its peak when Stoiber, buoyed by good polling data, attempted to link the Sudeten question to the Czechs' bid for European Union membership. By seeking political advantage in a conflict rooted in the past, the region's leaders were playing a dangerous game. Even Schröder, who initially leaned on the 1997 "Good Neighbors" Declaration, found it impossible to rise above the rancor.

It is remarkable that this episode, which seriously dampened enthusiasm for European Union enlargement among both members and applicants, did not completely derail the process. Just when the various parties seemed ready to go over the edge, outside intervention defused the crisis. After sending ambiguous and often conflicting signals for several months, the European Union's commissioner for enlargement, Günter Verheugen, stepped forward in April 2002 to reassure the Czechs that the Beneš decrees would not threaten their accession bid. Speaking in Brussels, Verheugen called for an end to the recklessness: "It is in the interest of all the parties involved in the discussion to moderate their statements and seek to find a political understanding. This understanding should be based on the principle that the postwar situation is in the past and that we want to establish a new system and a new architecture in Europe and by [doing] this to open a path toward peace and stability of all European countries."[69] Verheugen's appeal proved helpful. The Czechs continued their negotiations in Brussels and formally joined the European Union in 2004. By emphasizing the primacy of the present and the considerable stakes for the future, Verheugen convinced the key players to give up their gambit with the past. It also helped that Schröder's Social Democrats prevailed, albeit narrowly, in the German federal elections that took place on September 22, 2002.

While the flare-up in 2002 served as a warning regarding the dangers that history and historical thinking pose in the realm of international affairs, it is important to see how historical dialogue helped lay the groundwork for Verheugen's intervention. While Verheugen urged all parties in the debate not to make the past into a political obsession, there had already been two important initiatives to tame the history that Stoiber, Haider, and Zeman sought to weaponize.

The first initiative was a textbook project similar in scope and design to the German-Polish Textbook Commission described in the preceding section. Unlike its counterpart, however, the German-Czech Commission, which was launched as a UNESCO initiative in 1967, struggled to devise a workable agenda.[70] Brief periods of engagement in 1967–68 and 1976–77 were followed by longer intervals of inactivity. Following the Prague Spring (1968) and throughout most of the period of "normalization," Czechoslovak officials discouraged contact with foreigners, even within the Eastern Bloc. A brief thaw in 1976 was halted after one year, following the emergence of the Charter 77 dissident movement. When the commission resumed its work in 1987, the two sides discussed the portrayal of Czechoslovak-German relations in textbooks and school curricula, but again, external events—this time the dissolution of the Czechoslovak Federation—stymied the conversation. Whereas the work of the German-Polish Commission benefitted from a gradual process of rapprochement, the German-Czech Commission, for all practical purposes, had to begin from scratch in the post-Communist era.

Given this late start and the absence of meaningful political preparation, it is surprising how quickly the German-Czech Commission developed its program. After completing a broad survey of German-Czech relations in 1995, the commission dove into the emotionally charged topics and debates that the German-Polish Commission mostly avoided throughout the first two decades of its existence. Conferences in 1997 and 1998 explored nationalism and representations of the nation-state in German and Czech historiography. These seminars began from a critical vantage, viewing the nation as something contingent and constructed, but also potentially dangerous. The underlying idea, for the organizers, was to strip nationalist thinking of its apparent naturalness and timelessness.[71] This critique of "authentic" narratives eventually became one of the commission's core principles.

In 2002, after Zeman and Stoiber had tried to drag the past onto the bonfire of politics, the German-Czech Textbook Commission published new recommendations for classroom instruction. The guidelines encouraged teachers to lead students through a critical reevaluation of their national history and to call into question any historical narrative seeking to give an exclusive ethnic identity to a specific geographic territory. The achievements of the nation-state, according to the guidelines, ought to be considered from a variety of perspectives, including those of minority groups. Overall, the guidelines emphasized the value of "civic identity," which the commission considered "a prerequisite for 'national' identity," the importance of moving from content and coverage to critical thinking and historical habits of the mind (e.g., attention to context and skepticism toward monocausal arguments), and respect for divergent viewpoints, which the guidelines regarded as "by no means a deficit."[72]

It should be noted that the 2002 guidelines did not completely repudiate the concept of national identity. Rather, these recommendations reframed national identity as a complement and corollary to civic identity, which emphasizes cosmopolitan values (e.g., discouraging uncritical obedience to the state) over ethnonational belonging. This highlights one of the limitations of historical dialogue. The German-Czech Commission did not attempt, nor would it have managed, to strip students and instructors of their attachments to their respective national communities. Historical dialogue does not effect a magical transformation that begins with Germans (or Czechs) and ends with Europeans. Instead, by tracing history back to the migrations, negotiations, and contingencies that have imprinted particular ethnic identities onto specific European territories, the German-Czech Commission attempted to infuse a "civic" component into the common understanding of national identity. Rather than attachment to ancestry and ethnic "bloodlines," the commission focused on cultivation of democratic values and institutions as a way of making the nation less primordial and more open to critical analysis. In other words, the German-Czech Commission embraced what the philosopher Jürgen Habermas has referred to as "constitutional patriotism."[73] Understanding that political attachment and strong group identity are highly desirable for most humans, Habermas has pushed for affiliation on the basis of norms and values required for a functioning constitutional democracy. The German-Czech Textbook Commission appears to have envisioned something similar where it emphasized responsible citizenship as a possible antidote to "unreflective identification with the nation-state." Again, this conception of history and group identity does not ignore the more "organic" understandings of national identity so much as it seeks to balance these with what members of the commission saw as the overarching values of Europeanism and human rights.

The 2002 guidelines also make clear that commissioned history does not have to entail a homogenized view of the past that leaves no room for differences of perspective. The commission specifically noted that divergent views ought to be considered as a pedagogical asset rather than an impediment to understanding. While commissioned history cannot make room for untenable viewpoints that fly in the face of direct evidence, its scientific center is capacious enough to accommodate disagreement without suffering a breakdown in dialogue. The German-Czech guidelines demonstrate that mediating history is not about stripping down discussions of the past to a single, elemental strand or chaining the discussants to an inflexible statement of "official" truth. Instead, the work of historical commissions entails close scrutiny of the conflicts that divergent viewpoints generate in order to prevent these from jeopardizing the prospects for mutual understanding and cooperation. Choosing where to disagree and determining a mutually acceptable procedure for doing so (e.g., the German-Polish Commission's use of "metahistorical" commentary) is just as critical to the process as finding points of congruence.

Compared to its German-Polish counterpart, the German-Czech Textbook Commission has not enjoyed the same level of success. After attempting to create a joint history textbook based on the teaching guidelines developed in 2002, members of the commission decided in 2010 that the project was not feasible, given the differing requirements of the Czech and German school systems. Instead, the commission chose to focus on updating and supplementing the existing teacher's manual. In the interim, the commission organized a conference in 2009 called "History Lessons, Historical Awareness, and Cultivating History." A follow-up conference in 2012 took up the question of textbooks and teaching aids once more, but it also explored the role that mass media play in promoting historical awareness. Looking at the commission's website, one gets the feeling that the project has reached a kind of dead end, although there have been a handful of collaborative ventures with other organizations. Members of the commission have also published edited volumes on the role of nationalism in Central European history, World War II and its "difficult legacies" for Czech-German relations, and the depiction of the Communist period in German and Czech history books. In the final analysis, however, the German-Czech Textbook Commission seems noteworthy for what it failed to achieve in comparison with the German-Polish Commission.

Besides the textbook commission, another historical commission has tried to help the Germans and Czechs level the peaks and valleys of their relationship. The Czech-German Historians Commission was established in 1992 under the articles of the Treaty on Good Neighborhood and Friendly Cooperation, which the Czech and Slovak Republics signed with the Federal Republic of Germany. Unlike the textbook commissions, which were launched by a nongovernmental organization and developed outside of any official diplomatic channels, the Czech-German Historians Commission was the result of formal negotiations between the Czechoslovak and German governments. Under their agreement, a seventeen-member commission was established (seven Czech, six German, four Slovak; Slovak participation was voided after 1992) for regular meetings to discuss "issues related to the common past of the Czech Republic and the Federal Republic of Germany" and, in particular, the painful legacies of World War II.[74]

The Czech-German Historians Commission played an important role during the 2002 diplomatic crisis. Following the Zeman imbroglio and the cancellation of the European Union accession summit, members of the commission met in Berlin to draft a statement aimed at salvaging the Czech-German dialogue. Their position paper "against the reduction of Czech-German relations to the issue of [the] Beneš decrees" invoked the Declaration on Mutual Relations signed in 1997, but the emphasis of the commission's statement was even more deeply rooted in the need for careful historical contextualization. Citing a concern "about the misuse of historical arguments in the current political debate," the statement began by reprising the events that preceded the expulsion of Germans from Czechoslovakia. For the commission, the crucial point seemed to be that the course of international relations has always followed from historical events. In other words, the expulsions that took place from 1945 to 1947 did not occur spontaneously or in a vacuum. Rather, the commission stated, "The events immediately following the end of World War II were largely determined by the memory of the wartime atrocities and Nazi crimes."[75] The framework here is explanatory rather than accusatory or exculpatory. The commission explained that regulations were put in place to ensure that members of the Sudeten community were given an opportunity to demonstrate their loyalty to the Czech government, but their statement also noted that these safeguards "[were] not consistently observed in practice." The commission also agreed that while some consideration was given to the safety of the expellees, the expulsions were not carried out in the orderly and humane manner that the organizers had envisioned. The commission also tried to account for the shifting views of the Czechoslovak leaders in the course of the war and the ways in which the Beneš decrees represented the outcome of an evolutionary process: "The predominant view was that homogenous nation-states would be the best safeguard of a peace settlement in Central and Eastern Europe; there would be no national minorities. From late 1938, some Czecho-slovak exiled leaders and resistance fighters actually believed that Czechoslovakia should cede to Germany the areas inhabited by Germans beyond its line of defenses and resettle other groups of [the] population. However, their views changed during the war when the general trend was increasingly against any concessions."[76] Here, the commission used historical context to expose the violence of Zeman's rhetoric. In the commission's amended narrative, a conflict that might have ended peacefully in the prewar context descended into violence in the very different context of warfare characterized by mass violence, wide-spread terror, and genocidal killing.

The commission's statement specifically engaged events that took place in and around Lidice following the assassination of Reinhard Heydrich in May 1942. On Hitler's orders, Nazi troops in June 1942 drove the village's residents into a barn and systematically executed more than 60 percent of the population. Survivors were sent to concentration camps. In the aftermath of these killings, the desire for revenge greatly enhanced the potential for violence against ethnic Germans in the Czechoslovak territories. In the commission's view, the in-humane conditions that German expellees endured at the end of the war were a direct result of the violence that Germany's leaders sanctioned between 1939 and 1945. According to the historians' statement, this explained how and why "the original intention to judge Germans individually, on the basis of individual guilt and responsibility, was abandoned at this time." While the commission acknowledged that the expulsions failed to reflect "the basic idea of human rights," the removal of ethnic Germans was understood to be "one of the consequences of the war caused by the German political leadership." Simply put, Hitler's war had terrible consequences for Germans living in the East, including many innocents who had little or no sympathy for the National Socialist platform. Without providing details, the commission noted that prior to 1935 "most German-speaking voters [in the Czech territory] supported democratic German parties loyal to Czechoslovakia." So while the expulsions were carried out according to the faulty logic of "collective guilt," the commission held that the circumstances surrounding World War II made the Beneš decrees at least comprehensible, if not just.

The commission's statement, I want to suggest, is bolder than it appears. On the one hand, the commission produced a narrative that was already in wide circulation, and it built on facts that were largely uncontested. On the other hand, by developing a story in which the lines of causation are clearly traced and one atrocity begets the next, the commission opened new territory in terms of acknowledging co-responsibility for the injustices of the past. It overstates the significance of the Czech-German Historians Commission to say that the 2002 statement single-handedly salvaged bilateral relations. As previously discussed, Verheugen's intervention on behalf of the European Union played a key role, and there were a number of court cases concerning property restitution that favored the Czechs and closed the door on the Sudeten Germans.[77] While it is not particularly surprising that the Beneš decrees were upheld in the Czech courts, it is interesting to note that Czech judges at times relied on the same historical arguments made by the Czech-German Historians Commission in 2002. In rejecting a petition put forward by a Czech citizen of German descent seeking annulment of the Beneš decrees, the Czech constitutional court emphasized the importance of historical context over legal theory. Against the claim that the expulsions and confiscations carried out between 1945 and 1947 violated the legal norms of European society, the court held that "the present order . . . may not sit in judgment upon the order which prevailed in the past." The Beneš decrees were enacted "on the basis of the legal order then in force" and ought to be seen as "nothing other than a measure in reaction to the provocation represented by the elimination of state sovereignty, independence, territorial integrity, and the Czechoslovak Republic's democratic-republican form of government."[78]

The Sudeten Germans also took their claims to the European Court of Human Rights. In 2005, the ECHR heard a complaint from a group of ninety Sudeten Germans who asserted that the Beneš decrees contravened the human rights norms that govern international law. The court ruled the case inadmissible on the grounds that the petitioners had not exhausted their options in the Czech legal system but, even more crucially, in consideration of the fact that the European Convention for the Protection of Human Rights and Fundamental Freedoms did not come into effect until 1950.[79] Hailed as a "breakthrough verdict" by the Czech Ministry of Justice, the decision of the ECHR secured a legal peace for the Czechs, which, of course, the commission of historians could not.

The expulsion of the Sudeten continues to strain Czech-German relations, in spite of the ECHR's ruling and despite the best efforts of the bilateral commission. Elected to the presidency in 2013, Miloš Zeman has shown no sign of toning down his rhetoric or embracing the narrative offered by the commission. During a visit to Austria in April 2013, Zeman told reporters that the Sudeten ought to consider themselves lucky for having faced only expulsion and not something worse. Zeman reckoned, "When a citizen of some country collaborates with a country that has occupied his state, an expulsion is a subtler punishment than, for example, a death penalty."[80] While Zeman drew some domestic criticism for these comments (one Czech historian compared him to Slobodan Milošević), he also enjoyed a good measure of support in the political mainstream. A 2011 survey showed that 42 percent of Czechs still considered the expulsions to have been just, while 39 percent considered them unjust.[81] The Czechs and Germans have moved on to other disagreements, which do not carry the same historical significance,[82] but these issues have continued to put pressure on the fundamentals of the 1997 Declaration of Mutual Understanding, particularly the notion that bilateral relations "will not be burdened by political and legal questions coming from the past." There has not been another statement from the Czech-German Historians Commission concerning Zeman's latest remarks. The commission has continued to explore the history of Czech-German relations, including follow-up work on the expulsions and subsequent efforts to promote reconciliation. In October 2010, the commission held a conference on contradictory memories and the representation of mass violence in museums, with special consideration given to the Holocaust and the postwar expulsions.[83] In 2011, the commission organized a conference on property rights and property disputes, and participants explored these topics through the lens of the Czech-German borderlands and the violence committed there during the twentieth century. Since 1992, the commission has published its conference proceedings in a coedited, dual-language journal, covering a range of topics, including a comparative study of anti-Semitism in Central Europe; the history of Czech-German economic competition and cooperation from 1918 to 1945; "The Road to Disaster," which treated

German-Czechoslovakian relations between 1938 and 1947; and the expulsion of ethnic Germans from Eastern Europe in a comparative framework.[84] Since 2011, the commission has also awarded research scholarships to graduate students and young academics working on archives related to the history of Czech-German relations. Commission members are now appointed by the two country's respective professional historical associations with oversight from the Czech Ministry of Foreign Affairs and the German Foreign Office. While the commission enjoys broad autonomy over its research agenda and conference programs, financial support from the respective governments has enabled more than two decades of uninterrupted work. Even as high-ranking officials (in the case of Zeman, a head of state) have mined the past for the partisan memories that support their political ambitions and personal world-views, the commission's quasi-official status has helped create a countervailing force aimed at mutual understanding. Should a political framework for "deep" reconciliation present itself, the Czech-German Historians Commission will be in a strong position to support the process. In the meantime, other segments of civil society keep the expulsions in the public consciousness, although not always with the same thoroughgoing commitment to thoughtful contextualization.[85]

6

The International Commission on Holocaust-Era Insurance Claims

ost insurance assets resurfaced as an item of concern for the large Jewish organizations in Israel and the United States when the second wave of Holocaust restitution began in the 1990s. While some Holocaust survivors tried to collect on unpaid policies through the European courts in the 1950s, insurance firms were not pressed to give a full accounting of which policies had been paid and to whom. This changed in the mid-1990s as debates over property restitution in Eastern Europe and fresh revelations concerning so-called dormant accounts in the Swiss banks rekindled interest in the policies that European Jews had purchased prior to the Holocaust. During the interwar period, insurance policies had been a popular investment strategy for Jews (and others) seeking protection from economic volatility. These policies covered a variety of events and assets, not only life and property but also individual retirement and college savings funds, and even dowry for the betrothal of daughters. In the aftermath of the Holocaust, Jews who made claims on these policies were often rebuffed by the companies that had issued them, either because the beneficiaries lacked original policy documents or because the premiums had gone unpaid following the policyholder's internment or because the companies had transferred these assets to the Nazis and, therefore, considered them as paid. As part of an effort to sort out the legal complications that prevented Jewish policyholders and their heirs from reclaiming these assets, American insurance industry analysts estimated in the mid-1990s that these unpaid policies were likely worth between $1 billion and $4 billion.[1]

European Jews who purchased insurance policies prior to World War II did not fit a single profile. Many policies were purchased by bourgeois urbanites in Western and Central Europe, but poorer Jews who eked out a living in the shtetls of Eastern Europe also invested small sums. While the prewar data are difficult to recover, insurance regulators in Florida estimated in 1997 that up to one-third of all Holocaust survivors might hold a legitimate claim.[2] As the Nazi dictatorship solidified, insurance policies became increasingly attractive to Jewish customers, and some firms began to market policies that were payable in foreign currencies (e.g., dollars) or gave guarantees of continuous coverage if the policyholder elected to emigrate. Large firms, such as the Italian-based Assicurrazioni Generali, did exceptionally well selling policies in precisely the territories that were hardest hit by the Nazis after 1938–39 (e.g., Poland, Czechoslovakia, and Hungary).

Following the war, companies that received inquiries from would-be claimants frequently cited lack of adherence to administrative rules as their reason for declining to pay. According to representatives for the companies, these claims were made either too early (before the postwar governments had established an official protocol) or received too late (after the expiration of some arbitrary cutoff). Where policyholders had died or had been killed during the war, heirs often struggled to collect and present what the companies required for "proper" documentation. Many of the claimants had been small children when their parents purchased the original policy, and consequently they did not know—or could not remember—important details related to the coverage. Some legitimate heirs were never listed as beneficiaries and were disqualified on that basis, for example, nieces, nephews, and others outside the policyholder's immediate family. Complicating matters further, many insurance records were destroyed during the war, and some firms ceased operating after the war. Other companies were absorbed by their competitors. In cases where companies chose to pay on Jewish claims, they often disbursed insultingly low sums to the beneficiaries, claiming that the policy's value had eroded as a consequence of inflation.[3] In 1997, a French newspaper reported the story of one Holocaust victim who had made regular payments on a life insurance policy for eighteen years before being deported to a concentration camp, where he subsequently died. In 1945 his children received a payment of twenty-six centimes, the approximate cost of a subway ticket.[4] Given the prevalence of such stories and an estimated total for unpaid policies that reached into the billions, the eventual involvement of lawyers and public officials is hardly surprising. By 1997, a class-action lawsuit had been filed in New York against Generali and a handful of other European firms with business ties to the United States. At the time of the filing, attorneys for the plaintiffs estimated that the case could attract more than 10,000 claimants, and they predicted average awards in excess of $75,000.[5] Faced with the possibility of a nine-figure judgment and believing their actual exposure to be much lower, some of the companies named in the suit developed proactive strategies for clarification, for example, by establishing toll-free hotlines for potential claimants and by opening their company files to independent auditors. Other companies, fearing that the lawsuit in New York would open the floodgates to additional claims, took a more hard-line approach and promised to defend themselves vigorously against "misleading" claims aimed at "embarrassing [firms] into paying amounts that are not due."[6]

In September 1997, as attention to the plight of the beneficiaries mounted, the National Association of Insurance Commissioners (NAIC), headquartered in Kansas City, established a Holocaust-Era Assets Working Group. The purpose of the Working Group was (1) to communicate with survivors so as to further assess the scope of the problem, and (2) to establish a dialogue with the firms that sold these policies (or acquired the portfolios of those that did) to discuss the terms of a possible settlement. Noting that Holocaust survivors had waited more than fifty years for consideration, the NAIC urged that action be taken as quickly as possible. The Working Group convened informational hearings in American cities with large survivor communities, and elderly claimants gave emotional testimony in which they recounted their experiences during the Holocaust and described their unsuccessful efforts to collect on family policies afterward.

In March 1998, the Working Group formed a subcommittee to draft a memorandum of understanding (MOU) that defined the responsibilities of the NAIC and the European insurance firms and outlined plans to develop a comprehensive database for recording and investigating claims. In the memo, the Working Group identified several issues requiring further work: the development of adequate documentation standards (what would constitute proof of an unpaid claim); establishing a legitimate principle of valuation (how to determine the current value of unpaid policies); protocol for the resolution of heirless claims (how to process policies for which no beneficiaries could be located); and settlement terms for nationalized policies (how to proceed where insurance writers had been taken over by the state).[7]

The pressure of the class-action suit in New York and the determination of the NAIC to seek justice for the survivors produced a new framework for negotiation in the summer of 1998. Working closely with several Jewish NGOs as well as the State of Israel, the NAIC created a special task force whose purpose was to establish an international commission to resolve the unpaid insurance claims of Holocaust survivors.[8] Comprised of insurance regulators from the United States and Europe, the task force continued talks with six European companies that sold large numbers of policies in the inter-war period.[9] These discussions helped to finalize the MOU that established a new body, the International Commission for Holocaust-Era Insurance Claims (ICHEIC), whose subsequent role was to manage negotiations with the insurance companies on behalf of survivors.

From its inception, the ICHEIC argued that neither the claimants nor the insurance companies would be well served by adversarial litigation. For the aging claimants, a lengthy court battle might not be resolved within their life-time, while the insurance firms would be financially hamstrung during a protracted period of legal limbo. The MOU also highlighted the commission's determination to reach consensus on all key points in order to ensure a balance of interests. The commission was made up of three insurance regulators from the United States, two members appointed by Jewish survivor organizations, one member nominated by Israel, and six more who represented European insurance interests. Lawrence Eagleburger, a former secretary of state under George H. W. Bush, served as chairman. With its variegated membership, its strong commitment to negotiation and consensus, and the threat of a less desirable alternative looming over both sides, the ICHEIC promised a quick and just outcome. Petitioners in the New York class action, hopeful that the commission could deliver, dropped their suit in exchange for guaranteed representation at future settlement talks. Edward Fagan, the lead lawyer in the case, described his clients' optimism in an interview with the *New York Times*: "This puts everybody at one table to work out a mechanism for a speedy settlement."[10] The expectation was that a settlement could be secured if both sides engaged in open dialogue, and that the question of money could be re-solved once the larger issue of moral justice was addressed. At the same time, Fagan emphasized that no settlement could be reached without a direct role for the victims.

A Line to Nowhere?

Despite the optimism surrounding its creation, the ICHEIC failed to deliver the outcome that Fagan and his clients sought. The commission stumbled badly during the initial setup phase, and its members struggled to formulate clear operating guidelines. Before long, the ICHEIC drew sharp criticism from both claimants and outside observers, and ultimately the commission negotiated a settlement, which many saw as patently unjust. In 2003,

U.S. District Court Judge Michael B. Mukasey allowed for the resumption of class-action litigation, explaining that the ICHEIC resembled "a company store," whose close ties to European insurance firms negated any possibility of fair treatment for the claimants.[11] Deborah Senn, a member of the NAIC task force that created the ICHEIC, described its record as "a huge disappointment," and even John Garamendi, a member of the commission's board of directors, acknowledged that the ICHEIC "[had] failed miserably at its task."[12] In September 2003, two Holocaust survivors sued the ICHEIC, claiming that it had colluded with insurers to "diminish and deny claims" by allowing the insurers to withhold crucial documentation related to unpaid policies.[13]

Although the ICHEIC had promised to move quickly, the commission spent eight years trying to negotiate a settlement that satisfied both the claimants and the insurance companies. From the outset, there were significant obstacles that prevented the two sides from agreeing on a basic framework in which to pursue the negotiations. Two of these, the proper valuation of policies and the standard of proof employed in the investigation of claims, had been identified earlier in the MOU that the NAIC drafted just prior to the launch of the commission. As discussions to resolve these issues unfolded, representatives for the claimants argued that the overall process was slanted in favor of the insurance companies. Almost immediately following the creation of the commission, the participating insurance firms contributed $100 million toward a settlement fund, but these funds were held in escrow for the next three years as the disputes over valuation and standards of proof continued.[14] Whereas in an earlier deal, Dutch firms had agreed to pay twenty-two times the face value of polices written during the Holocaust era, Allianz initially refused to consider anything above 1.7 times. Despite the commission's stated commitment to consensus building, Eagleburger eventually intervened on a unilateral basis to set the payment standard at roughly ten times face value.[15]

At the same time that these debates over valuation were drawing negative attention, Jewish survivor organizations also complained that European insurers were thwarting their efforts to establish a comprehensive list of unpaid claims. For survivors, open access to insurance company records was a critical issue, since approximately 80 percent of potential claimants did not know the name of the company that issued their relatives' policies. While the ICHEIC made the publication of policy data one of its primary goals, the insurance firms dragged their collective feet by offering the least possible assistance, particularly in the early stages. By the end of 2000, Generali had released only 11,000 names, which represented 3.2 percent of the 340,000 listings that experts believed their records to contain.[16] Generali, these experts pointed out, had already released 100,000 names to Yad Vashem during the negotiation of a separate settlement with Israel with the provision that these were to remain confidential.[17] Allianz, which held an estimated 1.5 million unpaid policies, released fewer than 400 names, while AXA, citing privacy concerns, refused to release any of the names from its list of 570,000 Holocaust-era policies.[18] The ICHEIC eventually managed to publish a list of more than 500,000 policyholders.[19] But this roster, which was compiled in 2003, represented only a fraction of the 2.5 million policies that the commission had targeted in 2001.[20]

Disagreement over standards of proof also shadowed the ICHEIC. While the commission promised that claimants would benefit from "relaxed standards," in light of the historical circumstances, getting the insurers to accept the validity of specific claims proved to be extraordinarily difficult.[21] Allianz, for example, received 15,000 claims through the ICHEIC by 2001 but offered settlements in just four cases, while Winterthur, which received 6,500 claims, offered no settlements at all.[22] In November 2001, the Fort Lauderdale *Sun-Sentinel* reported that less than 2 percent of the 40,000 claims submitted through the ICHEIC had garnered settlement offers.[23] At the same time, a large number of claims, more than 33,000 according to one estimate, had been thrown out due to what the insurance firms judged as insufficient documentation.[24] A raft of complaints also came from claimants who received low settlement offers. One claimant, after having been matched to two separate life insurance policies, was offered $500.[25]

Criticism of the ICHEIC's settlement criteria was compounded by concerns over mismanagement and administrative overspending. Some critics highlighted the fact that Eagleburger, the commission's chairman, received a salary of $360,000, while others serving in similar roles (e.g., Paul Volcker, chair of the Independent Commission of Eminent Persons [ICEP/Volcker Commission] charged with investigating the Swiss Banks) provided their services pro bono.[26] Others pointed to the dismissal and eventual disbarment of the commission's chief of staff, Neal Sher, over unauthorized travel reimbursements.[27] The most prevalent criticisms related to administrative spending and the costs of overhead. The *New York Times* reported in 2002 that the ICHEIC had distributed $15 million in settlements, while spending $40 million on its own operations.[28] Other sources painted an even shadier picture. *Deutsche-Presse Agentur* ran a story in May 2001 alleging that the commission had spent ten times as much on its operations ($30 million) as it had on settlements ($3 million).[29] Eagleburger, who briefly resigned as chair of the commission when these expenditures were publicized, blamed the insurance firms for holding up the process and making the investigative process more expensive than it needed to be. While acknowledging that his commission had spent aggressively,

Eagleburger hit back by describing the importance of critical, but also expensive, projects aimed at promoting the ICHEIC's work and making potential claimants aware of the program. The ICHEIC, he pointed out, devoted substantial resources to global outreach and administration. Not only did the multinational composition of the claimant pool necessitate the use of extensive translation services, the commission also spent vast sums to "define the target audience."[30] The commission set up a twenty-four-hour call center in New York City to handle inquiries related to the claims process and to provide assistance, which was made available in more than twenty languages, to individuals filling out their claims forms. The commission also relied on both free and paid media to extend its reach and promote its work. Working with the same media strategists who conducted outreach for the Claims Resolution Tribunal in the case of the Swiss banks, the ICHEIC issued press releases, sent out posters and pamphlets to Jewish survivor organizations, and distributed informational packets in survivor communities.[31] Advertisements to facilitate the claims process appeared in both major media and in more parochial outlets. According to the ICHEIC, these outlays generated in excess of 100,000 claims from more than thirty countries.[32] Additional advertising was purchased as various filing deadlines approached. Concerns over spending and mismanagement escalated to the point that the U.S. House of Representatives requested that the commission be investigated by the State Department. The insurance companies that financed the ICHEIC also demanded reimbursement for some of their expenses, and German insurers pushed to deduct their own administrative costs ($76 million) from the final settlement sum.[33]

The NAIC had argued that an international commission would deliver a fuller measure of justice to aging victims than lawyers would (and more quickly), but it took eighteen months for the ICHEIC to establish a rudimentary framework for claims processing. When the commission finally attempted to implement this plan, it unraveled almost completely. Hundreds of millions of dollars sat in escrow, while the insurance companies who contributed these funds challenged the fundamental points of the commission's modus operandi. When the review process finally lurched into gear (February 2000), the results were underwhelming, and the commission faced charges of corruption and incompetence for the next several years. The deadline to file a claim, originally set for January 31, 2002, was extended several times with the final date pushed to December 31, 2003. In the end, all claims received by March 31, 2004, were given consideration. The ICHEIC claimed that these extensions were given when archival research showed that the scope of the problem was bigger than originally thought. However, based on what appears in the commission's own records, this scenario seems rather unlikely. According to its final report, the

ICHEIC resolved a total of 90,000 claims from 1998 to 2006. Out of this total, the commission offered $306 million in payments to 48,000 survivors.[34] Another $169 million was provided to support social welfare programs serving Holocaust survivors without a specific insurance claim and to pay for a variety of Holocaust education initiatives. But while the total settlement ($475 million) might look impressive to some, it is important to weigh these figures against the commission's own lofty expectations. After sparring with the insurance companies for nearly two years, the commission eventually published a list of 500,000 potential policyholders.[35] These figures suggest an average settlement of less than $6,400.[36] Even if one focuses on the total settlement of $306 million, this sum pales in comparison to the estimates that outside analysts provided—between $1 and $4 billion—when they pushed for the creation of the commission in 1997.[37]

All of this helps explain why a Federal District Court judge ruled in 2002 that Holocaust victims seeking to collect on unpaid insurance policies were not bound by the ICHEIC's process.[38] These calculations and comparisons also communicate something about the mind-set of individuals who submitted claims to the ICHEIC but then walked away when the insurance companies offered what they considered to be lowball settlements. In April 2003, the *New York Times* reported on several such individuals, including Suzanne Weiner-Zada, who had filed claims through the ICHEIC on multiple policies written by Generali, including one that covered her ten-year-old brother, who was killed in Auschwitz. Weiner-Zada received an initial settlement offer of $10,533 (it was later raised to $16,012), but she refused to accept this payout and instead sought relief through the courts when representatives for Generali asked her for a written statement acknowledging that the insurer bore no actual responsibility for her brother's unpaid policy. "It's like they're offering this money out of the goodness of their heart, that I should be grateful to them," Weiner-Zada railed. "But I'm not grateful to them. My father paid for this policy, and I should be able to enjoy the benefits."[39] In the same article, Eagleburger defended the ICHEIC, saying that the commission had "instituted a number of creative solutions that benefit claimants." He added that Generali had paid claims through the ICHEIC that "it would not have been required to under normal insurance practices."

Given the precedent of the Swiss banking scandal and the $1.25 billion settlement negotiated through the ICEP in August 1998, the difficulties of the ICHEIC are hard to fathom. Eagleburger stated that the struggles of his commission were due primarily to the large scope of the investigation, which, he asserted, no one involved in the process could have anticipated.[40] But the Volcker Commission faced a task no less daunting, and that body managed to produce a substantial settlement in just over two years.[41] If anything, the troubles of the ICHEIC can be pinned on the various ways in which the example of the Volcker Commission was not followed. This included Volcker's determination to subject the Swiss banks to an independent investigation and thus allow external oversight of the distribution of reclaimed assets. By contrast, the ICHEIC did not require the insurance companies to open themselves up to an independent investigation of their records, although Allianz, at one point, paid Arthur Anderson LLP to make a survey of their corporate records. Moreover, the insurers did not have to submit their settlement offers to an external review panel. Because of the negative publicity generated by some of the early settlement offers, the ICHEIC added an appeals process that utilized specially appointed judges, but this review was conducted behind closed doors. Whereas the Volcker Commission endeavored to maximize transparency and incorporate strict oversight, the ICHEIC instituted a secretive process, which gave the insurance firms considerable leverage in determining the framework for negotiation and settlement. It should also be pointed out that the insurance companies negotiated their total liability ($475 million) *five years before* the commission completed its archival research. Given this "cart before the horse" approach, it is not surprising that claimants like Weiner-Zada withdrew from the process and took their cases to the courts instead. Frank Kaplan, lead counsel in a lawsuit aimed at forcing the insurance companies to publish the full extent of their policy lists, pulled no punches when describing the ICHEIC's advocacy on behalf of the claimants: "These people are in a line to nowhere."[42] In September 2003, Eagleburger was called to testify in front of the U.S. House of Representatives Committee on Government Reform, and the ICHEIC was slapped with a lawsuit, filed in Los Angeles by two Holocaust survivors who claimed that the commission supported unfair business practices by accommodating the insurance companies to the point of negligence. It would be easy to argue that the ICHEIC never fully recovered from this crisis, despite the work it performed over the next three years.

Historiographical Assessment

Beyond the public relations skirmishes, the investigations, and the lawsuits, it is interesting to consider the work of the ICHEIC from a historiographical perspective. While the commission lurched from one problem to the next for most of the time it operated, its work also entailed a significant commitment to historical clarification and archival research. Prior to the launch of the ICHEIC, there was a great deal of secrecy and uncertainty surrounding the business practices of the major European insurers before, during, and after the Holocaust. The commission sought to shed light on the subject by initiating a large research project in key archives located in Central and Eastern Europe, Israel, and the United States. To this end, the commission contracted two experts, Yoram Mayorek (Israel) and Frank Drauschke (Germany), whose previous research gave them familiarity with the relevant materials. Mayorek and Drauschke assigned much of the legwork to a team of researchers, who combed through archival records in fifteen different countries, beginning in 2000. The ICHEIC initially gave the researchers six months to complete the investigation, but the project was extended several times to allow for a more thorough analysis of the relevant materials. The researchers completed their work in 2003, and Mayorek and Drauschke prepared a final report on the team's findings, which was released to the public in April 2004.

The research team focused on three types of records. The first set was pulled from Nazi files and was comprised of asset registration logs and confiscation inventories. The Nazis kept detailed records of their spoliation (one scholar recalls finding a receipt for a dog, which the Nazis "confiscated" prior to the owner's deportation), so this entailed considerable work for the research team. The second data category included claims forms prepared by Jewish survivors seeking to reclaim their plundered properties immediately following Germany's surrender. Once again, the sheer scale of Holocaust-era spoliation made for an enormous amount of work. The final category, also the smallest, included insurance company records, which were located in public and regulatory archives.[43] Except for Allianz, which invited a historian from the University of California–Berkeley to examine its corporate archives, the insurance companies did not make their own materials available, to the great consternation of many victims and others who viewed the ICHEIC as a toothless bureaucracy created to feed itself and rubber-stamp whatever settlement plan the insurance companies agreed to devise.

The ICHEIC researchers did a huge amount of work. Just counting the third category of findings (insurance records), the research teams located 77,518 policies written for 55,079 policyholders. These materials also included the names of 16,579 beneficiaries, although in many cases there was little accompanying information to track down these individuals. The insurance firms, as noted, did little to assist the researchers in their efforts to track down unpaid policies and locate the policyholders or heirs. In the final report, the ICHEIC indicates that the insurance companies, although initially reluctant to publish their own data, changed their stance over time and became committed "to making potential policyholder names available for use within the ICHEIC process."[44] It seems clear from the way the commission was received, and from the crises that arose between 2000 and 2003, that many outside observers questioned the depth of this commitment. In any case, the commission used the data it harvested to create a database, which it then ran through an elaborate matching protocol. In the final report, the commission makes a great deal of the "electronic tools," which it used to scan the names in the database and the way this protocol streamlined what otherwise would have required a cumbersome manual review. The matching protocol and the use of electronic sorting, according to the report, "added significant value to the claims process."

One issue that the ICHEIC did not engage in any meaningful way is the quality and character of the evidence located by their researchers. Jewish claimants, in many cases, asserted that their primary concern was not money but rather the "larger" question of justice. Some, like Suzanne Weiner-Zada, were interested in reclaiming what was rightfully theirs, but many stated that what they wanted more than anything was some acknowledgment from the insurers that those unpaid policies represented another kind of injury, another wound on top of what they and their families had already suffered. The archival materials that the ICHEIC researchers worked with discouraged this kind of acknowledgment. The Nazi records (i.e., property registries and confiscation inventories) and the publically recorded insurance documents that the ICHEIC investigated held limited value for those who sought a nuanced explanation for past injustice. Given the nature of their task, the commission's research teams focused on documentation of material loss. Their job was to find policies, estimate their value, and, if possible, locate the beneficiaries to produce a settlement. But this work plan did not intersect with the larger concerns expressed by the victims, meaning their desire to receive acknowledgment of wrongdoing. In offering to settle with Weiner-Zada, Generali sought full exculpation in the form of a written statement releasing the company from any legal or concrete obligation. It is difficult to find anything in the ICHEIC research reports that challenges or subverts this kind of formula, in which monetary compensation is offered in exchange for the effacement of injustice.

Both Catherine Lillie and Gerald Feldman have written on this tension between historical research as a search for lost/pilfered assets and as a potential remedy to injustice, more broadly conceived.[45] To different degrees and in different ways, both have wrestled with the problem of shaping historical narratives on the basis of fragmentary records. Whereas Lillie has emphasized the richness of the insurance archives (e.g., as compared to the records related to Swiss bank accounts, where secrecy was paramount), Feldman has addressed the difficulties of compiling source materials where companies have not been thoroughly committed to historical preservation and where historical events have led to the unintentional destruction of important materials.[46] But the larger point here deals less with how much material historians have at their disposal, and more with the types of material that commissions like the ICHEIC dig for, compile, and use as evidence in their accounts of the past. If one is interested chiefly in the relationship between the insurance business and the Nazi regime, then the sources considered by the ICHEIC prove to be illuminating. If, on the other hand, one is interested in reconstructing what is owed to Holocaust survivors as a consequence of nonpayment on insurance policies purchased in the interwar period and thus wants to understand the full implications of that injury for the victims, then the commission's work appears to have been insufficient. While the ICHEIC's final report includes a smattering of victims' testimony, understanding their perspective was not a major aspect of the commission's work. Painful memories that victims shared in the hearings that preceded the creation of the commission and the artifacts they supplied to substantiate their claims are mentioned anecdotally in the final report, but the commission's subsequent research ignored these sources in favor of Nazi records and insurance company records in public and regulatory archives. The question is whether one can truly understand the full meaning and impact of nonpayment on these policies from the victims' perspective through the kinds of sources collected by the commission.

In April 2004, the ICHEIC published its "Final Report on External Research."[47] This eighteen-page document with two appendices, each with eight items, summarized the commission's key findings. Reading the document, one starts to understand not only the commission's research process on a general level but also the decision-making that led the researchers to privilege some kinds of records while ignoring others. The most striking feature of the research report is the absence of individual victims, or more properly, the distance that exists between the commission's tabulations and the individual policyholders whose savings the insurance companies misdirected or refused to disgorge. For example, appendix A-5 (Statistics According to Country of Residence) is significant because of the way it condenses and articulates the data. Rather than counting policyholders (individuals), this table counts only policies (accounts), which it then maps onto specific countries of origin. And although the research report includes other tables in which the individual policyholders are made visible, there is a general trend toward depersonalized accounting, like the information provided in A-5. The report includes a country-by-country overview of the commission's research, which is noteworthy for its many references to "files" and "records" as well as the pronounced absence of the defrauded victims as individuals. For example, the overview for

Hungary (section 2.13) describes the review of "no less than 100 record groups and collections," but there is no mention at all of the individuals whose lives intersect with these records. One could argue that the researchers used a kind of shorthand here and that the presence of the victims can be easily inferred from their notations. But again, what seems important here is the unarticulated distance between the two, whether intentional or not. To what extent does a survey of "record groups" illuminate the experience of Holocaust victims or, to turn the question around, how might the inclusion of these sources and the exclusion of others dull our understanding of Holocaust-era insurance practices and their long-term effects by pushing us away from the victims?

Gerald Feldman's work is instructive here. In his monograph on Allianz and the German insurance industry during the Nazi era, Feldman approached the collection of source materials in a completely different manner from that of the ICHEIC. Not only was Feldman allowed to examine Allianz's corporate archive, a privilege that was never extended to the ICHEIC, his study incorporated the private papers (i.e., victims' correspondence) that the commission ignored. Describing his methodology, Feldman stated, "Periodically . . . one does find valuable and usually painful, but also very illuminating, correspondence in the policies which reveal the situation of the Jews [who] had insurance as well as the way in which Allianz dealt with them."[48] Whereas the ICHEIC chose not to include these letters in the final research report, Feldman describes them as "[his] primary interest." In other words, Feldman's history privileges not the policies themselves or the "record groups" into which they were collected, but instead the personal letters of Jewish victims describing what these assets represented in terms of their ability to rebuild their lives in the aftermath of the Holocaust.

Of course, there is no reason why statistical data cannot support rich and nuanced historical analysis. It makes sense that the commission's researchers sought out the materials they did, given that their overall aim was "to locate and register information on Holocaust-era life insurance policies and their owners."[49] However, the issue here pertains to the meaning of the word "information." Does it refer to the financial details of specific policies (i.e., purchaser, accrued payments, policy terms, etc.), or might it refer to the added pressures—financial and otherwise—that unpaid claims placed on survivors following more than a decade of racial persecution and violence? In what ways did the claimants' unsuccessful requests for payment after the war exacerbate the loss of dignity, which demonization, spoliation, internment, deportation, and genocide had already produced? How might the personal letters of policyholders enhance our understanding of Jewish disenfranchisement *before* the war? For example, what could the ICHEIC's inquiry have taught us about "[the] harried struggle to maintain adequate premium payments" as Nazi racial laws spread through Europe?[50]

Another thing the ICHEIC might have illuminated, but failed to, are the strategies that Jews used to cope with their deteriorating situation. As Catherine Lillie has shown, the personal letters that the commission overlooked reflect the difficult choices that Jewish policyholders were forced to make as their economic and social standing became increasingly imperiled.[51] Some chose to cash in their policies, despite penalties for doing so, in order to pay the costs associated with their emigration attempts, while others did the same merely to cover the next month's rent. In some cases, insurers advised policyholders that they could take out loans using their policies as collateral, or else convert the policies to maturity at a lower value. The point is that the recovery of insurance assets might have served as an opportunity to develop the history of the Holocaust, rather than as a mechanical exercise in the negotiation of material debts. The research report compiled by the ICHEIC has the character of what Hayden White has called an "annal."[52] It is more or less a list of events (policy purchases, policy lapses, policy claims and settlements, etc.) arranged chronologically or geographically, but it lacks what White termed a "social center," meaning that these events are not clearly linked to a specific point of view nor are they imbued with any moral meaning. The focus of the study is tabulation and computation, rather than moral instruction or political advocacy. Purists might claim that historians have no business in either of these arenas, but as I have argued throughout this study, the withholding of such commitments is also a moral and political stance. At the very least, it would seem that the ICHEIC missed an opportunity to compare the Nazi paper trail against the letters and recollections of the victims. Without the victims' perspective, there is no way for the ICHEIC's study to mediate the past, and this might explain the decision of some of the claimants to take their cases back to the courts.

Regarding the potential of historical commissions to clarify the past and mediate conflict, the record of the ICHEIC should temper expectations. Large Jewish organizations that initially supported the ICHEIC have not hesitated to express their disappointment, and outside observers, in some cases, have actively pushed for the resumption of class-action litigation.[53] There can be no doubt about the relative size of the settlements brokered by the ICHEIC compared to the awards ordered by the courts or the settlements negotiated by lawyers who feared an even more damaging outcome in front of a jury. The commission's report suggests an average settlement of roughly $6,400 (actual payments ranged from $1,000 to more than $1 million). In November 1999, Adolf Stern, an Auschwitz survivor, received a settlement from Generali in the amount of $1.25 million for unpaid life insurance policies purchased by his father.[54] When Stern had tried to collect on these policies immediately after the war, Generali bizarrely demanded that he present a death certificate for his father, who died in Auschwitz, in addition to copies of the original policy papers. Peter Simhauser, Generali's counsel, told the *New York Times* that Stern's settlement reflected the company's policy of working to resolve all Holocaust-era claims fairly. Generali contributed more than $120 million to the ICHEIC settlement fund (one-quarter of the total disbursements) and offered settlements of several hundred thousand dollars to some of the claimants who applied for relief through the commission. On the other hand, Generali is the firm that pressed Suzanne Weiner-Zada for written acknowledgment that her settlement offer was made on the basis of charity, rather than as the fulfillment of a legal obligation (and this action is what prompted her to sue). Moreover, in the first two years of the commission's work, Generali released the names of just 11,000 policyholders out of an estimated 340,000.

Although the ICHEIC ceased operations in 2006, Jewish survivors and their heirs have continued to press for compensation on unpaid policies. In 2007, Generali agreed to pay $175 million to settle its class-action suits, a sum that more than doubled what the company paid to survivors while working through the ICHEIC. Some of the plaintiffs, meanwhile, complained that Generali still got off cheaply. Sidney Zabludoff, an economist with the Jerusalem Center for Public Affairs, estimated that Generali had sold 110,000 "Jewish" policies by the time of the Holocaust, and he calculated their present-day value at $4.5 billion.[55] In June 2007, the USHMM released a trove of documents, which were recovered from a vacant apartment in Vienna.[56] Although authorities in Vienna sought to assure the public that these documents had no connection to bank or insurance assets, survivors were skeptical, since, as one lawyer put it, "every institution holding information about their past and their assets has concealed relevant information."[57] In March 2011, the U.S. House of Representatives debated a measure that would have forced European insurers doing business in the United States to disclose all of their documentation related to unpaid claims on Holocaust-era policies;[58] the State Department objected, however, arguing that the bill's passage would produce "significant problems in our foreign relations."[59] Instead, the State Department urged survivors to work with the European insurance firms to negotiate claims that were never registered with the ICHEIC. In a "fact sheet," which could have been pulled from the commission's final report, the State Department commended the European insurance companies for working with the ICHEIC "even though most of the claimants had no documents about or records of the policies for which they filed claims."[60] One can only guess at the diplomatic considerations that led the State Department to take the side of the ICHEIC. Whatever the case, it is a useful reminder of the limitations of the commission model for achieving justice. Where truth-seeking impinges on the political interests of the state and commissions are unwilling or unable to circumnavigate government policy, claimants will find themselves at a significant disadvantage. Under the administrations of George W. Bush and Barack Obama, the federal government has actively discouraged Holocaust survivors from using the U.S. courts to pursue their insurance assets. Nonetheless, a handful of survivors have pushed their claims through legal channels, and in these cases, the compensation they garnered far outweighed what the ICHEIC achieved on their behalf. The poor performance of the ICHEIC can be explained several ways: weak leadership, cost overrun, ambiguous mandate, and poorly conceived research methodology being just a few. In the end, we must look to international politics, as well as a certain degree of fatigue regarding Holocaust justice. Coming on the heels of a $1.25 billion settlement with the Swiss banks (1998) and a $5 billion settlement with the German government on behalf of slave laborers (2000), the ICHEIC received no encouragement to press for maximum claims except from the victims, and it lacked sufficient authority to challenge the political cover that the U.S. government gave to the European insurance firms.

7

The International Catholic-Jewish Historical Commission

t is easy to see why Europe's large insurance firms pushed back against the claims of Holocaust survivors, given that billions of dollars hung in the balance. But if money is today's standard for symbolizing guilt and giving it a concrete expression, it is not always the most precious commodity for groups attempting to mediate the past. Where history crosses over sacred ground and claims of infallibility come up against secular skepticism, the possibilities for constructive dialogue are more limited than in cases, like that of unpaid insurance claims, where the stakes are firmly rooted in the material world.

Within Holocaust historiography, few topics have provoked the same degree of vitriol as the debates over Pope Pius XII (r. 1939–58) and the role of the Vatican during World War II. Despite several attempts by the Roman Catholic Church to improve relations with Jews during the past half century, interfaith reconciliation has proven to be elusive. Since 1963, when Rolf Hochhuth's play *Stellvertreter* (*The Deputy*) presented Pius XII as "a symbol of all men who are passive when their brother is harmed," the two sides have been engaged in a cycle of mutual recrimination, which waxes and wanes but never fully dissipates.[1] At one extreme, Pius's most severe critics have latched on to every crumb and kernel that seems to damage the papacy, no matter what the historical context or competing evidence might suggest. At the other end of the spectrum, Catholic apologists, including some who still adhere to the doctrine of papal infallibility, refuse to accept anything short of saintliness in the attitudes and actions of the Catholic leadership.[2] While several recent studies of Pius XII have navigated between these extremes, much of the public discourse still unfolds at the two outside poles.

Opinions regarding Pius XII were not always so deeply divided. At the time of his election in 1939, Jewish groups voiced strong support for Pius XII, noting his record as a defender of democracy and minority rights. The *Zionist Review* (London) commented on March 16, 1939, that Pius's appointment "confirms the view that the new Pope means to conduct an anti-Nazi and anti-Fascist policy."[3] Pius received accolades from some Jewish leaders, even in the last stages of the Holocaust. In April 1945, with the Nazi regime in its death throes, Moshe Sharrett, the future foreign minister and prime minister of Israel, met with Pius at the Vatican. In his report to the executive of the Jewish Agency, Sharrett wrote: "My first duty was to thank him, and through him, the Catholic Church, on behalf of the Jewish public, for all they had done in the various countries to rescue Jews, to save children, and Jews in general."[4] Pinchas Lapide, a low-ranking Israeli diplomat, who had worked for a time in Italy, argued in *The Last Three Popes and the Jews* that Pius XII rescued more Jews during the Holocaust (between 700,000 and 860,000) than any other person or organization in the world. Estimating that 1.3 million European Jews had survived Hitler's onslaught, Lapide subtracted from this sum all of the "reasonable" claims of rescue made by non-Catholic groups. The remainder, he concluded, had been saved "under the pontificate of Pius XII" (he did not actually say that these individuals were saved through Pius's personal intervention).[5] Lapide's "rubbery figures" have reappeared in several quasi-academic works written by staunch defenders of Pius XII.[6] The Internet is also awash with websites and "discussion boards" where Lapide's numbers are cited with uncritical acceptance. But while we can downplay what transpires on the front lines of the popular war to define Pius's legacy, it is important to see how the Catholic Church responded to the debate, as the rhetoric around Pius's legacy became increasingly incendiary.

In 1964, in response to Hochhuth and his characterization of Pius XII as a passive onlooker to the horrors of the Holocaust, Pope Paul VII authorized a project to collect and publish materials from the Vatican Secret Archives that would reveal the mind-set and inner workings of the Holy See during the period of the Nazi dictatorship. The task of collecting and preparing these materials was given to four Jesuit priests, all of whom were trained as historians: Pierre Blet (France), Angelo Martini (Italy), Burkhart Schneider (Germany), and Robert Graham (U.S.). Over a period of sixteen years (1965–81), the four priests searched the archives for relevant material, which the Vatican then published in eleven volumes under the title *Actes et documents du Saint-Siège relatifs à la période de la Seconde Guerre Mondiale* (hereafter *ADSS*).[7] Each volume presented archival documents in their original language—there are more than five thousand documents altogether—and included a short introduction aimed at contextualizing and summarizing the contents. Taken together, the *ADSS* provided a partial overview of the Vatican's diplomatic relations between 1939 and 1945, and a condensed record of the Vatican's efforts to intervene on behalf of noncombatants, including the Jewish victims of Nazism.[8] Volumes 2 and 3, which were organized along slightly different lines, contained a selection of Pius XII's correspondence with German bishops and a collection of documents showing the persecution of the Catholic Church in Poland and the Baltics before and during World War II. At the time of their publication, the *ADSS* received little attention outside a small circle of Church historians. The size of the collection (5,089 documents collected in eleven volumes) and the long process of their compilation discouraged a concentrated discussion of their content. Although the *ADSS* are a crucial resource for historians hoping to understand the role of the Vatican during World War II, there are different opinions regarding how much one can extract from them. While one researcher considers them "a comprehensive portrait" of the Vatican's policies and actions, the Holy See has acknowledged that the full archival record is much larger.[9] According to one report, the Vatican has close to sixteen million documents that pertain to Pius's response to the Holocaust.[10] Moreover, while the editors of the *ADSS* were instructed to collect a "representative" selection of the full archive, their assignment arose in the context of severe criticisms directed at Pius XII and at the Church more generally. In other words, the *ADSS* should be seen as a defensive measure on the part of the Church, regardless of the academic credentials of its editors.

Setting aside the question of their utility for unbiased scholarship, the *ADSS* sat mostly untouched until 1998. Their content and limitations became important once more when the Vatican released an official statement on the Holocaust, "We Remember: A Reflection on the Shoah."[11] The statement reignited the controversy over Pius XII, whose beatification appeared imminent.[12] Viewed as "too little, too late"[13] and characterized as "incomplete repentance,"[14] "We Remember" was criticized for failing to establish a direct link between the Vatican's wartime actions—particularly Pius XII's 1942 Christmas address wherein the pope made no explicit mention of anti-Semitism or the plight of Jews—and the Nazi-led genocide, which was accelerating at the same time.[15] Although the Church acknowledged a tradition of anti-Jewish discrimination among its members (including both clerics and laity), critics still felt that "We Remember" refused to accept full responsibility, since the failings it highlighted were attributed to individual and anonymous Christians rather than to the Church as a whole or to the pontiff who presided over it.

Although it addressed a history of anti-Judaism within its ranks, "We Remember" also distanced the Church from the Nazi regime, calling it "a thoroughly neo-pagan regime" that developed its racial laws "outside of Christianity." For some, "We Remember" encouraged its readers to think that because the Nazis also persecuted Catholics, no doctrinal continuity between the two groups could have existed. Pius's critics found it especially troubling that "We Remember" appeared to place Catholic suffering on par with Jewish suffering. "The document rings hollow," said Abraham Foxman of the Anti-Defamation League. "It is an apologia full of rationalizations for Pope Pius XII and the Church. It takes very little moral and historical responsibility for the Church's historic teaching for the contempt of Jews. It talks about the past in question marks rather than providing an answer."[16] Yehuda Bauer, the head of Yad Vashem's International Center for Holocaust Studies, called the Church's statement "an easy way out."[17] And while one rabbi expressed hope that "We Remember" might pave the way to further access to the Vatican archives, there was no immediate movement toward a formal inquiry.

It is ironic, sadly so, that the debates over Pius XII intensified at the same time that the Church was reaching out to the Jewish community to cultivate a new relationship. Though some viewed it as a weak and belated attempt at self-exculpation, "We Remember" was not the first attempt on the part of the Vatican to improve Catholic-Jewish relations. While the Vatican exhibited a similar amnesia with respect to the Holocaust that many Europeans (and some Jews) did in the immediate postwar period, the 1960s marked a turning point in the Church's attitudes and teachings regarding Jews and Judaism. After taking a passive role in the debates over Jewish restitution in the 1950s, and having kept silent about the pogroms and cemetery desecrations that occurred in Poland and Germany as Jewish survivors returned home following the war, the Church energetically pursued a policy aimed at interfaith reconciliation following the election of Pope John VI in 1963.[18]

The publication of *Nostra Aetate* following the Second Vatican Council in 1965 marked a wholesale change in the Church's attitude toward Judaism,[19] and it represented a sweeping reassessment of the Church's own history.[20] After lengthy deliberations, the Church's Council of Fathers renounced the long-standing view that blamed Jews, as a collective, for Christ's crucifixion, and they repudiated the teaching that Jews were a "cursed people," who broke their covenant with God. By highlighting these changes, *Nostra Aetate* (also known as *In Our Time*) sought to repair the rift that Hochhuth's *The Deputy* helped to produce. Although the Church's proclamation did not include an explicit apology, many Jews regarded it as "an implicit acknowledgment of Christian guilt for the Holocaust, and for Christian anti-Semitism down through the ages."[21] Ratified by an overwhelming majority of bishops who voted on it (2,221 in favor, 88 opposed), *In Our Time* was well received by most Jewish leaders, including many who understood it as a useful point of departure for further dialogue. Despite the absence of an unqualified apology, *Nostra Aetate* was the Church's first unequivocal statement on the common heritage of Christians and Jews, and it laid a foundation for subsequent pronouncements along the same lines in 1974 and 1985.[22] Unfortunately, there were also several well-publicized setbacks on the road to Catholic-Jewish reconciliation. In 1982, the Church angered many Jews when Pope John Paul II decided to meet with Yassir Arafat, the leader of the Palestinian Liberation Organization. Another incident occurred in 1984 when a group of Carmelite nuns in Poland established a convent on the periphery of Auschwitz I, where they also erected a large cross.[23] Notwithstanding such controversies, *Nostra Aetate* and Vatican II still represented a turning point in Catholic-Jewish relations. When the previously ignored *ADSS* became a matter of public interest again following the release of "We Remember," both sides expressed hope that clarification of the past could help to relieve the conflict. Despite potent criticisms of "We Remember," this optimism was a clear product of the push for reconciliation, which began more than thirty years earlier following the release of *Nostra Aetate*.

Launch of the International Catholic-Jewish Historical Commission (ICJHC)

Speaking to a group of Christian and Jewish scholars in April 1999, Cardinal Edward Idris Cassidy, president of the Vatican's Commission for Religious Relations with Jews and the main architect of "We Remember," highlighted the references that the document made to the Church's "sinful sons and daughters." Those who neglected to execute their moral duties during the Nazi era, according to Cassidy, included not only lay Catholics but also the highest officials of the Church, and "even renowned teachers of faith."[24] Although Cassidy stopped short of accepting institutional responsibility for the Holocaust (i.e., not the Church itself but some who acted in its name had erred), his concern with moral failure signaled to some that the Vatican might be ready to open its archive for further study. In fact, Cassidy had already proposed the creation of a joint panel of Catholic and Jewish scholars to study the *ADSS*, but Seymour Reich, chairman of the International Jewish Committee for Inter-Religious Consultations, rejected the Cardinal's invitation, saying that his group would not endorse an investigation without a promise of unimpeded access to the Vatican archive. "Until access to the full record is available to independent researchers," Reich wrote in the *New York Times*, "Pius's role will remain an enigma."[25] The clear inference was that the *ADSS* had been selectively edited, not to bring out the truth but to venerate Pius XII and whitewash the past.

For reasons that are unclear, Reich reversed himself in October 1999 and agreed to facilitate a joint scholars' initiative.[26] After tapping two project coordinators, Cassidy and Reich assembled a bipartisan commission (three Catholic, three Jewish) to study the *ADSS* in their entirety. On the Catholic side, Cassidy appointed Rev. Gerald Fogarty (University of Virginia), Eva Fleishner (Montclair State University), and Rev. John F. Morley (Seton Hall University). On the Jewish side, Reich appointed Michael Marrus (University of Toronto), Robert Wistrich (Hebrew University), and Bernard Suchecky (Free University, Brussels). In keeping with Cassidy's original proposal, the commission was asked to make a critical examination of the *ADSS* and to raise relevant questions where those documents did not supply sufficient data. Concerns over the formulation of this mandate would later affect the commission's work adversely, but the ultimate failure of the ICJHC entailed other factors, too. Looking at the commission's work record and the preliminary report that led to the project's suspension in July 2001, it is not hard to conclude that the project was fatally flawed from the start.[27]

Concerns over the commission's composition and personnel arose almost immediately. Five of the commission's six members (Fleischner, Morley, Marrus, Wistrich, and Suchecky) had already expressed reservations about Pius's conduct prior to joining the project. Wistrich was quoted as saying, "Pius XII did not perform in a way that reflects any credit on the Vatican or on the Catholic Church. He wound up in a position where he was complicit in German policy."[28] Marrus had also been critical of Pius. The pope's priorities, Marrus told the *Toronto Star*, focused on shielding "the institutions of the Church so souls [could] be saved. . . . This was the supreme value over everything else, including the victims of the Holocaust."[29] Wistrich and Marrus both made conciliatory statements after being appointed to the ICJHC, but the panel's objectivity was already compromised in the eyes of some.[30] Although Cardinal Cassidy handpicked three of the commission's six members, the perception that the commission reflected an anti-Catholic bias undermined its credibility from the outset.

Every commission must wrestle with the politics of history to some extent. The intensity of these debates will run in direct proportion to the proximity of specific historical claims to the core elements of a particular group identity. While responsible scholars strive to base their conclusions on empirical evidence, some degree of subjectivity is unavoidable. Marrus, himself, acknowledged as much: "Everyone has preconceptions."[31] The structure and organization of the commission—with three from the "Catholic side" and three from the "Jewish side"—already supposed that the Church's history could not be studied except through the prejudicial lens of competing faiths. By appointing equal numbers on both sides, Reich and Cassidy may have believed that these biases would be balanced and, therefore, negated. The Vatican also had certain preconceptions; while the commission was still taking shape, preparations for Pius's beatification were already moving forward in the Holy See. Marrus has maintained that the ICJHC reflected a diverse range of opinions; however, Catholic "hard-liners" were never convinced that the commission could give the *ADSS* a fair reading. Either they refused to believe that Reich's appointees were ready to work in good faith or they rejected, a priori, any suggestion that Pius's actions might deserve criticism. Overcoming this problem of perception proved to be difficult. The ICJHC lacked a single leader, who could control the commission's public outreach and media strategy. Comprised of six individuals with unique viewpoints and given no clear guidance beyond the original mandate, which was vague and problematic to begin with, the commission attempted to operate by consensus, but practical difficulties hampered the initiative from the beginning. With no central office, no research budget, and only a small number of assistants to depend on, the commission struggled to coordinate its work. E-mail communication was sporadic, and, according to Marrus, commission members did not always know what their peers were working on.[32] Cassidy and Reich did a small amount of organization to keep the project together, but their influence did little to overcome the perception of a partisan divide. Perhaps if it had been put under the direction of a disinterested "third party," the commission might have fared better. But then, one of the bedrock contentions of this study is that history is always already enveloped by politics. There is no outside perspective from which historical conflict can be cleanly adjudicated, only differing degrees of commitment to social scientific norms and peace-building practices. And if historical truth emerges through rigorous application of scientific methods, there is still no guarantee that this will be the salve that soothes and heals all wounds.

As we have seen already with the bilateral textbook commissions, one possibility for mediating history entails developing a narrative strategy that can encompass multiple perspectives. A history geared toward both truth and reconciliation must make space for a range of voices and highlight, rather than bury or politicize, ambiguous data that supports multiple interpretations. With respect to Pius, Michael Phayer's work offers a good model, as does the scholarship of Paul O'Shea.[33] Phayer argues that Pius did little to help European Jews once the war began, but rather than conclude that Pius was complicit in the Holocaust, Phayer explores a range of possible explanations for what others (e.g., Hochhuth) have taken for immorality. Was Pius XII silent during the Holocaust? According to Phayer, "Yes, if we take it to mean that the Pope did not speak out unequivocally against the murder of the Jews. No, if we take it to mean that the Pope failed to use the Vatican's offices to help in the rescue of Jews."[34] This is not a case of hedging bets either; Phayer deliberately engages the facts from rival perspectives in order to render a picture of the past that avoids crude moral judgment. He works the evidence toward what Catholic and Jewish partisans have taken to be an impossible paradox, that is, silence without complicity (from the Jewish perspective) or innocence without heroics (from the Catholic perspective). The Vatican, Phayer argues, followed a "serpentine course" of cautious intervention, punctuated by extended periods of inaction. "The image that emerges . . . is that of a pontiff whose deep concern about communism and the intact physical survival of the city of Rome kept him from exploring options on behalf of the Jewish people."[35] Phayer refuses to use Pius as an emblem of Catholic indifference, and he avoids judging the wartime pope against options that never existed. Could Pius XII have stopped the Holocaust by directly condemning Nazi racial policy in his 1942 Christmas address? Phayer is adamant that he could not. Could he have reduced the lethality of the Holocaust by influencing ordinary Catholics to resist Nazi violence (or at least refuse to abet it)? Phayer lets the question linger. He does note that thousands of Gentiles intervened on behalf of their Jewish friends and acquaintances—and even strangers—despite the Vatican's tentative messaging and inconsistent attempts at intervention. Given more in the way of direct encouragement, readers are left to wonder, might more Catholics have asserted themselves? Phayer underlines the fact of Jewish suffering, which he ties to the callousness that many Jews encountered, and he reaches a strong conclusion about the ineffectiveness of the Vatican's diplomacy, but he does so without pushing for an untenable moral judgment.[36] His assessment serves as an excellent example of multivocal history.

Members of the ICJHC claim to have used a similar strategy in drafting the preliminary report, which they submitted in October 2000. In their preface, they ask and answer a series of questions related to their credentials and overall goals: "What then can we bring to the discussion that others have not? We do not claim expertise on all of the subjects covered in the published volumes, although we are all part of the ongoing research and dialogue surrounding the Church and the Holocaust. Each of us came to the commission with distinct viewpoints based on previous work. We hope to provide a *multiple dimension* to the report that reflects scholarly difference and opinions inherent in any research."[37] Yet, in spite of this professed interest in crafting a report imbued by that "multiple dimension," the questions they pose throughout the rest of the document begin from a presumption of moral guilt, either Pius's during the war or the Vatican's in the decades that followed. In every instance, these questions come from the same general perspective in which unseen materials serve as cause for indictment. Instead of working in a scholarly mode, where explanations are qualified, partial, and open to revision, the authors of the report appear to favor a juridical framework, where a definitive verdict is preferred and open-and-shut cases are the most comfortable to the conscience. While there is a tendency in the field of conflict resolution to equate reconciliation with closure, mediating history resists the view that historical actors are like the characters in a morality play, who may be judged either wholly good or wholly bad. Ultimately, mediating history hinges on a determination to develop and defend thoroughly contextualized empirical assessments against easy moral judgments, although it is not an amoral endeavor either.

Returning to the ICJHC, the either/or pattern of thinking that emerged in the commission's preliminary report recalls the mandate provided by Cardinal Cassidy and Seymour Reich. From the outset, the project was conceived so that the professional standards of historical scholarship could not be upheld. The commission was expected to make a comprehensive evaluation of the Vatican's role during World War II, but their investigation was constrained by the limited source material that the Vatican supplied. The *ADSS* included more than five thousand documents from the Vatican's archive, but these were *handpicked* from a much larger trove of materials, which the commission was never permitted to see or study. While Paul O'Shea has argued that the *ADSS* provide a "comprehensive portrait" of the Vatican's considerations and diplomacy prior to and during the war, there is no way of knowing whether this is true, since nobody has yet made or published a complete assessment of the full contents.[38] To characterize something as comprehensive is to judge the quality of a part against that of the whole, which, in this case, is still unknown. The expectations for the commission's project and the materials for its execution were, therefore, totally incompatible. The commission was expected to "critically examine" the *ADSS* and pose questions for further study based on their findings, but there was never any real possibility of pursuing such questions because the Vatican refused to provide unfettered access to records beyond the *ADSS*. Ronald Rychlak, a legal scholar who has also written on Pius's role during World War II, has attempted to answer some of the questions in the preliminary report, but he has also criticized the commission for posing questions to which no answer was possible.[39] Rychlak, whose writings on

Pius XII and the Vatican have been disseminated through conservative (Spence Publishing) and Catholic (Genesis Press) outlets, maintains that the ICJHC "expect[ed] to find documents that do not exist." He calls the commission's preliminary report "a polemic" that "raised the heat of the debate, not the level of it." But, again, Rychlak cannot know whether other pertinent documents exist. Like every other scholar who has worked on Pius's wartime diplomacy, Rychlak has seen only what the Vatican has selected for publication and release. Until the Vatican catalogs and releases all of the documents that pertain to this chapter in the Church's history, there is no reason to conclude either that the *ADSS* give a "comprehensive portrait" or that a particular picture of Pius XII has been distorted by the partial nature of this collection.[40]

While Rychlak is adamant that the commission failed because of its prejudicial leanings, the source materials require further scrutiny. Although the *ADSS* include valuable material for historians working in this field, there are also significant lacunae, which can be located via cross-referencing and also deduced by means of comparison to other archival materials outside the Vatican.[41] These include letters exchanged between Pius XII and Konrad von Preysing, who was the bishop of Berlin from 1935 to 1950; materials referring to Alois Hudal, the "brown bishop" who published a book in 1937 praising Adolf Hitler and the Nazi Party; all traces of the so-called Riegner Report, in which details of the Final Solution were painstakingly rehearsed for the Vatican; and the Auschwitz Protocols, which described key details relating the Nazis' methods of mass murder. Paul O'Shea has discussed the possibility of using other archives outside of Rome to complement (or challenge) what appears in the *ADSS*, but this kind of work has, so far, been limited in scope. One possibility is the six-volume collection of letters written to Pius XII by German bishops, edited by Bernard Stasiewski and published between 1968 and 1985.[42] These lend credence to one possible interpretation of the *ADSS*. According to O'Shea, "What emerges very clearly . . . is the rapidly expanding scale of both the Vatican's attempts to help victims of the war, and the requests made of the Holy See by governments and aid agencies, including Jewish communal and international groups." O'Shea does not mention that "attempts to help victims of the war" often referred to attempts to help Catholic victims. It is also unclear from O'Shea's statement how the scale of the Vatican's efforts can be fully evaluated on the basis of a selective sampling of data. Historians cannot decipher on the basis of the *ADSS* alone whether the Vatican did as much as it could, as little as it could, or, as is likely, something in between.

There is no question that the *ADSS* reveal a degree of concern over the persecution of European Jews. Paul O'Shea has made a detailed analysis of the full eleven volumes of *ADSS* to show how (and what) the Vatican learned of anti-Semitic actions during the war and how it responded. According to O'Shea, 734 documents in the *ADSS* (14.5 percent of the entire contents) "relate directly to the persecution and murder of Jews." One can infer from this that the conditions of Jewish life under German occupation were an important subject for the Holy See, although there is clearly some variability in how each of the 734 documents "related" to Jewish suffering. Volume 8 of the *ADSS*, which deals with the persecution of Jews in Slovakia, shows that the Vatican's secretary of state, Cardinal Luigi Maglione, received news from Bratislava that Slovakia had introduced a Jewish Code, similar to the Nuremberg Laws, in September 1941. It also shows that Maglione wrote to Karel Sidor, the Slovakian minister to the Holy See, on November 11, 1941, objecting to the conditions imposed by the Jewish Code. When deportations began in Slovakia in March 1942, Maglione wrote to the papal nuncio in Switzerland with instructions to intervene on behalf of Slovakian Jews.[43] Maglione received news five days later that these deportations had been suspended, which the chargé d'affaires in Bratislava offered as evidence that the Holy See's interventions had been effective. When Maglione received a note the next day informing him that the deportations had *not* been suspended, as previously reported, Maglione jotted on the telegram: "I do not know what steps to take to stop these lunatics."[44] While deportations slowed temporarily after June 1942, allowing several thousand Slovakian Jews to escape to Hungary, they accelerated once again in 1944. In total, German and Slovak authorities deported 70,000 Jews from Slovakia, of whom 60,000 were killed. O'Shea says of the slowdown after June 1942: "The Holy Father wanted the trains stopped. And stopped they were for several months before resuming at a slower rate in September."[45] O'Shea does not explore other explanations for the slowdown, for example, the decreased "demand" at Auschwitz-Birkenau, nor does he explain why, if Pius had wanted them stopped, the deportations were subsequently resumed. He notes that the Church granted exemptions to baptized Jews, which spared a great number from deportation, but of course this protection was extended to these individuals because they were considered to be Christian under Church doctrine. Concern for "non-Aryan" Christians is a common theme throughout the *ADSS*, but it is misleading to count such comments as direct references to Jewish suffering.[46] What O'Shea's work really shows is the difficulty of commenting intelligently on the content of the *ADSS* without a clearer understanding of what they exclude, not to mention the transformation of the Vatican's concern over Catholic life during the war into opposition to anti-Semitism after the war.

The lacunae in the *Actes* and the impossibility of fully executing the mandate without a better understanding of their limitations are paramount in any consideration of the ICJHC's performance. When Cassidy first approached Reich about creating an interfaith commission, Reich complained that the *ADSS* were not sufficient for conducting a responsible inquiry, yet he later agreed to help organize the project anyway, despite receiving no assurance that the scope of the inquiry could or would be expanded. In the letter Cassidy and Reich sent to the Vatican in July 2001 announcing the suspension of their work, the five remaining members of the commission (Fleischner dropped out) noted that they had accepted an "unusually limited mandate" because "we were . . . hopeful that the process we began might promote the advisability of opening the archives for the period of the Second World War."[47] But the Vatican never hinted, let alone promised, that this would be possible, at least not publicly. Made to rely on materials that were already edited to support the Vatican's contention that Pius XII had worked diligently, but also quietly, to rescue Jews, the commission repeatedly ran up against the barriers and arguments that the compilers of the *ADSS* had laid down through their own interpretation. From the beginning, the commission experienced dissonance between the preselected questions (i.e., preconceptions) that they brought to the inquiry and the preselected materials supplied to them. Unfortunately, this dynamic pushed the commission straight into the juridical framework (i.e., guilty or not guilty) that they claimed to eschew. Frustration with this scenario comes through clearly in the commission's preliminary report: "The mandate given to us by our sponsoring bodies was to review the volumes that make up the *ADSS* and to raise relevant questions and issues that, in our opinion, have not adequately or satisfactorily been resolved by the available documentation, and to issue a report on our findings. In our review of the material, we have felt compelled to request additional documentation that could answer questions that arose as a result of our research."[48] Rychlak, who argued that the commission expected to find documents that do not exist, was correct about one thing anyway. There can be little doubt but that some members of the commission understood the mandate as a launching point for an accusatory study. The questions posed in their preliminary report related to "unresolved" matters in the *ADSS* were infused by deep moral suspicion. Members of the commission came to believe (or already did) that the limitations of the *ADSS* obscured an immoral position, which Pius never wished to adjust. Knowing that Pius XII was never a Nazi sympathizer, as some have claimed, the commission nevertheless failed to raise their inquiry above the "contentious portraits" that they hoped to surmount. While most of the forty-seven questions in the preliminary report are straightforward requests for additional documentation, there are several that treat the lacunae of the *ADSS* as likely sites of turpitude. For example, in question 14, which deals with the bishop of Berlin's letters to

Pius XII, the commission states that these had amounted to "a direct appeal to the Pope." They continue: "What impression did von Preysing's words make on Pius XII; what discussions, if any, took place about making such a public appeal as the German bishop requested, and was further information about Nazi anti-Jewish policy sought?" The implication here seems to be that the Vatican chose not to press the matter in Germany, when doing so might have improved the standing of Jews swept up in the violence there. Question 15 leads in a similar direction, where the commission notes that Pius XII informed von Preysing "that local bishops had the discretion when to be silent and when to speak out in the face of reprisals and pressures." Once again, there is a subtle, but also unmistakable, suggestion here that the pope elected not to intervene at the precise moment when doing so represented what von Preysing called "the last hope for many and the profound wish of all right-thinking people." Of course, Pius's decisions might have been part of a larger strategy to preserve the Vatican's neutrality, which is what some of his defenders have claimed, but the commission showed little inclination to explore that possibility. Instead, in question 17, the commission comes around to what we can read as the bottom line, morally speaking: "The Pope's reply to von Preysing did not give a specific commitment to make any public appeal for the Jews."

Many of the questions in the preliminary report aim at basic clarification and discovery. In question 3, the commission asks whether there are drafts or other materials related to a document that already appears in the *ADSS*. In question 5, the commission seeks "further documentation" that reflects the Vatican's internal deliberations regarding conditions in occupied Poland and whether the Holy See contemplated direct aid to the Poles. Other questions are more pointed. For example, in question 30, the commission refers to financial records showing donations made to the Vatican by Jewish organizations for civilian relief and rescue. The commission observes that the *ADSS* contain "no documents regarding the Vatican's own financial transactions relating to such efforts." The commission then asks: "Is there any archival evidence to indicate how the Vatican collected and disbursed its own or other funds in carrying out such activities, such as the annual Peter's Pence collection?"

While this is not a direct accusation of impropriety, one can certainly imagine how such a question might arouse indignation within the Vatican. The subtext seems to be that diplomacy without financial commitment is little more than an empty gesture. If the Vatican's rescue efforts were as robust as Pius's most ardent defenders have asserted, then there should be a paper trail that documents the expenditures related to these operations. Even if the question were posed innocently, that is, in the expectation that the Vatican *could* produce such documents, this moves the inquiry in an unexpected direction.

In a sense, the commission's question regarding financial transactions puts the Vatican in a "no-win" situation. If the Vatican elects not to release the records that document its expenditures, this could be taken as an acknowledgment of the insufficiency of Pius's efforts. On the other hand, if the Vatican does release these records, there is no level of financial commitment that will satisfy Pius's fiercest critics. Once the commission pushes into the realm of finances, the Vatican is exposed to varying degrees of suspicion: *Why not more? Why not twice as much? Why not every last nickel?* This is a good example of a question in the preliminary report that slips into a confrontational mode and gives validation to those interested in propagating the most damaging portrayals of Pius.

Reading the commission's preliminary report, one sees little effort to pose questions in conciliatory language or to frame potentially damaging questions, such as the one concerning financial records, in a way that anticipates and defuses partisan rhetoric. On the one hand, the preliminary report commends the four Jesuits who compiled the *ADSS* for providing a record of "the complexity and variety of the activities which the Holy See pursued on behalf of 'victims of the war.'" On the other hand, the commission chafed against the interpretative limitations of the *ADSS*. By selecting some documents for posterity, while rejecting others as irrelevant, redundant, or (as some inferred) unflattering, the editors of the *ADSS* had already established an interpretative framework, which discouraged fresh perspectives and invited suspicion about unexamined items deposited in the Vatican archives. According to the report:

> Scrutiny of these volumes of Vatican documents does not put to rest significant questions about the role of the Vatican during the Holocaust. No serious historian could accept that the published, edited volumes could put us at the end of the story. This is due neither to the complexity nor to the difficulty of the questions themselves, nor to the editorial quality of the documentary volumes. Rather, it reflects the fact that many of the documents are susceptible to *different interpretations*. Interpretation is unavoidable in the work of historians; it is particularly relevant and sensitive in this case because the Historical Commission is dealing with what the editors of the documents themselves acknowledge to be only a portion of the available evidence.[49]

Members of the commission saw their work as an entry point into the past rather than as a definitive account that would make further investigation superfluous. Unfortunately, this perspective did not prevent them from falling into a pattern of either/or thinking. Why did members of the commission, by delving into what they regarded (rightly) as an incomplete and partial record of the past, allow themselves to be drawn into the juridical framework that has characterized so much of the public debate concerning Pius XII?

As previously stated, some members of the commission clearly hoped that the preliminary report would open the way for a second phase of research, free from the limitations imposed by the *ADSS*. When the project began, Bernard Suchecky called the commission's work "part of a process of demanding a full opening of the Vatican archives."[50] Similarly, Robert Wistrich viewed the project as "a way into a whole thicket of contentious issues."[51] Unfortunately, there is nothing in the public record to suggest that the Vatican ever encouraged these hopes. If the preliminary report was a gambit aimed at forcing the Vatican's hand, then members of the commission badly underestimated the resistance they would face. Perhaps they felt that the Vatican had cracked opened the door in 1998 with "We Remember," or maybe they were struck by the conciliatory language that Pope John Paul II used in his sweeping millennial apology.[52] Whatever the case, because some portions of the report slipped into moral indictment and gave rhetorical space to those whose criticisms of Pius had been the most polemical, the Vatican's refusal to engage was hardly surprising, much less blameworthy.

For future commissions, the lesson here is important. These investigative bodies need to develop both a rhetorical style and a historiographical perspective that do not elicit reflexive defensiveness from the parties who open themselves to scrutiny. To nourish a working relationship with the Holy See, Suchecky's "demand" for additional information could have been expressed as "a most sincere wish" or, better yet, in words specifically chosen to strike a doctrinal chord. A reference to the questions that Jesus posed in the Gospels or the idea of Jesus as the deliverer of transformative questions might have softened the Vatican to the questions that the ICHJC submitted in the preliminary report. In cases such as this one, where secular curiosities overlap with sacred claims, commissions must work to develop a "bridging discourse" that makes communication easier and historical probing less overtly threatening.[53] Because the nature of religious difference is that sacred spaces are exclusionary and nonnegotiable, it is particularly important that members of interfaith commissions address their counterparts in a language that can disarm them. The same consideration applies to bilateral commissions that enlist ethnonational rivals. In order to mediate the past, commissions must realize that *how* they couch their findings is just as important as *what* they communicate. With more sensitivity to the tone and rhetoric in the preliminary report, it is at least conceivable that the ICJHC could have reached a more satisfying outcome. What makes this failure so lamentable is the burgeoning goodwill that existed in both the Catholic and Jewish communities prior to the release of the preliminary report and in spite of the alleged evasions contained in "We Remember."[54] Although the path to reconciliation is often a twisting one, the failure to capitalize on positive momentum must be regarded as a bad omen.

Some will argue that the Vatican can never accept a negative judgment of Pius XII, and therefore can never release the full extent of its archives. According to this line of thought, if the Church (or the pope himself) made mistakes in the past, then it is capable of making mistakes in the present and future. And the Church cannot make mistakes, ever, since it is guided by divine providence. This argument meshes with the doctrine of papal infallibility, which was established at the First Vatican Council in 1870. Papal infallibility, if it holds sway, would make it impossible for the Vatican to assist any historian in the development of a critical assessment of Pius, which means that the Holy See cannot release the full extent of its archives, if there is any possibility that those records might damage Pius's legacy. But the doctrine of papal infallibility has been denied by many prominent Catholics, and even by some popes, which means there is still a possibility that the Vatican will allow historians to investigate beyond the *ADSS*. During his papacy, John Paul II apologized for a variety of historical injustices, including Catholic involvement in the transatlantic slave trade, the role of Catholicism in the conquest of Mesoamerica, the persecution of Galileo Galilei, the Crusaders' siege on Constantinople, clerical sex abuses, and "[the] sins committed against the people of the covenant [i.e., Jews]." In 2000, John Paul II asked forgiveness for "the part that each of us has played in such evils thus contributing to disrupting the face of the Church."[55] While John Paul II did not officially depart from the doctrine of infallibility, his apology included a strong statement on historical justice and on the importance of amending the past "and purifying memory" where history is marked by immorality (sin). Only through acts of repentance, John Paul urged, could the Church hope to "[eliminate] from personal and collective conscience all forms of resentment and violence left by the inheritance of the past."[56] This helps to explain why John Paul in 2002 took the extraordinary measure of opening (ahead of schedule) a portion of the papers from the pontificate of Pius XI (1922–39), including documents from the Vatican's secretariat of state relating to the Holy See's relations with Germany. According to the Vatican's archivists, John Paul's decision reflected his desire "to put an end to thoughtless and unjust speculation" surrounding Cardinal Pacelli, Pius's secretary of state, who later became Pope Pius XII.[57]

While John Paul's interest in amending the past did not translate into success for the ICJHC, his apology in 2000 and his decision to grant additional archival access have kept open a possibility for further study, and subsequent popes have signaled that the Vatican still wishes to improve Catholic-Jewish relations. In his first audience with Jewish leaders, Benedict XVI (r. 2005–13) reiterated the importance of *Nostra Aetate* and emphasized his commitment "to implementing this decisive teaching." He also stated that he hoped to build on the process of reconciliation, which his predecessor initiated: "Remembrance of the past remains for both communities a moral imperative and a source of purification in our efforts to pray and work toward reconciliation, justice, respect for human dignity and for that peace which is ultimately a gift from the Lord himself."[58] In 2006, Benedict authorized the release of the remainder of the files from the pontificate of Pius XI, but he also angered many Jews in 2009 when he confirmed Pius XII's "heroic virtues," thereby moving the wartime pontiff another step closer to sainthood. More recently, the election of Pope Francis has been seen as a potential step toward interfaith healing. Francis cultivated a strong relationship with the Jewish community in Argentina while he served as bishop there, and some Jewish leaders who have worked closely with him suggest that Francis is interested in speeding up the opening of the Vatican archives from the pontificate of Pius XII. Rabbi Abraham Skorka, the rector of the Latin American Rabbinical Seminary in Buenos Aires and coauthor, with Francis, of *On Heaven and Earth: Pope Francis on Faith, Family, and the Church in the 21st Century*, has said that the new pope is likely to support the continuation of the inquiry into Pius XII's wartime actions.[59]

Where the Vatican has opened new portions of its archive since 2002–3, there has been some revealing scholarship, bringing new information to the debates over Pius XII. Robert Ventresca's *Soldier of Christ: The Life of Pius XII* integrates new materials on the pontificate of Pius XI that the Vatican released in 2006.[60] His study cuts an even-handed path between the two partisan camps, which have called out, alternately, for Pius XII's condemnation or his immediate canonization. Ventresca shows how Cardinal Pacelli (the future Pius XII) worked with Pius XI while serving as the Vatican's secretary of state to draft and disseminate an encyclical denouncing Nazism in 1937.[61] Ventresca also shows how Pacelli, following his election to the papacy in 1939, relied on diplomatic exchanges and sometimes conflicting reports from his bishops in the territories occupied by Germany to calibrate the Vatican's policy toward the Nazis. In so doing, Ventresca writes, Pius XII "many times acted more the part of a diplomat than the supreme pastor."[62] Although Pius XII was not an anti-Semite, Ventresca argues that he could have done more to assist Europe's Jews during the war. According to Ventresca, Pius XII admired German culture, but he abhorred the atrocities committed by the Nazis. If his Christmas radio address in 1942 did not *specifically* mention the Nazis or the Jews, Ventresca contends, that is because Pius XII was also deeply concerned with war crimes committed by other combatants, most notably the Soviet Union. In any case, concludes Ventresca, Pius's reference to "the hundreds of thousands of persons who, without any fault on their part, sometimes only because of their nationality or race, have been consigned to death" was understood at the time as a clear denunciation of Nazi policy, including by the Nazis themselves.

Ventresca's study points to a potential way forward for historical mediation and a missed opportunity on the part of the ICJHC. The Vatican has said that the release of all archival files pertaining to Pius XII will occur, at the earliest, in 2015; yet, so far, there has been no movement suggesting this will happen.[63] If and when these documents become available, historians will have an opportunity to review what the ICJHC requested but never received, and this will present a fresh opportunity for interfaith dialogue. There is already a legacy of rapprochement on which to build. In 1997, bishops in France and Germany apologized for their silence during Jewish deportations and lamented that the Church did not vigorously oppose Nazism or condemn the Holocaust.[64] Even before the creation of the ICJHC, Cardinal Cassidy had addressed the Church's past mistakes in unambiguous language. In reference to "We Remember," Cassidy said, "It's more than an apology. We feel the need to repent . . . for those members of our church who failed."[65] This is a potential point of departure for future negotiations. While Benedict's papacy ended under a dark cloud, the Church appears to have opened a new chapter with the election of Francis. Although the ICJHC's preliminary report did not fully capture the "multidimensional" history that its authors vaunted, future negotiations could still capitalize on the commission's preliminary work and the external scholarship that has appeared since then.

Besides Ventresca, others have used the Vatican archives to mediate between partisan perspectives. Gordon Thomas has argued that Pius XII chose to work clandestinely on behalf of Jewish victims rather than confront the Nazi regime openly because he gauged this to be a more effective strategy for humanitarian action.[66] Thomas covers Catholic rescue efforts in several European countries, for example, instructions sent from the Vatican to priests abroad to provide false certificates of baptism to Jews and operations to provide sanctuary to Jews in convents and monasteries. At the same time, Thomas argues that Pius's strategy failed in numerous instances, including the roundup of Jews in Rome (1943), which took place, as Susan Zucotti has put it, under Pius's "very windows."[67] This is another good example of mediating history, although it does not overcome or solve the main problem of archival access that derailed the ICJHC.

Hubert Wolf has shown another way forward. Working from the documents that Benedict released in 2006 (relating to Pius XI), Wolf asserts that the Vatican was *not* silent with respect to the evils of Nazi anti-Semitism *prior to the outbreak of World War II*, but he also documents how Pius XI was dissuaded by Cardinal Pacelli from taking a more confrontational stance.[68]

While Wolf rejects the idea that the Vatican took no position against Nazism, his study undercuts many of the arguments that Pius XII's defenders have used to protect and/or bolster his legacy. For example, Wolf shows that the Vatican, under Pius XI, viewed itself as a protector of universal rights, although some have argued that this was impossible since the concept of human rights had not yet entered international law. Wolf also documents, as others have, that the Vatican was informed of so-called brown priests in Germany, who supported the Nazi Party and promoted the persecution of Jews.[69] Although his study of the Vatican's prewar policies has not quelled the debates over Pius XII's record, Wolf's close attention to chronology, that is, his readiness to evaluate Pius XII over the course of decades and to judge his wartime policies against those of his predecessor, raises the scholarly discourse above the partisan rancor. Without resorting to heavy-handed judgments, Wolf provides an example of the way that scholars can dissect persistent myths and assumptions that energize intergroup conflicts, which are steeped in history.

The potential of historical commissions lies in their ability to remove the sharp edges from conflicting perspectives and offer new descriptions of the past, which both encompass and overcome the insecurities of groups locked in conflict. In the case of Pius XII, this means getting between the hagiographers, who have called for his immediate canonization, and the uninformed critics, who continue to revile Pius XII as "Hitler's Pope." While good history writing always depends on the availability of good sources, as Doris Bergen has written with respect to the debates over Pius, mediating history depends on the readiness of scholars to use the available material in a way that transcends and tames ideological conflict.[70] The ICJHC failed, in part, not only because it lacked access to the "good sources" that the Vatican has promised to release in the future but also because it deployed the available materials in a manner that fed an accusatory perspective. Although they backed away from such statements later, Wistrich and Suchecky, prior to joining the commission, had basically stated that Pius's inaction during the war amounted to complicity with the Nazis. Like others who have argued in the same vein, Wistrich and Suchecky observed in the *ADSS* a narrow fixation on diplomacy, an obsession with the threat of communism, and an inflexible personality in Pius, which discouraged implementation of new tactics when diplomacy failed to halt the violent treatment of Jews and "non-Aryan gentiles." Furthermore, they saw in the Vatican's unwillingness to grant full archival access corroboration of all their convictions.

Although it is premature to suggest a mediating narrative until the full contents of the Vatican archives have been studied, one can still imagine a possible strategy for dealing with this contested chapter of history. The available documentation already points to certain (tentative) conclusions, which the ICJHC failed to highlight in the preliminary report. For example, the *ADSS* communicate a great deal about the Vatican's determination to broker a diplomatic solution to the problem of Nazi foreign aggression as well as Pius's efforts to intervene on behalf of Europe's Jewish communities. At the same time, these records, when read against other data, reiterate the scope and magnitude of the Holocaust and the impotence of the Vatican—and other bystanders—to stem the tide of anti-Semitic violence. There is also a great deal to be said and learned about the positive legacy of Catholic resistance efforts and the courageous acts of Righteous Gentiles. To keep a place within the legitimate discourse, those who have pushed for humiliating guilt will need to give up their claims that Pius remained silent throughout the Nazi period. His first encyclical, "On the Unity of Human Society" (1939), rejects the claims of racial pseudo-science and was based, in large part, on the anti-Nazi encyclical of his predecessor. Also untenable are the claims that Pius's wartime policies were driven by an anti-Semitic inclination that made him "Hitler's Pope." On the opposite end of the spectrum, the hagiographers can no longer argue reasonably that Pius XII worked miracles through a policy of Christian love based on universal brotherhood. So far, the Vatican archives have not supplied evidence to support the contention that Pius's rescue efforts were more significant than any other relief agency, and the *ADSS* do not substantiate the claim that Pius's efforts led to the rescue of 860,000 Jews, as has been claimed.[71]

On the other hand, the *ADSS* do strongly suggest that Catholic interests had a higher priority in the Vatican's diplomatic calculations than the difficulties and suffering of so-called non-gentiles. In the final analysis, the currently available evidence points to an elemental, if somewhat dejecting, historical truth: that in spite of efforts to condemn the Nazi politics of anti-Semitism and rescue some of the Jews exposed to genocidal violence, Pius XII and the Vatican were unable to thwart the Nazi program because their authority and tactics were insufficient in the face of a totalitarian regime bent on military conquest and racial "purification." In this narrative, Pius XII appears as neither angel nor devil but merely as a man of his times who, like many others, failed to stop Hitler and the Nazi war machine even though he may have had some opportunity, theoretically speaking, to do so. Hitler and his retinue are entrenched as the primary perpetrators; European Jews remain the victims of an unprecedented industrial genocide; and Pius XII and the Holy See figure as high-profile bystanders, not entirely powerless to intervene but also not equipped to neutralize the dangers of Nazism. We should recall once more Cardinal Maglione's handwritten note on the cable he received in March 1942, informing him of the ongoing deportation of Slovak Jews: "I do not know what steps to take to stop these lunatics." This sentence encapsulates much of what the *ADSS* have to teach. It shows strong commitment to moral principle and a clear understanding of the urgency of the situation and also a painful consciousness of failure. While there are many possible responses to the cardinal's pronouncement, there is no historical evidence that other tactics could have averted the Holocaust.

Of course, the historical record has nothing to say about events that never transpired, so we need to be very careful with any speculative thinking. Clearly, though, there are still questions worthy of further research, and time will tell whether the Vatican archives contain useful answers to these. For example, why did Pius XII choose to excommunicate every Communist in the world but not a single Nazi? Why did he publicly protest some aspects of the Nazi racial ideology, for example, the euthanasia program, but not the Final Solution, which was predicated on a similar set of beliefs? Why did the Vatican intervene to stop the deportation of "non-gentile Catholics" (i.e., converted Jews) but not Jews who maintained their religious identity? Although we do not yet have the answers to these questions, we should be wary of any attempt to answer them that replicates the terrain of the current debates without also performing a rigorous analysis of the presuppositions contained within each contending point of view. All history is to some degree preconceived. There are no facts at all without some conception of what counts as fact, of which comparisons are relevant, and the like. The characteristic feature of mediating history is its commitment to drawing out these preconceptions and interrogating them in the open, which the ICJHC was not able to do convincingly, given its mandate, its limited resources, and its own miscues.

Conclusion

Truth-Telling, Narrativity, and the Right to History

The idea that truth-telling can reliably produce reconciliation and promote social harmony has been picked apart in various ways. From an empirical standpoint, Hugo van der Merwe, Audrey Chapman, Patrick Ball, David Mendeloff, and others have documented cases in which the formula that connects truth to reconciliation has either broken down over time or failed to adhere in the first place.[1] From a more philosophical perspective, Berber Bevernage has shown how the truth-and-reconciliation paradigm threatens to implode where different notions of temporality collide.[2] According to Bevernage, truth commissions attempt to accommodate a judicial concept of time, in which injustices committed in the past require an ethical response from the present while also relying on a historical concept of time, under which past events are unalterable and irreparable. Employing both of these concepts and trying to accomplish two different things at once, truth-telling commissions, Bevernage argues, frequently end up doing neither. They do not produce a unified understanding of the past so much as emphasize the divide between those who consider these events to be a closed chapter and those who still experience them as an open wound. This is a deep ontological rift, according to Bevernage, which makes each of the two concepts of time appear inferior from the perspective of the other.

Encompassing both of these critiques is a much larger epistemological question, which concerns objectivity, values, and various constraints on truth (e.g., social, technological, and methodological), and reaches well beyond the realm of truth commissions. Since Nietzsche, skeptics have argued that universal truths are not grounded in real substance but are merely successful exercises of desire, that is, the fulfillment of a group or individual's wish to have others see the world as they do. Morality, in this scheme, reflects the interests of the powerful. Rights become "a fancy cloak" for what one wants.[3] Scientific truths are recast as discursive conventions. And historical narratives can be freely emplotted to suit the tastes of the author (or his readers), since no version of the past is perfectly authentic. Despite their outward appearance of stability, the sacred and transcendent truths of this world, according to this perspective, are really neither. Truths come and go. "If a temple is to be erected," Nietzsche wrote, "a temple must be destroyed."[4] This is a problem for the historian if he wants to present himself as a full-fledged empiricist. It is a disastrous state of affairs, or at any rate seems to be, if he thinks that the past cries out for moral judgment. Not only would his judgments have no real anchor, but his ability to ascertain the truth of the past would be fatally compromised. So it goes.

With respect to the Holocaust and the ability of historians to represent its extremity or locate its ultimate meaning, this debate has played itself out several times over. While the academic mainstream has reacted strongly (and appropriately) to any whiff of Holocaust denial, Holocaust historiography is still dogged by the problem of "situated" knowledge, and the Holocaust commissions examined in this study do not offer a wholly reliable way out of this ditch. Even if historical evidence sets some limits on how it may be legitimately interpreted, as Perry Anderson has argued, there is still no entirely satisfactory way of deciphering which are the empirical mistakes and which are the literary or moral mistakes.[5] For example, if it is a fact that the Holocaust and the mass killing of ethnic Germans at the hands of the Red Army in 1944–45 both became possible thanks to the same idea concerning the desirability of ethnic cleansing, which is what Andreas Hillgruber asserted in his controversial book, *Two Kinds of Ruin*,[6] then there is no obvious reason for Hillgruber's critics to label this comparison as "[an] oblique reduction" except for their strong wish to capture these events in separate moral categories.[7] It does not mean that we cannot challenge Hillgruber's argument on moral grounds; it simply means that our criticisms will be shadowed by what Hayden White once called the "inexpungible relativity" of all representation.[8] Scientifically speaking, Perry Anderson's assertion that the Nazi Judeocide was more tragic and more grotesque than the mass killing of German civilians at the end of World War II is indistinguishable from Hillgruber's interpretation of both events as equally "ruinous," since the empirical content of both claims is the same (i.e., these two things actually happened, according to the record). But even if their claims appear equally valid when compared on the basis of their pure facticity, this does not mean that they are interchangeable. Anderson's determination to disassociate the events that Hillgruber melded together represents something crucial for anyone interested in thinking through the possibilities for historical justice and mediation. While they make the same empirical claims, Anderson and Hillgruber present these events in altogether different contexts, which gives their narratives distinctive moral qualities. Whereas the Red Army engaged in total war with the Nazis for three years leading up to Germany's collapse, there was no comparable conflict between the Aryan and Jewish "races," except in the imagination of Germans who sought a scapegoat for their nation's difficulties and a guiding principle for their vision of revolutionary rebirth. For Anderson, this is what makes the killing of German civilians in the east in 1944–45 categorically different, in comparison to the roundup, deportation, and mass murder of European Jews after 1938. Anderson's moral assertion, that is, his insistence that the Holocaust was more horrific than the reprisal killings undertaken by the Soviets, returns us to the historical commissions that are the subject of this study. As I have tried to make clear, the potential of these commissions to mediate the past depends on their ability to clarify the facts in a responsible and authoritative manner, but at the same time it also hinges on the willingness of their members to stake out, communicate, and defend moral positions like the one Anderson has taken with respect to Hillgruber. Although Anderson stopped short of calling Hillgruber a Nazi apologist, he questioned the morality of the latter's nationalist reading of the Nazi past. In so doing, Anderson highlighted a set of rights and responsibilities that treats any co-mingling of Jewish and German suffering as patently immoral. Mediation, in this case, entails probing the moral implications of two competing narratives, and then using historical evidence and argument to assert their incomparability and the primacy, in terms of inhumane violence, of one over the other.

Nothing in *Two Kinds of Ruin* suggests that Hillgruber wanted to purposely deceive his readers, and Anderson has acknowledged that the book was conceived in good faith. But what if *Two Kinds of Ruin* represents a "counter-history," which, according to Amos Funkenstein, is "inauthentic [and] unreal, not because their authors lie consciously . . . but rather because they are through-and-through derivative, altogether dependent in every detail on the story they intend to overthrow."[9] To examine this possibility through a different example, we might recall the work of the Commission of the Historians of Latvia (CHL) and, in particular, the conference that the CHL hosted in October 2009 shortly before disbanding. "Occupation, Collaboration, and Resistance: History and Perception" was intended to bring Latvian scholars together with their Western counterparts to talk about conflicting memories of World War II. Whereas the Western scholars who attended pushed for acknowledgment of Latvian complicity in the Holocaust, the Latvian historians who participated sought to win acknowledgment for what they saw as Latvia's own experience of genocide under Soviet occupation. This resulted in what one participant called "a dialogue of the deaf." Western scholars left the conference feeling that their Latvian counterparts still refused to accept responsibility for the annihilation of Latvian Jewry, while Latvian participants accused the Western contingent of willfully misreading their country's history. Of course, the crucial question here—and the main complication hanging over all of the commissions presented in this study—is this: "Which of these perspectives should be regarded as history and which as counterhistory?" Whose perspective prevails when there are divergent accounts of the same events?

Given what historians have learned about the role of Latvian SD auxiliary units and other local collaborationist groups, there is no way of avoiding some degree of Latvian responsibility for the Holocaust.[10] The only legitimate questions are "Responsible to what degree?" and "Under what circumstances?" There was considerable disagreement within the CHL regarding both of these questions and, in particular, over whether Latvians participated in the mass killing of Jews prior to the arrival of German troops, or only afterward. One member of the commission, Alfred Senn (U.S.), argued that Latvians, driven by anti-Soviet sentiment, began to terrorize and kill Jews prior to the installation of the German regime, whereas another member, Aivars Stranga (Latvia), asserted that there was "no spontaneous terror" until after the arrival of the German Einsatzgruppen. In Senn's account, Latvians undertook *self-initiated* killings of Jews, while in Stranga's view, the Judeocide was "initiated and administered by the Germans, though they tried to make it look like a local enterprise." What allows for these mutually exclusive accounts? Here, it is the availability of different kinds of evidence (e.g., Jewish testimonies, Latvian testimonies, German files, Soviet files, etc.) and the different possibilities for reading these with and against each other. This is a good example of the way evidence sometimes constrains truth-telling, and it is one of the methodological limitations inherent to historical inquiry. Each side regards the other as having descended into counterhistory, and this standoff goes a long way toward explaining the CHL's failure. Further study and the discovery of new sources may eventually validate one of these versions, but for now the two sides have reached an impasse. There is nothing left to negotiate here, historically speaking; what remains is merely a question of politics, that is, who wins? Meanwhile, failed mediation has reinforced unfortunate stereotypes on both sides.

Considered alone, the Latvian case is discouraging, but the commission model can succeed if it can foster intersubjective agreement regarding historical facts and the moral judgments these facts can accommodate. One of the best examples of this (largely untapped) capacity is the Mattéoli Commission (France). Jacques Chirac's apology in 1995 for France's contribution to the Holocaust was an extraordinary breakthrough, if we consider the hold that the Resistance myth previously exerted over broad segments of the French public. However, in terms of its substance, Chirac's apology was not unlike others mentioned in this study, such as Kaspar Villiger's apology (1995) in Switzerland for turning away Jewish refugees. Despite some small differences in their rhetoric, both leaders acknowledged essentially the same kind of guilt: through their actions and inactions, their countrymen had facilitated the Holocaust. What makes the French case compelling is not the fact of the apology itself but rather the lengths to which the French went afterward to recover the history of Vichy collaboration and develop it in a narrative that underscored France's moral guilt. Whereas the CHL unraveled over small but highly potent differences, which minimized or amplified Latvian guilt (depending on which side of the disagreement we refer to), France's Mattéoli Commission accepted unqualified moral responsibility for the Holocaust, even though France, according to the commission's report, exercised only partial sovereignty under Vichy's "vassal dictatorship." Chirac said that German criminality "was seconded by the French, by the French state." Consistent with this view, the Mattéoli Commission reported that officers of French banks interpreted to their advantage ambiguous orders from Berlin concerning the status of legal contracts with Jews, thereby initiating a "stunning" program of spoliation that enabled further assaults against Jewish culture and lives. The commission also determined that Vichy officials, assisted by French police, "organized and carried out" the deportations that Germany demanded. According to the commission's vice-chairman, Ady Steg, France bore clear responsibility for "the anguish, humiliation, suffering, and death" of French Holocaust victims, and for the travails and deprivations of those who managed to escape death. For that reason, the Mattéoli Commission determined that French Jews were entitled not only to financial restitution but to moral reparations as well. Instead of focusing exclusively on financial liabilities, which were considerable although not always easy to document, the commission urged the French government and France's large banks to consider and repay their moral debts to the Jewish community, which members of the commission regarded as "clearly more important" than any uncompensated property losses. France created a second historical commission, the CIVS, to process individual restitution claims, while the Mattéoli Commission focused on how to ensure collective payback. Although the Mattéoli Commission estimated the total value of unreturned Jewish assets at approximately $130 million (based on what they knew to be incomplete records), France's banks and the French government, by 2013, had paid out close to $990 million, not to absolve the nation of its guilt but to underscore it. These funds were disbursed to individual claimants, Jewish communal groups, and nonprofits devoted to Holocaust commemoration and education. Chirac argued that reparations were not only a matter of concern for the Jewish community but rather should be viewed as a *"grande cause nationale."* The Mattéoli Commission and the CIVS, more than any of the other commissions presented in this study, succeeded in realizing that aim. As compared with Latvia, where the period of interregnum (the interval, during the summer of 1941, between the withdrawal of Soviet forces and the installation of the Nazi regime) and the question of responsibility for the first Jewish pogroms (self-initiated or prompted by the Germans?) resulted in the breakdown of mediation, in France the parenthesis theory (Vichy was not France) was clearly marked as illegitimate counterhistory.

Of course, this judgment has not penetrated every corner of French society, and these commissions are far from being magic bullets. Even where they have scraped out a foundation for reconciliation and historical justice, their work has not always made a deep impression on the public. One of the biggest challenges these commissions face is how to capture and hold the attention and interest of the lay public without resorting to the incendiary rhetoric and boundary-pushing claims that both political partisans and popular media exploit to generate support. We can dissect the available commission reports to get a clearer picture of their inner workings, but if the media and political culture reward the accusatory narratives that inflame passions and feed conflict, then this analysis will be purely academic.

To date, there has not yet been an in-depth, comparative study of Holocaust commissions, like the heavily cited works that analyze truth commissions and other related mechanisms for promoting transitional justice.[11] Historical commissions, including the Holocaust commissions treated here, bear some resemblance to the truth commissions. It is tempting to think of Holocaust commissions and truth commissions as representing subsets of a larger phenomenon, as both entail "retrospective scrutiny" of past injustices and a concerted effort to establish the truth about these events.[12] Despite these similarities, however, historical commissions and truth commissions employ different methodologies. In general, the truth commissions rely on the oral testimonies of living individuals (victims and perpetrators); the historical commissions rely on the written record. Also, while both are backward-looking enterprises, truth commissions are typically engaged with the recent past; historical commissions investigate more distant episodes, which explains why the role of witnesses is typically reduced. The proponents of truth commissions have claimed that these exercises are critically important for drawing a sharp line between the abuses of previous regimes and the democratic commitment of the new regime. The same argument can apply to certain historical commissions, for example, in East Central Europe, where Holocaust clarification commissions in the 1990s operated in parallel with post-Communist democratization initiatives. In other locales, for example, Western Europe, the analogy is not quite so precise, although one could argue, as Dan Diner has, that Holocaust commissions there have helped in the construction of a "foundational narrative" for the so-called New Europe. One of the biggest differences between the truth commissions and the historical commissions is the relative ease with which the former manage to capture and hold public attention. This is almost certainly due to the media-friendly dynamic of the truth commissions and the slow, meticulous style of the historical commissions. In the case of the truth commissions, wrenching testimony from survivors and the opportunity to see perpetrators squirm under questioning make for a highly dramatic presentation, which also generates a strong aura of suspense. Although some truth commissions have tried to create informal settings in order to give victims a relaxed forum for self-expression, their proceedings still tend to have a sharp emotional edge. Archbishop Desmond Tutu could be seen crying on South African television during the proceedings of the TRC, whereas the emotional strain associated with archival research almost never registers with the public. As a consequence, it has been harder for the historical commissions to attract and hold the public's interest. Their work is punctuated by long pauses, and these periods of investigative silence do not always lead to exciting revelations. Ambiguous written records many times remain ambiguous, since there is no opportunity to pose follow-up questions, as there is with living victims. In general, the historical commissions have more difficulty than the truth commissions when it comes to amplifying the voices of the victims. This can be the result of specific methodological choices, but it is also one of the fundamental challenges (liabilities?) of the discipline. Both commission types rely on mediated access to the past, but historical commissions work with something cooler and less commanding than the truth commissions. Paper documents do not radiate the same pathos that living victims do, and cruelty incarnate trumps paper facsimiles of the same. The relative coolness of the historical commission model offers potential advantages, where the goal is to tone down and transcend the hyperbole of partisan debate, but the drawbacks may, at times, outweigh these. In general, the truth commissions have a performative quality that the historical commissions lack, which might explain why the latter have been less enticing to scholars.[13] In cases where historical commissions *have* managed to attract media attention—typically interest peaks with the publication of the final report and dissipates soon thereafter—a bright spotlight on their work has not always been beneficial. Commissions that have given sober accounts of the past and have carefully responded to reporters' questions with measured language have seen their findings poorly summarized under blistering headlines intended to manufacture scandal, for example, "Historians' Report Slams Swiss Wartime Policy."[14] The paradox here is clear. In order to deliver real benefits, historical commissions need buy-in from the public, but mediating history requires cautious thinking and sedate language, which is difficult to translate into riveting prose. Compared to the red-hot sensationalism of the popular culture, mediating history burns a pale blue.

Despite these challenges, the post–Cold War era has seen rising interest in historical justice and the potential contribution of mediating history to the same. Although it is a backward-looking enterprise, historical justice intersects with contemporary debates regarding the content and reach of human rights, the place of ethics in politics, the role of history in politics, and the possibilities for building peace where conflicting historical memories have fed intergroup conflict. While the Nuremberg and Tokyo war crimes trials set an important precedent for prosecuting the leaders and representatives of criminal regimes, Cold War realism interrupted and delayed the implementation of new norms for international justice. Ironically, the collapse of Communism in Eastern Europe, which some regarded as "the end of history," kindled an increased demand for historical justice. In the ensuing quarter century, the appetite for historical justice and redress has become "almost insatiable."[15] This book reflects and analyzes one aspect of that trend. While it is not possible to treat all of the Holocaust commissions in a single volume, I have presented more than a dozen cases here in an effort to develop a useful framework for comparative analysis. Other scholars know individual commissions better than I do— and this study has benefitted greatly from their expertise—but no other work to date has attempted to map so many cases in one constellation. In order to do this, I have employed what might be described as a triangular approach. In addition to dissecting the actual work of thirteen Holocaust commissions (fourteen, if my introductory comments on Norway are counted), I have also tried to gauge their public reception, and I have attempted to assess their historiographical significance. By weaving these three strands together, I have tried to show the typological potential of these commissions while still accounting for their distinctive features.

To varying degrees, all of the commissions in this study have addressed the difficult theme of how to establish responsibility for policies and practices, which today are widely considered to have been unjust (though clearly not universally so). Comparison of their output reveals a range of results. Both the

Mattéoli Commission (France) and the Independent Commission of Experts (Switzerland) performed admirably, though their approaches differed. Even if these commissions cannot be credited with single-handedly turning the tide, the retreat of nationalist myths in both countries suggests the overall relevance and efficacy of their work. The Mattéoli Commission distinguished itself by disassembling the parenthesis theory and showing which of its constitutive elements meshed with the facts (e.g., the commission took seriously the subordination of the Vichy government to the Nazi regime) and which did not (e.g., bank records revealed French initiative in the application of Jewish spoliation measures). Endeavoring to give a comprehensive assessment of the past, the Mattéoli Commission applied a strict principle of moral responsibility, which it translated into a pragmatic program for justice and repair. Unlike some of the other government-appointed commissions treated here, the Mattéoli Commission was empowered to make specific recommendations regarding appropriate measures for restitution. The commission found that Jewish assets worth at least $130 million had not been returned to their rightful owners (or heirs), but it urged the French government and citizenry to think of the nation's debt as something beyond the scope of monetary compensation. Chirac called the injustices committed by France "irreparable," and the Mattéoli Commission prepared a detailed history, which gave substance to this characterization. Spoliation was more than just plunder in the commission's view; it laid the groundwork for more coercive measures, which were introduced later. While some scholars have suggested that European Jews were killed so that they could be plundered, the Mattéoli Commission saw a dialectical relationship between expropriation and genocide. Killing allowed for large-scale theft, but theft made killing possible, too. For the commission, reluctance or refusal to remedy the effects of these thefts was seen as condonation of the killing, a kind of collaboration after the fact.

Inasmuch as this formula represents the Mattéoli Commission's "verdict" on Vichy, it is important to contemplate how this reading of the past tweaks our everyday understanding(s) of guilt and responsibility. While common sense strongly suggests that individuals cannot be held responsible for acts they did not commit themselves, a "moral duty to rescue" has entered into many of the civil law systems that operate in Europe. By contrast, in the common law systems that have been established in most English-speaking countries, there is no general duty to come to the aid of someone in harm's way, except where there is a "special relationship" (e.g., parent/child) or in cases where the person in danger has created a hazardous situation for others. What the Mattéoli Commission's narrative seems to imply is that the moral duty to rescue applies not only to the eyewitness or bystander but to the latecomer as well, at the moment that she becomes aware of the ongoing effects of a past harm. Whereas, under common law, I may walk past a semiconscious stranger who has just had her purse stolen, civil law imposes a duty on me to lend whatever aid I can. The Mattéoli Commission has pushed this concept a step further by urging me to take action, even if my arrival onto the scene is significantly delayed and others have stepped in ahead of me. The distance between the crime and my becoming aware of it are, to a large extent, inconsequential. Knowledge of the crime, when it arises, carries an obligation to explore its full meaning and support its remediation. Taken to the extreme, this principle would obviously impose an absurd duty. Can I really be responsible for securing justice wherever there has been a crime or an atrocity, just because, long after the fact, I happen to have strolled past the place where these events occurred? The answer, whether considered from a legal or moral perspective, is no. But then, the Mattéoli Commission was concerned with crimes of an altogether different character, not the depressingly commonplace purse snatching, which one individual carries out against another, but rather a systematic program of plunder, deportation, and mass killing perpetrated and/or facilitated by the state—by France—against a whole group. In other words, the commission's conception of guilt springs from a *specific* brand of injustice. We are no longer dealing here with a Good Samaritan parable, that is, the moral challenge given to the individual to accept every stranger as his brother. Instead, we are confronted by something different, more limited in some respects but also "bigger" in some ways. This refers to an ethical imperative to acknowledge and repair a specific violation of individual and group rights brought to light by responsible historians who have convincingly explained it as a collective moral failure. Unlike the story of the Good Samaritan, which is concerned with mankind, that is, the individual taken out of any specific institutional or historical context, the Mattéoli Commission's verdict applies to a particular group, in a specific place, at a fixed moment in time. On the other hand, the commission's report is more than just a pronouncement of past failure. It is also a statement on the accumulation of further injustice, where a society attempts to divorce itself from the past without making a thorough and deliberate effort to give to all what is their due. History and justice become a joint enterprise in this formula. Both seek to provide a narrative that is, as Charles Maier has put it, "on the one hand synthetic, and, on the other, open to conflicting testimony."[16] Both offer a "summation," which is intended to assess "choices made and damages done, or damages that were allowed to take place."[17]

Switzerland's ICE reveals both the potential and the limitations of the commission model. While it helped dispel the myth of neutrality that Swiss nationals had used to protect their positive self-image following the war, and although it led to a substantive program of restitution, the ICE, in some respects, skirted the question of moral responsibility that the Mattéoli Commission addressed directly. Given unrestricted archival access and a hefty budget, the ICE published twenty-five book-length studies between 1996 and 2002. Within this large body of work, the commission highlighted three major findings: (1) the Swiss government maintained an "unnecessarily restrictive" refugee policy, which adversely affected Jews whose lives were known to be in jeopardy; (2) Swiss firms cooperated with the Axis war economy to a significant degree and over a sustained period; and (3) Swiss banks, in the postwar period, were negligent in their handling of "dormant accounts" that contained Jewish assets. For the majority of Swiss historians and for many ordinary Swiss, these were not especially shocking revelations; most of what the ICE reported was already known. But if the ICE dropped no real bombshells, their reports still challenged persistent myths regarding Switzerland's "benevolent neutrality." When the ICE presented its final report in 2002, Jean-François Bergier, the commission's chairman, offered that the study aimed to promote "genuine dialogue" on topics that raised "highly charged and conflicting emotions." Whereas popular histories had emphasized Swiss heroism, for example, General Guisan's mobilization of the Swiss army in 1940 against a possible Nazi attack, the commission focused on Switzerland's "egregious failure[s]." According to the ICE, Switzerland failed to uphold its own humanitarian principles, just as France, according to Chirac, had betrayed the universal rights and Enlightenment values that it claimed to embody. But if both of these countries failed in essentially the same way, a key difference appears when we examine how their respective Holocaust commissions contextualized these failures. In France, the Mattéoli Commission accepted unqualified guilt for anti-Semitic persecution. Although French sovereignty was partially eclipsed after June 1940, the commission found that France's subordination occurred *within the context of its collaboration.* This formula preserved France's moral agency, whereas the parenthesis theory previously had held that Vichy arose from a moral vacuum. In the Mattéoli narrative, the continuity of moral agency engrains Vichy in France's national history.

By contrast, the ICE placed Switzerland's failures in a global context where the behavior of other countries suggested a more relaxed moral standard. Regarding Swiss xenophobia and anti-Semitism, the commission observed that similar attitudes were widespread in Europe for decades prior to the rise of Nazism. The commission also noted that Switzerland was not alone in refusing to assist imperiled refugees. Besides Switzerland, thirty-one other countries attended the Evian Conference in 1938, and all but one (the

Dominican Republic) declined to increase their quotas for Jewish immigration. By weaving these considerations into their narrative, the ICE made Swiss callousness and antipathy less exotic and, therefore, less egregious. If the Swiss denied asylum to Jews who faced the likelihood of extermination, they should be judged on the same basis as other liberal democracies, which also failed to offer assistance. Of course, the ICE also found important differences in comparison to other countries. In the final report, the ICE acknowledged that Switzerland requested that Germany mark the passports of its Jewish citizens with a *J* stamp. Moreover, the report revealed that Swiss border guards used their rifle butts to physically repel refugees at the border. But these examples of official "ruthlessness" are contrasted with other examples of individual Swiss citizens acting more "generously," including some consular officials who issued entry visas to refugees, despite receiving reprimands from their government for doing so. While this sort of contextualization might be seen as the stock-in-trade of responsible historical inquiry, the narrative in this section of the commission's final report seems to depend to an uncomfortable degree on the counterclaim that Swiss refugee policy was especially deleterious to Jews. Using Amos Funkenstein's terminology, we might call this aspect of the ICE narrative an example of international counterhistory. Conversely, one could argue that the ICE's comparisons do not go far enough. For example, both Great Britain and the United States, like Switzerland, refused to loosen their immigration quotas at the Evian Conference but, taking the comparison further, neither of these countries shared a border with Germany. Is it wrong to make Switzerland's geographical proximity to Germany a matter of moral concern? If one is better positioned than others to give life-saving assistance, is the responsibility to do so not somehow greater? Although the ICE report revolves around Swiss "failures," it includes several sections like this, where callousness and collaboration are depicted in ways that shield Switzerland from charges of immorality. Regarding Switzerland's economic cooperation with Germany, the ICE concluded that even if some segments of the Swiss business elite showed admiration for the fundamental tenets of Nazism, "such sympathies were not expressed through the intensity of economic exchange." Rather, Switzerland's economic entanglements with Germany stemmed from a "business first logic." They were not driven by racial ideology, according to the ICE, even if the instinct for profit sometimes blinded Swiss business leaders to the rights and suffering of Germany's so-called racial enemies.

It is certainly possible to make too much of these deflections, which are minor in comparison to the commission's overall criticism of the Swiss record. At the same time, it is important to recognize such nuances, since the efficacy of mediating history can be determined by what might appear to be small matters. Austria's Historikerkommission offers a good example here. Convened in 1998, the Austrian commission received a straightforward mandate with few obvious restrictions. The commission was created to investigate and clarify "the whole complex of [Nazi] expropriation" and to assess Austrian restitution efforts after 1945. But despite the wide latitude it was given to explore Nazi-era crimes, the commission conducted its investigation with a narrow, economic focus, which silenced important aspects of Holocaust history and allowed Austrians to avoid difficult questions concerning their nation's moral debts to the victims and survivors. The commission focused on compensable losses, that is, the monetary value of confiscated, looted, and destroyed properties, without exploring the experiences of victims beyond these limits. Virtually everything in the commission's final report related to shillings, reichsmarks, and dollars, while almost nothing dealt with the traumatic effects of anti-Semitic violence on those who were exposed to it. In the sections on Kristallnacht, the commission's report displayed a curious obsession with the materiality of broken glass. The report covers the number of windows broken, the total area (in square meters) of all shattered glass, the insured values of these panes, and which of these broken windows was the subject of an insurance claim. Readers gain little familiarity with the people who looked out from behind these windows and suffered profoundly, far beyond any financial losses, as a result of their shattering. Whereas Marion Kaplan saw these attacks as a "public degradation ritual," which led to a sharp spike in suicide among Jews, the Austrian commission was basically silent on the internal experiences of victims.[18] Reading the report, it seems the commission determined that broken glass and stolen furniture were compensable, whereas terrorizing one's neighbors in an open display of racial hatred—to the point that many Jews contemplated or committed suicide—was not. There is a preoccupation with quantitative analysis and forensic accounting throughout the report that precludes deep contemplation of Jewish suffering. This is an example of how methodological choices can shade the past, even where the stated goal of the exercise is clarification. Like the Mattéoli Commission in France, the Austrian Historikerkommission linked property confiscation and "Aryanization" to the Judeocide in a direct way. It also undercut the "victim thesis," which held that Austrians bore no responsibility for the Holocaust, since Austria did not exist as a sovereign state between 1938 and 1945. But these accomplishments are partly overshadowed by the commission's fixation on material losses, and overemphasis on crimes against property makes other dimensions of Jewish suffering seem less acute. The Austrian case shows that unless historical commissions deliberately push their investigations into the realm of victims' rights, including what I have called the right to history, their utility for peace-building and reconciliation will be limited.

Poland's Institute of National Remembrance (IPN) teaches a number of important lessons about the pros and cons of "thick description" for promoting historical reconciliation and the need to carefully calibrate the emotional temperature of mediating histories. The IPN's study of the Jedwabne massacre, which appeared several years after Jan Gross's international bestseller, *Neighbors*, which sparked a national debate over Poland's role in the Holocaust, does a very good job of avoiding the accusatory formulas that provoke nationalist backlash. Nonetheless, the cautiousness of the IPN study ends up being some-thing of a double-edged sword. On the one hand, by avoiding the literary stylization(s) that Gross uses in *Neighbors* to build suspense, encourage em-pathy, and arouse condemnation, the IPN produced a restrained, but still illuminating, account of the massacre. The IPN asserted that Gross's central claim that "one half of the village killed the other half" is not supported by physical evidence (e.g., a forensic study of human remains), to which Gross had no access.[19] On the other hand, the IPN's study partially confirmed another of Gross's contentions that homegrown Polish anti-Semitism was a factor (albeit to different degrees) in the pogroms that took place there during the war. However, while Gross used evidence of Polish anti-Semitism as a point of departure for a more sweeping judgment (i.e., that the Jedwabne killers were typical Poles who used Barbarossa as an excuse to vent their criminal desires), the IPN expanded their study beyond Jedwabne to show how circumstances differed from village to village and across different regions. Polish anti-Semitism, although real, did not always have the genocidal intention that Gross saw as one of its essential features. The overall effect of the IPN study is the way it cools off (without diminishing) the violent and difficult history that Gross composed in the form of a fiery national indictment. Whereas Gross launches *Neighbors* with grotesque eyewitness testimony that encourages readers to see the Jedwabne perpetrators as the inhuman embodiment of a primal hatred, the IPN study is less flamboyant in its treatment of the most gruesome details. But again, the IPN study does not deny Polish responsibility for the massacre nor downplay the viciousness of the event. The report is direct and unvarnished where it describes a pernicious tradition of anti-Semitism in parts of Poland and the role that this bigotry played in specific episodes of vio-lence, including some in which Poles killed Jews without being encouraged or coerced by German troops.

A second issue raised by the Polish case is the problem of generalization as it relates to historical knowledge. History deals with particularity, and trained historians typically avoid the temptation to draw "big lessons" from their studies, since the biggest claims are quite often the most tenuous. But it is extraordinarily difficult to write about events like the Jedwabne massacre without making reference to "Poles" and "Jews." In any case, historical commissions are created to provide context for the documents contained in the archival record. In the process, these commissions frequently raise the acts of individuals to the group level. In contrast with legal courts, where individual perpetrators matter only to the extent that lawyers can reveal their individual actions and motives, historical commissions are concerned with perpetrators and victims because of the possibility that these individuals reveal something important about larger, historical trends, currents, forces, and the like. History positions itself between poetry, which strives to relate universal truths, and legal discourse, which seeks to discover particular truths in order to compare them against particular rules. Because they migrate toward the group level, historical commissions, even if they make no claim to having universal insight, tend to conceptualize guilt in terms of its collective applicability. This is a problem if we want to argue that historical justice enriches democratic practice, since the liberal democratic framework normally does not recognize the idea of collective guilt. Yet commissions like the ones presented here almost invariably have something to say either about the guilt of the group or, conversely, about the circumstances that absolve the group of such guilt. In France, the Mattéoli Commission determined that Vichy was, in fact, France and that Vichy collaboration ought to be viewed as French collaboration. About the Vél d'Hiv roundup, Chirac insisted, and the Mattéoli Commission concurred, that Germany's crimes were "seconded by the French." This is a difficult proposition for French citizens who stood up to the regime and also for those who were not present at the time these crimes were committed. But historical justice is not principally about determining culpability, even though this may be an important component of commissioned history. Like truth commissions, historical commissions do sometimes "name names," but emphasis on specific personages can also undercut their potential for fostering intergroup reconciliation. Where empirical study verifies the culpability of a few, the rest may take this as proof of vindication and clearance. The best historical commissions have, for this reason, developed a different conception of guilt. Rather than culpability, these commissions have tried to impart a sense of collective responsibility, not for past acts of victimization per se but for contributing to a society that regards these as wrong and, therefore, in need of remediation. Historical justice does not require that individuals feel remorse for past crimes in which they were not directly involved. Instead, it asks for moral recommitment, a concrete expression of the will to see past wrongs righted and new wrongs prevented. Danielle Celermajer has described this concept in terms of "re-covenanting the national imagery."[20] More than just a demand for compensation, this concept of justice calls for "an expression of shame, where shame marks the recognition of ethical flaws in the identity of the collective, or rather its failure to live up to its ideal self as defined in its constitutional principals."[21] If Vichy was France, and France wants to claim attachment to the Rights of Man (referring to the 1789 *Déclaration des droits de l'homme et du citoyen*), then individuals claiming a French identity need to be concerned with any abridgment of these rights, whether contemporary or historical. When the Mattéoli Commission declared that France had a solemn responsibility to make moral reparations for the crime of collaboration, it meant that inclusion in the French national collective requires that individuals take offense to that crime and work to address, through a process of mediation, the abridgments of rights, which that crime entailed. Although the IPN study does not directly invoke this kind of formula, I would argue that its narrative for Jedwabne suggests something analogous in terms of Poland's responsibility for the massacre and the obligations of contemporary Poles toward Jewish victims and their descendants.

Still, it is troubling that recent discussions of Jedwabne have involved accusations of "Polish anti-Semitism," as if that were the disposition of all Poles. Through its examination of archival sources, the IPN study clearly documented that some Poles in the Białystok region, including officials of the Church and State, had expressed anti-Semitic views commensurate with those espoused through Nazi ideology and propaganda. Others Poles, the IPN showed, rejected these views. But the debates around Jedwabne, since the publication of *Neighbors*, have revolved largely around "Poles" and "Jews," as if these groups were monolithic. Trying to wring historical knowledge out of individual documents and artifacts, the IPN also relied on this terminology to a certain extent. Jacek Zakowski, the well-known Polish journalist, pointed out (correctly, in my view) that "large-scale quantifiers" of this type can reproduce a tribal logic that harbors a dangerous potential for ethnic violence. Gross's *Neighbors* was controversial precisely because of his willingness to draw general conclusions about the Polish collective from specific court documents related to Jedwabne. In his more recent work, Gross has tried to articulate more fully his conception of the relationship between particular artifacts and the general knowledge that historians attempt to derive from these. A "narrowly confined piece of information," Gross has argued, will "consolidate a general understanding about [the past]" so long as it reflects "a larger flow of events."[22] But while historical knowledge differentiates itself from anecdotal experience on the basis of its empirical richness, meaning the inductive collection of multiple data points prior to the suggestion of a general principle, there is no possibility of validating historical judgments by means of additional experimentation. The historical claim that $a + b + c = d$ can be examined for its logical coherence, for its relationship to other explanatory formulas, and for the integrity of its individual components, but there is no way to verify the claim in an absolute sense. On the other hand, it is relatively easy to recognize which historical claims and which tonal and rhetorical choices create conflict. The use of "large-scale quantifiers" has a pronounced tendency to do this, whereas qualified claims, which pass muster epistemologically without overstating their own significance, are more helpful to the process of mediation. What Gross tries to teach his readers about "Poles" or "Poland" is unverifiable, even if some Poles have left clear evidence of their anti-Semitic attitudes in the documentary record. This observation is not meant to fuel hyperskepticism, which is immensely appealing to revisionists and partisans who care nothing for the requirements of responsible history. Rather, it is offered as a reminder to those who wish to clarify difficult histories without reinforcing partisan memories. If there is any value to the large-scale quantifiers that historians rely on to communicate the greater significance of their findings, it is the way these labels make the past more readily digestible. If, for example, Poles feel animosity toward Germany, for the violence and destruction that the Nazi regime wrought in their country, a mediating history must give these individuals some opportunity to understand the "German" perspective. Poles might accept or reject this version of the past, depending on how thoroughly they felt it exposed the injustice of Germany's quest for "living space" and how accurately it communicated the full extent of their losses. Rather than offering some kind of "middle of the road" position, mediation would hinge on definitive documentation of German war guilt without minimizing the hardships that Germans in Poland endured at the end of the war as a result of their forced expulsion. Rather than compromise, mediating history would entail exposure and invalidation of propaganda on both sides of the conflict. This is one way of looking at the work of the Polish-German Historians' Commission presented in chapter 5 in this study.

Clearly, then, one of the crucial challenges for historical commissions is how to balance their judgments of large ethnonational collectives with their revelations about particular members of these groups. "Naming names" can facilitate mourning in some cases, but it is a poor strategy for promoting intergroup reconciliation, since it loads guilt onto the shoulders of a relative few. On the other hand, overgeneralization can deepen partisan discord. In the case of Germany, we know that there were Righteous Gentiles among the Germans at the time of the Holocaust; Yad Vashem honors 569 of them.[23] We also know that Nazi courts convicted tens of thousands of non-Jewish Germans for various "political crimes." We know that various anti-Nazi resistance groups existed in Germany from 1933 to 1945, even if their impact was limited. Besides this, there were millions of "bystanders," Germans who did nothing to oppose the Holocaust but did not proactively contribute to the genocide either. In other words, it is obvious that criminal guilt for Nazi crimes does not extend to every German who lived through this era, even if other types of guilt (e.g., moral and metaphysical) might apply, as Karl Jaspers famously suggested. At the same time, there are clear problems with the legal prosecutions that were undertaken to punish Nazi perpetrators after the war, including, primarily, the way these trials whittled down "German" guilt to a relative few. One of the main critiques of the Nuremberg Tribunal, when the first trial opened in November 1945, was the inadequacy of prosecuting two dozen individuals for crimes that implicated millions. To effectively mediate the past, historical commissions must scale their efforts appropriately. Holocaust narratives that demonize entire groups will trigger backlash from the nationalist set, while narrow concern for high-level perpetrators warps the past and does violence to the memory of the victims. In between these positions, we can find room for investigation. In the same way that Holocaust historians have had to work through the debate concerning functionalist and intentionalist interpretations of the genocide, Holocaust commissions have had to negotiate the dimensions of Holocaust guilt.[24] The most successful commissions have developed a formula that presents national guilt as both limited (materially) and unlimited (morally).

Besides negotiating the proportions and the quality of guilt, historical commissions have had to wrestle with the problem of detachment. In order to come to grips with the themes of collaboration and responsibility, it is necessary that historical commissions present their data in a manner that captures the moral imagination. At the same time, I have argued that thick description, especially when it supports an accusatory framework, has the potential to repel readers and, in particular, those who refuse to accept moral responsibility for crimes committed by their countrymen in a previous era. To take a different example, a film like *Twelve Years a Slave* (2013) depends on graphic, prolonged depictions of violence in the context of plantation slavery to raise the historical consciousness of its viewers and to convey the brutality of America's "peculiar institution." While some hailed the film as a masterpiece, others lambasted it as "torture porn" that "perpetuate[s] Hollywood's disenfranchisement of Black people's humanity."[25] Noting its limited earnings, even in comparison with other so-called black films, one writer for the *Independent* (London) wondered whether *Twelve Years a Slave* was not "too much for American audiences."[26] Decorated with numerous industry awards, but largely brushed aside by the public, how do we measure the film's social significance? Should we expect moviegoers to line up for a film that "chastens, shames, and mortifies"? Or do we conclude that the limited box-office returns for a film hailed by Henry Louis Gates Jr. as "the best film ever made about slavery from the point of view of a slave"[27] are an indication that "mainstream" America is still not ready for a serious conversation about race?

This study argues inter alia that the impact of historical commissions is demonstrably real and at least potentially positive in terms of fostering historical dialogue and accountability. Some of the case studies, however, point in the opposite direction. In Italy, the Anselmi Commission published a report that revealed widespread persecution of Italian Jews prior to the German invasion of 1943 and pervasive spoliation of Jewish property beginning in 1938. However, while the commission produced an extremely detailed picture of the infringements on Jewish life in Holocaust-era Italy, its work did little to overcome the indifference of most Italians to the full extent of Jewish suffering and losses. This failure, I have argued, was due not only to the government's lack of support for a new program of restitution but also to the arid quality of the commission's report, and in particular, the commission's attention to minute historical details that, in the end, detracted from the bigger picture of Holocaust history in Italy.[28] Whereas some accounts of the past fail to promote reconciliation because they are too visceral, others, like the Anselmi report, fall flat because of their clinical detachment. Much like Austria's Historikerkommission, the Anselmi Commission's excessive interest in quantifiable losses makes for numbing reading with little potential for mediation of divergent memories, which are experiential rather than statistical.

Other commissions have struggled mainly for technical reasons. The International Commission on Holocaust-Era Insurance Claims (ICHEIC), which, according to one of its own board members, "failed miserably at its task," committed many more technical and procedural errors than can be summarized here.[29] The commission developed a close relationship with the European insurance firms whose records were subject to investigation, and although this kind of cooperation has worked in other cases (e.g., the willingness of French banks to assist the Mattéoli Commission with a full review of their records), in the case of the ICHEIC it corrupted the process of negotiation. Not only did the insurance companies refuse to grant the commission full access to their archives, but they also dragged their feet and resisted the commission's attempts to negotiate a fair conversion rate for unpaid policies purchased during the interwar period. One judge, who presided over a class-action lawsuit filed in New York by individuals whose policy claims had been rejected, noted the commission's close ties with the companies being sued and concluded that the ICHEIC had been set up in the manner of "a company store." Others took the commission to task for administrative overspending and improper use of settlement funds (e.g., for the reimbursement of personal travel). The most perplexing aspect of the ICHEIC, however, was the commission's decision to accept a settlement from the insurance companies *prior* to the completion of its own independent investigation. The commission received $475 million from the European insurance companies that sold the majority of unpaid policies, but this settlement was negotiated five years *before* the commission concluded its research. Although the commission placed a premium on achieving a speedy resolution in light of the advanced age of many claimants and the long delay they experienced while waiting for consideration, numerous experts rated the settlement figure as exceedingly low. The American insurance analysts who originally pushed for the creation of the ICHEIC estimated the total value of unpaid Holocaust-era policies to be between $1 billion and $4 billion. Making matters worse, the settlement funds, whether sufficient or not, sat untouched in escrow for three years as the ICHEIC struggled to resolve key questions concerning valuation and standards of proof. The ICHEIC's "legacy document" (i.e., final report) does not detail how many claimants died during this three-year interval or the total value of "heirless" claims.

The results of the International Catholic-Jewish Historical Commission (ICJHC) are similarly discouraging. A restrictive mandate and the Vatican's unwillingness to provide the commission full access to its archives probably doomed this project from the beginning. The commission's preliminary report, which also turned out to be its final testament, failed to help matters. Concerned by the lacunae in their limited source material—the Vatican supplied more than five thousand documents for study but acknowledged that their archives contained millions more from the period in question—the commission dissolved itself after determining that the Vatican's lack of transparency made it impossible to resolve the most serious disputes concerning the Holy See's role in the Holocaust and the specific policies of Pope Pius XII. The staunchest Catholic supporters believed that the ICJHC was determined to defame the Church and its pontiff, no matter what evidence of Catholic benevolence was contained in the historical record. On the other side, Pius's harshest critics have maintained that the Vatican failed to protect and assist Jews to the full extent of its capabilities, and that Pius's "silence" with respect to the Holocaust signaled his tacit acceptance of Nazi ideology. While recent scholarship on the Vatican's policy of neutrality has done a commendable job of exploring the complex realities and difficult choices that the Catholic Church confronted during the war, the ICJHC failed to transcend the either/or dynamic that has characterized the partisan debates over Pius.[30] Although members of the commission stated that they wanted to explore the "multiple dimension[s]" of this historical episode, the preliminary report repeatedly pointed to the same general conclusion. Without directly accusing Pius of having turned a blind eye to Jewish suffering, the commission implied that whatever actions he may have taken and whatever measures he attempted "behind the scenes," these were overshadowed and undermined by his refusal to make a public appeal on behalf of Europe's imperiled Jews. The policy of neutrality, in other words, was not merely ineffective; it was immoral. For the Vatican, this judgment was obviously unacceptable. While the most successful Holocaust commissions have been forceful in their insistence on moral guilt as a consequence of national collaboration, the ICJHC attempted to inject moral guilt into a sacred space, where it could not be accepted. This is one of the unique challenges for commissions that wade into religious debates. To maintain their authority, sacred claims must be impervious to secular curiosity.

Commissioned history must contend with other potential pitfalls. As Peter Novick observed in his work on the aspirations of professional history and the ideal of objectivity, "Every group has its own historian."[31] In an age of skepticism and uncertainty, the tendency is toward greater fragmentation of historical understanding rather than convergence. In some cases, there is no realistic possibility of moving partisans away from dubious historical claims that satisfy deep internal longings for self-validation. The commission model does not easily or automatically override the fact that conflicts rooted in the past are sustained by competing groups, who each wish to claim the same "right to history." Commission reports that fail to support a particular perspective or claim may simply be viewed as the work of *their* historians rather than *ours*. On the other hand, where there is already some interest in reconciliation, the commission model supplies a potential route forward. While these commissions cannot single-handedly determine the course of international politics, they can be effective levers for reorienting key actors. An excellent example of this potential for driving reconciliation is the Polish-German Historians Commission presented in chapter 5 in this study. While this commission would never have existed except for the executive-level diplomacy that produced the Treaty of Warsaw (1970), more recently, following a period that has been characterized as another Polish-German "ice age" (1998–2007), the commission's work has been lauded by diplomats seeking a new foundation for confidence building and rapprochement. In 2007, when Germany's foreign minister Frank Walter Steinmeier met with his Polish counterpart for talks on how to reset relations between the two countries, he made the Polish-German

Historians Commission and, specifically, the commission's joint history text-book project, one of his major talking points. This commission was especially helpful in its response to widespread Polish concerns over German plans for a Center Against Expulsion.[32] Steinmeier acknowledged that the center had been promoted in a way that was offensive to Polish (and other) victims of Nazism, and he urged more work from historians to clarify the context in which ethnic Germans were expelled from Poland. Steinmeier's push for a joint textbook (originally expected in 2015) is a prime example of the way that history can enter politics and drive diplomacy geared toward the improvement of bilateral relations. Often viewed as an outward sign of reconciliation, historical commis-sions can also be effective agents of reconciliation.

Despite the epistemological radicalism of recent years, historical scholar-ship remains anchored in the social sciences. Even the most flamboyant theore-ticians have been reluctant to follow their own thinking "all the way down" where the question of emplotment has come up against events, like the Holo-caust, whose meaning seems to be intrinsic, at least within the mainstream discourse of ethics. Despite what they know regarding the inextricability of politics and history, historians have been steadfast in maintaining a distinction between fact and fiction, and they have pushed back against literary and nar-rative theory, that is, the linguistic turn, precisely because of its relativizing potential. With respect to the Holocaust, this emphasis on scientific orthodoxy and the inviolability of prelinguistic facts has melded with a concern for the singular nature of the event. As a consequence, Holocaust historiography in-cludes numerous warnings and admonitions concerning instrumental usage of the Shoah. Lucy Dawidowicz, for example, decried what she saw as the rise of an "activist agenda" within Holocaust Studies.[33] While acknowledging a poten-tial link between historical truth and justice, Dawidowicz strongly opposed Holocaust scholarship and pedagogy that aimed to indoctrinate its audience or tout a particular political perspective, even one consistent with the liberal values of multicultural democracy. This kind of approach, she argued, dis-couraged deep historical understanding of the Holocaust by treating Nazi anti-Semitism as an example of a more general (i.e., sociological) tendency toward prejudice, bigotry, and social scapegoating. Attempting to derive uni-versal lessons from a unique event, too many scholars and teachers, Dawidowicz lamented, have developed "imprecise and tendentious analogies," which en-courage lazy intellectual habits and shallow moralizing "inappropriate to the subject."[34]

Dawidowicz was right to worry about the potential dangers of compara-tive analysis and "analogic" thinking. Once this door is opened, there is nothing that prevents historians from proposing new readings of the Shoah based on idiosyncratic judgments of the direction and meaning of history. Historians cannot interpret the world without making a determination regarding which events are isolated and which are clustered (that is, causally related), but the very act of relating one episode to another is an assertion of subjectivity that reveals an ideological disposition. Looked at from this angle, Andreas Hillgruber's argument in *Two Kinds of Ruin* that "the end of European Jewry" and "the shattering of the German Reich" can both be traced to the same intellectual root cause is not substantively different than the lesson plans developed by Facing History and Ourselves, which link middle-school bullying and social ostracism today to the rise of anti-Semitism in interwar Germany.[35] While Hillgruber's book might be cast as German nationalism and the Facing History lesson might be seen as promoting multicultural tolerance, both are the products of interpretive clustering. For some, this will serve as a warning against the use of history in political debate. Once the latch is loosened, there is no telling what comes rushing in.

This concern for guarding the neutrality of fact-finding is crucial when thinking about the potential of historical commissions for mediating conflict. Whether a commission is able to develop a mutually acceptable version of the past that promotes reconciliation or decides to validate one narrative at the expense of another so as to "settle accounts," the legitimacy of the enterprise is likely to be challenged by those who equate instrumental history with irresponsible partisanship. "A historical clarification commission's legitimacy," Robert Rotberg has written, "depends entirely on its ability to sift the often contentious and muddled record objectively."[36] As this study hopefully makes clear, I take Rotberg's claim as both true *and* false. There is no question that commissioned history forfeits its mediating capacity if the findings and opinions it generates are seen as programmatic, rather than factual. While exploring various possibilities for how the past can be narrated (and with what effects), I have also stated that mediating history is not a postmodern enterprise that equates might and right, or one that replaces epistemological standards with aesthetic judgments. If the line between ordinary subjectivity and irresponsible subjectivity is not always clear, everything in this study begins from the belief that this line does, indeed, exist and that it can be located through a process of dialogue and negotiation. On the other hand, I have defended the practices of certain Holocaust commissions while questioning the work of others on the basis of an idea, borrowed from Thomas Haskell, that "objectivity is not neutrality."[37] In other words, my analysis of these commissions arises from the perspective that responsible historians can largely overcome themselves and establish a sufficiently detached position vis-à-vis the past without giving up their political commitments or renouncing their moral concerns. I do not mean to imply that historical detachment gives access to transcendent truths, but I do see this habit as permitting a lesser brand of certitude, which is the uncovering of non-empirical premises and recognition of how wishful thinking (including one's own) influences historical interpretation. So long as these boundaries are observed, there is no reason why responsible history cannot be buttressed by a particular set of values or a specific conception of obligation. Historical facticity, once established, is impervious to and independent of moral judgment. This is why one can say of Hillgruber's *Two Kinds of Ruin* that the work is empirically sound, while the thesis is morally dubious.

Called upon to clarify the past and to weigh in on the quality of competing narratives, historical commissions are easily caught out in the crossfire between *is* and *ought*. On the one hand, their task is descriptive, meaning these bodies are charged with recovering and communicating the facts in a detached, non-judgmental manner. On the other hand, there is frequently a prescriptive aspect to the work they perform. Depending on the mandate they receive, these commissions might be tasked with making policy recommendations to remediate past injustices, or they might be called upon to develop pedagogical materials for primary and secondary education. Regardless of any "extra" responsibilities they may or may not carry, these commissions invariably construct a moral philosophy by virtue of their suggesting meaningful connections between past events, or by virtue of their determination to keep certain events separate. In this regard, their work is not markedly different from that of individual historians, whose interpretation of the past, even when given from an appropriately detached position, is always already determined by non-empirical premises. Mediating history, which is the turning over and careful counting of ideological and rhetorical trump cards within historical narrative, does not resolve the problem of subjectivity so much as present it openly. Given that you have *your* facts and we have *ours*, as Simo Drljača maintained in 1997, where can we go from here? What might be gained (or lost) by launching a dialogue around our differences?

In the introduction, I stated that the proliferation of historical commissions since 1989 can be traced to three factors: (1) the rise of the Internet, which makes the recovery and recirculation of forgotten histories exceptionally easy and also allows for intense, public rumination on past injustices; (2) the rise of a human rights discourse and, in particular, the emergence of a right to truth and redress for victims of crime and abuse of power; and finally (3) the growing interest in truth commissions as a way of dealing with the past and effecting a measure of justice where criminal prosecutions are deemed impractical or imprudent. I briefly mentioned that both commission types—truth and historical—owe something to the commissions of inquiry and Royal

Commissions, which were implemented throughout the twentieth century to investigate a range of issues from police corruption to bridge collapses to questionable use of force by imperial troops to air travel disasters. Some of the earliest commissions, in fact, date back even farther, to the first half of the nineteenth century. For example, in the United Kingdom, there was a probe of Irish poverty (1833) and an investigation into child labor practices (1840). In this chapter I have made a quick methodological comparison of the truth commissions and the historical commissions in order to highlight some of their differences, and to explore some of the special liabilities and untapped potential inherent to the latter. What I have not discussed, at least not very thoroughly, are the external pressures that help encourage the launch of these commissions. If we examine these initiatives through the lens of realpolitik, it is easy to become convinced that these confrontations with the past are undertaken on a less than voluntary basis. Looking at Eastern Europe or the Baltics, for example, one notes the close alignment of the Holocaust commissions with negotiations surrounding the expansion of NATO and the enlargement of the European Union. Given what membership in these organizations represented and offered to the economically depleted and politically unsteady democracies that emerged from the former Soviet bloc, it is easy to think that these countries were manipulated into the performance of a ritual penance. Likewise, in the case of Western and Central Europe, there are external pressures to consider here as well. In France, large banks faced the prospect of costly class actions filed on behalf of Holocaust survivors in the United States. In Switzerland, the launch of the ICE came soon after revelations concerning "dormant" bank accounts and the shredding of documentation related to these. In Austria, Jörg Haider and the FPÖ prompted embarrassing questions about the resurgence of the radical Right and a perceived lack of commitment to liberal democratic values. But these countries could also have elected to "take their lumps" if they were determined not to reopen the Nazi era for investigation. Naturally, there would have been a price to pay for stonewalling, but history is filled with policies and decisions that do not support so-called rational choice theory. We know, for example, that France elected to pay out, through the CIVS (Drai Commission) and several educational and commemorative initiatives, far more than what the Mattéoli Commission had estimated as the total uncompensated losses for French Jews exposed to Nazi-era plunder. Even if the countries that created these commissions did so to minimize their exposure to greater liability, France's commitment to moral reparation shows that there can still be an idealist component in measures undertaken to "amend" shameful chapters from the past. And if this idealism seems weak against the rough-and-tumble realities of international politics, it is worth considering the motivations of the arm-twisters, too. Why, for example, did five congressional representatives from the United States write to the prime minister of Lithuania in December 2009 to urge greater support for the prosecution of Nazi war criminals? Looking at the signatures at the bottom of the letter, these are hardly the names that would point to the influence of a "Jewish lobby."[38] Does Paul Hodes, the representative for New Hampshire's 2nd district, really make it to Washington on the strength of "Jewish" money? Besides recalling one of the main planks of Hitlerism, this line of thinking simply strains belief. Or, to take a different example, does anyone honestly believe that "the Jews" persuaded Germany and Poland to form a joint historical commission? The World Jewish Congress, whose name appears around several of the commissions in this study, has considerable clout and has been a force in the global negotiations concerning Jewish restitution, but is there any realistic scenario in which the WJC could coerce the Holy See into creating a commission to investigate Pius XII's role in the Holocaust? Let us recall the facts: the ICJHC was put together by the Vatican, which approached Seymour Reich, not once but twice, in the hopes of securing Jewish partnership for a project aimed at promoting interfaith reconciliation. The unwillingness of the Vatican to accommodate the commission's demands later on must not overshadow the fact that the initiative, while it lasted, was a voluntary one on both sides. Besides the political pressures that can spur the decision of states to reopen the past, there can also be a genuine striving for mutual understanding on the part of large ethnonational collectives. Parties to the process of historical dialogue do not always appreciate the full price of justice and reconciliation, but this does not mean their desire to see these realized is less than sincere.

It is frequently said of the truth commissions that they represent a compromise. Where retributive justice is out of reach, the truth commissions are created to ensure that the memory and dignity of the victims is preserved, and to sanction the perpetrators, even if that amounts only to public shaming rather than jail time. The truth commissions, in other words, perform their work where political and practical constraints make "perfect" justice impossible, but also where forgetting and impunity are offensive to the moral conscience and contradictory to the emergent norms concerning the right to truth. While they employ different methodologies and have different capabilities, truth commissions and historical commissions are similar in this regard. Historical commissions have appeared where time and distance make criminal prosecution of perpetrators unlikely or impossible, and also where there is a desire to protect the memories of victims against oblivion, diminishment, and/or political attacks. The commissions in this volume have not always secured a "right to history" for the victims of the Holocaust, and they do not offer a perfect solution where rival groups conjure divergent memories of the past while invoking the same right to "their" history. In some cases, mediating history has managed to transcend ideology, but in other cases it has brought competing ideologies out into the open without pointing the way to a settlement. It relativizes history by identifying the nonempirical premises that underlie all historical narratives, but it does not abandon the commitment of social science to the idea of an Archimedean point. It strives for objectivity, but it does not require neutrality. Instead, mediating history takes as its starting point a recently consolidated and still evolving set of norms regarding the obligation of states to guarantee victims of international crimes (under treaty law) and crimes against humanity (under customary law) the rights to remedy, truth, justice, and reparations. Clearly, these rights are still far from being universally embraced, and there has been significant disagreement in some cases about their exact content, for example, differing opinions regarding what constitutes legitimate and effective reparation. Still, the overall trend and the sociological type that emerges from a comparative analysis of recent Holocaust commissions is strongly suggestive of a growing consensus about the importance of these rights and the potential pros and cons of their observance. Some of the proponents of truth commissions have defended these initiatives against the charge of impunity by invoking their potential for creating new forums for democratic deliberation.[39] These commissions, they argue, get people talking about the meaning of peace and justice and how to secure an acceptable balance between the two, which they proffer as an intrinsic good. Critics of the truth commissions, on the other hand, have pointed to a deficit in exactly the same area. The TRCs, in certain cases, have been an effective device for convincing clashing groups to schedule democratic elections, but this does not mean that victims have been well represented in the initial negotiations that led to their creation.[40] Historical commissions are similar in this regard. They are capable of fostering democratic dialogue on sensitive historical topics, such as the meaning of collaboration, different degrees of moral agency and free will under military occupation, historical arguments that take particular acts of violence as representative (or not) of a larger group, and so on. Conversations like these can take place between and among members of historical commissions, and they can be pursued with more involvement from the public if the commissions can effectively communicate their findings in terms that have a clear moral resonance. There are also examples of commissions whose work has had no measurable public impact. Where bilateral commissions are concerned, the potential for fostering historical dialogue is more pronounced, but so is the risk of re-entrenchment. With enough savvy and a good sense of symbolism, a bilateral commission can project its dialogue into the sphere of international politics, as the Czech-German commission did when Miloš Zeman, Jörg Haider, and Edmund Stoiber nearly scuttled the European Union's expansion plans by using the Beneš decrees as a tool of domestic politics.

The rhetoric around truth-seeking is seductive. Democracies, one hears, are strengthened when historical myths are dismantled. Reconciliation is achieved by exposing the empirical and moral inadequacies of irresponsible histories. To believe these things feels good, particularly for historians who want their work to serve pragmatic ends. But we should be careful about embracing an overly sanguine perspective. The historical commissions are no panacea. The Holocaust commissions presented here have ranged from good to bad to ugly. This tells us several things. To begin, truth-telling exercises obviously do not guarantee reconciliation. If historians wish to have a meaningful role in conflict mediation, they will need to give careful consideration to *how* they construct and communicate their findings, rather than just what they have learned from their research. For better or worse, history and narrative have become nearly inseparable, and so the former will not escape the realm of politics any time soon. Second, a comparative study of recent Holocaust commissions shows that historians can be important players in conflict mediation so long as they do not shy away from the politics of history. To a surprising extent, academic historians enjoy powerful influence over the public imagination. Where there is an appetite for historical narrative, these are seen as more satisfying when they have passed muster with trained scholars. But historians cannot give ground to partisan perspectives simply because they fear having their "subjectivity" discovered in their writing. It is a mistake to believe that objectivity requires absolute neutrality. While the historian must be even-handed and unbiased and resistant to political influence in order to legitimate her findings, she can responsibly maintain her "external loyalties,"[41] providing these do not prevent her from suspending her own perceptions "long enough to enter sympathetically into the alien and possibly repugnant perspectives of rival thinkers."[42] What we have seen from at least some of the Holocaust commissions is a disciplined commitment to objectivity with an accompanying interest in applying the emergent norms of the human rights discourse, particularly those aspects concerned with the right to truth and redress. Finally, mediating history can set the stage for rapprochement where the past has unsettled intergroup relations. It can also do the opposite, setting intergroup relations back a step where "wounds of the past" had previously shown signs of healing. The power of the past to create and sustain conflict is mirrored by its potential to foster reconciliation. In the same way that history written for utilitarian purposes poses certain risks and dangers, history that refuses to consider any possibility for advocacy carries unhappy consequences, too. Charles Maier has put this in the form of a musical analogy. Mediating history will be "contrapuntal, not harmonic." In other words, "it must allow the particular histories of national groups to be woven together linearly alongside each other so that the careful listener can follow them distinctly but simultaneously, hearing the whole together with the parts."[43] The work of historical commissions ought to be evaluated on that basis. The criteria for judgment are, in the end, pragmatic: How will rivals and adversaries regard and treat each other once their narratives, testimonies, and perspectives have been judiciously evaluated and thoughtfully intertwined?

Notes

Introduction

1. Quoted in "Swiss President Says Pleas for a Holocaust Compensation Fund Are Blackmail," *New York Times*, January 1, 1997.

2. The ICE built a rich website to document the various aspects of its work. See http://www.uek.ch/en/. For a full analysis of the ICE, see chap. 1 in this study.

3. "International List of Current Activities Regarding Holocaust-Era Assets Including Historical Commissions, and Forced and Slave Labor," December 3, 1998, http://www.ushmm.org/information/exhibitions/online-features/special-focus /holocaust-era-assets. See n. 31 for further discussion of this list.

4. "Under Secretary Eizenstat's Introductory Comments," June 30, 1998, http:// www.ushmm.org/information/exhibitions/online-features/special-focus/holocaust-era-assets/eizenstat-comments. The published proceedings for the April 1999 "Washington Conference on Holocaust-Era Assets" are archived at http://1997-2001.state.gov /www/regions/eur/holocaust/heac.html.

5. Jean-François Bergier, "Commissioned History in Switzerland," in *Revisiting the National Socialist Legacy*, ed. Oliver Rathkolb (Vienna: Studien Verlag, 2002), 44.

6. Saul Friedlander, *The Years of Extermination: Nazi Germany and the Jews, 1939–1945* (New York: HarperCollins, 2007).

7. See Mark Bevir, "Objectivity in History," *History and Theory* 33, no. 3 (October 1994): 328–44.

8. See, for example, Michel Foucault, "Nietzsche, Genealogy, and History," in *The Foucault Reader*, ed. Paul Rainbow (New York: Vintage, 1984), 76–100.

9. "Students Stumble Again on the Basics of History," *Wall Street Journal*, June 15, 2011.

10. In March 2010, the Texas Board of Education approved a new social studies curriculum that aimed to put a more conservative stamp on history textbooks. According to one board member who voted in support of the measure, the new curriculum aimed at "adding balance" to a discipline that had been "skewed too far to the left."

Quoted in James C. McKinley Jr., "Texas Conservatives Win Curriculum Change," *New York Times*, March 12, 2010.

11. Debates over the Yasukuni war shrine in Tokyo and the visits of Japanese politicians to pay homage to their nation's war dead have been covered extensively. See, for example, Taku Tamaki, "An Unholy Pilgrimage? Yasukuni and the Construction of Japan's Asia Imaginary," *Asian Politics and Policy* 1, no. 1 (2009): 31–49.

12. Germany is one of thirteen European countries that have made Holocaust denial illegal. There have been several convictions under German statutes that prohibit individuals from expressing views that "incite racial hatred." Each of these prosecutions renewed the debate over the criminalization of speech, as was the case in 2007, when Ernst Zündel, a sixty-seven-year-old German citizen, was sentenced to five years of imprisonment on fourteen separate counts of Holocaust denial. See "Jail for German Holocaust Denier," *BBC News*, February 15, 2007.

13. As part of its "Sunday Nights" radio series, the Australian Broadcasting Corporation in July 2011 aired a discussion of Middle Eastern politics and current events, which it advertised to its listeners as a debate on "Arab Spring or Caliphate?" A podcast of the full discussion is available at http://www.abc.net.au/sundaynights/stories/s3259815.htm.

14. "History wars" has been a recurrent phrase in recent discussions on the politics of history. Margaret MacMillan has discussed the meaning of these debates in a particularly eloquent way in her book *Dangerous Games: The Uses and Abuses of History* (New York: Modern Library, 2010), esp. 113–38.

15. "In the national contests for power depicted here, history becomes a weapon in the struggle for symbolic capital, wielded to acquire legitimacy for one's own side while delegitimizing the opposition." Max Paul Friedman and Padraic Kenney, eds., *Partisan Histories: The Past in Contemporary Global Politics* (New York: Palgrave Macmillan, 2005), 2.

16. Quoted in Charles W. Ingrao and Thomas A. Emmet, eds., *Confronting the Yugoslav Controversies: A Scholars' Initiative* (West Lafayette, IN: Purdue University Press, 2009). Drljača was shot and killed by NATO troops attempting to serve his arrest warrant in July 1997.

17. Friedman and Kenney, *Partisan Histories*, 2.

18. Charles Maier, *The Unmasterable Past: History, Holocaust, and National Identity* (Cambridge, MA: Harvard University Press, 1988), 61. Maier has pursued the same thread more recently in "Doing History, Doing Justice: The Narrative of the Historian and the Truth Commission," in *Truth v. Justice: The Morality of Truth Commissions*, ed. Robert I. Rotberg and Dennis Thompson (Princeton, NJ: Princeton University Press, 2000), 261–78. See also Charles Maier, "Overcoming the Past? Narrative and Negotiation, Remembering and Reparation: Issues at the Interface of History and the Law," in *Politics and the Past: Repairing Historical Injustices*, ed. John C. Torpey (Lanham, MD: Rowman and Littlefield, 2003), 295–304.

19. Elazar Barkan, "Historians and Historical Reconciliation," *American Historical Review* 114, no. 4 (2009): 907.

20. In "What Makes an Interpretation Acceptable?" Stanley Fish offers this: "Rather than being proof of the stability of objects, [the fact of agreement] is a testimony to the power of an interpretative community to constitute the objects upon which its members (also and simultaneously constituted) can then agree." Reprinted in Russell B. Goodman, ed., *Pragmatism: A Contemporary Reader* (New York: Routledge, 1995), 253.

21. The literature on truth commissions is massive. The seminal text is Priscilla Hayner's *Unspeakable Truths: Transitional Justice and the Challenge of Truth Commissions* (New York: Routledge, 2001).

22. Helen B. Junz, "The Bergier Commission" (paper presented at "International Conference on Confronting History: The Historical Commissions of Inquiry," Yad Vashem, Jerusalem, December 29, 2002–January 1, 2003).

23. One example is the Hunter Commission, which the British government in India established in 1919 to investigate "disturbances" throughout Bombay, Delhi, and the Punjab, as well as "the measures taken to cope with [these]." The commission was formed six months after the Amritsar Massacre, in which British-led troops fired on unarmed demonstrators, killing a great number (estimates have ranged from more than three hundred up to one thousand).

24. The Oklahoma Historical Society published its report (with a recommendation that the state pay reparations to the victims) on the Tulsa Race Riot online. See "Tulsa Race Riot: A Report by the Oklahoma Commission to Study the Tulsa Race Riot of 1921," February 28, 2001, http://www.okhistory.org/research/forms/freport .pdf. The Florida Board of Regents assembled a committee of five professors employed in the state university system to produce a history of the Rosewood riot. See "Documented History of the Incident Which Occurred at Rosewood, Florida, in January 1923," December 22, 1993, http://www.displaysforschools.com/rosewoodrp.html.

25. For more on the Ugandan initiative, see "Roco Wat I Acoli: Restoring Relationships in Acholi-land: Traditional Approaches to Reintegration and Justice," September 2005, http://www.ligi.ubc.ca/sites/liu/files/Publications/JRP/15Sept2005_Roco_ Wat_I_Acoli.pdf.

26. Elazar Barkan, "Historical Reconciliation: Redress, Rights, and Politics," *Journal of International Affairs* 60, no. 1 (2006): 1–15.

27. See IHJR, "Ani, Kars and Gyumri: Journey Towards Understanding," http:// www.historyandreconciliation.org/armenia-turkey/.

28. Ingrao and Emmett, *Confronting the Yugoslav Controversies*, 948.

29. Ibid., 950.

30. In Sri Lanka, the Lessons Learned and Reconciliation Commission (LLRC), which was created in 2010 following a twenty-six-year civil war, concluded that the Sri Lankan military had not deliberately targeted civilians, but that the Tamil rebels had done so routinely. The LLRC has been heavily criticized by human rights organizations, as well as the United Nations, who assert that the commission was not an independent body and that the government endorsed its findings in order to prevent an international investigation of its human rights abuses.

31. It is difficult to give a precise count of Holocaust commissions. The United States Holocaust Memorial Museum (USHMM) maintains a list of "Activities Regarding Holocaust-Era Assets Including Historical Commissions and Forced and Slave Labor." See n. 3. There are close to 150 initiatives listed in this document. Originating in Europe in most cases, the list covers a range of activities; however, the majority of these are devoted to Holocaust-era property restitution, the tracing and recovery of financial assets, and the identification and return of stolen and looted artworks. Among European countries, the Netherlands accounts for more activities (twenty) than any other country. France is next with thirteen, followed by Austria with twelve, and Switzerland with ten. While the USHMM list includes legislative acts, some of which can be described as token measures, there were serious historical commissions created in each of the countries mentioned here, with some countries sponsoring more than one initiative concurrently. In addition to the activities listed by country, the USHMM supplies information for another fifteen international initiatives. The USHMM previously maintained a separate list exclusively for government-appointed Holocaust commissions; that information is now integrated into the larger "activities" list. The U.S. State Department also maintains a web page devoted to "Holocaust Issues," which includes links to some of the international commissions presented in this study, as well as information related to major Holocaust-era assets conferences. See "Holocaust Issues," http://www.state.gov/p/eur/rt/hlcst/index.htm. Elazar Barkan has compiled an expansive (though still only partial) list of resources related to historical commissions in the footnotes section of his essay "Historians and Historical Reconciliation." See n. 19.

32. Dan Diner spoke of the desire of Europeans for a "foundational narrative" at the UCLA conference "Confronting the Past: Memory, Identity, and Society" in February 2001. He returned to this theme in a subsequent article, where he described the Holocaust as having "transformed into a veritable foundational, seminal event." See Dan Diner, "Restitution and Memory—The Holocaust in Europe's Political Cultures," *New German Critique* 90 (Fall 2003): 36.

33. One of the event's cosponsors, the German Historical Institute (Washington, DC), produced a conference report, "Commissioning History in the United States, Germany, and Austria: Historical Commissions, Victims, and World War II Restitution," *GHI Bulletin* 2003 (Spring 2003): 170–79, http://www.ghi-dc.org/publications/ghipubs/bu/032/32.165-174.pdf.

34. A brief description of the conference program can be found in "International Conference Opens Sunday at Yad Vashem: Confronting History—The Historical Commissions of Inquiry," December 24, 2002, http://www1.yadvashem.org/yv/en/pressroom/pressreleases/pr_details.asp?cid=511.

35. More information related to this event, including video recordings of all of its panels, can be found at http://humanrightscolumbia.org/historical.

36. This theme was explored again at the more recent "Historical Justice and Memory Conference," which was hosted at the Swinburne Institute for Social Research (Melbourne, Australia) in February 2012. A conference report is available at http://

pandora.nla.gov.au/pan/138121/20130208-1520/www.historicaljusticeandmemory conference.net/wp-content/uploads/2012/04/HJMRN-inaugural-conference-report-2012.pdf.

37. Hayner, *Unspeakable Truths*, 22–74.

38. Erin Daly has conducted important work along these lines. See, for example, "Truth Skepticism: An Inquiry into the Value of Truth in Times of Transition," *International Journal of Transitional Justice* 2 (2008): 23–41. Daly outlines several "intrinsic concerns" regarding the difficulty of using truth to promote reconciliation (e.g., multiple truths, subjectivity, relativism, and the recalcitrance of partisans to meaningful psychological transformation). She also points to several of what she calls "consequentialist concerns" (e.g., the possibility of illegitimate governments sponsoring sham commissions, her concerns about commissions undermining democracy by demanding conformity with their views, and the return to violence that some fragile democracies have suffered following unsuccessful attempts to use truth as a basis for reconciliation).

39. The Innovative Publishing Group (Chicago) maintains a website to promote sales of what appears to be the only title in its catalogue, *The Rape of Nanking: An Undeniable History in Photographs*. See http://www.tribo.org/nanking/.

40. See Japan Society for History Textbook Reform, http://www.tsukurukai.com/index.html.

41. See, for example, the website created by the Bund der Vertriebenen (German League of Expellees), http://www.bund-der-vertriebenen.de/.

42. See http://www.heroesofserbia.com/.

43. See http://theremakingrwanda.blogspot.com/2011/04/remaking-rwanda-only-rwandans-can-do-it.html.

44. See, for example, Barkan, "Historical Reconciliation," 1–15.

45. Mark Philip Bradley and Patrice Petro, "Introduction," in *Truth Claims: Representation and Human Rights*, ed. M. P. Bradley and P. Petro (New Brunswick, NJ: Rutgers University Press, 2002), 3.

46. "International Covenant on Civil and Political Rights," December 16, 1966, http://www.ohchr.org/EN/ProfessionalInterest/Pages/CCPR.aspx.

47. See Antoon De Baets, "The Impact of the Universal Declaration of Human Rights on the Study of History," *History and Theory* 48 (February 2009): 29.

48. Ibid.

49. Ibid., 35.

50. Ibid., 37.

51. Ibid., 38.

52. "Declaration of Basic Principles of Justice for Victims of Crime and Abuse of Power," November 29, 1985, http://www.un.org/documents/ga/res/40/a40r034.htm.

53. Ibid., item 6b.

54. See Theo van Boven, "The United Nations Basic Principles and Guidelines on the Right to a Remedy and Reparation for Victims of Gross Violations of International Human Rights Law and Serious Violations of International Humanitarian Law," 2010, http://legal.un.org/avl/pdf/ha/ga_60-147/ga_60-147_e.pdf.

55. See Antoon De Baets, *Responsible History* (New York: Berghahn Books, 2009), 4.

56. Jeremy Waldron, "Superseding Historical Injustice," *Ethics* 103 (October 1992): 7.

57. Ibid.

58. Diane Orentlicher, "Independent Study on Best Practices, including Recommendations, to Assist States in Strengthening Their Domestic Capacity to Combat All Aspects of Impunity," February 27, 2004, http://daccess-dds-ny.un.org/doc/UNDOC /GEN/G04/113/55/PDF/G0411355.pdf?OpenElement.

59. Information was provided by the following governments: Argentina, Bulgaria, Canada, Chile, Colombia, Croatia, Cuba, Ethiopia, Germany, Italy, Madagascar, Mauritius, Mexico, Namibia, Panama, Portugal, Romania, the Russian Federation, Sierra Leone, and Switzerland.

60. These included representatives from the Office of the High Commissioner for Human Rights, the International Committee of the Red Cross, Amnesty International, the International Center for Transitional Justice, the International Commission of Jurists, Human Rights Watch, the International Human Rights Academy and the War Crimes Research Office of the American University Washington College of Law, the Open Society Justice Initiative, the World Council of Churches, and the World Organization Against Torture.

61. Orentlicher, "Independent Study," 5, 5, 6, 11, 19, 5.

62. Alexander Karn, "Holocaust Commissions as Narrators of Trauma" (paper presented at "(Un)Silencing the Past: Narratives of Trauma in Comparative Perspective," University of New Mexico, October 25, 2013).

63. Orentlicher, "Independent Study," 7.

64. Ibid., 8.

65. Martha Minow, *Between Vengeance and Forgiveness: Facing History after Genocide and Mass Violence* (Boston: Beacon Press, 1998), 78.

66. Ibid.

67. Desmond Tutu, *No Future Without Forgiveness* (New York: Doubleday, 1999).

68. See Comisión para el Esclarecimiento Histórico, *Guatemala: Memory of Silence* (Guatemala, CEH, 1999).

69. Mary Poovey, *A History of the Modern Fact: Problems of Knowledge in the Sciences of Wealth and Society* (Chicago: University of Chicago Press, 1998).

70. Material for the Skarpnes Commission, including both the majority and minority reports, is available at the website for the Norwegian Department of Justice, under the title "Inndragning av jødisk eiendom i Norge under den 2. verdenskrig," June 1997, http://odin.dep.no/jd/norsk/dok/andre_dok/utredninger/012005-020017 /hov029-bn.html.

71. For an English summary of the minority report, see https://www.regjeringen .no/nb/dokumenter/nou-1997-22/id141043/?docId=NOU199719970022000DDDEPIS &q=Inndragning av jodisk eiendom i Norge under den 2. verdenskrig&navchap=1& ch=5.

72. Walter V. Robinson, "Norway Says Its Probe Downplays WWII Guilt," *Boston Globe*, June 14, 1997, emphasis mine.

Chapter 1. France and Switzerland

1. Henry Russo, *The Vichy Syndrome: History and Memory in France since 1944* (Cambridge, MA: Harvard University Press, 1994). Besides Russo, there are other authors to consider. For a helpful review of the literature on Jewish spoliation in France, see Claire Andrieu, "Ecrire l'histoire des spoliations antisémites (France, 1940–44)," *Histoire@Politique* 9 (2009): 1–17.

2. The Vélodrome d'Hiver was an indoor bicycle track near the Eiffel Tower where French police interned large numbers of (mostly non-French) Jews in July 1942. Over the course of two days, approximately 12,800 individuals, including 4,000 children, were arrested in Paris and processed for deportation. Approximately 7,000 individuals were held at the bicycle stadium before being sent to camps outside the city. Most of these individuals were eventually deported to the East, where they were gassed or killed by other means.

3. Quoted in Julie Fette, "The Apology Moment: Vichy Memories on 1990s France," in *Taking Wrongs Seriously: Apologies and Reconciliation*, ed. Elazar Barkan and Alexander Karn (Stanford: Stanford University Press, 2006), 261.

4. Ibid., 262.

5. Ibid.

6. French President François Hollande went a step farther than Chirac. Marking the seventieth anniversary of the Vél d'Hiv roundup, Hollande called the event "a crime committed in France, by France." See "French President Apologizes for Nation's Role in WWII," *Los Angeles Times*, July 22, 2012, http://latimesblogs.latimes.com/world_now/2012/07/french-president-apologizes-for-role-in-wwii.html.

7. Mitterrand attended the fiftieth anniversary commemoration of Vél d'Hiv in 1992, but he remained silent there (while being subjected to a chorus of boos). In 1993, Mitterrand established July 16 as a day of national commemoration for the racist and anti-Semitic persecutions "committed under the de facto authority of the government of the French State (1940–1944)." Soon afterward, Mitterrand announced that he would no longer lay a wreath on Petain's grave in observance of the Veterans Day holiday. Of course, Mitterrand had personal reasons to deflect attention away from the past. In 1994, Pierre Péan published a biography, *Une Jeunesse Française* (Paris: Le Grand Livre Du Mois), in which he described Mitterrand's support for Marshall Petain and the Vichy regime. In addition to being a leader in the Resistance, Mitterrand, according to Péan, had been a civil servant in the Vichy government. In a televised interview (September 12, 1994), Mitterrand attempted to justify his personal history, but he also refused to accept personal responsibility for injustices that unfolded under the Vichy regime.

8. Ady Steg, "Statement to the U.S. House of Representatives on the Work of the Mattéoli Commission," September 14, 1999, http://democrats.financialservices.house.gov/banking/91499ste.shtml.

9. Claire Andrieu, "Statement to the U.S. House of Representatives on the Work of the Mattéoli Commission," September 14, 1999, http://democrats.financialservices .house.gov/banking/91499and.shtml#main_content.

10. Ibid.

11. Access to government files had been a topic of debate in France since 1994, when Sonia Combe published *Archives Interdite* (Paris: A. Michel, 1994), in which she claimed that historians were routinely denied access to official documents pertaining to Vichy.

12. See "Commission Says France Owes Millions for Looted Jewish Assets," *Associated Press Worldstream*, April 16, 2003.

13. Marilyn Henry, "French Banks to Return WWII-Era Accounts," *Jerusalem Post*, March 25, 1999.

14. Steg, "Statement to the U.S. House of Representatives."

15. Quoted in Xavier Ternisien, "The 62,000 Cases of Shame," *Le Monde*, April 16–17, 2000, translation mine.

16. Jean Mattéoli, "Mission d'étude sur la spoliation des Juifs de France: Rapport général" (summary report), December 2000, http://www.ladocumentationfrancaise .fr/rapports-publics/004000897-mission-d-etude-sur-la-spoliation-des-juifs-de-france- rapport-general#book_sommaire.

17. "The essential, fundamental aspect of the restitution question," Hajdenberg said, "is historical knowledge and its dissemination. A foundation to teach the history of totalitarian movements would help make sure something like the Holocaust could never happen again." Quoted in Craig R. Whitney, "France Confronts Holocaust Claims," *New York Times*, November 30, 1998.

18. It is important to understand that the commission's estimates for looting and restitution were very rough and also, in key respects, imprecise. For example, regarding the extent of restitution after the war, the estimate of 90 percent could apply to registered and easily traceable assets, such as apartments, bank accounts, and certain cultural objects. On the other hand, this figure does not provide a clear understanding of the looting that occurred at a more personal level, for example, the "frisking" at camps, which deprived Jews of their cash, personal effects, jewelry, and the like. I will return to this issue in the discussion of financial restitution and moral reparation.

19. Detailed information on these deportations can be found in Annette Wieviorka and Françoise Rosset, "Jewish Identity in the First Accounts by Extermination Camp Survivors from France," *Yale French Studies* 85 (1994): 136.

20. See Robert Paxton, *Vichy France: Old Guard and New Order, 1940–1944* (New York: Columbia University Press, 2001), 182.

21. Ibid., 183.

22. Although others have cited higher figures for the total number of deportees, the Mattéoli Commission gave an estimate of 76,000. In her statement to Congress in 1999, Claire Andrieu noted that this was the second lowest percentage of Jews deported in Europe, behind only Italy. She also stated that 68,000 non-Jewish French were deported for participating in the Resistance.

23. Steg, "Statement to the U.S. House of Representatives."

24. For more on the impact of the yellow star, see Renée Poznanski, "From Drancy to the Yellow Star," in *Jews in France during World War II* (Waltham, MA: Brandeis University Press, 2001).

25. Claire Andrieu used this terminology in her statement to the U.S. Congress.

26. For more on French pacifism, see Eugen Weber, "A Wilderness Called Peace," in *The Hollow Years: France in the 1930s* (New York: W. W. Norton, 1994), 11–25.

27. Ibid., 21. Weber describes an initiative from the mid-1920s that sought to produce new history textbooks for the secondary schools, which would present both France and its enemies in "a more balanced light." For more on Franco-German textbook revision, see chap. 5 in this study.

28. Andrieu, "Statement to the U.S. House of Representatives."

29. Quoted in Steg, "Statement to the U.S. House of Representatives."

30. Ibid.

31. "French Banks Announce Comprehensive Measures of Restitution and Reparation for Holocaust Victims," *PR Newswire*, March 24, 1999.

32. See M. Henry, "French Banks to Return WWII-Era Accounts."

33. At the time, nine French banks faced a class-action suit in the United States, and the collective statement came only days before a federal court in Brooklyn was scheduled to open hearings on the case.

34. Two non-French banks, Barclays and J. P. Morgan, had already reached separate settlements. Details of the executive agreement with the French banks were published in an advertisement that appeared in major newspapers around the world in October 2001. See "Notice to Victims of Anti-Semitic Persecution in France," *Sunday Telegraph* (Sydney), October 7, 2001.

35. Tom Heneghan, "French Study to Reveal Shoah Plunder of Jews," *Jerusalem Post*, April 17, 2000.

36. Suzanne Daley, "French Issue First Study of Wartime Thefts from Jews," *New York Times*, April 18, 2000.

37. Ibid. Henri Hajdenberg, president of the Conseil Représentatif des Institutions juives de France (CRIF, Representative Council of French Jewish Institutions), declared, "We are 700,000, the Diaspora's second-largest community, and capable of handling this by ourselves."

38. "Agreement between the Government of the United States of America and the Government of France Concerning Payments for Certain Losses Suffered During World War II," January 18, 2001, http://www.state.gov/documents/organization/28994.pdf.

39. Jean-Marc Dreyfus, "France Confronts the Holocaust," *Brookings Institution*, December 1, 2011, http://www.brookings.edu/research/articles/2001/12/france-dreyfus.

40. Anne Grynberg, personal correspondence, September 1, 2014.

41. Andrieu, "Statement to the U.S. House of Representatives."

42. Ibid. See also Claire Andrieu, "Two Approaches to Compensation in France: Restitution and Reparation," in *Robbery and Restitution: The Conflict of Jewish Property*

in Europe, ed. Martin Dean, Constantin Goschler, and Philipp Ther (New York: Berghahn Books, 2007), 134–54.

43. Cited in Andrieu, "Statement to the U.S. House of Representatives."

44. Ibid.

45. Ibid.

46. Ibid.

47. Steg, "Statement to the U.S. House of Representatives."

48. Program details for Mémoire de Justes can be found at http://www.fondation franceisrael.org/actions/education.

49. European Court of Human Rights, "Cinquième section décision sur la recevabilité," November 24, 2009, http://www.lph-asso.fr/images/stories/documents/cour_europ.pdf.

50. Independent Commission of Experts, *Switzerland, National Socialism, and the Second World War: Final Report* (Zurich: Pendo Verlag, 2002), 428–29, hereafter ICE, *Final Report*. The report is available at http://www.uek.ch/en/schlussbericht/synthesis/ueke.pdf.

51. Ibid.

52. George Kreis, "Introduction: Four Debates and Little Dissent," in *Switzerland and the Second World War*, ed. Georg Kreis (London: Frank Cass, 2000), 3.

53. See Allen Dulles, "Switzerland's Benevolent Neutrality," in *Switzerland Under Siege, 1939–45: A Neutral Nation's Struggle for Survival*, ed. Leo Schelbert (Rockport, ME: Picton Press, 2000).

54. Kreis, "Introduction: Four Debates," 2–3.

55. Switzerland was the primary hub of the Continental gold trade during World War II. Between 1940 and 1945, Germany sold large quantities of looted gold—valued at more than 1.3 billion Swiss francs—to Swiss commercial banks and also to the Swiss National Bank. While the Allies condemned these transactions and demanded full restitution of all looted gold at the end of the war, Swiss purchases continued unabated, and Switzerland sought to justify its trading role via several different legal arguments. Following the war, Switzerland agreed to pay 250 million Swiss francs into a fund for Holocaust victims in exchange for an Allied promise to drop further claims related to "incriminating gold transactions." In May 1997, the U.S. government published a detailed study of so-called Nazi gold transactions and the fate of other assets plundered in the course of the Holocaust. See *Preliminary Study on U.S. and Allied Efforts to Recover and Restore Gold and Other Assets Stolen or Hidden by Germany During World War II* (Washington, DC: Department of State, 1997).

56. For more on Villiger's speech and challenges to Swiss patriotic memory, see Regula Ludi, "Waging War on Wartime Memory: Recent Swiss Debates on the Legacies of the Holocaust and the Nazi Era," *Jewish Social Studies* 10, no. 2 (2004): 116–52.

57. Quoted in Alan Scham, "A Survey of Nazi and Pro-Nazi Groups in Switzerland, 1930–1945," Report to Simon Wiesenthal Center, 1998, http://www.wiesenthal.com/site/pp.asp?c=lsKWLbPJLnF&b=4441317.

58. Alfred A. Häsler, *Das Boot ist voll: Die Schweiz und die Fluchtlinge*, 1933–1945 (Zurich: Ex Libris, 1967).

59. Research reported in 1996, after Villiger's apology, showed that Swiss border guards in some cases turned over Jewish asylum seekers directly to the German police. See ICE, *Final Report*, 109.

60. Ibid., 108. Beginning in April 1938, Switzerland and Germany held talks to establish measures that would allow Swiss border guards to differentiate between Jewish and non-Jewish German citizens. The two countries initially discussed an entry visa requirement for all German citizens. Germany, however, fearing the impact on its foreign affairs if other countries were to follow suit, instead agreed to identify the passports of German Jews with a *J* stamp.

61. In addition to Bergier, the commission included eight other scholars, four Swiss, and four non-Swiss. By 2001, when the mandate expired, eleven individuals had served on the commission: Władysław Bartoszewski (Poland), Saul Friedlander (Israel), Harold James (U.S.), Georg Kreis (Switzerland), Sybil Milton (U.S.; died in October 2000), Helen Junz (Netherlands/U.S.), Jacques Picard (Switzerland), Jakob Tanner (Switzerland), Joseph Voyame (Switzerland; resigned in April 2000), and Daniel Thürer (Switzerland).

62. See "Introductory Speech by Prof. Jean-François Bergier at the Press Conference of 22 March 2002," http://www.uek.ch/en/presse/pressemitteilungen/220302 redebergier.htm.

63. An index of all published studies with summaries in PDF format is available at the ICE's website, http://www.uek.ch/en/.

64. See "Introductory Speech by Prof. Jean-François Bergier."

65. Ibid.

66. The ICE estimated that Switzerland accepted approximately 60,000 civilian refugees, including somewhere between 7,000 and 8,000 Jews. Regarding the number turned away, the ICE report suggested 10,000 as an "absolute minimum," but the authors also speculated that the number was probably closer to 20,000. See ICE, *Final Report*, 117–18.

67. See "Introductory Speech by Prof. Jean-François Bergier."

68. ICE, *Final Report*, 113.

69. Ibid., 115. This was due primarily to an inability to effectively patrol the border as per the official policy, but also as a result of public outcry and a strong protest from the Swiss Federation of Jewish Communities.

70. Ibid., 119: "The assumption that the Swiss authorities were inadequately informed and would have acted differently 'if one had known what was happening' in the Third Reich is false."

71. The figures established in the ICE's refugee report have been challenged by revisionists seeking to minimize Switzerland's responsibility. Among other claims, these individuals have argued that only expulsions at the border can be counted, since document loss has made it difficult to determine with precision the number of individuals who were denied an entry visa.

72. ICE, *Final Report*, 180.

73. Ibid.

74. Ibid., 181.

75. Ibid., 186.

76. Ibid.

77. Ibid., 189.

78. Helen Junz, "The Bergier Commission" (lecture, Yad Vashem, Jerusalem, December 29, 2002).

79. ICE, *Final Report*, 193.

80. See "Introductory Speech by Prof. Jean-François Bergier."

81. ICE, *Final Report*, 423.

82. Ibid., 429.

83. Ibid., 484–85.

84. Ibid., 493.

85. Jean-François Bergier, "On the Role of the 'Swiss Independent Expert Commission on the Second World War,'" in Kreis, *Switzerland and the Second World War*, 353–61.

86. While digitizing its archives in July 2013, the Bank of England uncovered a document that showed its officers had helped Germany sell off looted gold from Czechoslovakia in 1939. See "Bank of England Helped in Sale of Looted Nazi Gold," *BBC News*, July 31, 2013.

87. Jean-François Bergier, "Commissioned History in Switzerland," in *Revisiting the National Socialist Legacy*, ed. Oliver Rathkolb (Vienna and Munich: Studien Verlag, 2002), 43.

88. In 2010 Somm debated one of the members of the ICE, Jakob Tanner, on the Swiss television program *Streitgespräch* (Straight Talk). See "Streitgespräch: Jakob Tanner und Markus Somm," April 14, 2010, video available at http://www.srf.ch/play /tv/rundschau/video/streitgespraech-jakob-tanner-und-markus-somm?id=dc225053-ea40-4e29-b3bf-2e171274bb44.

89. ICE, *Final Report*, 517.

90. Ibid., 116.

91. Ibid., 164.

92. The League of Nations gave assistance to both Russian and Armenian refugees in the 1920s. The Nansen International Office for Refugees, which was authorized by the league, was the recipient of the Nobel Peace Prize in 1938, primarily for its assistance to non-Jewish Germans who fled the Reich after 1933.

93. The commission's interim report on refugees included a lengthy section on rescuers and other helpers.

94. Bernhard C. Schär and Vera Sperisen, "Switzerland and the Holocaust: Teaching Contested History," *Journal of Curriculum Studies* 42, no. 5 (2010): 652.

95. Quoted in ibid.

96. The textbook was financed by the Canton of Zürich's Ministry of Education.

97. Schär and Sperisen, "Switzerland and the Holocaust," 652.

98. Ibid., 657.

99. Ibid., 658.

100. Daniel Levy and Natan Sznaider, *The Holocaust and Memory in the Global Age*, chap. 2 (Philadelphia: Temple University Press, 2006), 23–38.

101. Tony Judt, *Postwar: A History of Europe Since 1945* (New York: Penguin, 2006), 803.

102. Kreis, *Switzerland and the Second World War*, 1–8.

103. This is how Regula Ludi and Jean-Marc Dreyfus have interpreted the Swiss ICE and the French Mattéoli Commission. See Ludi and Dreyfus, *Historians as Political Trouble-Shooters: Officially Commissioned Surveys of Holocaust Legacies in France and Switzerland*, Center for European Studies Working Papers 80 (Cambridge, MA: Minda de Gunzburg Center for European Studies, Harvard University, 2001).

104. "Swiss Jews Fault President on Holocaust Statement," *Associated Press*, January 28, 2013.

105. Ibid.

106. Maurer attracted media attention in 2008 when he commented, in the context of discussing European integration and the place of foreigners in Swiss society: "So long as I talk about Negroes, the cameras stay on me." See Gieri Cavelty and Gaby Szollosy, "Maurer: Der Scharfmacher kann durchaus angenehm sein," *Berner Zeitung*, November 25, 2008.

107. Kreis, *Switzerland and the Second World War*, 10.

108. Ibid., 16.

Chapter 2. Poles and Jews

1. Jan Gross's study originally appeared in Polish in 2000. All references here are to the English translation, *Neighbors: The Destruction of the Jewish Community in Jedwabne, Poland* (Princeton, NJ: Princeton University Press, 2001).

2. While Gross accepts that the Nazis and Soviets "called the shots" in the Polish territories they occupied, he also writes that "one should not deny the reality of autonomous dynamics between Poles and Jews within the constraints imposed by the occupiers." See Gross, *Neighbors*, 9.

3. James Young, "The Biography of a Memorial Icon: Nathan Rapoport's Warsaw Ghetto Monument," *Representations* 26 (Spring 1989): 69–106.

4. Ibid., 69.

5. Antony Polonsky and Joanna Michlic, eds., *The Neighbors Respond: The Controversy Over the Jedwabne Massacre in Poland* (Princeton, NJ: Princeton University Press, 2004), 5.

6. Ibid., 6–7.

7. See Joanna Michlic, "The Holocaust and Its Aftermath as Perceived in Poland: Voices of Polish Intellectuals," in *The Jews Are Coming Back: The Return of Jews to Their Countries of Origin After WWII*, ed. David Bankier (Jerusalem: Yad Vashem/ Berghahn, 2005), 206–30.

8. Polonsky and Michlic, *The Neighbors Respond*, 6.

9. Ibid., 7.

10. See David Engel, *Facing a Holocaust: The Polish Government-in-Exile and the Jews, 1943–45* (Chapel Hill: University of North Carolina Press, 1993).

11. Polonsky and Michlic, *The Neighbors Respond*, 6.

12. "Poland Apologises to Jews," *BBC News*, July 10, 2001.

13. Quoted in Polonsky and Michlic, *The Neighbors Respond*, 15. All of this is further explored in Joshua D. Zimmerman, ed., *Contested Memories: Poles and Jews during the Holocaust and Its Aftermath* (New Brunswick, NJ: Rutgers University Press, 2003).

14. Polonsky and Michlic, *The Neighbors Respond*, 10.

15. Gross, *Neighbors*, 47.

16. Ibid., 150.

17. Quoted in Polonsky and Michlic, *The Neighbors Respond*, 4.

18. Gross, *Neighbors*, 123, emphasis mine.

19. Ibid., 124.

20. In his introduction, before engaging the pogrom that is the centerpiece of his study, Gross mulls over the "demographic catastrophe" that befell Poland between 1939 and 1945. Close to 20 percent of Poland's population died as a consequence of the war. Besides the near-total elimination of its largest minorities (i.e., Jews, Ukrainians, and Germans), close to 2.5 million ethnic Poles died or were killed. Elites were hit especially hard: "Over a third of its urban residents were missing at the conclusion of the war. Fifty-five percent of the country's lawyers were no more, along with forty percent of its medical doctors and one-third of its university professors and Roman Catholic clergy." See Gross, *Neighbors*, 7.

21. Polonsky and Michlic refer to this as the "parallel fates" narrative. See *The Neighbors Respond*, 7.

22. Cimoszewicz's letter was published by the *National Post* (Toronto), the *Ottawa Citizen*, and the *Vancouver Sun* on August 18, 2004.

23. See Wojciech Roszkowski, "After *Neighbors*: Seeking Universal Standards," *Slavic Review* 61, no. 3 (2002): 460–65.

24. Gross, *Neighbors*, 12.

25. Reprinted in Polonsky and Michlic, *The Neighbors Respond*, 76.

26. Ibid., 80–83.

27. See Antoni Macierewicz, "The Revolution in Nihilism," in Polonsky and Michlic, *The Neighbors Respond*, 98–99.

28. Ibid., 98–99.

29. Ibid., 98.

30. Most of Strzembosz's writings are unavailable in English. An obscure outfit in Victoria, Australia, has translated some of his work on the massacre. See Tomasz Strzembosz, *Jedwabne, 1941* (Footscray: Strzelecki Holding, Ltd., 2001).

31. Zakowski's article, "Każdy sąsiad ma imię" (Every Neighbor Has a Name), appeared in *Gazeta Wyborcza*, November 18–19, 2000. Cited in Polonsky and Michlic, *The Neighbors Respond*, 77.

32. Cited in Dawid Warszawski, "Responsibility and the Lack of Responsibility," *Gazeta Worborcza*, December 9–10, 2000.

33. Ibid.

34. Ibid. Zakowski writes, "I am irritated by the language of large-scale quantifiers which attempts to implicate me in culpability for a crime committed half a century ago *only because I am a Pole*" (emphasis mine).

35. Gross, *Neighbors*, 139–40.

36. Krzysztof Persak, "IPN: Polish Model of Dealing with the Totalitarian Past" (paper presented at "Historical Commissions: Comparative Perspectives," Columbia University, March 12–13, 2010).

37. For an overview of the IPN's activities, see its website, http://ipn.gov.pl/en. The figures here are taken from a talk Persak gave in 2010 (see n. 36). Additional information is taken from Persak's unpublished report, "Coming to Terms with the Wartime Past: The Institute for National Remembrance and its Research on the Jedwabne Case" (paper presented at "International Conference on Confronting History: The Historical Commissions of Inquiry," Yad Vashem, Jerusalem, December 29, 2002—January 1, 2003).

38. Paweł Machcewicz and Krzysztof Persak, eds., *Wokół Jedwabnego*, vols. 1 and 2 (Warsaw: Instytut Pamięci Narodowej, 2002).

39. Persak, "Coming to Terms with the Wartime Past," 15.

40. Gross, *Neighbors*, 16.

41. Persak, "Coming to Terms with the Wartime Past."

42. See Dariusz Stola, "Jedwabne: Revisiting the Evidence and Nature of the Crime," *Holocaust and Genocide Studies* 17, no. 1 (Spring 2003): 144. Anti-Semitic violence in these communities reached genocidal proportions within a short time. Stola's point is that the first episodes of killing were more limited compared to what took place after the consolidation of the German occupation.

43. Ibid.

44. Others have made the same point. Alexander Rossino has emphasized Gross's decision not to include German documents and sources. See Rossino, "Polish 'Neighbors' and German Invaders: Contextualizing Anti-Jewish Violence in the Białystok District During the Opening Weeks of Operation Barbarossa," *Polin* 16 (2003): 431–52.

45. Stola, "Jedwabne: Revisiting the Evidence and Nature of the Crime," 141.

46. Ibid.

47. Stola makes essentially the same point. See ibid., 142–43.

48. Ibid.

49. See, for example, Elazar Barkan, Elizabeth A. Cole, and Kai Struve, eds., *Shared History—Divided Memory: Jews and Others in Soviet-Occupied Poland, 1939–1941* (Leipzig: Leipziger Universitätsverlag, 2007).

50. Joanna Michlic, "Anti-Polish and Pro-Soviet? 1939–1941 and the Stereotyping of the Jew in Polish Historiography," in ibid., 68.

51. Persak, "Coming to Terms with the Wartime Past," 16, emphasis mine.

52. Ibid.

53. Piotr Wrobel, "Double Memory: Poles and Jews after the Holocaust," *East European Politics and Societies* 11, no. 3 (1997): 567.

54. Based on Mieczysław Orłowicz's study of public records, the IPN estimates that approximately 1,000 Jews lived in Jedwabne in 1939. See Orłowicz, *Przewodnik ilustrowany po województwie białostockim* (Białystok, 1937), 168. Persak writes: "Even if we take into account the presence of some Jewish refugees from the vicinity on the day of the massacre, it seems that the figure of 1,600 victims remembered by local residents is at least twice as many as there were in reality." Persak, "Coming to Terms with the Wartime Past," 18.

55. According to one report, a Lenin statue was also found in the smaller of the two graves (thirty to fifty bodies present). See "Śledztwo IPN w sprawie mordu Żydów w Jedwabnem," *Gazeta Wyborcza*, December 20, 2001, cited in Stola, "Jedwabne," 140.

56. Stola, "Jedwabne," 141.

57. Ibid.

58. Jan Gross, personal correspondence, January 23, 2014.

59. Persak, "Coming to Terms with the Wartime Past," 18.

60. Ibid., 19.

61. Ibid.

62. The literature on transitional justice is much too vast to rehearse here. A few of the major works are Neil J. Kritz, ed., *Transitional Justice: How Emerging Democracies Reckon with Former Regimes*, vols. 1–3 (Washington, DC: United States Institute of Peace, 1995); Alex Boraine and Sue Valentine, eds., *Transitional Justice and Human Security* (Cape Town: International Center for Transitional Justice, 2006); Hayner, *Unspeakable Truths*; and Minow, *Between Vengeance and Forgiveness*.

63. See, for example, David Crocker, "Punishment, Reconciliation, and Democratic Deliberation," in *Taking Wrongs Seriously: Apologies and Reconciliation*, ed. Elazar Barkan and Alexander Karn (Stanford: Stanford University Press, 2006), 50–82.

64. For those who work on projects that aim at reconciliation, it is essential to take stock of the empirical projects that yield skeptical assessments. Even where transitional justice mechanisms have been celebrated for promoting reconciliation, there is reason for caution regarding the durability of peace. David Backer's longitudinal study of victims' attitudes toward transitional justice in South Africa is sobering for the way it reveals eroding support for key aspects of the negotiated peace between the ANC and the apartheid-era government. See Backer, "Watching a Bargain Unravel? A Panel Study of Victims' Attitudes about Transitional Justice in Cape Town, South Africa," *International Journal of Transitional Justice* 4 (2010): 443–56. Janine Clark describes an even darker scenario for Bosnia, where, she says, "there is no agreement on the basic facts of what happened" and, therefore, no hope for "meaningful reconciliation." See Janine Natayla Clark, "From Negative to Positive Peace: The Case of Bosnia and Herzegovina," *Journal of Human Rights* 8 (2009): 360–84.

65. See Vamik Volkan, "What Some Monuments Tell Us About Mourning and Forgiveness," in Barkan and Karn, *Taking Wrongs Seriously*, 115–31.

66. Data as of February 2012.

Chapter 3. Austria and Italy

1. Hermann Langbein, "Darf man vergessen?," in *Das grosse Tabu: Österreichs Umgang mit seiner Vergangenheit*, ed. Anton Pelinka and Erika Weinzierl (Vienna: Verlag der Österreichischen Staatsdruckerei, 1987), 8–20.

2. Waldheim and his wife were deemed personae non grata by American customs and immigration officials due to their Nazi affiliations and were barred from entering the United States for the remainder of their lives. Waldheim died in June 2007 and was given a state funeral.

3. For more on the Waldheim affair and the impediments that unresolved history presents in Austrian politics and diplomacy, see Richard Mitten, *The Politics of Anti-Semitic Prejudice: The Waldheim Phenomenon in Austria* (Boulder, CO: Westview Press, 1993).

4. See, for example, Anton Pelinka, *Austria: Out of the Shadow of the Past* (Boulder, CO: Westview Press, 1989). David Art has also analyzed these debates in *The Politics of the Nazi Past in Germany and Austria* (Cambridge: Cambridge University Press, 2006).

5. Langbein, "Darf man vergessen?"

6. The declaration described Austria as "the first free country to fall victim to Hitlerite aggression." In the next lines, however, the document hits a different note, reminding Austria "that she has a responsibility, which she cannot evade, for participation in the war at the side of Hitlerite Germany. See "The Moscow Conference; October 1943," http://avalon.law.yale.edu/wwii/moscow.asp.

7. See Bruce F. Pauly, "From Splinter Party to Mass Movement: The Austrian Nazi Breakthrough," *German Studies Review* 2, no. 1 (1979): 7–29.

8. The term "wild Aryanization" comes from the final report (2003) of Austria's Historikerkommission. See note 28.

9. For more on Vranitzky's role, see Sonja Riekmann, "The Politics of *Ausgrenzung*: The Nazi Past and the European Dimension of the New Radical Right in Austria," in *The Vranitzky Era in Austria*, ed. Gunther Bischof, Anton Pelinka, and Ferdinand Karlhofer (New Brunswick, NJ: Transaction Publishers, 1999), 78–105.

10. Quoted in Greer Cashman and Batsheve Tsur, "Vranitzky Says Austria Accepts Moral Responsibility for Nazi Era," *Jerusalem Post*, June 10, 1993.

11. See Batsheva Tsur and David Makovsky, "Klestil Admits Austria's Role in the Holocaust," *Jerusalem Post*, November 14, 1994.

12. Dan Izenberg and Batsheva Tsur, "Klestil: No Apology Can Expunge Agony of Holocaust," *Jerusalem Post*, November 15, 1994.

13. Klestil traveled to Israel with an entourage of one hundred business and financial leaders, representing some of Austria's largest firms and banks. The presence of these individuals speaks to the subtext of Klestil's visit.

14. Haider and the FPÖ topped out at 26.9 percent in the 1999 election. David Art delves into the "Haiderization of the FPÖ" and analyzes electoral data for Austria during the period from 1986 to 1999. See Art, *Politics of the Nazi Past*.

15. Melissa Eddy, "History Commission Stresses Need for Speedy Compensation to Slave Laborers," *Associated Press*, February 17, 2000.

16. Besides Jabloner and Mikoletzky, the other Austrian appointees were Brigiette Bailer-Galanda, Bertand Perz, Roman Sandgruber, Georg Graff, Karl Stuhlpfarrer, and Alice Teichova. The British historian Robert Knight was appointed to the commission after Avraham Barkai (Israel) and Raul Hilberg (U.S.) declined to participate.

17. The Jabloner Commission created a rich website, http://www.historikerkommission.gv.at/english_home.html.

18. See Clemens Jabloner, "The Austrian Historical Commission: Motives, Results, and Impact," in *Revisiting the National Socialist Legacy: Coming to Terms with Forced Labor, Expropriation, Compensation, and Restitution*, ed. Oliver Rathkolb (New Brunswick, NJ: Transaction Publishers, 2004), 54.

19. Ibid., 51.

20. The "difficult history" of four paintings in Rudolf Leopold's Schiele Collection came to light in 1997. See Judith H. Dobrzynski, "The Zealous Collector," *New York Times*, December 24, 1997. This article put a spotlight on Austria's Holocaust restitution practices and led to the creation of a research commission in February 1998, which was charged with investigating the provenance of artworks in Austria's public museums.

21. Clemens Jabloner, "Scholarly Investigation and Material Compensation: The Austrian Historical Commission at Work," in *Restitution and Memory: Material Restoration in Europe*, ed. Dan Diner and Gotthart Wunberg (Oxford: Berghahn Books, 2007), 107.

22. Ibid.

23. Ibid., 105.

24. Clemens Jabloner, "The Legacy of Nazi-Expropriation in Austria: The Impact of the Historical Commission on Research and Restitution" (lecture, Austrian Embassy, London, England, March 3, 2009), 3. A transcript is available at http://www.doew.at/english/1938-2008-legacies-and-lessons-in-post-war-austria.

25. Jabloner, "The Austrian Historical Commission," 54.

26. Jabloner, "Scholarly Investigation and Material Compensation," 106.

27. Among these private sector reports, the commission reviewed the findings of the VOEST Steel Company and the Österreichische Postsparkasse (PSK, Austrian Postal Savings Bank). For more on these commissions, see Oliver Rathkolb, "Private Industry and Banking Commissions and the Holocaust Era Assets Debate," *Studia Germanica et Austriaca* 2 (2002): 48–54.

28. The commission's summary ("Final Report," January 24, 2003) is available at http://www.historikerkommission.gv.at/pdf_hk/INTENGLISCHEPRESSEINFO.pdf.

29. Jabloner, "The Legacy of Nazi-Expropriation in Austria," 13.

30. Jabloner, "The Austrian Historical Commission," 53.

31. Chancellor Wolfgang Schuessel appointed Maria Schaumayer, a former president of the Austrian National Bank, to lead the negotiations.

32. William Hall, "Austrians Get to Grips with 'Aryanisation,'" *Financial Times* (London), March 8, 2000.

33. Historikerkommission, "Final Report," 2; see n. 28. Besides the suggestion that property expropriation and genocidal intent could only be appreciated "in retrospect," one might also ask about the commission's interest in "Jews who stayed [*verbleiben*] within the areas of Nazi rule." In particular, it is worth asking whether this formulation is, to any degree, faithful to the experience of Jewish victims, who reported feeling trapped and imprisoned in German-controlled territories (as opposed to simply remaining or "staying" there).

34. Ibid.

35. Statistics on Austria's Jewish emigration are available in the United States Holocaust Memorial Museum's "Encyclopedia of the Holocaust." See http://www .ushmm.org/wlc/en/article.php?ModuleId=10005447.

36. Historikerkommission, "Final Report," 4.

37. Ibid.

38. Ibid.

39. Ibid., 5.

40. Ibid., 3.

41. In 1953, the Committee for Jewish Claims on Austria estimated total "occupational damages" to Jews at $300 million, but their report provided little information about the validity of this figure. Regarding a different estimate, made by the Federal Ministry of Finance in 1947, the Jabloner Commission described the calculations as "arbitrary and superficial."

42. Marion Kaplan, *Between Dignity and Despair: Jewish Life in Nazi Germany* (Oxford: Oxford University Press, 1998). See, in particular, chap. 5 on the November Pogrom and its aftermath.

43. Jabloner, "Scholarly Investigation and Material Compensation," 108.

44. Ibid.

45. Historikerkommission, "Final Report," 16.

46. It is interesting that Austrians could easily see how a German successor state would have to bear the costs of Nazi era crimes, but they still refused to accept any notion of continuity between the Austrian State that entered the war and the Republic that emerged in the aftermath.

47. Historikerkommission, "Final Report," 16.

48. Ibid., 17.

49. Ibid., 17. West Germany passed two laws regulating restitution and compensation. Victims who appealed for justice there encountered a more open and straightforward process aimed at compensating Jewish losses. See chap. 4 on German "guilt management" in Regula Ludi, *Reparations for Nazi Victims in Postwar Europe* (Cambridge: Cambridge University Press, 2012).

50. Historikerkommission, "Final Report," 18–19.

51. Ibid., 19.

52. Ibid., 20.

53. Although the act has been modified sixty-two times since its initial passage, usually as the result of pressure from Jewish victims' groups or the intervention of the Allies, this legislation, according to the Jabloner report, has always applied a "selective definition" regarding the identity of victims.

54. Historikerkommission, "Final Report," 24.

55. Using a conversion of RM 2.5 to $1, the total value of registered Jewish properties following the Anschluss ranged from $737 million to $1.16 billion.

56. Conference on Jewish Material Claims Against Germany (Claims Conference), "Mauerbach Hardship Fund," http://www.claimscon.org/what-we-do/negotiations /austria/mauerbach-hardship-fund/.

57. Claims Conference, "Austrian National Fund," http://www.claimscon.org /about/history/closed-programs/austrian-national-fund/.

58. Claims Conference, "Austrian General Settlement Fund," http://www.claims con.org/about/history/closed-programs/general-settlement-fund/.

59. See J. D. Bindenagel, "Justice, Apology, Reconciliation, and the German Foundation," in Barkan and Karn, *Taking Wrongs Seriously*, 286–310.

60. A database for worldwide compensation programs is available at http://forms .claimscon.org/comp_guide/comp_guide.php.

61. Historikerkommission, "Final Report," 31.

62. Jabloner, "The Legacy of Nazi-Expropriation in Austria," 3.

63. Ibid., 12.

64. Jabloner, "The Austrian Historical Commission," 54.

65. Historikerkommission, "Final Report," 31.

66. Karl Jaspers, "The Question of German Guilt," in *Perspectives on the Nuremberg Trial*, ed. Guénaël Mattraux (New York: Oxford University Press, 2006), 676.

67. This sentiment is far removed from what Jaspers understood as the chief consequences of metaphysical guilt: "Pride is broken. This self-transformation by inner activity may lead to a new source of active life, but one linked with an indelible sense of guilt in that humility which grows modest before God and submerges all its doings in an atmosphere where arrogance becomes impossible." Ibid.

68. Jabloner, "Scholarly Investigation and Material Compensation," 106.

69. Jabloner, "The Austrian Historical Commission," 54.

70. Jabloner, "The Legacy of Nazi-Expropriation in Austria," 12.

71. See Austrian Federal Chancellery, "Bundesgesetz über den Fonds für freiwillige Leistungen der Republik Österreich an ehemalige Sklaven-und Zwangsarbeiter des nationalsozialistischen Regimes (Versöhnungsfonds-Gesetz)," http://www.ris.bka.gv .at/Dokument.wxe?Abfrage=Erv&Dokumentnummer=ERV_2000_1_74.

72. Jabloner, "The Legacy of Nazi-Expropriation in Austria," 4.

73. Jabloner, "Scholarly Investigation and Material Compensation," 95.

74. Jabloner, "The Legacy of Nazi-Expropriation in Austria," 4.

75. Pelinka, *Austria: Out of the Shadow of the Past*, 201.

76. Lutz Musner, "Memory and Globalization: Austria's Recycling of the Nazi Past and Its European Echoes," *New German Critique* 80 (2000): 79.

77. Jabloner, "The Legacy of Nazi-Expropriation in Austria," 13.

78. See Yad Vashem, Database of the Righteous Among the Nations, "Palatucci Family," http://db.yadvashem.org/righteous/family.html?language=en&itemId =4043708.

79. In 2002, Pope John Paul II declared Palatucci a Catholic "martyr," which opened a path for his beatification. Until June 2013, when damaging revelations emerged concerning Palatucci's war record, the International Raoul Wallenberg Foundation included a tribute to him on their website. The tribute has since been removed.

80. Quoted in the withdrawn tribute on the International Raoul Wallenberg Foundation website.

81. This letter was prepared in 1953 by Rozsy Arvay Neumann following a tree-planting ceremony in the Israeli settlement of Ramat Gan to commemorate Palatucci's bravery. In addition to her general assessment of his character, Neumann stated that Palatucci invited her to Christmas lunch while she was jailed in Fiume.

82. "Some Were Neighbors: Collaboration and Complicity in the Holocaust" was opened in 2013 to mark the twentieth anniversary of the USHMM. The online exhibition can be viewed at http://somewereneighbors.ushmm.org/.

83. The project was coordinated by Natalia Indrimi (Centro Primo Levi, New York). Twelve others contributed to the research or reviewed the final report: Anna Pizzuti, Marco Coslovich, Michele Sarfatti, Liliana Picciotto, Susan Zuccotti, Spartaco Capogreco Mauro Canali, Sergio Minerbi, Federico Falk, Davide Rodogno, Silva Bon, and Micahel Ebner.

84. Quoted in Patricia Cohen, "Italian Praised for Saving Jews Is Now Seen as Nazi Collaborator," *New York Times*, June 19, 2013.

85. The CPL's research drew on documents located in Italian, German, British, Swiss, Israeli, and Croatian archives. While the full report has not yet been made available to the public, a copy was provided to the author. Palatucci's collaboration with the Nazis is covered in part 2 of the report in "Palatucci's Participation in the Arrest of Fiume's Jews."

86. Quoted in ibid.

87. The CPL report states, "The analysis of documents concerning Jewish relief in Fiume and Trieste does not substantiate the idea that someone at the Fiume Police Headquarters was involved in helping the Jews."

88. See "Vatican Paper Contests Study on Alleged Nazi Collaborator," *Reuters*, June 22, 2013.

89. Cited in Cohen, "Italian Praised for Saving Jews Is Now Seen as Nazi Collaborator."

90. Given the difficulties of documenting a transnational genocide, precise numbers are hard to confirm. Estimates of Jewish deaths in Italy range from 7,600 (Yehuda Bauer) to 9,000 (Raul Hilberg). We can extrapolate a death rate of 15–17 percent.

91. See Michele Sarfatti, *The Jews in Mussolini's Italy: From Equality to Persecution* (Madison: University of Wisconsin Press, 2006).

92. David Ward traces the Italian parenthesis theory back to Benedetto Croce in 1944. See "Croce Versus Vico in the Construction of Post-Fascist Italy," in *Italian Fascism: History, Memory, and Representation*, ed. Richard Dogliani and Patrizia Dogliani (New York: St. Martin's Press, 1999), 65.

93. Ibid.

94. Robert Gordon, "The Holocaust in Italian Collective Memory: *Il giorno della memoria*, 27 January, 2001," *Modern Italy* 11, no. 2 (June 2006): 167.

95. Ibid., 168.

96. Ibid., 170.

97. Ibid.

98. This phrase (emphasis mine) is taken from Article 1. The full text of the law is available at http://www.parlamento.it/parlam/leggi/00211l.htm.

99. Article 2, law no. 211, emphasis mine.

100. Alexis Herr has written a dissertation on the Campo di Fossoli (Carpi) site and the role that Italian contractors and service industries played in building and operating the camp. See "Remembering Fossoli di Carpi: From Death's Waiting Room to Ruins" (PhD diss., Clark University, 2013).

101. Quoted in Gordon, "The Holocaust in Italian Collective Memory," 175.

102. Robert Gordon, *The Holocaust in Italian Culture, 1944–2010* (Stanford: Stanford University Press, 2012), 21.

103. Ibid.

104. According to the USHMM, 8,564 Jews were deported from Italy and Italian-controlled territories.

105. Quoted in Ruth Ellen Gruber, "Italy Still Years Away from First Holocaust Museum," *Times of Israel*, January 23, 2013.

106. For additional background on Italy's role in the Holocaust, see Sarfatti, *The Jews in Mussolini's Italy*; Renzo De Felice, *The Jews in Fascist Italy: A History* (New York: Enigma Books, 2001); and Susan Zuccotti, *The Italians and the Holocaust: Persecution, Rescue, and Survival* (New York: Basic Books, 1987).

107. R. J. B. Bosworth and Patrizia Dogliani offer a thorough review of the historiography in their introduction to *Italian Fascism: History, Memory, and Representation* (Basingstoke, UK: Palgrave Macmillan, 1999).

108. See D. Ward, "From Croce to Vico: Carlo Levi's *l'Orologio* and Italian Anti-Fascism, 1943–46," in Bosworth and Dogliani, *Italian Fascism*, 65.

109. Patrizia Dogliani, "Constructing Memory and Anti-Memory: The Monumental Representation of Fascism and its Denial in Republican Italy," in Bosworth and Dogliani, *Italian Fascism*, 21.

110. D. Ward, "From Croce to Vico," 68. See also R. J. B. Bosworth, "Film Memories of Fascism," in Bosworth and Dogliani, *Italian Fascism*, 111.

111. Bosworth and Dogliani, introduction to *Italian Fascism*.

112. Richard Bosworth, "Coming to Terms with Fascism in Italy," *History Today* 55, no. 1 (2005): 18–20.

113. Renzo De Felice, *Mussolini*, 7 vols. (Turin: Einaudi, 1965–97).

114. Emilio Gentile, "Fascism, Totalitarianism, and Political Religion: Definitions and Critical Reflections on Criticism of an Interpretation," *Totalitarian Movements and Political Religions* 5, no. 3 (2004): 326–75.

115. Ibid., 352.

116. In English, the full title of the commission runs (approximately) as follows: Commission with the Task of Enquiring into the Actions Undertaken by Public and Private Bodies in Italy with the Aim to Acquire the Property of Jewish Citizens and the Results Thereof.

117. Sarfatti, "The Work and Findings of the 'Commissione Anselmi' on Italian Jewish Assets, 1998–2001" (lecture, Yad Vashem, Jerusalem, December 29, 2002).

118. Ilaria Pavan, "Indifference and Forgetting: Italy and Its Jewish Community, 1938–1970," in Dean, Goschler, and Ther, *Robbery and Restitution*, 171–81.

119. In 1997, Italy returned a small collection of ritual objects that Nazi officials stole from Jews in Trieste. Since then, the government has passed only one law pertaining to restitution. While Italian judges have attempted to clear the way for further claims, lawmakers have shown no interest in pursuing the matter. This is a reversal of the immediate postwar scenario, when most Italian legislators supported restitution and judges, in general, did not.

120. Sarfatti, "The Work and Findings of the 'Commissione Anselmi,'" 5.

121. The commission's final report ("Rapporto Generale," April 2001) is available at http://www.governo.it/Presidenza/DICA/beni_ebraici/index.html. See p. 64.

122. Ibid., 78.

123. Sarfatti, "The Work and Findings of the 'Commissione Anselmi,'" 6.

124. Ibid., 15.

125. The biggest firms were Assicurrazione Generali, Allianz, and Riunione Adriatica di Securita (Adriatic Insurance Company).

126. See chap. 6 for more on the ICHEIC.

127. See "Areas Not Included in the Commission's Tasks," in the "Rapporto Generale," 13.

128. Sarfatti, "The Work and Findings of the 'Commissione Anselmi,'" 15.

129. For more on France and the effort to negotiate moral reparations there, see chap. 2.

130. Pavan, "Indifference and Forgetting."

131. See section 2.1 in the "Rapporto Generale," 12.

132. Titho was arrested by U.S. troops at the Bolzano camp at the end of the war. He was later sent to The Hague, where he was convicted of war crimes in 1949 and sentenced to six years in prison. Italy attempted to retry Titho on separate charges in 1954, but Germany (which is where Titho ended up after serving out his sentence) refused to extradite him.

133. It is revealing to compare the inaction of the Italian government in 2001 with the uproar that resulted from Erich Priebke's case a few years earlier. In 1996, following his extradition from Argentina, Priebke was convicted on charges related to the Ardeatine Cave Massacre but was subsequently released when it was determined that

the statute of limitations had run out. Despite this, public outcry led an Italian court of appeals to retry Priebke in 1998, and he received a life sentence for his part in the killing.

134. Tina Anselmi, introduction to "Rapporto Generale," 3.

135. Ibid., 7.

136. See "Concluding Remarks," in "Rapporto Generale."

137. The report includes a long section on the repeal of the racial laws and the restitution of stolen assets. See http://www.governo.it/Presidenza/DICA/beni_ebraici /english_version/261_299_fg.pdf.

138. Anselmi, introduction to "Rapporto Generale," 7.

139. "Concluding Remarks," in "Rapporto Generale."

140. Anselmi, introduction to "Rapporto Generale," 5.

141. See, for example, Carlo Ginzburg, "Just One Witness," in *Probing the Limits of Representation: Nazism and the "Final Solution,"* ed. Saul Friedlander (Cambridge, MA: Harvard University Press, 1992), 82–96.

142. See section 2.a.4.1 in the "Rapporto Generale," available at http://www.governo .it/Presidenza/DICA/beni_ebraici/english_version/89_114_js.pdf.

143. This term is taken from Hayden White, "The Burden of History," *History and Theory* 5, no. 2 (1966): 111–34.

Chapter 4. Lithuania and Latvia

1. Even with all of the available archival documentation and scholarship, it is hard to provide definitive figures for total Holocaust victims on a country-by-country basis. Bauer and Rozett offer the following estimates: Estonia, 1,500–2,000; Latvia, 70,000–71,500; and Lithuania, 140,000–143,000. See Yehuda Bauer and Robert Rozett, "Estimated Jewish Losses in the Holocaust," in *Encyclopedia of the Holocaust* (New York: Macmillan, 1990), 1799.

2. Again, these are informed estimates. For Estonia, 50,000 killed; Latvia, 230,000 killed; and Lithuania, 350,000 killed.

3. Lithuania has its own judicial definition of the term "genocide," which is broader than the definition applied by the UN and includes attempts to eradicate both social and cultural groups. Some non-Jewish Lithuanians have seized on this to argue that the Soviet campaign against their nation's intellectual elite was, in fact, genocidal.

4. See chap. 2.

5. See, for example, Vello Pettai and Eva-Clarita Pettai, "The Baltic States and Russia: Bi-Lateral Lessons from Unilateral Commissions" (paper presented at "Historical Commissions, Comparative Perspectives," Columbia University, March 10, 2010). The authors have devised a scoring system for the Baltic commissions based on four categories with scores of 1–5 in each: (1) fact-finding (2) multiperspectival initiative (3) societal impact, and (4) engagement of third parties. The aggregate scores for the three Baltic commissions were: Latvia (15), Lithuania (13), and Estonia (12).

6. Australia and Canada also received the Wiesenthal Center's lowest possible grade. The full report ("SWC Annual Nazi War Criminal Report," April 11, 2010) is

available at http://www.wiesenthal.com/site/apps/nlnet/content2.aspx?c=lsKWLbPJL
nF&b=4441467&ct=8180041.

7. Quoted in Paul Frysh, "The Holocaust in Lithuania: One Man's Crusade to
Bring Justice," CNN, June 3, 2010, http://www.cnn.com/2010/WORLD/europe/06/03
/lithuania.nazi.prosecutions/index.html.

8. See the section "Gauging the ICL's Achievements."

9. An account of how the Lithuanian military assisted in the mass murder of the
Jewish population can be found in *U.S. v. Stelmokas* 100 F.3rd 302 (3rd Cir.; 1996).
The court opinion is available at http://scholar.google.com/scholar_case?case=5543670
345632486233&hl=en&as_sdt=2&as_vis=1&oi=scholarr.

10. The quotation appears in an extract from Jaeger's report. See Yad Vashem,
"Extract From a Report by Karl Jaeger, Commander Of Einsatzkommando 3, on the
Extermination Of Lithuanian Jews, 1941," http://www.yadvashem.org/about_holocaust
/documents/part3/doc180.html. To read the complete report in English, see Ernst
Klee, Willi Dressen, and Volker Riess, *The Good Old Days: The Holocaust as Seen by Its
Perpetrators and Bystanders* (New York: Free Press, 1991), 46–58.

11. The court held: "The evidence shows that when Stelmokas joined the *Schutzmannschaft*, service of all its officers was voluntary as there was an ample supply of candidates and conscription was not necessary. Indeed, for at least several months after Stelmokas joined the *Schutzmannschaft*, its members could be released at their own request."

12. Zingeris was a signatory to Lithuania's independence declaration in 1990.

13. Information related to the commission can be viewed at the ICL's website,
http://www.komisija.lt/en/. An overview of the research process is available at http://
www.komisija.lt/en/body.php?&m=1183459740. As of this writing, the ICL website
was unavailable, but an archived version is located at http://web.archive.org/web
/20141129225846/http://www.komisija.lt/en/.

14. For more on the Arad affair, see "Lithuania Wants to Grill Top Israeli Historian over War Crimes," *Agence France-Presse*, September 12, 2007.

15. The rules of procedure are elaborated in a nine-page document, available at
http://www.komisija.lt/en/body.php?&m=1187781478.

16. See the Research Works Database, available at http://www.komisija.lt/en/body
.php?&m=1194863084.

17. In a public talk given in 2002, Markas Zingeris, the ICL's research coordinator
for the period of Nazi occupation (and also the chairman's brother), noted: "For the
great part of the Lithuanian public, mainly the youth, World War II [is] almost ancient
history, and for [older] generations the main instrument for the perception of totalitarian regimes were the atrocities which the population of mainly ethnic Lithuanians
suffered under the Soviets. It means the 'last occupation' has overshadowed everything
else." See Markas Zingeris, "Commission for the Historical Truth and the Reshaping
of Public Mentality in the New Republic of Lithuania: Issues of Holocaust Research
and Dissemination of Knowledge" (paper presented at "International Conference on
Confronting History: The Historical Commissions of Inquiry," Yad Vashem, Jerusalem, December 29, 2002–January 1, 2003).

18. It should be pointed out that the ICL makes no comparisons along these lines (i.e., Jewish versus Lithuanian). I only mention the numbers of victims here to indicate how the commission used its resources and tailored its agenda.

19. Valdas Adamkus arrived on the political stage as a prominent member of the liberal circle known as "Santara-Sviesa" (Concord and Enlightenment). After fleeing Lithuania with his family in 1944, Adamkus immigrated to the United States in 1949. Following his graduation from college, Adamkus took a position with the Environmental Protection Agency, where he served a long stint before deciding to return to Lithuania and enter political life there.

20. Quoted in Virgil Krapauskas, "Post-Soviet Lithuania," in *Antisemitism: A Historical Encyclopedia of Prejudice and Persecution*, vol. 2, ed. Richard S. Levy (Santa Barbara: ABC-CLIO, 2005), 429–30.

21. Quoted in M. Zingeris, "Commission for the Historical Truth."

22. The most widely discussed issue was the trial of Aleksandras Lileikis, a former Lithuanian policeman accused of handing Jews over to Nazi death squads during the war. Lileikis immigrated to the United States after the war, but he returned to Lithuania in the 1990s when American investigators began to pursue a case against him. The Lithuanian government initially refused to put Lileikis on trial but finally did so in 1998 under pressure from American and EU diplomats. Lileikis died at the age of ninety-three before a verdict was reached.

23. M. Zingeris, "Commission for the Historical Truth."

24. Quoted in ibid.

25. Timothy Snyder made the same point after a monument to Jewish victims near Ponary was vandalized in July 2011. See Timothy Snyder, "Neglecting the Lithuanian Holocaust," *New York Review of Books*, July 25, 2011, http://www.nybooks.com/blogs /nyrblog/2011/jul/25/neglecting-lithuanian-holocaust/.

26. In his memoir, Arad recounted: "We broke into the village from two directions, and the defenders fled after putting up feeble resistance. We took the residents out of several houses in the section of the village where our two comrades fell and burned down the houses. Never again were partisans fired on from their village." Quoted in Nick Bravin, "In Other Words: Baltic Ghosts," *Foreign Policy*, April 15, 2009.

27. Ibid.

28. Ibid.

29. See "Lithuania Wants to Grill Top Israeli Historian over War Crimes."

30. Ibid.

31. Bravin, "In Other Words."

32. Printed on congressional letterhead, the missive to Kubilius (dated December 9, 2009) was signed by Paul Hodes, Howard Berman, Shelley Berkley, Robert Wexler, and James P. Moran. In addition to Secretary Clinton, three Lithuanian officials were also copied: President Dalia Grybauskaite; Vygaudas Usackas, the minister of foreign affairs; and Irena Degutiene, speaker of the Seima. It is archived at http://www.holocaust inthebaltics.com/2009Dec3USCongressProtestsOnMargolis.pdf.

33. Bravin, "In Other Words."

34. Cited in M. Zingeris, "Commission for the Historical Truth."

35. A list of the commission's members is available at http://www.komisija.lt/en/body.php?&m=1173522142.

36. M. Zingeris, "Commission for the Historical Truth."

37. The New Jersey Commission on Holocaust Education website is http://www.state.nj.us/education/holocaust/.

38. M. Zingeris, "Commission for the Historical Truth."

39. This point is nicely summarized in the ICL document "The Preconditions for the Holocaust in Lithuania," http://www.komisija.lt/en/body.php?&m=1194863779.

40. The commission reviewed data on Communist Party membership and showed that Jews accounted for just 12.6 percent of the total party membership in June 1941 (down from 16.2 percent earlier that year). As a percentage of the total Jewish population in Lithuania (208,400), membership in the Communist Party never exceeded 0.28 percent (593 Jewish party members out of a total Jewish population of more than 208,000). See "The Preconditions for the Holocaust in Lithuania," Annex 1.

41. Ibid.

42. See Markas Zingeris, "Scrambling out from the Abyss of the Holocaust," *Lithuanian Foreign Policy Review*, August 2001, http://www.lfpr.lt/uploads/File/2001-8/Zingeris.pdf.

43. Ibid.

44. Ibid.

45. Researchers at Yad Vashem put the number of victims at 9,200. See http://www.yadvashem.org/yv/en/about/institute/killing_sites_catalog_details_full.asp?region=Kaunas.

46. Jonathan Freedland, "I See Why 'Double Genocide' Is a Term Lithuanians Want. But it Appalls Me," *Guardian*, September 14, 2010. A photo of the Ninth Fort plaque is available on the website for the Florida Center for Instructional Technology. See "A Teacher's Guide to the Holocaust," http://fcit.usf.edu/HOLOCAUST/photos/ninth4/ninth426.htm.

47. Quoted in Raul Hilberg, *The Destruction of the European Jews* (New York: Holmes and Meier, 1985), 122.

48. Freedland, "I See Why 'Double Genocide' Is a Term Lithuanians Want."

49. The museum's mission statement, as well as information on its exhibitions and collections, is available at http://genocid.lt/muziejus/en/98/c/.

50. See Museum of Genocide Victims, "The History of the Building," http://genocid.lt/muziejus/en/711/c/. In e-mail correspondence with the head of the museum's history department, I asked about the relative lack of coverage for the period between 1941 and 1944. I was informed that the museum's exhibitions are based only on materials that were housed at the museum site when Lithuania established its independence in 1991. A video on the ground floor of the museum deals briefly with the period of Gestapo activity, but nothing else in the current collection deals with the subject in any depth.

51. A description of the "Katastrofa" (Catastrophe) exhibit is available in English at http://www.jmuseum.lt/index.aspx?Element=ViewArticle&TopicID=163&Article ID=3032.

52. See Vilna Gaon Jewish State Museum, "Catastrophe—Shoah," September 25, 2009, http://www.jmuseum.lt/index.aspx?Element=ViewArticle&TopicID=422& ArticleID=4147.

53. Details from another Kaunas pogrom (June 27, 1941) are even more disturbing. According to the museum's documentation, Lithuanians beat and bludgeoned a group of forty to fifty Jews with crowbars, shovels, and rifle butts. The attackers also forced hoses into the mouths of some victims, pumping them with water to the point of bursting.

54. Danielle Singer, "Lithuania Accuses Holocaust Survivors of War Crimes," *Jerusalem Post*, May 28, 2008.

55. See n. 32.

56. The memoir appears in English as Rachel Margolis, *A Partisan from Vilna* (Brighton, MA: Academic Studies Press, 2010).

57. One of the members of the ICL, Saulius Suziedelis, made this point in a talk he gave on the public perception of the Holocaust in Lithuania at the Wilson Center on September 26, 2007. See Saulius Suziedelis, "The Perception of the Holocaust: Public Challenges and Experience in Lithuania," Wilson Center, Meeting Report 341, http://www.wilsoncenter.org/publication/341-the-perception-the-holocaust-public-challenges-and-experience-lithuania.

58. Basic information pertaining to the CHL is available on the website of the Latvijas Valsts prezidenta kanceleja (Latvian State Chancellery of the President), http://www.president.lv/pk/content/?cat_id=7&lng=en.

59. Latvia's official presidential website provides material on the CHL, which includes this statement: "Academic research on the Holocaust will represent a certain criterion for the maturity of the scholars as well as the community as a whole." See n. 58.

60. The absence of formal rules of procedure had major repercussions when the commission experienced turbulence later.

61. The CHL later split the fourth category into two separate projects, one dealing with the period from 1944 to 1956 and another focused on the years from 1956 to 1990.

62. See "Latvia to Shut Commission on Soviet 'Occupation' to Save Money," *Ria Novosti*, June 12, 2009, http://rianovosti.com/world/20090612/155235137.html.

63. This is actually quite rare. It is more common that historical commissions give a new reading to materials that have already been examined before. The CHL unearthed previously unknown documents and security files, which had been stored in archives in Riga and elsewhere throughout Europe. These included German and Soviet propaganda materials that members of the CHL used to trace the origins of various historical myths. For more on this, see "Collection of Documents About German Occupation in Latvia Presented," *Baltic News Service*, May 23, 2002.

64. Valters Nollendorfs and Erwin Oberländer, eds., *The Hidden and Forbidden History of Latvia under Soviet and Nazi Occupations 1940–1991: Selected Research of the Commission of the Historians of Latvia*, Symposium of the Commission of the Historians of Latvia 14 (Riga: Institute of the History of Latvia, 2005).

65. Professor Oberländer's conference summary is available at http://www.president.lv/pk/content/?cat_id=9076&lng=en.

66. Nollendorfs and Oberländer, *Hidden and Forbidden History*.

67. Ibid., 16.

68. Ibid., 11, 10.

69. According to Senn, Jewish communists in Latvia held posts in the Soviet security force NKVD, and Jews "constituted half, if not more" of the Communist Youth League (Komsomol). See Alfred Erich Senn, "Baltic Background" in Nollendorfs and Oberländer, *Hidden and Forbidden History*, 24.

70. Ibid., 26, emphasis mine.

71. For an analysis of Gross's work, see chap. 2.

72. Senn, "Baltic Battleground," 26.

73. Quoted in Nollendorfs and Oberländer, *Hidden and Forbidden History*, 12.

74. Aivars Stranga, "The Holocaust in Occupied Latvia: 1941–1945," in Nollendorfs and Oberländer, *Hidden and Forbidden History*, 168.

75. Ibid. "Thus, the so-called interregnum periods were very short and no pogroms took place during them, to say nothing about any mass-scale executions of Jews by Latvians."

76. Nollendorfs and Oberländer, *Hidden and Forbidden History*, 12.

77. Stranga, "The Holocaust in Occupied Latvia," 162.

78. Ibid., 165–67.

79. For more on the Arājs Commando, see Andrew Ezergailis, "The Role of the Self-Defense Commandantures in the Holocaust," in *Latvija Otraja Pasaules Kara* (Riga, Latvia: Rīga Latvijas Vēstures Inst. Apgāds, 2000), 235–52 (conference proceedings from June 14–15, 1999).

80. Stranga, "The Holocaust in Occupied Latvia," 165.

81. Senn, "Baltic Battleground," 26.

82. Nollendorfs and Oberländer, *Hidden and Forbidden History*, 16.

83. Ibid.

84. Eva-Clarita Pettai (née Onken), "The Politics of Finding Historical Truth: Reviewing Baltic History Commissions and Their Work," *Journal of Baltic Studies* 38, no. 1 (March 2007): 113.

85. The Skarpnes Commission in Norway encountered a scenario like this. See the introduction for more on this. See also Walter V. Robinson, "Norway Says Its Probe Downplays WWII Guilt," *Boston Globe*, June 24, 1997.

86. Pettai (Onken), "The Politics of Finding Historical Truth," 114.

87. Conference proceedings were published (in Latvian) and are available at http://www.president.lv/images/modules/items/LVK%2026%20PDF.pdf.

88. See n. 65.

89. One participant recalled: "What really struck me was the peculiar silence or disinterest of established Latvian historians in relation to arguments and suggestions put forward by Western colleagues; and the barely concealed frustration that this elicited amongst some of the Western scholars of Baltic history." Quoted in Eva-Clarita Pettai, "The Convergence of Two Worlds: Historians and Emerging Histories in the Baltic States," in *Forgotten Pages in Baltic History: Inclusion and Exclusion in History*, ed. Martyn Housden and David J. Smith (Amsterdam: Rodopi, 2011), 264.

90. Ibid.

91. See De Baets, *Responsible History*, part I.

92. See M. Zingeris, "Commission for the Historical Truth": "I see the meaning of the Commission's work more in the process than in the result which is destined to materialize in [a] pile of volumes on the library shelf." Norman Naimark, a member of both the Lithuanian and Latvian commissions, made similar remarks at the conference "Historical Commissions: Comparative Perspectives," which was held at Columbia University on March 12 and 13, 2010. Conference video is available at http://human rightscolumbia.org/historical.

Chapter 5. Germany and Its Neighbors

1. François Heisbourg, "Reconciliation Between Countries and Societies: The Example of the French-German Experience" (lecture, Institute for Cultural Diplomacy, Berlin, November 6, 2010).

2. See below for more on the Franco-German Historians Agreement of 1951, its roots in the interwar period, and its impact on subsequent reconciliation initiatives.

3. Kim Seungryeol, "International History Textbook Work from a Global Perspective: The Joint Franco-German History Textbook and its Implications for Northeast Asia," *Journal of Northeast Asian History* 6, no. 2 (December 2009): 78.

4. The French edition is published by Éditions Nathan; the German edition by Ernst Klett Verlag. French and international press coverage is summarized at "Une couverture média importante au niveau national et international," http://www.nathan .fr/manuelfrancoallemand/ressources/Revue_de_presse_mfa.pdf.

5. Alain Auffray, "Le Manuel d'histoire, noveau symbole franco-allemand," *Liberátion*, May 4, 2006.

6. See *Histoire/Geschichte*, vol. 3, 127.

7. Leopold von Carlowitz, "Post-war Reconciliation through Joint Textbook Revision: The Cases of Franco-German and Polish-German History Books," *International Journal for Education Law and Policy* (2010): 51.

8. Cited in Seungryeol, "International History Textbook Work," 88–89.

9. "Franco-German Textbook Launched," *BBC News*, May 5, 2006.

10. Quoted in *Deutsche Welle*, July 10, 2006.

11. Etienne François, quoted in Seungryeol, "International History Textbook Work," 82.

12. Wojciech Roszkowski, "Opinion on French-German Secondary School History Textbook *Histoire/Geschichte*," available at http://www.euroclio.eu/download/2009/Wojciech%20Roszkowski%20-%20Criticism%20of%20New%20History%20Textbook.pdf.

13. Ibid., 3.

14. Ibid., 15.

15. Carlowitz, "Post-war Reconciliation through Joint Textbook Revision," 54.

16. Ibid., 47.

17. Corine Defrance and Ulrich Pfeil, "German-French School Textbook: Some Considerations about the Origins of the First Two Volumes" (lecture, Networking European Citizenship Education, Sofia, Bulgaria, November 6–8, 2008).

18. Official election results ("Référendum du 29 mai 2005") are available at http://www.interieur.gouv.fr/Elections/Les-resultats/Referendums/elecresult__referendum_2005/(path)/referendum_2005/000/000.html.

19. Jaime Smyth, "Germany Proposes Common EU History Textbook for Students," *Irish Times*, March 2, 2007.

20. Mona Siegel and Kirsten Harjes, "Disarming Hatred: History Education, National Memories, and Franco-German Reconciliation from World War I to the Cold War," *History of Education Quarterly* 52, no. 3 (2012): 378.

21. Ibid., 377.

22. Quoted in ibid., 380.

23. Ibid., 383.

24. See "Les Manuels d'histoire allemands et français: Résolutions adoptées par la Commission d'historiens allemands et français," *l'École libératrice* 11, no. 31 (May 15, 1937).

25. Cited in Corine Defrance, *La Politique culturelle de la France sur la rive gauche du Rhine, 1945–55* (Strasbourg: Presses Universitaires, 1994), 265, n. 10.

26. Cited in Siegel and Harjes, "Disarming Hatred," 397.

27. Quoted in ibid., 397.

28. Ibid., 399.

29. Election results ("Reichstagswahl November 1932") are available at http://www.gonschior.de/weimar/Deutschland/RT7.html.

30. Siegel and Harjes, "Disarming Hatred," 400.

31. On the direction of history teaching and textbooks in West Germany and for a revealing comparison to East Germany, see Julian Dierkes, "The Decline and Rise of the Nation in German History Education," in *The Nation, Europe, and the World: Textbooks and Curricula in Transition*, ed. Hanna Schissler and Yassemin Nuhoglu Soysal (New York: Berghahn Books, 2005), 82–102.

32. The term "alternative culture" is taken from Michael G. Müller, "The Joint Polish-German Commission for the Revision of School Textbooks and Polish Views of German History," *German History* 22, no. 3 (2004): 433–47. In English, there is one more indispensable overview of the commission: Krzysztof Ruchniewicz, "The History of the Polish-German Textbook Commission," an October 2008 presentation

available at http://ece.columbia.edu/files/ece/images/HistoryoftheGerman-Polish TextbookCommission-3.pdf.

33. Müller, "The Joint Polish-German Commission," 434.

34. See Basil Kerski, Thomas Kycia, and Robert Żurek, *"Wir vergeben und bitten um Vergebung": Der Briefwechsel der polnischen und deutschen Bischöfe von 1965 und seine Wirkung* (Osnabrück: Fibre, 2006).

35. Müller, "The Joint Polish-German Commission," 436.

36. This was especially true on the Polish side, where the work was often highly innovative. See ibid., 436–37. Müller writes, "Many Polish contributions to the respective conference volumes could be cited as evidence for a major shift in perspective: from a discussion of German *Polenpoltik* and its exclusive focus on economic, social, and cultural impacts of German developments on Poland, towards a broader debate over the role of German historical experiences in European history."

37. Ruchniewicz, "The History of the Polish-German Textbook Commission," 11–12.

38. Müller, "The Joint Polish-German Commission," n. 32.

39. See Włodzimierz Borodziej and Hans Lemberg, eds., *"Unsere Heimat ist uns eins fremdes Land geworden . . .": Die Deutschen östlich von Oder Neisse, 1945–1950* (Marburg: Verlag Herder-Institut, 2000).

40. Müller, "The Joint Polish-German Commission," 443.

41. Robert Maier, "German Textbook Cooperation since 1989" (lecture, Korean Educational Development Institute, Seoul, Korea, October 16, 2002).

42. In media accounts, German demands were attached to exorbitant (i.e., eleven-digit) financial figures. See, for example, Roger Boyes, "Poland Fears War Payback Demands," *Times* (London), September 25, 2003.

43. Quoted in Robert Maier, "German Textbook Cooperation since 1989."

44. Ibid.

45. Ibid.

46. Ibid.

47. Ibid.

48. Piotr Jendroszczyk, "Steinmeier Counting on Poland," *Rzeczpospolita*, February 1, 2008.

49. Ibid.

50. Ruchniewicz, "The History of the Polish-German Textbook Commission."

51. Ibid.

52. Lily Gardner Feldman, "German-Polish Reconciliation in Comparative Perspective: Lessons for Japan?," *Asia-Pacific Journal*, April 19, 2010. By the same author, see also *Germany's Foreign Policy of Reconciliation: From Enmity to Amity* (New York: Rowman and Littlefield, 2012).

53. The recommendations are available (in Polish and German) on the website of the Georg Eckert Institute for International Textbook Research, at http://www.gei.de /en/research/europe-narratives-images-spaces/europe-and-the-national-factor/german-polish-history-textbook.html.

54. Ibid.

55. Quoted in Jan Friedmann, "Can a Jointly Written History Erase Centuries of German-Polish Strife?," *Spiegel Online*, June 20, 2011.

56. Ibid.

57. Charles Maier, *The Unmasterable Past: History, Holocaust, and National Identity* (Cambridge, MA: Harvard University Press, 1988), 61. For more on Maier's conceptualization of mediating history, see the introduction to this study.

58. German and Polish publishing partners have been secured, but there are no further publication details as of the time of this writing. For more on the plans and objectives for this project, see n. 53.

59. R. M. Douglas, *Orderly and Humane: The Expulsion of Germans after the Second World War* (New Haven, CT: Yale University Press, 1012). See, in particular, chap. 8.

60. For more on the legal aspects of the expellees' claims, refer to the next section, "Germany and the Czech Republic."

61. Charles Hawley, "Germany and Its World War II Victims: Historians Condemn Commemoration Day Proposal," *Spiegel Online*, February 15, 2011.

62. Ibid.

63. Ibid.

64. "Czech Ministry Sees No Need for Commission to Study Post-War Deportations," *BBC Worldwide Monitoring*, May 12, 2008.

65. Cited in "The Beneš Decrees: A Spectre over Central Europe," *Economist*, August 15, 2002.

66. These figures are taken from Timothy W. Ryback, "Dateline Sudetenland: Hostages to History," *Foreign Policy* 105 (1996/97): 162–78.

67. "Deutsch-Tschechische Erklärung über die gegenseitigen Beziehungen und deren künftige Entwicklung," signed by Helmut Kohl and Vaclav Klaus, January 1997, http://eudocs.lib.byu.edu/index.php/Deutsch-Tschechische_Erkl%C3%A4rung. An English translation is available at http://eudocs.lib.byu.edu/index.php/Czech-German_Declaration.

68. Ibid.

69. "EU Commissioner Says Czech Legal System Meets EU Standards," *CTK News Agency* (Prague), April 9, 2002.

70. Until the "Velvet Divorce" in 1993, the commission was a trilateral project, as it involved not only Czechs and Germans but also Slovaks.

71. The commission has its own page within the Georg Eckert Institute's website, available at http://www.gei.de/en/research/europe-narratives-images-spaces/europe-and-the-national-factor/german-czech-textbook-commission.html.

72. Ibid.

73. See, for example, Jürgen Habermas, "Citizenship and National Identity: Some Reflections on the Future of Europe," in *The Condition of Citizenship*, ed. Bart van Steenbergen (New York: Sage, 1994).

74. The commission was originally co-chaired by Jiří Pešek (Czech) and Hans Lemberg (German).

75. "The Czech-German Historians Commission against the Reduction of Czech-German Relations to the Issue of [the] Beneš Decrees" is available at http://www.mzv.cz /jnp/en/foreign_relations/archiv/second_world_war_and_its_impact/joint_czech_ german_historians_commission/index.html.

76. Ibid.

77. Czech restitution laws were challenged repeatedly in the mid-1990s. Rudolf Dreithaler, a Czech citizen of German descent, brought a case to the Czech Constitutional Court, seeking the annulment of the Beneš decrees and the return of property that had been seized from his family. Dreithaler argued that the expulsions and confiscations were in direct conflict with international treaties to which the Czech Republic was party (e.g., Article 17 of the UDHR); however, the court rejected his petition in a judgment handed down on March 8, 1995. For more on this, see Mark Gillis, "Facing Up to the Past: The Czech Constitutional Court's Decision on the Confiscation of Sudeten German Property," *Parker School Journal of East European Law* 2, no. 6 (1995): 709–59.

78. Quoted in ibid., 743.

79. "European Court Rejects Sudeten German Complaint Against Czech Republic," *Czech News Agency* (CTK), December 29, 2005.

80. "The Expulsion of Sudeten Germans Is Still Raw," *Economist*, May 7, 2013.

81. Cited in ibid.

82. Angela Merkel's visit to Prague in early 2012 focused on disagreements over fiscal policy and the Czechs' continuing reliance on nuclear energy. See "German Chancellor Merkel Visits Czech Neighbors," *Deutsche Welle*, April 3, 2012.

83. The conference program (in German) for "Erinnern—Ausstellen—Speichern: Deutsch-tschechische und deutsch-slowakische Beziehungsgeschichte im Museum" is available at http://www.dt-ds-historikerkommission.de/programm.pdf.

84. The commission (Česko-německá a Slovensko-německá komise historiků) maintains a list of past and future publications available at http://www.dt-ds-historiker kommission.de/publikationen_t.html.

85. In 2013, the National Technical Museum in Prague opened a photography exhibition titled "The Art of Killing." The exhibit featured new works by Lukas Houdek, which featured Barbie dolls posed in grim scenes depicting mass rape and executions. In an interview, Houdek stated that the photos were based on archival records and eyewitness testimonies related to the expulsion of Sudetenlandern. See Ian Willoughby, "Barbies and Barbarity: Exhibition Takes Novel Approach to Post-war Massacres of Germans," February 6, 2013, http://www.radio.cz/en/section/curraffrs /barbies-and-barbarity-exhibition-takes-novel-approach-to-post-war-massacres-of-germans#0.

Chapter 6. The International Commission on Holocaust-Era Insurance Claims

1. Adrienne Scholz, "Restitution of Holocaust-Era Insurance Assets: Success or Failure?," *New England Journal of International and Comparative Law* 9 (2003): 297–333.

2. Ibid., 299.

3. Following the war, the Allies devalued the German currency at a ratio of ten to one. Some insurance companies argued that policies purchased with reichsmarks should therefore be paid at one-tenth their original value.

4. Cited in "Insurance and the Holocaust," *Economist*, March 13, 1997.

5. Marilyn Henry, "Holocaust Survivors Sue Generali in U.S. Class Action," *Jerusalem Post*, April 1, 1997.

6. Quoted in "Insurance and the Holocaust."

7. Lawrence S. Eagleburger and M. Diane Koken with Catherin Lillie, "Finding Claimants and Paying Them: The Creation and Workings of the International Commission on Holocaust Era Insurance Claims," June 18, 2007, 17, http://www.icheic.org/pdf/ICHEIC%20Legacy%20Document.pdf.

8. Three NGOs participated: the World Jewish Congress, the World Jewish Restitution Organization, and the Conference on Jewish Material Claims Against Germany.

9. The six firms were Allianz (Germany), Generali (Italy), AXA (France), Winterthur (Switzerland), Basler (Switzerland), and Zurich (Switzerland).

10. David Clay Johnston, "Accord Signed to Name Tribunal on Holocaust Insurance Claims," *New York Times*, May 7, 1998.

11. Joseph B. Treaster, "Holocaust Survivors' Insurance Ordeal," *New York Times*, April 8, 2003.

12. Garamendi called for the resignation of the commission's chair, Lawrence Eagleburger, describing his performance and leadership as "abominable." See "Holocaust Insurance: Bad Policies," *Economist*, October 16, 2003.

13. Joseph B. Treaster, "Two Holocaust Survivors Sue Group Set Up to Collect Insurance," *New York Times*, September 25, 2003.

14. Henry Weinstein, "Hope Raised for Holocaust Claim Payouts," *Los Angeles Times*, April 14, 1999.

15. Cited in Scholz, "Restitution of Holocaust-Era Insurance Assets," 317.

16. Ibid., 318.

17. Ibid.

18. Ibid.

19. The ICHEIC described its research database as "the most extensive project ever conducted to investigate and record information on insurance policies from Holocaust-era archives from around the world." The commission also claimed that the effort to acquire policy lists from participating insurers was "largely successful." Some of the data related to its policy research and matching protocol are available at http://www.icheic.org/research.html.

20. Scholz claims to have picked out this figure from a news release (November 2001) on the ICHEIC website. As of this writing, however, the site includes no news releases prior to March 2004.

21. For more on the commission's considerations relating to admissible evidence, see Eagleburger and Koken, "Finding Claimants and Paying Them," 23.

22. Cited in Scholz, "Restitution of Holocaust Era Insurance Assets," 319.

23. Nicole Brochu, "Holocaust Compensation Failing Many," *Sun-Sentinel* (Fort Lauderdale), November 9, 2001.

24. Henry Waxman's testimony to Congress, November 8, 2001. Cited in Michael J. Bazyler, "The Holocaust Restitution Movement in Comparative Perspective," *Berkeley Journal of International Law* 20, no. 1 (2002): 21.

25. Scholz, "Restitution of Holocaust-Era Insurance Assets," 319.

26. Treaster, "Two Holocaust Survivors Sue Group."

27. "Holocaust Insurance: Bad Policies."

28. Philip Shenon, "Holocaust Claims Commission Falling Into Turmoil," *New York Times*, January 25, 2002.

29. "Holocaust Insurance Body Spends 30 Million to Award 3 Million," *Deutsche Presse-Agentur*, May 17, 2001.

30. Eagleburger and Koken, "Finding Claimants and Paying Them," 22.

31. For more information on the settlement with the Swiss banks, see Roger P. Alford, "The Claims Resolution Tribunal and Holocaust Claims Against Swiss Banks," *Berkeley Journal of International Law* 20, no. 1 (2002): 250–81.

32. Eagleburger and Koken, "Finding Claimants and Paying Them," 22.

33. Henry Weinstein, "Holocaust Claims Still Going Unpaid," *Los Angeles Times*, July 9, 2001.

34. Not all of these offers were accepted. While the commission developed an appeals process for individuals whose claims were rejected or who felt their settlement offer was unsatisfactory, some claimants walked away without taking what the commission offered, presumably to preserve a possibility for subsequent litigation.

35. Eagleburger and Koken, "Finding Claimants and Paying Them," 4.

36. According to the commission's final report, individual claimants received between $1,000 and $1 million. With respect to the low end of the range, the commission noted the prevalence of "small sum policies" in prewar Europe. There is no mention of reportedly lower settlement offers, which claimants rejected or submitted for appeal.

37. Michael Bazyler, a legal scholar specializing in Holocaust restitution, estimated that prewar insurance policies held by European Jews might be worth as much as $10 billion. Cited in "Insurers and the Holocaust: Line to Nowhere," *Economist*, August 2, 2003.

38. Joseph B. Treaster, "Court Favors Families in Suits Over Holocaust-Era Insurance," *New York Times*, September 30, 2002.

39. Treaster, "Holocaust Survivors' Insurance Ordeal."

40. For Eagleburger and the ICHEIC this became a standard refrain. See, for example, "Insurers and the Holocaust: Line to Nowhere"; and Eagleburger and Koken, "Finding Claimants and Paying Them," 22. Mara Rudman, the commission's chief operating officer, took the same position in June 2004, saying that all sides had underestimated the complexity and time requirements for settling claims: "Everybody expected too much." Quoted in Tom Tugend, "Holocaust Claims Commission Mired in Strife," *Jerusalem Post*, June 15, 2004.

41. The Volcker Commission audited approximately 300,000 individual accounts and found that 54,000 "[had] a probable or possible relationship to victims of Nazi persecution." Detailed information on the settlement with the Swiss banks, including the ICEP final report, is available at the website of the *Swiss Banks Settlement: In re Holocaust Victim Assets Litigation*, at http://www.swissbankclaims.com/Overview.aspx.

42. Quoted in "Insurers and the Holocaust: Line to Nowhere."

43. An overview of the commission's research appears in Eagleburger and Koken, "Finding Claimants and Paying Them," 34.

44. Ibid., 35. The final report states that the ICHEIC published a list of 500,000 potential policyholders. Subtracting what the commission's researchers found on their own (55,079 policyholders), one can infer that the insurance companies provided approximately 445,000 names. To put this figure in perspective, Allianz alone wrote approximately 1.5 million policies in the period leading up to World War II.

45. Lillie and Feldman presented their work at a 1998 symposium, hosted by the National Archives, on records and research related to Holocaust-era assets, available at http://www.archives.gov/research/holocaust/articles-and-papers/.

46. Feldman did extensive work in Allianz's corporate archive, although he notes that the company's headquarters were badly damaged, and many important materials lost, as the result of Allied bombing. See Gerald Feldman, *Allianz and the German Insurance Business, 1933–1945* (Cambridge: Cambridge University Press, 2001).

47. ICHEIC, "Final Report on External Research," April 2004, http://www.icheic.org/pdf/Research%20Report-0404.pdf.

48. Gerald D. Feldman, "Insurance in the National Socialist Period: Sources and Research Problems," December 4, 1998, http://www.archives.gov/research/holocaust/articles-and-papers/symposium-papers/insurance-in-national-socialist-period.html.

49. ICHEIC, "Final Report on External Research," 2.

50. Catherine Lillie, "Researching Unpaid and Unclaimed Holocaust-Era Insurance Policies: Documentary Evidence for Claims," December 4, 1998, http://www.archives.gov/research/holocaust/articles-and-papers/symposium-papers/researching-unpaid-unclaimed-insurance-policies.html.

51. Ibid.

52. See Hayden White, *The Content of the Form: Narrative Discourse and Historical Representation* (Baltimore: Johns Hopkins University Press, 1990), 5.

53. Scholz, "Restitution of Holocaust-Era Insurance Assets," 332. She writes: "The robbers continue to go unpunished. The restitution efforts thus far have resulted in a mere pittance of what could possibly be considered just compensation. . . . The brightest promise for the future seems to rest in . . . two class-action suits."

54. "Holocaust Insurance Settlement Reported," *New York Times*, November 25, 1999.

55. Joseph Treaster, "Holocaust Victims Settle with Generali," *New York Times*, January 30, 2007.

56. Marjorie Backman, "Survivors Complain of Delay in Release of Holocaust Files," *New York Times*, June 9, 2007.

57. Ibid.

58. See the Holocaust Insurance Accountability Act of 2011 (H.R. 890), available at http://thomas.loc.gov/cgi-bin/query/z?c112:H.R.+890:.

59. Leslie Scism, "Collecting Unpaid Insurance," *Wall Street Journal*, March 3, 2012.

60. See U.S. State Department Fact Sheet, "Seeking Compensation for Unpaid Holocaust Era Insurance Claims," November 15, 2011, http://www.state.gov/r/pa/prs/ps/2011/11/177217.htm. The sheet ends with the following advice: "This voluntary process . . . is a better and more efficient way to ensure payment of Holocaust-era policies than is litigation. Such litigation is unlikely to succeed in any case because of jurisdictional issues, higher evidentiary standards in court, and otherwise unavailable legal defenses that defendants could raise in a legal proceeding."

Chapter 7. The International Catholic-Jewish Historical Commission

1. The quotation is taken from an interview in 1964 with Hochhuth and Hannah Arendt. See "Rolf Hochhuth Discusses His Play 'The Deputy' with Hannah Arendt," http://www.catarchive.com/detailPages/640315.html. For those who wish to read the play, see Rolf Hochhuth, *The Deputy*, trans. Richard and Clara Winston (Baltimore: Johns Hopkins University Press, 1997).

2. The literature on Pius XII is vast. The most damaging and sensational portrait is John Cornwall's book *Hitler's Pope: The Secret History of Pius XII* (New York: Viking, 1999). Cornwall depicts Pius as a flagrant anti-Semite eager to accommodate the genocidal aims of the Nazi regime. Catholic publishers have countered with their own slanted portraits. See, for example, Margherita Marchione, *Pope Pius XII: Architect for Peace* (New York: Paulist Press, 2000), in which the author claims that during World War II and for twenty years after "Pius XII was almost universally regarded as a saintly man, a scholar, a man of peace, a tower of strength, and a compassionate defender and protector of all victims of war and genocide that had drowned Europe in blood for six years." Quoted in Carol Rittner and John K. Roth, eds., *Pope Pius XII and the Holocaust* (London: Leicester University Press, 2002), 6.

3. Quoted in Dimitri Cavalli, "The Good Samaritan: Jewish Praise for Pope Pius XII," *Inside the Vatican* (October 2000): 72–77.

4. Quoted in ibid.

5. Quoted in Jose Maria Sanchez, *Pius XII and the Holocaust: Understanding the Controversy* (Washington, DC: Catholic University of America Press, 2002), 140.

6. See, for example, Ronald Rychlak, *Hitler, the War, and the Pope* (Huntington, IN: Our Sunday Visitor, 2010); and David G. Dalin, *The Myth of Hitler's Pope: How Pope Pius XII Rescued Jews from the Nazis* (Washington, DC: Regnery, 2005).

7. The *ADSS* are available at http://www.vatican.va/archive/actes/index_fr.htm.

8. While the *ADSS* contain 5,089 documents, the Vatican acknowledges that these were selected from a much larger collection numbering in the millions.

9. Paul O'Shea, "The Vatican, the Holocaust, and the Archives," in *Genocide Perspectives IV: Essays on Holocaust and Genocide*, ed. Colin Tatz (Sydney: UTSePress, 2012), 199–233.

10. See Andrea Gagliarducci, "Pope Francis Thinking about Declaring Pius XII a Saint," *Catholic News Agency*, July 31, 2013.

11. Commission for Religious Relations with the Jews, "We Remember: A Reflection on the Shoah," March 16, 1998, http://www.vatican.va/roman_curia/pontifical_councils/chrstuni/documents/rc_pc_chrstuni_doc_16031998_shoah_en.html.

12. In December 2009, Pope Benedict XVI signed a decree approving Pius XII's "heroic virtues." This moved Pius to the third of four steps that culminate in canonization.

13. Lisa Palmieri-Billig, "Document Defends Pope Pius XII," *Jerusalem Post*, March 17, 1998.

14. "Incomplete Repentance," *Jerusalem Post*, March 18, 1998.

15. "Radiomessaggio di sua Santità Pio Xii," December 24, 1942, http://www.vatican.va/holy_father/pius_xii/speeches/1942/documents/hf_p-xii_spe_19421224_radiomessage-christmas_it.html.

16. Palmieri-Billig, "Document Defends Pope Pius XII."

17. Elli Wohlgelernter, "A First Step to Repentance," *Jerusalem Post*, June 12, 1998.

18. While the Roman Catholic Church issued at least one statement in support of restitution, its leaders lent no direct assistance to ensure that such programs were enacted fairly. For more on the position of the Church in the early debates on Jewish restitution, see Michael Phayer, *The Catholic Church and the Holocaust, 1930–1965* (Bloomington: Indiana University Press, 2000), 194.

19. The full title is *Declaration on the Relation of the Church to Non-Christian Religions (Nostra Aetate)*; it was released on October 28, 1965. See http://www.vatican.va/archive/hist_councils/ii_vatican_council/documents/vat-ii_decl_19651028_nostra-aetate_en.html.

20. See Phayer, *The Catholic Church and the Holocaust*, 203–16.

21. Ibid., 214.

22. In 1974, the Church published formal guidelines for the implementation of *Nostra Aetate*. In 1985, it supplemented these guidelines with another statement, "Notes on the Correct Way to Present the Jews and Judaism in the Preachings and Catechesis in the Roman Catholic Church." See http://www.vatican.va/roman_curia/pontifical_councils/chrstuni/relations-jews-docs/rc_pc_chrstuni_doc_19820306_jews-judaism_en.html.

23. Genevieve Zubrzycki offers a probing treatment of this controversy in *The Crosses of Auschwitz: Nationalism and Religion in Post-Communist Poland* (Chicago: University of Chicago Press, 2006).

24. Peter Steinfels, "Beliefs," *New York Times*, April 3, 1999.

25. Quoted in "Israel and Vatican: Improper Request?," *New York Times*, November 7, 1998. Stuart Eizenstat also pressed the Vatican to open its archives so that historians could learn the fate of looted artworks and other assets plundered during the war.

See Jay Bushinsky, "Eizenstat Wants More Access to Information on Nazi Looting," *Jerusalem Post*, June 18, 1998.

26. My e-mail queries to Seymour Reich, seeking clarification, went unanswered.

27. ICJHC, "The Vatican and the Holocaust: Preliminary Report on the Vatican during the Holocaust," October 2000, http://www.jewishvirtuallibrary.org/jsource /Holocaust/vatrep.html.

28. Quoted in Dimitri Cavalli, "The Commission That Couldn't Shoot Straight," *New Oxford Review* 69 (July/August 2002): 33–39.

29. Quoted in ibid.

30. See Marilyn Henry, "Jewish, Catholic Scholars Convene on Vatican's WWII Role," *Jerusalem Post*, December 9, 1999. Wistrich promised: "This is not a tribunal passing a verdict. That is not our brief or approach. The idea of pronouncing those kinds of dramatic verdicts is not a historian's task." Marrus asserted that the commission's research would be "an open inquiry that leaves behind the polemics and caricatures."

31. Michael Marrus, e-mail correspondence with author, June 22, 2005.

32. Ibid.

33. Phayer, *The Catholic Church and the Holocaust*; Paul O'Shea, *A Cross Too Heavy: Pope Pius XII and the Jews of Europe* (New York: Palgrave Macmillan, 2011).

34. Phayer, *The Catholic Church and the Holocaust*, xv.

35. Ibid.

36. Berel Lang takes more or less the same approach in "'Not Enough' vs. 'Plenty': Which Did Pius XII Do?," *Judaism* 50, no. 4 (2001): 448–52. Regarding Pius and the debates that have clouded his legacy, Lang writes: "It may well be (it almost certainly is) that Pius XII did not do enough and yet that he did a great deal" (448).

37. ICJHC, "The Vatican and the Holocaust," emphasis mine.

38. O'Shea, "The Vatican, the Holocaust, and the Archives."

39. Ronald J. Rychlak, "A Response to 'The Vatican and the Holocaust,'" was originally posted online in November 2002 by the Catholic League for Religious and Civil Rights. See http://www.catholicculture.org/culture/library/view.cfm?id=3098& CFID=32012285&CFTOKEN=64765173.

40. Documents from the Vatican archive are normally made available to the public after a period of seventy-five years. In some cases, the Vatican has taken longer to prepare documents for academic study. According to Paul O'Shea, the Vatican pledged to release all files from the papacy of Pius XII in 2014; however, that has not happened as of the time of this writing.

41. O'Shea, "The Vatican, the Holocaust, and the Archives."

42. *Akten Deutscher Bischöfe über die Lage der Kirche, 1933–1945*, cited in ibid.

43. While O'Shea does not offer details on what, specifically, constituted such "intervention," the source material in the *ADSS* strongly suggests that intervention entailed a flurry of letter writing.

44. Quoted in O'Shea, "The Vatican, the Holocaust, and the Archives."

45. Ibid.

46. Ariella Lang, who worked as a research assistant for the ICJHC, published an insightful study on "Aryan rhetoric" and the linguistic style of the *ADSS*. See Ariella Lang, "The Politics and Poetics of Vatican Holocaust Discourse," *Judaism* 52, nos. 3–4 (2003): 216–24.

47. See "Catholic-Jewish Scholars Panel Suspends Study of Holy See's Archival Material, Citing Lack of 'Positive' Response from the Vatican," July 22, 2001, http://www.bc.edu/content/dam/files/research_sites/cjl/texts/cjrelations/news/ijcic.htm.

48. ICJHC, "The Vatican and the Holocaust."

49. Ibid., emphasis mine.

50. Quoted in Henry, "Jewish, Catholic Historians Convene on Vatican's WWII Role."

51. Ibid.

52. See Rory Carroll, "Pope Says Sorry for Sins of Church," *Guardian*, March 13, 2000.

53. See R. Scott Appleby, *The Ambivalence of the Sacred: Religion, Violence, and Reconciliation* (Lanham, MD: Rowman and Littlefield, 2000), 293. Appleby argues that reconciliation depends on the ability of rivals to find a mutually intelligible vocabulary that minimizes the friction between sacred convictions and secular curiosity.

54. Tullia Zevi, the president of the Federation of Italian Jewish Communities, gave "We Remember" a more generous reading than most others. "One must know [the Church's] language," Zevi said in March 1998, "and if it speaks of *teshuva* [repentance] that means it recognizes past errors." Quoted in Palmieri-Billig, "Document Defends Pope Pius XII."

55. See James Warner, "Infallible Apologies," *SAIS Review of International Affairs* 25, no. 2 (2005): 67–68.

56. Ibid., 68.

57. "Vatican Archivists Rush to Declassify WWII Documents," *Catholic World News*, February 20, 2002.

58. Philip Pullella, "Pope Tells Jews He Is Committed to Good Relations," *Reuters*, June 9, 2005.

59. Cited in Stewart Ain and Steve Lipman, "Opening Wartime Archives?," *Jewish Weekly*, March 14, 2013. Skorka repeated this assertion in January 2014 following a visit to the Vatican several months earlier: "What we said to each other was between us, but I believe that, yes, he will open the archives." Quoted in John Follian, "Francis Searches for Secrets of Holocaust Pope," *Sunday Times* (London), January 19, 2014.

60. See Robert A. Ventresca, *Soldier of Christ: The Life of Pius XII* (Cambridge, MA: Belknap Press, 2013).

61. Published in March 1937, *Mit brennender Sorge* (With Burning Concern) criticized the Nazi regime for breaking its agreements with the Holy See and for promoting an ideology based on the supremacy of one race above all others. Michael Phayer (*The Catholic Church and the Holocaust*) offers important details on this encyclical, as does Frank J. Coppa in *The Life and Pontificate of Pius XII: Between History and Controversy* (Washington, DC: Catholic University of America Press, 2013).

62. Ventresca, *Soldier of Christ.*

63. "Vatican Stalls Jewish Bid for Truth on Nazi-Era Pope," *West Australian* (Perth), November 1, 2008.

64. Palmeri-Billig, "Document Defends Pope Pius XII."

65. Ibid.

66. Gordon Thomas, *The Pope's Jews: The Vatican's Secret Plan to Save Jews from the Nazis* (New York: Thomas Dunne, 2012).

67. Susan Zucotti, *Under His Very Windows: The Vatican and the Holocaust in Italy* (New Haven, CT: Yale University Press, 2002).

68. Hubert Wolf, *Pope and Devil: The Vatican Archives and the Third Reich*, trans. Kenneth Kronenberg (Cambridge, MA: Belknap Press, 2010), emphasis mine.

69. See, for example, Kevin P. Spicer, *Hitler's Priests: Catholic Clergy and National Socialism* (DeKalb: Northern Illinois University Press, 2008).

70. See Doris Bergen's review essay, "Speak of the Devil: Hubert Wolf on Pope Pius XI and the Vatican Archives," *Harvard Theological Review* 105, no. 1 (2012): 115–21.

71. This claim appears to have originated with Pinchas Lapide, whose book *Three Popes and the Jews* (New York: Hawthorn Books) was published in 1967. Lapide was a Jewish theologian and historian who served in the Israeli diplomatic corps as consul to Milan.

Conclusion

1. See, for example, Audrey Chapman and Patrick Ball, "The Truth of Truth Commissions: Comparative Lessons from Haiti, South Africa, and Guatemala," *Human Rights Quarterly* 23, no. 4 (2001): 1–42; Laurel E. Fletcher and Harvey M. Weinstein, "Violence and Social Repair: Rethinking the Contribution of Justice to Reconciliation," *Human Rights Quarterly* 24, no. 3 (2002): 573–639; David Mendeloff, "Truth-Seeking, Truth-Telling and Post-Conflict Peacebuilding: Curb the Enthusiasm?," *International Studies Review* 6, no. 3 (2004): 355–80; and Hugo van der Merwe, Victoria Baxter, and Audrey R. Chapman, eds., *Assessing the Impact of Transitional Justice: Challenges for Empirical Research* (Washington, DC: United States Institute of Peace, 2009).

2. Berber Bevernage, "Time, Presence, and Historical Injustice," *History and Theory* 48 (2008): 149–67. See also Bronwyn Anne Leebaw, "The Irreconcilable Goals of Transitional Justice," *Human Rights Quarterly* 30, no. 1 (2008): 95–118.

3. Thomas L. Haskell, "The Curious Persistence of Rights Talk in the Age of Interpretation," *Journal of American History* 74 (1987): 984–1012.

4. Friedrich Nietzsche, *On the Genealogy of Morals and Ecce Homo*, trans. Walter Kaufmann (New York: Vintage, 1989), *Genealogy*, essay 2, section 24, p. 95.

5. Perry Anderson, "On Emplotment: Two Kinds of Ruin," in *Probing the Limits of Representation: Nazism and the "Final Solution,"* ed. Saul Friedlander (Cambridge, MA: Harvard University Press, 1992), 54–65.

6. Andreas Hillgruber, *Zweierlei Untergang: Die Zerschlagung des Deutschen Reiches und das Ende des europäischen Judentums* (Berlin: W. J. Siedler, 1986).

7. Anderson, "On Emplotment," 57.

8. Hayden White, "Historical Emplotment and the Problem of Truth," in Friedlander, *Probing the Limits of Representation*, 37.

9. Amos Funkenstein, "History, Counterhistory, and Narrative," in ibid., 79.

10. The relevant scholarship is encapsulated in Peter Longerich, *Holocaust: The Nazi Persecution and Murder of the Jews* (Oxford: Oxford University Press, 2010). See, in particular, chaps. 1–13.

11. There has been good comparative work at the regional level, however. See, for example, Eva Clarita-Pettai and Vello Pettai, *Transitional and Retrospective Justice in the Baltic States* (Cambridge: Cambridge University Press, 2015). See also Ludi and Dreyfus, "Historians as Political Trouble-Shooters."

12. Robert Rotberg, "Apology, Truth Commissions, and Intrastate Conflict," in *Taking Wrongs Seriously: Apologies and Reconciliation*, ed. Elazar Barkan and Alexander Karn (Stanford: Stanford University Press, 2006), 33–49.

13. Teresa Godwin Phelps, *Shattered Voices: Language, Violence, and the Work of Truth Commissions* (Philadelphia: University of Pennsylvania Press, 2004).

14. Michael Shields, "Historians' Report Slams Swiss Wartime Policy," *Reuters News Service*, March 22, 2002.

15. Elazar Barkan, "Engaging History: Managing Conflict and Reconciliation," *History Workshop Journal* 59 (2005): 237. For a more recent perspective on the continuation of this trend, see Klaus Neumann, "Historians and the Yearning for Historical Justice," *Rethinking History* 18, no. 2 (2014): 145–64.

16. Charles Maier, "Doing History, Doing Justice: The Narrative of the Historian and the Truth Commission," in *Truth v. Justice: The Morality of Truth Commissions*, ed. Robert I. Rotberg and Dennis Thompson (Princeton, NJ: Princeton University Press, 2000), 270.

17. Ibid.

18. See chap. 5 in Marion Kaplan, *Between Dignity and Despair: Jewish Life in Nazi Germany* (Oxford: Oxford University Press, 1998).

19. In a recent discussion with Gross (2014), he described his concerns over the inadequacy of this exhumation. According to Gross, the IPN's Jedwabne study, which he admires and considers as vindication of his own work, is nevertheless flawed by its reliance on weak "scientific" evidence.

20. Danielle Celermajer, *Sins of the Nation and the Ritual of Apology* (Cambridge: Cambridge University Press, 2009).

21. Danielle Celermajer, "The Apology in Australia: Re-covenanting the National Imaginary," in Barkan and Karn, *Taking Wrongs Seriously*, 153–84.

22. Jan Gross, *Golden Harvest: Events at the Periphery of the Holocaust* (Oxford: Oxford University Press, 2012), 17.

23. See Yad Vashem, "Righteous Among the Nations Honored by Yad Vashem by

1 January 2015"; for the complete list of names, see http://www.yadvashem.org/yv/en/righteous/statistics/germany.pdf.

24. Both sides of the debate are richly explored in Thomas Childers and Jane Kaplan, *Reevaluating the Third Reich* (New York: Holmes and Meier, 1993).

25. Armond White, "Can't Trust It," *cityArts* (New York), October 16, 2013.

26. Rupert Cornwell, "Steve McQueen's Acclaimed film *12 Years a Slave* Is Brutal in Its Honesty. But Is It Too Much for American Audiences?," *Independent* (London), January 10, 2014.

27. Quoted in ibid.

28. Cf. Saul Friedlander, introduction to *Probing the Limits of Representation*, 20. He writes: "The documentary material itself often carries the story of minute incidents which seem to escape the overwhelming dimension of the overall catastrophe."

29. See chap. 6 for detailed analysis.

30. See chap. 7 for more on recent historiography.

31. See chap. 14 in Peter Novick, *That Noble Dream: The "Objectivity Question" and the American Historical Profession* (Cambridge: Cambridge University Press, 1988).

32. See chap. 5 in this study.

33. Lucy Dawidowicz, "How They Teach the Holocaust," in *What Is the Use of Jewish History?*, ed. Neal Kozody (New York: Schocken, 1992), 65–83.

34. Ibid., 77.

35. Cf. Facing History's unit on "Decision-Making in Times of Injustice," available at https://www.facinghistory.org/for-educators/educator-resources/lessons-and-units/decision-making-times-injustice-unit.

36. Rotberg, "Apology, Truth Commissions, and Intrastate Conflict," 40.

37. Thomas L. Haskell, "Objectivity Is Not Neutrality: Rhetoric vs. Practice in Peter Novick's *That Noble Dream*," *History and Theory* 29, no. 2 (1990): 129–57.

38. See chap. 4, n. 32.

39. See, for example, Louise Mallinder, "Can Amnesties and International Justice be Reconciled?," *International Journal of Transitional Justice* 1 (2007): 208–30.

40. David Crocker, "Punishment, Reconciliation, and Democratic Deliberation," in Barkan and Karn, *Taking Wrongs Seriously*, 68–69.

41. Novick, *That Noble Dream*, 2.

42. Haskell, "Objectivity Is Not Neutrality," 132.

43. C. Maier, "Doing History, Doing Justice," 274.

Index

apologist discourse, 67, 73, 86, 137, 207, 231

apology discourse: Austria and, 89; Czech-German bilateral relations and, 182; France and, 33–34, 40, 44–45, 233; Lithuania and, 134, 138; Polish-German bilateral relations and, 156, 166; Switzerland and, 49–50, 233, 269n59; Vatican and, 210–11, 221–22

Appleby, R. Scott, 299n53

Arad, Yitzhak, and affair, 130, 133, 135–36, 139–40, 284n26, 284n32

archival documentation: Anselmi Commission and, 116; CHL and, 286n63; historical commissions' clarification of, 16; ICHEIC and, 200–203; ICJHC and, 215–20, 224, 225; insurance assets/claims and, 192, 201–2, 295n43; in Latvia, 144; Mattéoli Commission and, 35, 37, 39–40, 266n11; Vatican and, 208–12, 215–16, 218, 222–26, 297n25, 298n40, 299n59; Vichy government and, 35, 37, 266n11

Argentina, 18, 223, 281n133

Armenian-Turkish case, 13, 16

artworks looted and stolen, 90, 276n20

Aryanization (Jewish spoliation). *See* banking practices and accusations; insurance assets and claims; Jewish spoliation (Aryanization); *specific commissions and countries*

assets, Holocaust-era. *See* Jewish spoliation (spoliation, Jewish or Aryanization)

Assicurazione Generali (Generali), 192–93, 195–96, 198, 201, 204–5, 281n125, 293n5

Austria: Anschluss in 1938 and, 88–90, 95, 98–99, 103–4, 278n55; anti-Semitism and, 88; apology discourse and, 89; artworks looted/stolen and, 90, 276n20; Austrian victimhood and, 87–90, 94; Catholic Church and, 88; civil society/organizations' assistance in, 91–92, 276n27; collective guilt and, 88; commemoration of Holocaust in, 92, 104; compensation funds/payments and, 89, 93, 100–101; concentration camps in, 101; deportee documentation/compensation and, 95; dignity of human beings discourse and, 97, 241; external pressures and, 90, 253; the Far Right and, 89, 105, 253; historical

commissions' contributions and, 15; Holocaust denial and, 105; Israel's bilateral relations with, 88–89, 275n13; Jewish population in, 94–95; Jewish spoliation and, 88, 93–95, 205, 241; Kristallnacht pogrom and, 88, 97, 102, 241; KVSG and, 100; liberal democratic discourse and, 253; methodology and, 92, 276n27; Moscow Declaration in 1943 and, 88, 94, 275n6; national identity/myths and, 87–88; national myth and, 87–88; Nazi racial policy and, 88, 100, 241; politics of history and, 89–90, 100, 275n14; racial cleansing actions and, 88, 90; resistance myth and, 88; responsibility for historical injustices and, 88–89, 275n6; restitution documentation/settlements and, 88–89, 91–93, 98–100, 273n31, 278n53; Settlement Fund Act in 1961 and, 100; slave labor documentation/settlements and, 89; SS and, 105; Third Restitution Act in 1947 and, 98; transitional justice and, 90–91; Victims Welfare Act in 1947 and, 100, 278n53; Waldheim affair and, 87–88, 275n2; Washington Agreement and, 100–101, 104; World War I and, 95. *See also* Jabloner Commission (Historikerkommission)

AXA, 196, 293n9

Backer, David, 274n64

Ball, Patrick, 229

Baltic states: anti-Semitism in, 127, 147; "double genocide" narrative and, 127–28, 130, 137, 141, 145, 282nn1–2; ethnonational communities in, 14; external pressures and, 128, 138, 253; Jew-communism myth and, 147; Jewish communists in, 146–47, 287n69; Jewish memories and, 127, 145; NATO and, 128, 138, 253; Nazi occupation/collaborators and, 127–30, 134, 141–42, 283n11, 284n22, 285n50; Nazi occupation of, 127; "parallel fates" narrative in, 127–28; post–Cold War era and, 127; Soviet Russia's occupation of, 127, 144–46, 148. *See also specific states*

banking practices and accusations: in France, 36–37, 39–41, 43, 46–47, 253, 267nn33–34;

in Switzerland, 3, 49–51, 198–99, 206, 253, 268n22, 295n41; in U.S. lawsuits/settlements with French banks, 41–42, 253, 267nn33–34. *See also* Jewish spoliation (spoliation, Jewish or Aryanization)

Barkan, Elazar, 262n31

Basic Principles and Guidelines on the Right to a Remedy and Reparation . . . , 21–23

Bauer, Yehuda, 210

Bazyler, Michael J., 294n37

beatification, 106, 209, 213, 279n79

Benedict XVI (pope), 222–23

Beneš decrees, 180–83, 186–88, 256, 292n77

Bergen, Doris, 225

Bergier, Jean-François, 5, 50–53, 55–56, 61, 239, 269n61. *See also* Independent Commission of Experts (ICE, Bergier Commission)

Bergier Commission (Independent Commission of Experts, ICE). *See* Independent Commission of Experts (ICE, Bergier Commission)

Berlusconi, Silvo, 123

Bevernage, Berber, 229

bilateral relations and commissions, 5, 15, 255–56. *See also* Czech-German bilateral relations; French-German bilateral relations; Polish-German bilateral relations

Blet, Pierre, 208–9

Bonjour, Edgar, 48

Borodziej, Włodzimierz, 169–70

Bosnia-Herzegovina, 8, 72, 274n64

Bousquet, René, 38

Brandt, Willy, 156, 166

Brauzauskas, Algirdas, 134, 143

brava gente (good and decent people) concept, 106, 109–10, 112–13

Bund der Vertriebenen (German League of Expellees/German Expellees Federation/Germany's Federation of Expellees), 168–69, 171

Bush, George W., 206

Cassidy, Edward Idris, 211–13, 215, 218, 224

Catholic Church diocese: apologists and, 207; bishops' apology/ies and, 224; Catholic victimhood/rescues and, 210, 217, 226–27;

Jewish victimhood/rescues by, 88, 224; Polish "Pastoral Letter" and, 167–68, 174; resistance efforts and, 226

Celermajer, Danielle, 244

Center Against Expulsions, Germany, 173, 179, 250

Centro Primo Levi (CPL), 106–8, 279n83, 279n85, 279n87

Chapman, Audrey R., 229

Chile, 18

Chirac, Jacques, 33–34, 42, 44–45, 157, 233–34, 237, 239, 243, 265n6

CHL (Commission of the Historians of Latvia). *See* Commission of the Historians of Latvia (CHL); Latvia

Cimoszewicz, Włodzimierz, 69

civil society/organizations: Anselmi Commission's assistance from, 116–17, 120, 281n125; in Austria, 91–92, 276n27; Czech-German bilateral relations and, 190, 292n85; external pressures and, 254; France and, 234; historical commissions initiatives from, 5, 13, 15; ICHEIC assistance from, 117; ICL and, 131; intergroup relationships and, 17, 243; Jedwabne pogrom in context of, 72, 75–76, 80, 92; Mattéoli Commission assistance from, 40–42, 46–47, 91, 267n37; moral judgments and, 234

CIVS (Commission for the Compensation of Victims of Spoliation Resulting from Anti-Semitic Legislation, Drai Commission), 35, 37, 42–44, 118, 123, 233–34, 253

Claims Conference (Conference on Jewish Material Claims Against Germany), 3, 101, 118, 193, 293n8

Clark, Janine, 274n64

coal and steel industry, in Europe, 155, 174

Cold War and post–Cold War era, 4, 12, 55, 109, 127, 155, 167, 236

collective guilt, 72–73, 80, 82, 88. *See also* responsibility for historical injustices (guilt)

Colombo, Furio, 110

commemoration sites, for war crimes, 141, 143, 285n45

commemorations of Holocaust: Anselmi Commission and, 118, 123; Austria and, 92, 104; France and, 34, 42, 47; in Israel, 47, 56–57, 105–6, 226, 245, 279n81; rescuers/heroic activities discourse and, 106, 108, 279n81; righteous gentiles list and, 47, 56–57, 105, 226, 245. *See also* Holocaust (Shoah)

Commission for the Compensation of Victims of Spoliation Resulting from Anti-Semitic Legislation, Drai Commission (CIVS), 35, 37, 42–44, 118, 123, 233–34, 253

Commission of the Historians of Latvia (CHL): overview and evaluation of, 15, 128, 144–51, 232, 282n5, 286nn59–61; archival documentation and, 286n63; counterhistory and, 232; genocidal intent and, 147–48, 287n75; historians' mediation of history and, 28, 145–46, 148–51, 234, 288n89, 288n92; intergroup relationships and, 145, 151; intersubjective agreement/disagreement and, 28, 144–45, 148–50; Jewish-Latvian communists and, 146–47, 287n69; Latvians' role in Holocaust and, 145–48, 232; memories of World War II and, 145, 231–32; methodology and, 144, 149, 286n60; multivocal/rival narratives and, 149; Nazi German occupation and, 144–48; "Occupation, Collaboration, Resistance . . ." conference and, 145, 150, 231–32, 288n89; publications of, 131, 144–48; responsibility for historical injustices and, 145, 232–34; right to history and, 28; SD and, 148; Soviet Russia's occupation and, 144–46, 148; SS and, 146. *See also* Latvia

communism: Jew-communism myth and, 83, 132, 139–40, 147, 285n40; Jewish-Latvian communists and, 146–47, 287n69; Pius XII and, 214, 227; Poland and, 64–66, 83; Polish-German bilateral relations and, 168; Vatican and, 225

compensation funds and payments: historical commissions and, 18; Internet websites and, 19; Jabloner Commission and, 90, 93, 97–98; Mattéoli Commission and,

44; national, 43–48, 89, 93, 100–101; Nazi slave labor documentation/settlements and, 89, 93–94, 101, 117–19, 206, 273n31; Switzerland and, 13

concentration camps, 47–48, 87, 101, 107, 110, 120, 126, 187. *See also* death/extermination camps

Conference on Jewish Material Claims Against Germany (Claims Conference), 3, 101, 118, 193, 293n8

cosmopolitanism, 31, 162, 184–85

counterhistory, 231–32, 234, 240. *See also* history

CPL (Centro Primo Levi), 106–8, 279n83, 279n85, 279n87

Czech-German bilateral relations: overview and history of, 155, 180, 190–91; apology discourse and, 182; Beneš decrees and, 180–83, 186–88, 256, 292n77; civil society/organizations role in, 190, 292n85; cosmopolitanism and, 184–85; Czech-German Historians Commission and, 186–90, 291n74; "Declaration on Mutual Relations . . ." in 1997 and, 182; diplomatic activities and, 181–83, 186, 188, 255–56; ethnonational communities and, 184–85; European Union accession and, 181–83, 188, 255–56; expulsions/confiscations lawsuits and, 188–89, 292n77; expulsions of Sudeten Germans discourse and, 30, 180–82, 187–90, 292n77, 292n85; German-Czech Textbook Commission and, 183–84; human rights discourse and, 185, 188–89; Jewish spoliation and, 181, 292n77; justice/injustices and, 180–81; mediation of history and, 181, 183–85, 187; memories and, 187; national identity/myths and, 184–86; partisan discourse and, 190; politics of history and, 181–84; the Resistance in Czechoslovakia and, 187; responsibility for historical injustices and, 187–88; restitution documentation/settlements and, 188–89, 292n77; symbolism and, 257–58; textbooks/teachers guidelines and, 180, 183–86, 291n70

Czech-German Historians Commission, 186–90, 291n74

Daly, Erin, 263n38
Dawidowicz, Lucy, 250–51
Day of Memory (*Il giorno della memoria*), 110, 113, 123
DBPJ (Declaration of Basic Principles of Justice for Victims of Crime and Abuse of Power), 21–22
death/extermination camps, 39, 69, 95. *See also* concentration camps
death statistics: ethnonational communities and, 282n2; Jewish, 82–83, 108, 128, 141, 274n54, 279n90, 282n2, 285n45
De Baets, Antoon, 23
Declaration of Basic Principles of Justice for Victims of Crime and Abuse of Power (DBPJ), 21–22
"Declaration on Mutual Relations . . ." in 1997, 182
De Felice, Renzo, 113
de Gaulle, Charles, 33, 35, 45–46, 155–56
Delamuraz, Jean-Pascal, 3
deportee documentation and compensation: Anselmi Commission and, 117–19, 118, 125–26; Austria and, 95; insurance assets/claims and, 192; Italy and, 46, 107–8, 110–12, 280n104; Jabloner Commission and, 95; Mattéoli Commission and, 37–38, 46, 266n22; Slovakian Jews and, 217, 298n43; Vichy government and, 33–34, 37–38, 40, 46–50, 192, 243, 265n2, 265nn6–7
Derrida, Jacques, 6, 10
Deutsche Nationalsozialistische Arbeiterpartei, German National Socialist Workers Party (DNSAP), 96
Diggelmann, Jakob, 54–55
dignity of human beings (public degradation) discourse, 24, 26, 52, 97, 121–22, 203–4, 241
Diner, Dan, 235, 262n32
diplomatic activities: bilateral commissions and, 176; Czech-German bilateral relations and, 181–83, 186, 188, 255–56; French-German bilateral relations and, 162–63; ICHEIC and, 205–6; of Pius XII, 223, 225; Polish-German bilateral relations and, 166, 171, 173, 179, 249; of Vatican, 209, 214–16, 219, 223, 226
Dmitrov, Edmund, 79

DNSAP (Deutsche Nationalsozialistische Arbeiterpartei, German National Socialist Workers Party), 96
Dominican Republic, 57, 239–40
Donskis, Leonidas, 128
"double genocide" narrative, 127–28, 130, 137, 141, 145, 282nn1–2. *See also* "parallel fates" narrative
Drauschke, Frank, 200
Drljača, Simo, 8, 252, 260n16
Dulles, Allen, 48

Eagleburger, Lawrence S., 194–99, 293n12, 294n40
ECHR (European Court of Human Rights), 47–48, 188–89
economic damage documentation, 91–97, 115, 277n33
educational projects: Anselmi Commission and, 118; France and, 42, 47; historical commissions and, 26; ICE and, 61; ICL and, 130, 138–40; Mattéoli Commission and, 46–47; Switzerland and, 59–61; Yad Vashem and, 47, 138
Eidintas, Alfonsas, 134
Eizenstat, Stuart, 4, 297n25
elite versus grassroots perspectives, 134–37, 139, 284n25
El Salvador, 18
Élysée Treaty in 1963, 155–57, 166, 174
epiphenomenal negotiations, 174
Estonia, 128, 282nn1–2, 282n5
ethnic and racial cleansing actions, 79, 81–82, 88, 90, 120, 129, 141, 230
ethnonational communities: Anselmi Commission and, 119; in Baltic states, 14; bilateral relations/commissions and, 221, 254; Czech-German bilateral relations and, 184–85; Gross on Jedwabne pogrom and, 72, 75; historical commissions and, 15, 245; IPN's Jedwabne pogrom study and, 75, 83; racial cleansing actions and, 79, 81–82, 88, 90, 120, 129, 141, 230–31; responsibility for historical injustices and, 72
European Court of Human Rights (ECHR), 47–48, 188–89

European integration and future, 155–56. *See also* Czech-German bilateral relations; French-German bilateral relations; Germany (Federal Republic of Germany); historical commissions (Holocaust historical commissions); Polish-German bilateral relations

European Union: overview and history of, 174, 182–83, 253; Czech-German bilateral relations and, 181–83, 188, 255–56; historical commissions and, 15, 253; responsibility for historical injustices and, 89, 117, 128, 136, 138, 156; textbooks on common history and, 162

Evian Conference in 1938, 57, 239–40

exculpation, 5–6, 19, 39, 75, 198, 201, 205, 210

expulsions discourse: Center Against Expulsions and, 173, 179, 250; Polish border, 168–71, 173, 178–80, 290n42; Sudetenland/ern, 30, 180–82, 187–90, 292n77, 292n85

extermination/death camps, 39, 69, 95. *See also* concentration camps

external pressures: overview of, 253–54; Anselmi Commission and, 117; Austria and, 90, 253; Baltic states and, 128, 138, 253; civil society/organizations and, 254; ICE and, 62; Jabloner Commission and, 90; Lithuania and, 136–37, 254; NATO and, 128, 138, 165, 253; NGOs and, 42, 193–94, 254, 293n8; performativity and, 253; Switzerland and, 62. *See also* European Union; United States

Fagan, Edward, 194

the Far Right, 39, 62, 89, 105, 138, 161, 253

Federal Republic of Germany (Germany). *See* Czech-German bilateral relations; French-German bilateral relations; GDR (German Democratic Republic, East Germany); Germany (Federal Republic of Germany); Nazism and Nazi Germany; Polish-German bilateral relations; West Germany

Federal Republic of Yugoslavia (formerly Yugoslavia), 8, 13–14, 18

Federation of Jewish Communities, Switzerland, 55, 269n69

Feldman, Gerald D., 201, 203, 295n46

Feldman, Lily Gardner, 176

Final Solution, 36, 141, 209, 216–17, 227

Fish, Stanley, 261n20

Fiume (now Rijek, Croatia), 106–7, 279n81, 279n85, 279n87

Fleishner, Eva, 212, 218

FMS (Foundation for the Memory of the Shoah), 36, 41, 43, 47, 118

Fogarty, Gerald, 212

forgetting, ritual (ritual forgetting), 65–66, 83–84. *See also* memory/ies

Foucault, Michel, 6

Foundation for the Memory of the Shoah (FMS), 36, 41, 43, 47, 118

Foxman, Abraham, 210

FPÖ (Freiheitliche Partei Österreichs, Freedom Party of Austria), 89–90, 104–5, 181–82, 253, 275n14

France: anti-Semitism in, 39; apology discourse and, 33–34, 40, 44–45, 233; banking practices and accusations in, 36–37, 39–41, 43, 46–47, 253, 267nn33–34; Catholic Church's apology in, 224; civil society/organizations and, 234; CIVS and, 35, 37, 42–44, 118, 123, 233–34, 253; commemoration of Holocaust in, 34, 42, 47; compensation funds and payments and, 43–48; ECHR on reparations in, 47–48; educational projects and, 42, 47; the Far Right and, 39; historical commissions and, 15, 262n31; human rights discourse and, 40; Israel's bilateral relations with, 47; Jewish community leaders in, 42, 267n37; Jewish refugee policies and, 57; the Left and, 39; liberal democratic discourse and, 45; moral judgments and, 234; pacifist movements and, 39; parenthesis theory and, 33–34, 36, 45, 48; reparations claims/payments and, 35, 47–48; the Resistance in, 33, 265n7, 266n22; resistance myth and, 33–34, 46, 88; restitution documentation/settlements and, 43–44, 253; righteous gentiles and, 47; self-image/self-understanding and, 244;

U.S. banking practices lawsuits and, 41–42, 253, 267nn33–34. *See also* Mattéoli Commission (Study Mission on the Spoliation of Jews); Vichy government

France-Israel Foundation, 47

Francis (pope), 223–24

Franco-German Historians Commission in 1935, 163–65

Free France, 35, 45–46. *See also* France; Vichy government

free speech, and history, 7, 260n12

Freiheitliche Partei Österreichs (FPÖ, Freedom Party of Austria), 89–90, 104–5, 181–82, 253, 275n14

French-German bilateral relations: overview/history of relations and, 39, 155–57, 166, 174; cosmopolitanism and, 162; diplomatic activities and, 162–63; divided/divergent memories and, 166; Élysée Treaty in 1963 and, 155–57, 166, 174; the Far Right and, 39, 161; Franco-German Historians Commission and, 163–65; *Histoire/Geschichte* textbook initiative and, 157–62, 164, 173–74, 267n27; historians' mediation of history and, 164; the Left and, 39, 160; liberal democratic discourse and, 159–60; mediation of history and, 25, 161, 164; memories and, 160, 166; moral judgments and, 161; multivocal/rival narratives and, 159–60; national identity/myths and, 161–64, 166; NATO and, 165; objectivity and, 161; partisan discourse and, 159, 161; politics of history and, 160–61, 164–65; reparations claims/payments and, 164; responsibility for historical injustices and, 159–60, 164–65, 253; right to history and, 25; symbolism and, 158; textbooks/textbook revisions and, 157–64, 166, 173–74, 267n27

Friedlander, Saul, 5, 302n28

Funkenstein, Amos, 231

Garamendi, John, 195, 293n12

GDR (German Democratic Republic, East Germany), 158–59, 167, 171. *See also* Germany (Federal Republic of Germany)

GEI (Georg Eckert Institute for International Textbook Research), 177, 291n58

Geiss, Peter, 157–60

Generali (Assicurazione Generali), 192–93, 195–96, 198, 201, 204–5, 281n125, 293n5

General Settlement Fund (GSF), 100–101, 104

genocide and genocidal intent: CHL and, 147–48, 287n75; Final Solution and, 36, 141, 209, 216–17, 227; genocide defined and, 282n5; Gross on Jedwabne pogrom and, 78–79, 273n42; Jabloner Commission and, 94, 277n33; Poland and, 82. *See also* Nazism and Nazi Germany

Gentile, Emilio, 113

Georg Eckert Institute for International Textbook Research (GEI), 177, 291n58

Gérin, René, 39

German-Czech Textbook Commission, 183–84

German Democratic Republic (GDR, East Germany), 158–59, 167, 171. *See also* Germany (Federal Republic of Germany)

German League of Expellees/German Expellees Federation/Germany's Federation of Expellees (Bund der Vertriebenen), 168–69, 171

German victimhood: Soviet Russia's ethnic cleansing activities and, 230–31; Sudetenland/ern expulsions discourse and, 30, 180–82, 187–90, 292n77, 292n85

Germany (Federal Republic of Germany): Allianz insurance and, 192–93, 195–96, 198, 201, 204–5, 281n125, 293n9; bilateral relations with, 170; Catholic Church's apology in, 224; Center Against Expulsions in, 173, 179, 250; Holocaust denial in, 260n12; Israel's restitution settlement with, 155; Polish-German bilateral relations and, 170; Remembrance, Responsibility, and the Future Fund and, 101, 118–19; restitution documentation/settlements and, 99, 155, 277n49; righteous gentiles as German and, 245; slave labor documentation/settlements and, 118–19; textbooks/textbook revisions and, 167. *See also* Czech-German bilateral relations; French-German bilateral relations; GDR (German Democratic Republic,

Germany (*continued*)
East Germany); Nazism and Nazi Germany; Polish-German bilateral relations; West Germany
Gestapo, 65, 69, 79, 96–97, 141, 285n50
Il giorno della memoria (Day of Memory), 110, 113, 123
Gomułka, Władysław, 65, 168
good and decent people (*brava gente*) concept, 106, 109–10, 112–13
Gordon, Robert, 110
Graham, Robert, 208–9
grassroots versus elite perspectives, 134–37, 139, 284n25
Gross, Jan, *Neighbors: The Destruction of the Jewish Community in Jedwabne, Poland*: overview of, 84–85; accusatory narratives and, 68, 75, 81–82; anti-Semitism and, 67–68, 78, 147; apologist discourse and, 73; civic society in Poland's role and, 72, 75–76, 92; collective guilt and, 72–73, 82; ethnonational communities and, 72, 75; genocidal intent and, 78–79, 273n42; group identities and, 71–73, 243–45, 272n34; historians' mediation of history and, 70–71; IPN's Jedwabne pogrom study exhumation data and, 242, 301n19; Jewish anti-Polonism and, 71; Jewish collaboration with Soviet Russia and, 67, 71, 147; Jewish death statistics and, 82–83; Jewish identity and, 71–72, 243–45; Jewish memories and, 73; Jewish victimhood and, 66–68, 78, 81; "large-scale quantifiers" and, 71–72, 244–45; lawsuits/settlements and, 75; mediation of history and, 70–71, 73, 75; methodology and, 70; Nazi occupation and, 64–65, 79, 273n42, 273n44; objectivity and, 85; partisan discourse and, 64, 76–77, 245; Poles as victimizers and, 68–69; Polish collaboration with Soviet Russia and, 67, 71; Polish identity and, 71–72, 243–45; Polish memories and, 73; Polish victimhood and, 66, 68–69, 71, 272n34; politics of history and, 69–70; reconciliation and, 73; responsibility for historical injustices and, 72, 75–76, 272n34; right

to history and, 73; ritual forgetting and, 69; Soviet Russia's occupation and, 64, 67, 71, 147; thick description and, 76–77, 242; universality versus particularity and, 68, 80–82, 242–43; on World War II history of Poland, 272n20. *See also* IPN's Jedwabne pogrom study; Poland
group identity/ies: Gross on Jedwabne pogrom and, 72–73, 272n34; history and, 7, 243–45; individual identities/experiences versus, 110, 115–16, 124–26; Jewish, 71–72, 243–45; "large-scale quantifiers" and, 71–72, 124, 244–45; Polish identity and, 71–72, 243–45
GSF (General Settlement Fund), 100–101, 104
Guatemala, 18, 27
guilt (responsibility for historical injustices). *See* justice/injustices, historical; responsibility for historical injustices (guilt)
Guisan, Henri, 56, 239

Habermas, Jürgen, 185
The Hague, 47, 281n132
Haider, Jörg, 89–90, 104–5, 181–83, 253, 255–56, 275n14
Hajdenberg, Henri, 36–37, 266n17
Harjes, Kirsten, 165
Haskell, Thomas L., 251
Häsler, Alfred, 50
Havel, Václav, 181
Hilberg, Raul, 129
Hillgruber, Andreas, 230–31, 251–52
Histoire/Geschichte textbook initiative, 157–62, 164, 173–74, 267n27
historians: Holocaust historiography and, 230–31, 252; ICE and, 3; instrumental history and, 8–9, 250–51; intersubjective agreement/disagreement and, 12, 260n20; justice/injustices and, 5; "large-scale quantifiers" and, 71–72, 124–25, 244–45; narratives and, 250; objectivity and, 6, 11, 85, 249, 255, 256; partisan discourse and, 8–11; politics of history and, 6, 9, 30, 256; social sciences and, 9, 70, 250–51. *See also* history
historians' mediation of history: overview of, 10–12, 26–30, 251–52; CHL and, 28,

145–46, 148–51, 288n89, 288n92; French-German bilateral relations and, 164; Gross on Jedwabne pogrom and, 70–71; IPN's Jedwabne pogrom study and, 76, 80; Polish-German bilateral relations and, 173–75, 177, 185; Switzerland and, 63. *See also* history; mediation of history

historical commissions (Holocaust historical commissions): overview and evaluation of, 4, 12–17, 19–20, 206, 232, 238–39, 261nn23–24; archival documentation and, 16; challenges for, 234–36, 245, 249; civil society/organization initiatives and, 5, 13, 15; compensation funds/payments and, 18; dignity of human beings restoration and, 26; educational projects and, 26; epiphenomenal negotiations and, 174; ethnonational communities and, 15, 245; European Union and, 15, 253; historical redress and, 14, 16, 20–21; historiography and, 16–17; human rights discourse and, 4–5, 16–20, 30, 252; intergroup relationships and, 5, 16, 26, 234, 243–44; Internet websites and, 17–19, 252; on Jewish spoliation, 3–4; judicial/juridical framework and, 103, 215, 218; justice/injustices and, 16, 26; liberal democratic discourse and, 61, 243, 255; mediation of history and, 257; methodology and, 17, 26, 30, 254; moral judgments and, 26; multivocal/rival narratives and, 29–30; narratives and, 14–15, 29–30, 235, 262n32; objectivity and, 79–80, 246–47, 251–52, 256; partisan discourse and, 16, 29–30; political knowledge and, 5; politics of history and, 5, 14, 25–26, 30, 261n30; reconciliation and, 5, 14, 16–17, 26; reparations claims/payment and, 26; reparations/moral reparations and, 22, 26; responsibility for historical injustices and, 16, 18, 25–26; restitution documentation/settlements and, 26; right to history and, 255; symbolism and, 25, 158, 166, 172–73, 176, 255–58; thick description avoidance and, 76–77, 242, 246; transitional justice and, 4, 17–18; TRCs compared with, 18, 252–53; truth-telling

and, 18, 30, 234; victimhood and, 26, 30. *See also* Roman Catholic Church; *specific commissions and countries*

historical justice/injustices. *See* justice/injustices, historical

historical redress, 14, 16, 20–25, 46, 256

Historikerkommission (Jabloner Commission). *See* Austria; Jabloner Commission (Historikerkommission)

historiography: historical commissions and, 16–17; of Holocaust, 5, 14, 61, 207, 216, 230–31, 250–51, 252, 298n36; ICHEIC and, 199–206, 221, 295n46; insurance assets/claims and, 192, 201–3, 295n43, 295n46; justice/injustices and, 5; Pius XII and, 207, 216, 298n36; Polish-German bilateral relations and, 168–70, 290n36; Vatican and, 207–9, 221, 296n8; Vichy government and, 33–34, 36, 40, 45, 234, 237, 239

history: counterhistory and, 231–32, 240; free speech and, 7, 260n12; group identity and, 7, 243–45; history wars ,and, 7, 260n14; instrumental, 8–9, 250–51; intergroup relationships and, 7, 260nn12–14; multivocal/rival narratives and, 11; narratives and, 11, 256; partisan discourse and, 7–11, 251, 260n15; popular culture/public consciousness and, 6–7, 109, 234, 246–47; relativism and, 7–8, 57, 230–31, 250; reparations claims/payments and, 40; thick description and, 246–47. *See also* historians; historians' mediation of history; mediation of history; politics of history (history of politics); right to history

history of politics (politics of history). *See* history; politics of history (history of politics)

Hitler, Adolf, 64, 66, 88, 108, 157, 165, 187–88, 208, 216, 225–26. *See also* Nazism and Nazi Germany

Hochhuth, Rolf, 207, 214

Hodes, Paul, 254

Hollande, François, 265n6

Holocaust (Shoah): Baltic states and, 127, 282n1; cosmopolitanism and, 31; denial of, 7, 105, 140, 230, 260n12; description

Holocaust (*continued*)

of, 5; historiography of, 5, 14, 61, 207, 216, 230–31, 250–51, 252, 298n36; Italians' role in, 107–10, 120, 123, 125; Latvians' role in, 145–48, 232; Poles' role in, 65, 69, 80; popular culture/public consciousness and, 44–46; racial cleansing actions and, 230; transitional justice and, 17–18, 84, 90–91, 234, 274n64; transnational character of, 51, 58, 110–11, 279n90. *See also* commemoration/s of Holocaust; commemorations of Holocaust

Holocaust-Era Assets Working Group, 193, 293nn8–9

Holocaust historical commissions (historical commissions). *See* historical commissions (Holocaust historical commissions); Roman Catholic Church; *specific commissions and countries*

Holocaust studies, 250

human rights discourse: overview of, 20–21; Basic Principles and Guidelines on the Right to a Remedy and Reparation . . . and, 22–23; Czech-German bilateral relations and, 185, 188–89; DBPJ and, 22–23; dignity of human beings discourse and, 24; France and, 40; historical commissions and, 4–5, 16–20, 30, 252; historical redress nexus with, 20–25, 46, 256; international law and, 30; lawsuits/settlements and, 25, 47–48, 188–89; Mattéoli Commission and, 46, 244; multivocal/rival narratives and, 62; NGOs and, 20–21, 24; right to history and, 21–22, 24, 30; TRCs and, 18; UDHR and, 21–23, 292n17; universality versus particularity and, 20–21, 61; victimhood and, 23–24

IACHR (Inter-American Court of Human Rights), 25

ICE (Independent Commission of Experts, Bergier Commission). *See* Independent Commission of Experts (ICE, Bergier Commission); Switzerland

ICEP/Volcker Commission (Independent Commission of Eminent Persons), 198–99, 295n41

ICHEIC (International Commission on Holocaust-Era Insurance Claims). *See* International Commission on Holocaust-Era Insurance Claims (ICHEIC)

ICTY (International Criminal Tribunal for the Former Yugoslavia), 8

identity/ies. *See* group identity; individual identity/ies

IHJR (Institute for Historical Justice and Reconciliation), 13

Independent Commission of Eminent Persons (ICEP/Volcker Commission), 198–99, 295n41

Independent Commission of Experts (ICE, Bergier Commission): overview and findings of, 3, 5, 13, 50–52, 55–58, 60, 62–63, 90, 238–40, 259n2, 269n61; amending the past and, 56; anti-Semitism and, 54, 57; banking practices and accusations by, 3, 50–51, 253; counterhistory and, 240; dignity of human beings discourse and, 52; educational projects and, 61; external pressures and, 62; German threat of Swiss leniency and, 51–52, 60; historian' s role and, 3; Jewish refugee policies and, 52, 56, 269n66, 269n69; Jewish spoliation and, 50–51; Mattéoli Commission compared with, 236–40; moral judgments and, 53–55; Nazi economic relationship and, 50–51, 53–54; partisan discourse and, 58; politics of history and, 59, 62; questions/answers or openended discourse and, 55–56; refugee policies and, 50–52, 56, 269n66, 269n70; relativized victimhood and, 57; reparations claims/payments and, 54–55; rescuers/heroic activities discourse and, 56–57, 239, 270n93; resistance myth and, 53; restitution documentation/settlements and, 50–51, 54; righteous gentiles and, 56–57; Swiss neutrality myth and, 3–4, 50; textbook revisions and, 59–60; transnational character of Holocaust and, 51. *See also* Switzerland

individual identity/ies: Jewish identity and, 65–66, 71–72, 243–45; Polish identity and, 71–72, 243–45

Mattéoli Commission (*continued*)
and, 35–39, 42–44, 46, 91, 266n18; right
to history and, 36–37, 266n17; yellow
star regulation and, 38
Maurer, Ueli, 62, 271n106
Mayorek, Yoram, 200
mediation of history: overview of, 256–57; bilateral relations and, 25, 161, 164, 173–75,
177, 181, 183–85, 187, 245; Czech-German
bilateral relations and, 181, 183–85, 187;
Gross on Jedwabne pogrom and, 70–71,
73, 75; ICL and, 140–41; IPN's Jedwabne
pogrom study and, 74–77, 79–80, 86;
Italy and, 112; Japan and, 7, 19; Lithuania and, 143; moral judgments and, 215,
231; Norway and, 29–30; objectivity and,
251, 255; Pius XII and, 213–14, 224–26,
298n36; reconciliation and, 11; relativized history and, 255; social sciences and,
79; Switzerland and, 60, 63; textbooks/
textbook revisions and, 7, 19, 259n10;
Vatican and, 213–14, 224–27, 298n36.
See also historians' mediation of history;
history
Memorandum of Understanding (MOU),
and insurance assets/claims, 193–95
memory/ies: in Baltic states, 127, 145, 231–32;
CHL and, 145, 231–32; conflicts or "hot"
wars and, 7; Czech-German bilateral relations and, 187; divided/divergent, 82,
108–10, 112, 166, 254–55; French-German
bilateral relations and, 160, 166; International Conference for the Teaching of
History and, 163; Jewish, 65, 67, 73, 82,
127, 145; of Poles, 67, 73, 82; ritual forgetting versus, 65–66, 83–84; Switzerland and, 49
Mendeloff, David, 229
Merkel, Angela, 179, 292n82
methodology/ies: Anselmi Commission and,
114–16, 120; Austrian historical commissions and, 92, 276n27; CHL and, 144,
149, 286n60; Gross on Jedwabne pogrom and, 70; historical commissions
and, 17, 26, 30, 254; ICL and, 132–33,
149; TRCs and, 254
Michlic, Joanna, 65, 272n21

Mikoletzky, Lorenz, 90
Mitterrand, François, 34, 156, 265n7
moral judgments, 19, 26, 53–55, 161, 204, 214–
15, 231–34
moral relativism, 39, 46, 57–58, 80–81. *See also*
relativism
moral reparations. *See* reparations claims and
payments
moral responsibility. *See* responsibility for historical injustices (guilt)
Morley, John f., 212
Morocco, 18
Moscow Declaration in 1943, 88, 94, 275n6
MOU (Memorandum of Understanding),
and insurance assets/claims, 193–95
Müller, Michael G., 173, 175, 177
multiculturalism, 8, 62, 176, 251, 271n106
multivocal (rival) narratives: CHL and, 149;
French-German bilateral relations and,
159–60; historical commissions and, 29–
30; history and, 11; human rights discourse and, 62; ICHEIC and, 202–4;
ICL and, 133; insurance assets/claims
and, 193–94; justice/injustices and, 5–6;
Polish-German bilateral relations and,
169–70, 177; Vatican and, 214–15
Museo della Shoah, Italy (to date unopened),
111–13
Museum of Genocide Victims, Vilnius, 141–
42, 285n50
Mussolini, Benito, 107–9, 111, 113, 118, 120,
121

NAIC (National Association of Insurance
Commissioners), 193, 195, 197
Narodnyï Kommissariat Vnutrennikh Del,
People's Commissariat of Internal Affairs
(NKVD), 67, 78, 287n69
narratives: accusatory, 75, 81–82, 212, 218–20,
225–26, 298n30; historians and, 250; historical commissions and, 14–15, 29–30,
235, 262n32; history and, 11, 256. *See also*
multivocal (rival) narratives
National Association of Insurance Commissioners (NAIC), 193, 195, 197
national Holocaust commissions, 14–15. *See
also specific commissions and countries*

policy and, 66; "parallel fates" narrative in, 65–66, 127–28, 272n21; pogroms in, 78, 82, 83–84, 273n42; Poles as victimizers in, 68–69, 78, 80–82; Poles' role in Holocaust and, 65, 69, 80; Polish-Jewish relations and, 65–66, 75–76, 271n2; Polish memories and, 67, 82; Polish victimhood and, 66, 68, 78, 81, 272n20; racial cleansing actions and, 79, 81–82, 141; relativism and, 57–58; righteous gentiles and, 57; ritual forgetting in, 65–66, 83–84; Soviet Russia and, 64–65, 67, 71, 74–75, 77–78, 81, 147; Warsaw Ghetto (Heroes) Monument in, 65, 156, 166; World War II history in, 64–65, 272n20; "Zydokommunizm" myth and, 83. *See also* Gross, Jan, *Neighbors: The Destruction of the Jewish Community in Jedwabne, Poland*; IPN (Instytut Pamięci Narodowej, Institute of National Remembrance); IPN's Jedwabne pogrom study

Polish-German bilateral relations: overview and history of, 155–56, 166–68, 172–73, 249–50; apology discourse and, 156, 166; Cold War era and, 167; communism and, 168; diplomatic activities and, 166, 171, 173, 179, 249; ethnonational communities and, 168; expulsions of Germans discourse and, 168–71, 173, 178–80, 290n42; GDR and, 167, 171; Germany and, 170; historians' mediation of history and, 173–75, 177, 185; historiography and, 168–70, 290n36; mediation of history and, 173–75, 177, 185, 245; multiculturalism and, 176, 251; multivocal/rival narratives and, 169–70, 177; national identity/myths and, 178; partisan discourse and, 170; Polish-German Historians Commission and, 167–71, 173–76, 178–80, 183–84, 245, 249; Polish "Pastoral Letter" and, 167–68, 174; politics of history and, 168, 170–74, 178–79, 290n36; realpolitik and, 174, 176; the Resistance in Poland and, 168, 170; responsibility for historical injustices and, 168–69; SS and, 171; symbolism and, 166,

172–73; textbooks/teachers guidelines and, 169, 171–74, 177–80; Treaty of Warsaw and, 166–68, 174, 249; universality versus particularity and, 172

Polish-German Historians Commission (Joint Polish-German Commission of Historians and Geographers for the Revision of School Textbooks) in 1972, 167–71, 173–76, 178–80, 183–84, 245, 249

political knowledge, 5, 7, 72

politics of history (history of politics): Austria and, 89–90, 100, 275n14; Czech-German bilateral relations and, 181–84; the Far Right and, 39, 62, 89, 105, 138, 161, 253; French-German bilateral relations and, 160–61, 164–65; Gross on Jedwabne pogrom and, 69–70; historians and, 6, 9, 30; historical commissions and, 5, 14, 25–26, 30, 261n30; historical redress and, 20; ICE and, 59, 62; ICJHC and, 212; Internet websites and, 19; IPN's Jedwabne pogrom study and, 83; Italy and, 113, 119; Jabloner Commission and, 104–5; the Left and, 8, 39, 110, 160; Lithuania and, 132, 134, 138, 139; Polish-German bilateral relations and, 168, 170–74, 178–79, 290n36; relativized victimhood and, 169; Switzerland and, 3, 58–60; textbook revisions and, 251; truth-seeking and, 206. *See also* history

politics of knowledge, 5

Polonsky, Antony, 65, 272n21

Polska Zjednoczona Partia Robotnicza, Polish United Workers Party (PZPR), 65–66, 68

Poovey, Mary, 28–29

popular culture/public consciousness, 6–7, 33, 11–16, 109, 234, 246–47

post–Cold War and Cold War era, 4, 12, 55, 109, 127, 155, 167, 236

"Promotion and Protection of Human Rights: Impunity" report, 21, 24

Prost, Antoine, 35–36

public degradation (dignity of human beings) discourse, 24, 26, 52, 97, 121–22, 203–4, 241

PZPR (Polska Zjednoczona Partia Robotnicza, Polish United Workers Party), 65–66, 68

questions/answers (openended) discourse, 29, 55–56, 79, 214, 216, 218–19, 298n36

racial and ethnic cleansing actions, 79, 81–82, 88, 90, 120, 129, 141, 230
racial laws (*leggi razziali*), 108–9, 111, 114–15, 119–20, 282n137
racial policy, and Nazi Germany, 54, 66, 88, 100, 108, 241, 282n137
racial terminology, 119–20, 125
Rapoport, Nathan, 65
realpolitik, 174, 176, 253
reconciliation: overview of, 84, 274n64; Gross on Jedwabne pogrom and, 73; historical commissions and, 5, 14, 16–17, 26; mediation of history and, 11; transitional justice and, 84, 274n64; truth-seeking and, 256; truth-telling's link with, 18, 30, 229, 256, 263n38. *See also* bilateral relations and commissions; Czech-German bilateral relations; French-German bilateral relations; Polish-German bilateral relations; truth and reconciliation commissions (TRCs); *specific commissions*
redress, historical, 20–25, 46, 256
refugee policies: ICE and, 50–52, 56, 269n66, 269n70; Jewish, 49–50, 52, 56–57, 269n66, 269n69; Switzerland and, 49–50, 57, 269nn59–60; U.S., 50, 57
Reich (Third Reich). *See* Nazism and Nazi Germany
Reich, Seymour, 211–13, 215, 218, 254
Reich Citizens Act (*Reichsbürgergesetz*) in 1941, 95
relativism: history and, 7–8, 57, 230–31, 250; Holocaust historical commissions in context of postmodern, 58; ICL and, 137; IPN's Jedwabne pogrom study and, 80–81; Italy and, 111, 121; Mattéoli Commission and, 39, 46; moral, 39, 46, 57–58, 80–81; Poland and, 57–58; Switzerland and, 57–58
relativized victimhood and history, 57, 169, 255

Remembrance, Responsibility, and the Future Fund (Stiftung EVZ), 101, 118–19
Renner, Karl, 88, 98
Renouvin, Pierre, 164–65
reparations claims and payments: Anselmi Commission and, 121–22; ECHR on, 47–48; France and, 35, 47–48; French-German bilateral relations and, 164; historical commissions and, 22, 26; history and, 40; ICE and, 54–55; Mattéoli Commission and, 35–37, 39–41, 44–46, 122, 266n18; right to history and, 25, 40; symbolism of, 45; truth-seeking and, 25
Repubblica Sociale Italiana, Italian Social Republic (RSI), 106–7
rescuers/heroic activities discourse, 210, 217, 224, 226–27; Catholic diocese and, 88, 224; Catholic victimhood and, 210, 217, 226–27; commemorations in Israel of, 47, 56–57, 105–6, 226, 245, 279n81; ICE and, 56–57, 239, 270n93; Italy and, 105–8, 279n79, 279n82, 279n87; Jewish victimhood and, 88, 208, 210, 217–19, 224, 226, 298n36, 300n71; Jewish victimhood/rescues and, 208, 210, 217–19, 224, 226, 298n36, 300n71; Lithuania and, 142; Pius XII and, 208, 218–19, 224, 226, 298n36, 300n71; Vatican and, 106–8, 210, 217, 224, 226–27, 279n79; Yad Vashem database and, 106, 108
the Resistance/resistance efforts: Baltic states, 135–36, 143, 146; Catholic, 226; Czech, 187; French, 33, 265n7, 266n22; ICJHC and, 226; Italian, 113, 118, 125; Jewish fighters in, 135–36, 143, 284n26; in Nazi Germany, 168, 246; in Poland, 168, 170; resistance myths and, 33–34, 46, 53, 88, 108–9, 112–13
responsibility for historical injustices (guilt): Anselmi Commission and, 120–21, 123; Austria and, 88–89, 275n6; CHL and, 145, 232–34; collective guilt and, 72–73, 80, 82, 88; Czech-German bilateral relations and, 187–88; ethnonational communities and, 72; European Union and, 89, 117, 128, 136, 138, 156; French-German bilateral relations and, 159–60,

164–65; Gross on Jedwabne pogrom and, 72, 75–76, 272n34; historical commissions and, 16, 18, 25–26, 61–62, 246, 247; ICL and, 133; IPN's Jedwabne pogrom study and, 75–76, 79, 81, 244; Italy and, 109–11; Jabloner Commission and, 93, 103–4, 278n67; justice/injustices and, 5; Lithuania and, 134, 143–44, 284n22; Mattéoli Commission and, 41–42, 45, 233; Pius XII and, 215, 219; Polish-German bilateral relations and, 168–69; right to history and, 26; Switzerland and, 49; Vatican and, 209–11, 210–11, 215. *See also* justice/injustices, historical

restitution documentation and settlements: Anselmi Commission and, 117–18, 122–23, 282n137; Austria and, 88–89, 91–93, 98–100, 273n31, 278n53; Czech-German bilateral relations and, 188–89, 292n77; France and, 43–44; Germany and, 99, 155, 277n49; historical commissions and, 26; ICE and, 50–51, 54; Israel's settlements with Germany and, 155; Italy and, 114, 281n119; Jabloner Commission and, 90, 97–100; Mattéoli Commission and, 35–39, 42–44, 46, 91, 266n18; Norway and, 29; USHMM and, 4; Vatican and, 210, 297n18. *See also* insurance assets and claims

Right, the Far, 39, 62, 89, 105, 138, 161, 253

righteous gentiles, Yad Vashem, 47, 56–57, 105, 226, 245

right to history: overview of, 4–5, 30, 249; CHL and, 28; divided/divergent memories and, 254–55; French-German bilateral relations and, 25; Gross on Jedwabne pogrom and, 73; historical commissions and, 255; historical redress and, 23; as human right, 21–22, 24, 30; ICL and, 131; international law and, 25; justice/injustices and, 25–26; Lithuania and, 137, 143; Mattéoli Commission and, 36–37, 266n17; Norway and, 30; reparations claims/payments and, 25, 40; responsibility for historical injustices and, 26. *See also* historical commissions (Holocaust historical commissions); history

Rijek, Croatia (formerly Fiume), 106–7, 279n81, 279n85, 279n87

Ringelblum, Emanuel, 67

Ritter, Gerhard, 164–65

ritual forgetting (forgetting, ritual), 65–66, 83–84. *See also* memory/ies

rival (multivocal) narratives. *See* multivocal (rival) narratives

Roman Catholic Church (Vatican). *See* Catholic Church diocese; Vatican (Roman Catholic Church)

Rosewood riot, Florida, 13, 261n24

Roszkowski, Wojciech, 69–70, 160–61

Rotberg, Robert, 251

Royal Commissions, 252–53

RSI (Repubblica Sociale Italiana, Italian Social Republic), 106–7

Rudman, Mara, 294n40

Russo, Henry, 33–34

Rwanda, 19, 72

Rychlak, Ronald J., 215–16, 218

sacred convictions versus secular curiosity, 207, 221, 249, 299n53

Sarfatti, Michele, 115, 117–18

Schär, Bernhard, 59–61

Schmittlein, Raymond, 163

Schneider, Burkhart, 208–9

Schochat, Azreal, 147

Scholars' Initiative for the Former Yugoslavia, 13–14

Scholz, Adrienne, 293n20, 295n53

Schröder, Gerhard, 157, 173, 182–83

Schuman Plan of 1950, 155, 165

Schutzstaffel, Protection Squadrons (SS), 37, 49, 105, 110, 120, 129, 141, 146, 171

SD (Sicherheitsdienst, Security Service, or SS intelligence agency), 148, 232

Second Vatican Council (Vatican II), 210–11

secular curiosity versus sacred convictions, 207, 221, 249, 299n53

self-image/self-understanding, 107–9, 112–13, 120, 244

Senn, Alfred Erich, 146 49, 232, 287n69

Senn, Deborah, 195

Serbia, 8, 19

Settlement Fund Act in 1961, Austria, 100

269nn59–60; relativism and, 57–58; responsibility for historical injustices and, 49; righteous gentiles and, 56–57; SS and, 49; textbook revisions and, 59–61, 270n96; Washington Agreement and, 54. *See also* Independent Commission of Experts (ICE, Bergier Commission)

symbolism, and commissions, 25, 158, 166, 172–73, 176, 255–58, 257–58

Sznaider, Natan, 61

terms/terminology, and Anselmi Commission, 116, 119–20, 125

textbooks and textbook revisions: Czech-German bilateral relations and, 180, 183–86, 291n70; European Union and, 162; French-German bilateral relations and, 157–64, 166, 173–74, 267n27; in Germany, 167; ICE and, 59–60; League of Nations and, 162; mediation of history and, 7, 19, 259n10; multiculturalism and, 176, 251; objectivity and, 161; Polish-German bilateral relations and, 169, 171–74, 177–80; politics of history and, 251; Slovaks and, 291n70; social sciences and, 60, 160; Soviet, 167; Switzerland and, 59–61, 270n96; UNESCO and, 163, 167, 183

thick description, 76–77, 242, 246–47

Third Reich (Reich). *See* Nazism and Nazi Germany

Third Restitution Act in 1947, Austria, 98

Thomas, Gordon, 224

Timor-Leste, 18

Titho, Karl Friedrich, 120–21, 281n132

Tokarska-Bakir, Joanna, 70–71

Tokyo war crimes trials, 246

Traba, Robert, 177

transitional justice, 4, 17–18, 84, 90–91, 234, 236, 252, 274n64

transnational understandings of history, 51, 55, 58, 110–11, 279n90

TRCs (truth and reconciliation commissions): overview and contributions of, 12, 16, 18, 234–35, 252–53, 263n38; historical commissions compared with, 18, 252–53; historical concept of time and,

229; human rights abuses and, 18; judicial concept of time and, 229; liberal democratic discourse and, 255; methodology and, 254; objectivity and, 229–30; performativity and, 77, 235; reconciliation's link with truth and, 18, 30, 229, 263n38; South Africa and, 27, 77, 235; thick description and, 77; truth discourse and, 229–30; victims' suffering relief and, 18, 30

Treaty of Warsaw in 1970, 166–68, 174, 249

Truska, Liudas, 132

truth and reconciliation commissions (TRCs): overview and contributions of, 12, 16, 18, 234–35, 252–53, 263n38; historical commissions compared with, 18, 252–53; historical concept of time and, 229; human rights abuses and, 18; judicial concept of time and, 229; liberal democratic discourse and, 255; methodology and, 254; objectivity and, 229–30; performativity and, 77, 235; reconciliation's link with truth and, 18, 30, 229, 263n38; South Africa and, 27, 77, 235; thick description and, 77; truth discourse and, 229–30; victims' suffering relief and, 18, 30

truth-seeking, 25, 140, 145, 206, 256

truth-telling, 18, 30, 229–30, 232, 234, 256, 263n38

Tulsa race riot, Oklahoma, 13

Tutu, Desmond, 235

Twelve Years a Slave (film, 2013), 246–47

Two Plus Four Agreement, 171

UDHR (Universal Declaration of Human Rights), 21–23, 292n17

Ugandan project, 13

Ulmanis, Guntis, 144, 286n59

UNESCO (United Nations Educational, Scientific, and Cultural Organization), 163, 167, 183

United Kingdom, 50, 57, 252–53, 270n86

United Nations, 20–25

United Nations Educational, Scientific, and Cultural Organization (UNESCO), 163, 167, 183

United States: Arad affair protests from, 136, 284n32; Austrian restitution and, 88,

United States (*continued*)
98–99; House of Representatives of, 35,
136, 197, 199, 205, 254, 284n32; Jewish
refugee policies and, 50, 57; lawsuits and,
41–42, 46, 90, 117, 192–95, 198–99, 205–
6, 247–48, 267nn33–34, 296n30; Nazi
collaborators criminal cases in, 129–30,
283n11; righteous gentiles and, 57; State
Department of, 197, 205–6, 262n31,
296n60; Waldheim affair and, 87, 275n2;
Washington Agreement and, 54, 100–
101, 104
United States Holocaust Memorial Museum
(USHMM), 4, 106, 205, 262n31, 279n82,
280n104
Universal Declaration of Human Rights
(UDHR), 21–23, 292n17
universality versus particularity, 20–21, 61, 68,
80–82, 172, 202–3, 242–43
USHMM (United States Holocaust Memorial
Museum), 4, 106, 205, 262n31, 279n82,
280n104

Valentukevicius, Rimvydas, 135–36
van der Merwe, Hugo, 229
Vatican (Roman Catholic Church): overview
and historiography of, 207–9, 221, 296n8;
ADSS publication by, 208–9, 211–13, 215–
22, 225–27, 296n8, 298n43; amending
the past and, 222; anti-Semitic beliefs
and, 67–68, 76, 81–83, 207–11; apology
discourse and, 210–11, 221–22; archival
documentation and, 208–12, 215–16, 218,
222–26, 297n25, 298n40, 299n59; beatification and, 106, 209, 213, 279n79;
Catholic-Jewish relations and, 210–11,
221–23, 254, 299n54, 299n59, 299n61;
Catholic victimhood/rescues and, 210,
217, 226–27; communism and, 225; diplomatic activities and, 209, 214–16, 219,
223, 226; exculpation and, 210; Final Solution and, 209, 216–17, 227; Jewish vic-
timhood/rescues and, 210, 217, 224, 226;
Judaism/anti-Judaism and, 210–11, 222,
297n22; mediation of history and, 213–
14, 224–27, 298n36; moral judgments

and, 214; multivocal/rival narratives and,
214–15; Nazism/anti-Nazism and, 223–
24, 299n61; *Nostra Aetate* and, 210–11,
217–18, 222, 297n19, 297n22; *Nostra
Aetate* (*In Our Time*) and, 210–11, 217–
18, 222, 297n19, 297n22; questions/solu-
tions or openended discourse and, 214,
218–19, 298n36; rescuers/heroic activities discourse and, 106–8, 210, 217, 224,
226–27, 279n79; responsibility for historical injustices and, 209–11, 210–11,
215; restitution documentation/settle-
ments and, 210, 297n18; self-image/self-
understanding and, 107; Slovakian Jews
deportations intervention and, 217,
298n43; "We Remember" statement on
Holocaust and, 209–11, 221, 224, 299n54.
See also Catholic Church diocese; International Catholic-Jewish Historical
Commission (ICJHC); *specific popes*
Vatican II (Second Vatican Council), 210–11
Vél d'Hiv action, 33–34, 37, 40, 49–50, 243,
265n2, 265nn6–7
Vélodrome d'Hiver (Vél d'Hiv), 33–34, 37, 40,
49–50, 243, 265n2, 265nn6–7
Ventresca, Robert A., 223–24
Verheugen, Günter, 183, 188
Vichy government: archival documentation
and, 35, 37, 266n11; deportee documen-
tation/compensation and, 33–34, 37–38,
40, 46–50, 192, 243, 265n2, 265nn6–7;
Final Solution and, 36; Free France
during era of, 35, 45–46; historiography
and, 33–34, 36, 40, 45, 234, 237, 239; SS
and, 37; "subordination within collaboration" and, 41, 45, 91, 237, 239; Vél
d'Hiv action and, 33–34, 37, 40, 49–50,
243, 265n2, 265nn6–7; yellow star regulation and, 38. *See also* France
victimhood: Catholic, 210, 217, 226–27; historical commissions and, 26, 30; human
rights discourse and, 23–24; Italian, 110–
12, 118–19; Jewish, 65–68, 78, 81, 88,
110, 112, 119, 208, 210, 217–19, 224, 226,
298n36, 300n71; marginalization of
Jewish, 65–66, 110, 112, 119; Poles as

victimizers and, 68–69, 78, 80–82; Polish, 66, 68–69, 71, 78, 81, 272n34; relativized, 169, 255
Victims Welfare Act in 1947, Austria, 100, 278n53
Vike-Freiberga, Vaira, 144
Villiger, Kaspar, 49–50, 233, 269n59
Vilna Gaon Jewish State Museum, Lithuania, 142–43, 286n53
Volkan, Vamik, 84
von Preysing, Konrad, 216, 219
Vranitzky, Franz, 88–89

Waldheim, Kurt, and affair, 87–88, 275n2
Waldron, Jeremy, 23–24
Ward, David, 280n92
Warsaw Ghetto (Heroes) Monument, 65, 156, 166
Warszawski, Dawid, 72–73
Washington Agreement in 1946, 54, 100–101, 104
Weber, Eugen, 267n27
Weiner-Zada, Suzanne, 198–99, 201, 205
"We Remember" (Vatican), 209–11, 221, 224, 299n54
West Germany, 155–56, 166, 168, 277n46. See also Germany (Federal Republic of Germany)
White, Hayden, 204, 230
Wieviorka, Annette, 35
Wistrich, Robert, 212, 221, 225, 298n30
WJC (World Jewish Congress), 3, 35, 42, 193, 254, 267n37, 293n8

Wolf, Hubert, 224–25
WorldCat database, 85
World Jewish Congress (WJC), 3, 35, 42, 193, 254, 267n37, 293n8
World War I, 19, 95, 156–57, 159, 162–64
World War II. *See* Nazism and Nazi Germany; *specific commissions and countries*
Worldwide Investigation and Prosecution report, Simon Wiesenthal Center, 128, 282n6
Wrobel, Piotr, 82

Yad Vashem, Jerusalem: Arad and, 130, 135; Austria's responsibility for historical injustices and, 88–89; educational projects and, 47, 138; insurance assets/claims lists and, 195–96; Jewish deaths statistics and, 285n45; rescuers/heroic activities database at, 106, 108; righteous gentiles listed in, 47, 56–57, 105, 226, 245. *See also* Israel (State of Israel)
Yugoslavia (now Federal Republic of Yugoslavia), 8, 13–14, 18

Zabludoff, Sidney, 205
Zakowski, Jacek, 71–73, 244, 272n34
Zeman, Miloš, 181, 189–90, 255–56
Zevi, Tullia, 299n54
Zingeris, Emanuelis, 130, 132–33, 283n12
Zingeris, Markas, 138–39, 142, 283n17
Zucotti, Susan, 224
"Zydokommunism" (Jew-communism) myth, 83

Critical Human Rights

www.ingramcontent.com/pod-product-compliance
Lightning Source LLC
Chambersburg PA
CBHW061001280326
41935CB00009B/785